Culture as the Core

Perspectives on Culture
in Second Language Learning

A Volume in
Research in Second Language Learning

Series Editor: JoAnn Hammadou Sullivan, University of Rhode Island

Culture as the Core

Perspectives on Culture
in Second Language Learning

Edited by

Dale L. Lange (Emeritus)

and

R.Michael Paige

University of Minnesota–Twin Cities Campus

INFORMATION AGE
PUBLISHING

80 Mason Street • Greenwich, Connecticut 06830 • www.infoagepub.com

Library of Congress Cataloging-in-Publication Data

Culture as the core : perspectives on culture in second language
education / edited by Dale L. Lange and R. Michael Paige.
    p. cm. – (Research in second language learning)
Includes bibliographical references and index.
  ISBN 1-931576-23-8 (Hardcover) – ISBN 1-931576-22-X (Paperback)
  1. Language and languages–Study and teaching. 2. Intercultural
education. I. Lange, Dale L. II. Paige, R. Michael, 1943- III. Series.
  P53.45.C86 2003
  418'.0071–dc21

                                                      2003000044

Copyright © 2003 Information Age Publishing Inc.

Printed in the United States of America

CONTENTS

Part I. Culture as the Core:
Interdisciplinary Perspectives on Culture Teaching and Learning in the Second Language Curriculum

**Part II. Culture as the Core:
Integrating Culture into Second Language Curriculum**

LIST OF CONTRIBUTORS

Wendy Allen   St. Olaf College
                        Northfield, Minnesota.

Janet M. Bennett   Intercultural Communications Institute
                        Portland, Oregon

Milton J. Bennett   Intercultural Communications Institute
                        Portland, Oregon

Jill Brody   Louisiana State University
                        Baton Rouge, Louisiana

Jeanette Colby   University of Minnesota, Twin Cities Campus
                        Minneapolis, Minnesota

Linda M. Crawford   Osseo Area Public Schools
                        Osseo, Minnesota

Louise Damen   Educational Consultant,
                        Tampa, Florida

Helen L. Jorstad   Professor Emerita
                        University of Minnesota, Twin Cities Campus
                        Minneapolis, Minnesota

Francine Klein   Viterbo University
                        LaCrosse, Wisconsin

Claire Kramsch   University of California-Berkeley
                        Berkeley, California.

Robert C. Lafayette Louisiana State University
                        Baton Rouge, Louisiana.

Dale L. Lange

Professor Emeritus
University of Minnesota, Twin Cities Campus
Minneapolis, Minnesota

Peter McLaren

University of California-Los Angeles
Los Angeles, California

R. Michael Paige

University of Minnesota, Twin Cities Campus
Minneapolis, Minnesota

June K. Phillips

Weber State University
Ogden, Utah

Muriel Saville-Troike

University of Arizona
Tucson, Arizona.

Laura Siaya

American Council on Education
Washington, D.C.

Shelley L. Smith

University of Minnesota, Twin Cities Campus
Minneapolis, Minnesota

Inge Steglitz

Michigan State University
East Lansing, Michigan

INTERDISCIPLINARY PERSPECTIVES ON CULTURE LEARNING IN THE SECOND LANGUAGE CURRICULUM

Introduction

Dale L. Lange and R. Michael Paige

This volume presents the very important issue of integrating culture into the second language classroom. Some of its chapters were originally presented at two symposia on Culture Learning and Interdisciplinary Perspectives on Culture learning in the Second Language Curriculum, held at the University of Minnesota in 1991 and 1994. Other chapters were developed at a third conference, Culture as the Core: Transforming the Language Curriculum. The latter brought scholars and practitioners together to reflect on the earlier theoretical discussions, refine those ideas in light of subsequent theoretical developments, and translate theory into classroom practice.

Culture as the Core: Perspectives in Second Language Education, pages ix–xvii
Copyright © 2003 by Information Age Publishing

WHY CULTURE?

The late 20th and early 21st centuries have seen a renewed interest in language education and language learning/acquisition due in part to economic globalization and the aftermath of September 11, 2001. This focus includes the recent effort to differentiate aspects of language competence into grammatical, sociolinguistic, discourse, and strategic domains (Canale & Swain, 1980). Yet the inclusion of culture in language teaching remains an unresolved issue for the following reasons: (1) Culture is complex and elusive, incorporating as it does elements such as attitudes, beliefs, ideologies, perceptions, ways of behaving and thinking, and values. These elements cannot be included in language programs in the linear and objective instructional formats that have traditionally been employed. (2) Many teachers say: "Culture is not language, so why should we have to deal with it and its complexities? It takes away from the needed focus on language and communication." (3) Any discussion of cultural differences could cause language learners to change their own ways of thinking and behaving. In other words, culture takes the learning experience far beyond the realm of comfort, experience, and interest of both teacher and the learner (Paige, 1993). It is simply too challenging. Each of these three concerns has played a role in maintaining the diminished position of culture in the language classroom. In spite of this, the debate about the role of culture in the language curriculum refuses to go away; for 50 plus years it has been a topic of discussion in the language education field.

During this past half-century, several scholars have made notable efforts to include culture in language learning. Brooks (1960), for example, enumerated a variety of culture-related topics that could be included in language programs. Later, Nostrand (1978) provided us with a taxonomic structure that could be applied generally to any culture. Seelye (1976, 1993) demonstrated how practitioners could set culture-learning goals and objectives, effectively utilize alternative teaching strategies in the teaching of culture, and appropriately evaluate culture learning. Stern (1983) showed us how culture could be integrated into the language curriculum through the interweaving of four syllabi (linguistic, cultural, communicative, and general language education). Crawford-Lange and Lange (1984) created a process by which the intertwining of language, culture, communication, and language learning could be directed toward higher levels of learning in both the cognitive and affective domains (Bloom, 1956; Krathwohl, Bloom, & Masia, 1964). Allen (1985) directed student learning toward awareness and appreciation of other cultures through progressive discovery in three content areas: information, experience, and authenticity. Damen (1987) discussed the teaching of culture in language education from the intercultural communication perspective. Within a dialectic of contradiction and boundary crossing, Kramsch (1993) pushed us to recognize that cultural context allows us multiple ways of viewing, talking, writing, reading, and listening. These scholars have made an important contribution to the discussion by articulating how culture learning can occur in the second language classroom.

At this particular point in culture learning and teaching, we are at a crossroads. On the one hand, we can safely say that culture in the second language classroom is still treated like a second cousin, twice removed; it is not recognized as the core, for language continues to be taught as language. On the other hand, as with almost every school subject at this moment, new national standards have been written for foreign languages, and culture figures much more prominently than previously. Within the broader environment of five goal areas (communication, culture, connections, comparisons, and communities), culture plays the central role because it is now viewed as the context and content of communication in any form, the link to any discipline, the opportunity to contrast and compare cultures and cultural contexts, and the most authentic way to connect the individual language learner to the broader target language community. We argue, then, that culture is the core of language learning/acquisition. And we present this book as a vehicle for the reader to better understand this proposition.

PART I. CULTURE AS THE CORE: INTERDISCIPLINARY PERSPECTIVES ON CULTURE TEACHING AND LEARNING IN THE SECOND LANGUAGE CURRICULUM

The first part of this volume comprises a collection of chapters resulting from the two symposia entitled, "Interdisciplinary Perspectives on Culture Learning in the Second Language Curriculum," that were held at the University of Minnesota in 1991 and 1994. One of the primary purposes of these symposia was to provide a forum in which to examine the contributions of a variety of fields in the humanities and social sciences to the teaching and learning of culture in the second language classroom.

The symposia brought together teachers and research scholars working in the fields of sociolinguistics, intercultural communication, anthropology, textual culture, and second languages to determine what each of these fields could contribute to an analysis of the connection between language and culture, and how these concepts could be applied to second language learning and teaching in the context of the high school and college classroom. Specialists in sociolinguistics, anthropology, intercultural communication, and discourse theory presented overviews of recent developments pertaining to *culture* in their fields of study. Each was paired with a scholar in second languages, who related these developments to the teaching of culture in the second language classroom.

The contributions of sociolinguistics to language teaching are apparent, as the focus of instruction has been broadened during the last three decades to include the development of communicative competence, although specialists in second language education often define this term somewhat differently. In her chapter entitled "Extending Communicative Concepts in the Second Language Curriculum: A Sociolinguistic Perspective," Muriel Saville-Troike explores the dimensions of communicative competence from a sociolinguistic perspective, focusing on the relationship of second language competence to membership in a speech community. She describes the implications of this relationship for second language acquisition, raising the issues of feasibility and even desirability of teaching and testing certain types of cultural knowledge in the second language classroom. She advocates for a differentiation between receptive and productive competence, stating that students should be helped to understand the native speaker's communicative intentions, but should not be expected to behave in a native-like manner. Claire Kramsch, in "Toward a Pedagogy of Cross-Cultural Competence" takes a somewhat different approach. Instead of focusing on the development of communicative competence related to a specific speech community, Kramsch suggests that culture teaching should focus on developing general sociolinguistic competence and social awareness across cultures. It should help students develop an awareness of their own ways of speaking, reading, and writing, as well as understanding the way their own discourse is culturally marked. She describes culture in discourse as a social symbolic construct that is the product of self and other perceptions. To allow students to develop social awareness across cultures, she outlines four steps that can be used in the second language classroom and that result in the teaching of culture as sociopragmatic competence and the understanding that "culture is dialogically created through language in discourse."

Emerging in the 1950s, the field of intercultural communication has had some impact on culture teaching in second language classrooms through the incorporation of certain instructional techniques such as culture capsules, culture assimilators, and simulations. Louise Damen in her chapter, "Interdisciplinary Perspectives on Culture Teaching in the Second Language Curriculum," briefly describes how the field of intercultural communication developed and notes that, in spite of the use of the techniques described above, it is a discipline that has largely been ignored by foreign language teachers until recently. After reviewing some of the challenges of teaching culture in a second language classroom, she notes that the field of intercultural communication can provide guidance for curriculum organizers and classroom teachers in overcoming some of these diffi-

culties and examines the classroom and curricular *lessons* of this discipline
for language teachers.

Shelley L. Smith, R. Michael Paige, and Inge Steglitz in their chapter,
"Theoretical Foundations of Intercultural Training and Applications to the
Teaching of Culture," summarize current perspectives, concepts, and models from the field of intercultural communication. They first describe the
intercultural perspective, defining it as difference-based, face-to-face interactive, processual, holistic, humanistic, phenomenological/socially-con-
structed, developmental, and contextual. They then present various
theoretical frameworks pertaining to culture, language, and communication. The authors conclude that communication and culture are interdependent and that the concept of intercultural communication competence
can help bridge the conceptual gap between language educators and interculturalists.

Jill Brody, in "A Linguistic Anthropological Perspective on Language
and Culture in the Second Language Curriculum," presents anthropological perspectives on culture. She notes that the concept of culture in the
second language teaching literature is often used in an unconsidered, constrained, and taken-for-granted fashion and believes that a linguistic
anthropological perspective can offer illumination to second language
educators in three general areas: (1) expertise regarding the concept of
culture, the practice of the investigation of culture, and the ways in which it
can be taught; (2) an understanding of the relationship between language
and culture; and, (3) the methodologies of ethnographic observation and
discourse analysis to understand the dynamics of the second language
classroom. After describing the concept of culture which is at the core of
the discipline of anthropology, she notes that the goals of the student in
the second language classroom are often more comparable to those of
anthropologists in the field than they are to those of children learning
their first language in a cultural setting. Like Kramsch, she advocates for
the use of discourse analysis to facilitate an understanding of the subtleties
of language and culture.

Robert C. Lafayette expands on the classroom implications of an
anthropological approach to culture in "Culture in Second Language
Learning and Teaching: Anthropology Revisited." From the point of view
of a second language specialist, he discusses the past, present, and future
roles of anthropology in the teaching of culture in the second language
classroom. Following a historical overview of culture teaching in second
language classrooms in the United States, he reviews concepts in anthropology that are helpful in the teaching of culture. He then analyzes the
relationships between the concepts of *awareness, comparison,* and *other dependent learning* and two recent curricular models, Edwards (1992) culture
teaching model and Lange's (1990) conceptualizations of curriculum. He

further discusses their potential contributions to the teaching of culture in the second language classroom of the future.

The chapter written jointly by Linda M. Crawford, a second language specialist, and Peter McLaren, an expert on critical theory, is entitled, "A Critical Perspective on Culture in the Second Language Classroom." The authors frame their discussion of culture teaching within the contemporary debate between neo-conservative and postmodernist views of culture. They challenge the neo-conservative agenda, which they define as "grounded in a concept of a homogeneous and monumentalized master culture predominating over diverse subordinate cultures," and argue for a rethinking of culture from postmodernist, postcolonial, and poststructuralist perspectives that incorporate a wide array of conflicting and competing discourses. They then examine culture in relation to the concepts of plurivocalism, tradition, resistance, individual subjectivity, discourse of the other, and the discourse of liberation, advocating for a critical pedagogy that can guide students in: (1) discovering the codes, ideologies, and social practices that make social life meaningful; (2) understanding how these meanings have been constructed; and, (3) learning how alternative discourses are associated with power. Such a perspective permits teachers to move beyond the prevailing conception of culture and empowers students to critically examine both their own culture and the culture of the other.

PART II. CULTURE AS THE CORE: INTEGRATING CULTURE INTO THE SECOND LANGUAGE CURRICULUM

The second part of this volume contains chapters from the 1996 Minnesota Conference on Culture as the Core: Transforming the Language Curriculum. Its primary goal was to bring leading language and culture researchers together with second language and culture practitioners in order to: (1) articulate a conceptual framework for culture and culture learning in the language classroom, one which would synthesize and build upon the earlier work of the project; (2) discuss the existing research on culture learning in language education settings with the goal of helping establish agendas for future research and practice; and, (3) generate a set of principles based on theory and research to guide practitioners, most importantly language educators, in incorporating culture into the curriculum.

To facilitate discussion around these objectives, the Intercultural Studies Project team commissioned three related working papers to be presented at the conference: a conceptual/theoretical paper linking culture and language learning by Janet M. Bennett, Milton J. Bennett, and Wendy Allen; a review of the research literature by R. Michael Paige, Helen Jorstad, and a team of research associates—Laura Siaya, Francine Klein, and Jeanette Colby; and, the development of principles for culture teaching and learning by Dale L. Lange.

These three papers represent the core of the second part. They were presented in draft form at the conference and then substantially revised as a result of the discussions that occurred there, as well as extensive follow-up work among the authors. As the work progressed, it became increasingly clear that a substantive discussion of the national standards (*Standards*, 1996) was needed. Accordingly, June K. Phillips was invited to write a chapter that would frame our volume in terms of the standards. Dale L. Lange summarizes the work of all of the authors in his concluding chapter, in which he reminds us of the key questions that remain to be addressed. His work underscores the daunting nature of the task, but it also encourages all of us in the field to go forward with it.

In order to fully understand the genesis of the three core chapters in this part, it is important to say a few words about the 1996 conference itself. It consisted of two components. The first part of the conference was a two-day round of discussions among invited participants from a variety of disciplines, all of whom were experts on culture and language learning. Most of them had participated in the 1994 conference and they had agreed at that time that a follow-up conference focusing on the aforementioned three themes would advance their work and be important for the field. One of the goals of the so-called expert round was to provide extensive discussion and feedback to the authors so that their papers could be revised and eventually published.

The second component of the conference was a one-day session with second language teachers and other practitioners in the field. More than 120 teachers and practitioners learned about and discussed various key aspects of curriculum design, pedagogy, and assessment related to culture teaching and learning. In a broader sense, we were all searching for answers on how to put culture at the core of language education.

The central theme of the conference was the proposition that studying a language must include significant learning about another culture, that language and culture are inseparable. In the National Standards for Foreign Language Learning (*Standards*, 1996) it is stated that students, "cannot truly master . . . language until they have also mastered the cultural context in which the language occurs" (p. 27). Our goal at the conference was to explore how this could become a reality in second language education.

This second section of the book presents the results of our collective efforts to articulate theoretically, empirically, and pragmatically what it means to put culture at the core of language education. Phillips leads off the discussion with her reflections on the role of culture in the national standards. Next, Paige et al. provide a comprehensive review of the literature that is organized around the themes of context, setting, teacher variables, learner variables, curricular materials, and assessment. Bennett et al. then present an elaborate conceptual framework regarding intercultural development, language development, and the relationship between the two. Based on those three chapters and several additional theoretical frameworks (e.g., Egan, 1979; Gardner, 1993a,b), Lange then discusses the principles, concerns, and questions associated with putting culture at the core of the second language curriculum. In the concluding chapter, also written by Lange, the works of all the authors are summarized and an agenda for the future is suggested.

We sincerely hope that this volume will encourage language educators to place culture at the center of their work. It is also our hope that readers of this volume will be as stimulated by these writings as the authors were in preparing them. All of those involved with this volume look forward to continued work with our colleagues on putting culture at the core of the second language curriculum.

REFERENCES

Allen, W. (1985). Toward cultural proficiency. In A.C. Omaggio (Ed.), *Proficiency, curriculum, articulation: The ties that bind* (pp. 127–166). Northeast Conference Reports. Middlebury, VT: The Conference.

Bloom, B.S. (Ed.). (1956). *Taxonomy of educational objectives: The classification of educational goals: Handbook I: Cognitive domain.* New York: David McKay.

Brooks, N. (1960). *Language and language learning: Theory and practice.* New York: Harcourt, Brace & World.

Canale, M., & Swain, M. (1980). Theoretical bases of communicative approaches to second-language teaching and testing. *Applied Linguistics, 1,* 1–47.

Crawford-Lange, L.M., & Lange, D.L. (1984) Doing the unthinkable in the second-language classroom: A process for the integration of language and culture. In T.V. Higgs (Ed.), *Teaching for proficiency, the organizing principle* (pp. 139–177). The ACTFL Foreign Language Education Series. Lincolnwood, IL: National Textbook.

Damen, L. (1987). *Culture learning: The fifth dimension in the language classroom.* Reading, MA: Addison-Wesley Publishing Company.

Edwards, J.D. (1992). Quelle culture enseigner?: Réflexions et pratiques, l' expérience MICEFA/TRIADE. In R.C. Lafayette (Ed.), *La culture et l' enseignement du français.* Paris: Didier-Erudition.

Egan, K. (1979). *Educational development.* New York: Oxford University Press.

Gardner, H. (1993a). *Frames of mind: The theory of multiple intelligences* (2nd ed.). New York: Basic Books.

Gardner, H. (1993b). *Multiple intelligences: The theory in practice* (2nd ed.). New York: Basic Books.

Giroux, H.A. (1992). *Border crossings: Cultural workers and the politics of education.* New York: Routledge.

Kramsch, C. (1993). *Context and culture in language teaching.* New York: Oxford University Press.

Krathwohl, D.R., Bloom, B.S., & Masia, B.B. (1964). *Taxonomy of educational objectives: The classification of educational goals: Handbook II: Affective domain.* New York: David McKay.

Lange, D.L. (1990). Sketching the crisis and exploring different perspectives in foreign language curriculum. In D.W. Birckbichler (Ed.), *New perspectives and new directions in foreign language education* (pp. 77-09). The ACTFL Foreign Language Education Series. Lincolnwood, IL: National Textbook.

National Standards in Foreign Language Education Project. (1996). *Standards for foreign language learning: Preparing for the 21st Century.* Yonkers, NY: The American Council on the Teaching of Foreign Languages.

Nostrand, H.L. (1978). The 'emergent model' (structured inventory of a sociocultural system) applied to contemporary France. *Contemporary French Civilization, 2,* 277–294.

Paige, R.M. (1993). On the nature of intercultural education and intercultural experiences. In R.M. Paige (Ed.), *Education for the intercultural experience* (pp. 1–19). Yarmouth, ME: Intercultural Press.

Seelye, H.N. (1976). *Teaching culture: Strategies for foreign language educators.* Skokie, IL: National Textbook.

Seelye, H.N. (1994). *Teaching culture: Strategies for intercultural communication* (3rd ed.). Lincolnwood, IL: National Textbook Company.

Stern, H. H. (1983). Toward a multidimensional foreign language curriculum. In R.G. Mead, Jr. (Ed.), *Foreign languages: Key links in the chain of learning* (pp.120–146). Northeast Conference Reports. Middlebury, VT: The Conference.

Part I

**CULTURE AS THE CORE:
INTERDISCIPLINARY PERSPECTIVES
ON CULTURE TEACHING AND LEARNING IN THE
SECOND LANGUAGE CURRICULUM**

CHAPTER 1

EXTENDING "COMMUNICATIVE" CONCEPTS IN THE SECOND LANGUAGE CURRICULUM

A Sociolinguistic Perspective

Muriel Saville-Troike

INTRODUCTION

The discipline we label *sociolinguistics* has been identified as a distinct perspective on language study since the 1960s. For a number of years, linguists had been isolating pieces of language for analysis by abstracting them from context, and had been regarding such elements as independent objects in their own right. This strategy of *autonomous linguistics* was—and is—very fruitful, to be sure, but the argument was made by the founders of sociolinguistics that just as the study of cadavers cannot teach us all there is to know about human physiology, a much broader analytical approach is needed if we are to achieve understanding of the role of language in com-

Culture as the Core: Perspectives in Second Language Education, pages 3–17
Copyright © 2003 by Information Age Publishing

3

munication. Indeed, understanding how communication can occur at all requires a consideration of much more than just language. Descriptions of the function of language use in social context (e.g., Gumperz & Hymes, 1972; Halliday, 1970) raised serious questions about the autonomy of linguistics and about the so-called "ideal speaker-hearer" in the "completely homogeneous speech-community" (Chomsky, 1965, p. 3), which were central concepts in the dominant theoretical model of the 1960s for linguistic analysis. By the end of that decade, merely accounting for *what* can (and cannot) be said without concern for *when, where, by whom, to whom, in what manner,* and *under what particular social circumstances* was considered an inadequate goal for linguistic description by those who by then identified themselves as sociolinguists.

No single, unifying theory has developed within sociolinguistics, in part because its practitioners came from diverse disciplinary perspectives themselves (e.g., linguistics, anthropology, sociology), with different foci of interest and different methodological traditions. A survey of the field today would range from quantitative studies on language variation, to ethnographies of language patterns within communities, to conversational and interaction analyses.

COMMUNICATIVE COMPETENCE

In spite of the divergent foci and traditions of sociolinguistics, there is one significant unifying construct which has emerged. That is the notion of *communicative competence* introduced by Hymes (1966). A deceptively simple definition I would offer is, "what a speaker needs to know to communicate appropriately within a particular speech community" (Saville-Troike, 2003). A critical observation by Hymes was that speakers who could produce any and all of the grammatical sentences of a language (per Chomsky's 1965 definition of *linguistic competence*) would be institutionalized if they indiscriminately went about trying to do so. The concept of communicative competence became a basic tenant in the then-emerging field of sociolinguistics. The phrase was soon adopted by specialists in the field of second language instruction as well, although from the beginning, sociolinguists and second language specialists have not been using it to refer to exactly parallel phenomena (see Hymes, 1987).

It is my intent on this occasion to explore some of the dimensions of communicative competence from a sociolinguistic perspective, as they are related to both first and second language acquisition and use. I will suggest that while the concept of communicative competence has important implications for selection and sequences in the second language curriculum, there are significant limitations on the extent to which the construct can (or should) transfer from first to second language contexts, particularly because of the different relationships that hold between first and second languages and *culture*. Exploration of these limitations should help define what we might mean by *Culture Learning in the Second Language Curriculum*, and perhaps raise issues of feasibility—and even desirability—for second language teaching and testing.

SPEECH COMMUNITY

Returning to the definition of communicative competence as "what a speaker needs to know to communicate appropriately within a particular speech community," let us first explore what sociolinguists mean by *speech community*. Widely accepted criteria for membership in the same speech community include shared language use (Lyons, 1970), shared rules of speaking and interpretation of speech performance (Hymes, 1972), and shared sociocultural understandings and presuppositions with regard to speech (Sherzer, 1975). The key concept is one of shared knowledge and skills for contextually appropriate use and interpretation of language in a community. In other words, communicative competence essentially refers to the communicative knowledge and skills shared by a socially constituted group of speakers, although these (like all aspects of culture) reside variably in its individual members.

The different relationships, which hold between first and second languages and culture, derive in part from the different social functions of first and second language learning, including the construction of *community*. First language learning for children is an integral part of their *enculturation* into their native speech community from three perspectives: (1) language is part of culture, and thus part of the body of knowledge, attitudes, and skills which are transmitted from one generation to the next; (2) language is a primary medium through which other aspects of culture are transmitted; and (3) language is a tool which children may use to explore and manipulate the social environment and negotiate their status and role-relationships within it. The relationship of second language competence to membership in a speech community is more complex, and no such across-the-board generalizations can be made.

I have thus far been using *second* language learning in the inclusive sense of adding another language to one's first (or native) language, but it is important at this point to make a distinction among *second* language learning, *foreign* language learning, and *auxiliary* language learning in relation to contexts and motivation for acquisition, as well as to speech community membership.

Students learning a *foreign* language within the context of their native culture generally have little opportunity even to interact with members of the speech community that speaks the foreign language natively, and little opportunity (or need) to become part of it. They may learn about different norms of interaction, different values and beliefs related to ways of speaking, but without direct knowledge and experience of the community's social and cultural organization, this is an academic exercise.

Students learning a *second* language within the context of the speech community whose members speak it natively will not be acquiring it automatically as part of enculturation, but of *acculturation*, or second culture learning and adaptation. Here I am referring primarily to minority language immigrant populations. Except for children, few of these second language learners are likely to become full-fledged members of the second language speech community. In this second language context, it is useful to distinguish between participating in a speech community and being a member of it; speaking the same language is sufficient for some degree of participation, but not for full membership. Unlike learners of a foreign language within the context of their own native culture, learners in second language contexts, who are not able to function effectively within the second language speech community, may be discriminated against socially, academically, politically, and economically. The nature and extent of potential discrimination and degree of participation in the second language speech community, as well as the possibility of eventual full membership, are likely to vary tremendously depending on age of entry. Even here, however, functioning effectively within a speech community does not necessarily require full membership.

Other students are learning a language in a context where it will function as an auxiliary language for political or technological purposes. Examples can be found in India and Africa, for instance, where English or French is required as an official language of government, or where access to current technological development and interaction with peers in other countries requires knowledge of a common linguistic code. No membership or even participation in native British, American, or French speech communities is required to use English or French for indigenous Indian and African sociocultural purposes, and very little participation in British, American, or French speech communities is required for communication within the domains of science and technology. I will return to this point in my discussion of the relationship of language and culture.

Within the definition of communicative competence then, the content of *what a speaker needs to know* depends on the social context in which he or she is using the language. From this perspective, native language norms in many cases may constitute an inappropriate target for instruction or assessment, even though these are often considered the ultimate goal of *commu-*

nicative approaches. Native language norms are most likely to be inappropriate targets for learners in foreign or auxiliary language contexts. Even for learners of a second language who will function within the native language speech community, however, native norms for communicative competence may not be a feasible (and perhaps not a desirable) goal. In discussing what may constitute more attainable and reasonable goals of instruction, I will focus in turn on linguistic, interactional, and cultural dimensions of competence.

LINGUISTIC KNOWLEDGE

First, let us consider what linguistic knowledge is involved in native communicative competence. Descriptive linguists have traditionally limited concern to the phonological, grammatical, and lexical components of a language, and to their denotational and referential meaning. While the study of systematic variation of linguistic elements in relation to geography (regional dialectology) dates back to the 19th century, it was only with the establishment of sociolinguistic research in the 1960s (most notably by Labov, 1966) that correlations among linguistic variables and other social factors were established, and that knowledge of such correlations was recognized as an ingredient of native speaker competence. Since then, sociolinguists have been crucially concerned with speaker/hearer knowledge and production of the range of linguistic variables which function to transmit social, as well as referential, information. These carry meaning in part by indicating speakers' ethnic as well as regional origin, education level, and social status. Selection among possible variants conveys information about what social group and point of view speakers choose to identify with in a specific communicative situation, and shifts in variables may be used by speakers to redefine the situation itself, including the role-relationship of its participants and the tone or mood of an exchange.

Although knowledge of these variants and their social meaning is usually held and processed unconsciously, it is as much a part of native speakers' communicative competence as is the knowledge of what constitutes a possible grammatical sentence in a language, or what a word's referential meaning might be.

Paulston (1974) was among the first to suggest that language instruction should be extended to include goals for conveying and interpreting social information in a second or foreign language, saying that even approaches to teaching then being developed, which emphasized communicative skills, were limited to referential meaning (cf. Savignon, 1971, p. 24, "the emphasis was always in getting the meaning across"). Social meaning rather involves "the social values implied when an utterance is used in a certain context" (Gumperz, 1971, p. 285).

Although we are not sure exactly how acquisition is accomplished, children learn variation and its social meaning in their first language as part of their native speaker intuition. In contrast, native-like intuitions for the social meaning of variability are rarely developed for second and foreign language speakers—even if they become highly proficient in other aspects of the phonological, grammatical, and lexical components of the code.

For instance, foreign students in the United States who hear a native English speaker say, "I ain't got none," usually recognize that the utterance is nonstandard from an academic perspective, but often cannot tell if the variant *means* that the speaker is uneducated, joking, or using an alternative grammar to establish solidarity. Also, while foreign students of English tend to be fascinated by slang, even when they reside for several years in an English-speaking setting, they rarely learn to use it appropriately. One example is provided by a very proper Japanese girl who was in a class I taught several years ago. She used the phrase "and all that crap" in place of "etc." in a term paper she wrote for me, although the tone of the paper was otherwise serious and scholarly. (I was amused in this case, although I would not have been amused at all if an American student had used the same phrase—unless it was clearly for some special effect. This example thus also illustrates that a variable will not convey the same social meaning when it is used by a nonnative versus a native speaker.)

There is also an element of potential transfer and/or miscommunication related to variation which has thus far received very little attention in second language research or pedagogy: even when advanced students of English *do* perceive variable features which mark differences in regional origin, social class, and style, their interpretation of the social meaning which the features convey commonly differs from that of native English speakers.

I believe that the conclusion we must inevitably come to is that appropriate production and interpretation of variable elements is very difficult to teach or learn in a nonnative language, even though this is a *natural* part of first language development. This may be because variation and its social meanings cannot be taught apart from social context and understanding of the social structure of the community, or because there is some (poorly understood and largely undocumented) *critical* or *sensitive* period for inter-relating linguistic and social development—perhaps essentially related to age and processes of enculturation. This is a highly speculative proposal, but we do know that even when there is significant interaction with the target language speech community, it is very difficult (to say the least) for students to manage multiple varieties of a second or foreign language, and extremely rare for even very advanced students to master fully this component of communicative competence.

Because realistic goals for beginning and intermediate levels of language production are quite limited in this domain, the selection of regional variety and register becomes an important issue when deciding on curricular priorities. One factor to consider is the attitude of the target speech community, including what communicative behavior its members believe is appropriate for a nonnative speaker of the language. Particularly for individuals who have had experience interacting with people from different language and cultural backgrounds, there are not the same expectations or interpretive frames in force; again, native communicative norms do not generally apply. Learners are probably best served when instruction aims for a relatively formal variety of the second or foreign language first, whether primary contact with native speakers is likely to be face-to-face or through written texts. This is typically the style *expected* from foreign speakers, and is thus less likely to carry the unintended informational load of a more *marked* variety.

INTERACTION SKILLS

A second component of native communicative competence consists of interaction skills. These include both knowledge and expectation of who may or may not speak in certain settings, to whom one may speak, when one should remain silent, how one should talk to people of different statuses and roles, what nonverbal behaviors are appropriate for one to use in various contexts, what routines one should use for turn-taking in conversation, how one should ask for and give information, how one should make a request, how one should offer or decline assistance or cooperation, how one should give commands, and how one should enforce discipline. In other words, communicative competence comprises everything one should know involving the appropriate use of language and other communicative devices as they are situated in particular social settings.

Referential meaning may be ascribed to many of the elements in the linguistic code in a static manner, but production and interpretation of socially situated meaning must be seen as an emergent, dynamic, and sensitive process. Describing and understanding speakers' interaction with others in their native language requires accounting for the perception, selection, and interpretation of salient features of the code used in actual communicative contexts, integrating these with other cultural knowledge and skills, and implementing appropriate strategies for achieving communicative goals—again, all aspects of communicative competence.

At least in part because this complex of knowledge, skills, and strategies for interaction is less likely to be consciously recognized as language-specific at the surface level than are grammatical patterns and lexicon, their transfer from first to another language is often both pervasive and persistent. Such transfer is positive in many respects, and accounts for the ability of second language learners to interact successfully in some social contexts even in the absence of a common linguistic code (see documentation in Saville-Troike, 1987; Saville-Troike, McClure, & Fritz, 1984).

Particularly where formalized verbal routines are involved, inappropriate literal translation to second language structures has already been widely recognized. The English speaker learning Chinese may respond to a compliment with *xie-xie* ("thank you") instead of the appropriate *nali* ("where"), for instance, while the native Chinese speaker may respond "Where? Where?" to a compliment in English. Similarly, there are reports by Americans that soon after meeting a Turkish speaker at a cocktail party they may be asked, "How much money do you make?" Such examples have already had significant impact on foreign language curricula, influencing the content of so-called *communicative* exercises and drills.

Less widely recognized are general differences in interaction patterns, which can and do result in more serious communicative conflicts, or may inhibit communication. For example, members of some American Indian speech communities (including Navajo and Apache) wait several minutes in silence before taking a turn in conversation or responding to a question, while the native English speakers they may be talking to find silences of that length embarrassing because of very short acceptable time frames for responses or conversational turn-taking. Additionally, important differences can be found not only with the forms and patterns that interaction takes, but with how interaction functions in the establishment of social relations and status, and in the identification of individuals and groups for themselves and others—in Goffman's (1967) terms, the establishment of *face*.

When differences in interaction patterns are consciously recognized, speakers may refuse to adopt those used by natives of the second language speech community even when they have no hesitancy in using their grammar and vocabulary. I will illustrate speaker sensitivity and resistance to adopting second language interaction rules by recounting three brief examples:

The first example involved another former Japanese graduate student of mine who bowed to professors when greeting and leave-taking. She became very upset when an English professor told her it was not appropriate for her to bow to Americans. (He was obviously giving her an informal lesson in sociolinguistics.) The student said she knew that Americans don't bow, but that *she* must in order to show respect. Although she felt guilty for not following the professor's instructions, she could not stop bowing to professors without becoming a *bad* person; that is, without becoming *not Japanese.* (I have had analogous reactions from some former students whom I invited to address me as *Muriel* after they completed their doctorates. One of them recently admitted that she had avoided writing to me for years because she could not do so.)

The second example occurred at a conference on American Indian education that I attended several years ago. One of the sessions was intended to be a discussion about educational problems in schools attended by American Indian students, and an important goal of the organizers was to get input from teachers who were members of the same cultural groups. This goal was thwarted in that while more than 75% of the teachers in attendance were Navajo, not one of them spoke. The interactional difference that blocked the teachers' participation in this case was the temporal pattern of silence in turn-taking between questions and answers that I alluded to earlier, which occupies a significantly longer time-space for Navajos than that generally used by non-Navajo English speakers. The Navajo teachers were effectively kept out of the discussion because the time-space was never allowed to reach an appropriate extent for them to respond. The teachers recognized what the problem was, and a few discussed it with me afterward. They considered the non-Navajo timing pattern quite impolite, and the short time between questions and answers a sure sign that those who did speak had no sincere concern for the issues that were being addressed. Although all of the Navajo teachers were fluent English speakers, they obviously did not wish to add such *impolite* behavior to their bilingual repertoire.

The third example shows that this phenomenon is by no means limited to learners of English as a second language. Valdman (1992, citing research by Wieland, 1990) says that even Americans who are quite fluent in French report being frustrated and uncomfortable in conversations with native French speakers, who interrupted and "talked out of turn." He reports:

> Although the Americans recognized the differences between the French and American conversational styles, they stated that they could not bring themselves to adopt the speech interaction behavior of the French because they consider interruptions, for example, impolite. Their own culture had conditioned them to show that one cares about what others have to say by listening attentively and not interrupting until one's turn comes up. (p. 83)

These three examples illustrate differences in rules for interaction held by members of Japanese, Navajo, and American English speech communities, which have been maintained in second language use, even when the speakers have a conscious awareness that different behavior would be more *appropriate.* Such resistance to the productive use of new rules in this domain probably occurs because the meaning carried by social interaction patterns is largely affective rather than referential in nature. Adopting the norms of another speech community may require violations of culture—of values and beliefs—that merely using second language surface structure does not (see Saville-Troike, 1992, for further discussion of this point).

Such phenomena suggest that when we leave the surface linguistic structures in language teaching and approach the deeper levels of communication into which interaction skills appear to tap, we need to be sensitive to the social psychological, as well as the sociolinguistic factors that may be involved. These add very important considerations to issues of what should and can be taught in a second language, and of what should be tested.

In some situations, particularly those involving second language contexts where minority language students are being acculturated to the dominant language and culture, expecting or requiring productive use of second language interaction patterns may in fact have very negative effects on learners. Paulston (1974) claims, "It is the process of trying to eradicate an existing set of social interactional rules in order to substitute another which is so counterproductive." She goes on to speculate that the reason why middle and upper socioeconomic class children generally do not suffer ill-effects from initial schooling in a second language (as lower socioeconomic class children often do) "may well be that there is no attempt to interfere with the rules for communicative competence of the upper-class children ... (while) with the lower-class children one insists that they adopt the social interactional rules of the target language" (p. 354).

Such considerations raise not only issues of pedagogical feasibility when we set second language instructional goals, but those of ultimate desirability and ethicacy when we consider broader educational and social objectives.

CULTURAL KNOWLEDGE

Finally, for reasons I have already suggested, the concept of communicative competence requires reference to the notion of cultural competence, or the total set of knowledge and skills which speakers bring into a situation. As defined by such anthropologists as Geertz (1973) and Douglas (1970), systems of culture are patterns of symbols, and language is only one of the symbolic systems in this network. Most sociolinguists would accept this definition. It entails that interpreting the meaning of linguistic behavior requires knowing the cultural meaning in which it is embedded. While ultimately all aspects of culture are potentially relevant to communication, those that have the most direct bearing on the interpretation of communicative forms and processes are (1) the social structure, (2) the values and attitudes held about language and ways of speaking, and (3) the network of conceptual categories which results from shared experiences (for an extended discussion of these points, see Saville-Troike, 1996, 2003).

In discussing the components of native communicative competence from a sociolinguistic perspective, I have thus far suggested that at the level of linguistic knowledge, it is unlikely that students who begin learning a second language beyond childhood can completely master the variability of its forms and interpret the social meaning they convey, that it is a nearly impossible goal for foreign language learners, and that it is largely irrelevant in an auxiliary language. I believe that the limits on learnability of such skills may have important implications for selection and sequencing of the second or foreign language curriculum. I have also suggested that at the level of interaction skills, norms of the second or foreign language speech community may be learned *about*, but adoption of new rules for interaction for productive use in some domains could violate deep-rooted beliefs and values and threaten students' identity and sense of *face*. I believe that making a distinction between receptive and productive competence is essential here, and that students who are interacting with native speakers should be helped to understand those speakers' communicative intentions, but not necessarily expected or required to behave likewise.

The limits on teaching cultural knowledge in the second, foreign, or auxiliary language classroom should also be recognized, including what needs to be, can be, and should be taught. For one thing, all students of another language already have knowledge of their own native culture, and particularly in early stages of learning, the second/foreign language will make sense largely to the extent that it can be assimilated into their existing cultural schema. In research that Kleifgen and I (e.g., Saville-Troike & Kleifgen, 1989; Kleifgen & Saville-Troike, 1992) have done on children learning English as a second language in U.S. schools, we found heavy reliance on *top-down* processing strategies for interpretation of meaning. On the positive side, when children understand the context of communication, verbal forms are often correctly decoded, even with very limited language proficiency. On the negative side, we found that even the same verbal forms often cannot be interpreted in an alien context.

The children Kleifgen and I studied were all from well-educated families. In spite of the many different countries of origin, similarities in social class background, family educational level, and shared conventions of formal schooling among the children, enabled them and their English-speaking teachers to draw upon a large fund of congruent cultural knowledge to communicate successfully even with little or no comprehensible linguistic code in common. This picture contrasts instructively with the examples of unsuccessful communication documented in Pride (1985) between Aboriginal and White Australians, where large cultural as well as linguistic differences were involved. It is particularly striking, in fact, that the children we studied, in spite of their lack of English ability, were often able to function more successfully in the same school setting than were native English-speaking students from a less affluent and less well educated social class background.

Our finding reinforces the recognition that the Westernization of elites in various countries and the spread of formal schooling have created an international middle class culture and school culture which, despite national borders, is more similar cross-culturally than with traditional and working class cultures within the same country (including the United States).

The main point I want to illustrate here is that although communicative competence is clearly embedded in cultural competence, there is not a necessary relationship between a *specific* language and a *specific* culture. Shared cultural knowledge is indeed essential for the usage and interpretation of language, but much of that knowledge may be shared among speakers of unrelated language. Conversely, there is no necessary reason why the structures and vocabulary of one language cannot be used by diverse speech communities to express the different cultures of those communities, and in ways in keeping with their own rules of appropriate interaction.

In my discussion of the function of language learning and use in different types of speech communities, I made reference to *auxiliary* language status, in contrast to the *foreign* vs. *second* language statuses that are more frequently mentioned. Auxiliary languages best illustrate the arbitrary relationship of language and culture because they are generally instances of a colonial language being developed and used creatively in the enactment of different cultural values and beliefs. These have been discussed at length by Braj Kachru, who refers particularly to "World Englishes" (e.g., see Kachru, 1986; Kachru & Nelson, 1996). In India, for instance, English "functions in the Indian sociocultural context in order to perform those roles which are relevant and appropriate to the social, educational and administrative network of India" (Kachru, 1986, p. 100). The use of English for these indigenous purposes is, of course, the legacy of empire building, but it has ceased to serve those original functions, and has been adapted to the post-colonial needs of groups that have adopted it.

Not denying the importance of the focus on teaching culture, I do want to emphasize the arbitrariness of the language-culture link because I believe that failure to recognize it can foster cultural imperialism and mask important issues of ethnic identity.

While I am expressing a view that is generally held by sociolinguists, many second and foreign language teachers disagree. Many of them see the teaching of a language as essentially promoting learning about its culture, as though the two were inextricably linked (this is certainly an underlying motivation for USIA support for English teaching around the world, and for other nationally sponsored organizations such as the British Council, the Goethe Institute, and the Alliance Française). Some ESL (English as a Second Language) teachers I have worked with display surprise or annoyance, or propose remedial treatment, if they find English being used in an "un-American" way. I suspect this observation could be generalized to teachers and teachers-in-training of most foreign languages.

As with linguistic knowledge and interaction skills, I would claim that what aspects of culture need to be, can be, or should be, taught in conjunction with a second, foreign, or auxiliary language again depend on the social context in which that language is being learned and in which it will be used. In conclusion, I want to extend this point beyond the content of instruction to assessment and evaluation.

Just as the theoretical linguistics of the 1950s and 1960s (which gave rise to and supported the mechanical audio-lingual method) erred by attempting to extract language from its sociocultural matrix, so recent movements in the field of language teaching and testing have erred in the opposite direction by taking native-speaker norms of use as the point of departure. A sociolinguistic perspective tells us that language teaching and testing cannot be divorced from the sociocultural context, which determines their purposes, opportunities, and imperatives, and that these are not the same for native and nonnative speakers—nor indeed for subgroups within these categories. Teaching English to Spanish-speaking children in Chicago or to Hmong adults in Minneapolis, where it is an instrument of social and economic survival, is vastly different from teaching German to English speaking high school students in St. Louis or Spanish to native Spanish speakers in New York or Tucson. The organization of the curriculum and the choice of methods, as well as the design of testing, must be based on the goals of instruction and the background of the student, and thus must recognize the communicative needs of the learner (both receptive and productive, and graphic as well as oral) within the constraints of sociolinguistic realism. To do otherwise is to threaten the entire enterprise with failure, to the detriment of learners and ultimately, of the society.

REFERENCES

Chomsky, N. (1965). *Aspects of the theory of syntax.* Cambridge, MA: MIT Press.

Douglas, M. (1970). *Natural symbols: Explorations in cosmology.* New York: Random House.

Geertz, C. (1973). *The interpretation of cultures.* New York: Basic Books.

Goffman, E. (1967). *Interaction ritual: Essays on face-to-face behavior.* Garden City, NY: Doubleday.

Gumperz, J.J. (1971). *Language in social groups.* Stanford, CA: Stanford University Press.

Gumperz, J.J., & Hymes, D. (Eds.). (1972). *Directions in sociolinguistics: Ethnography of communication.* New York: Holt, Rinehart and Winston.

Halliday, M.A.K. (1970). Language structure and language function. In J. Lyons (Ed.), *New horizons in linguistics* (pp. 140–65). Harmondsworth: Penguin Books.

Hymes, D. (1966). *On communicative competence.* Paper presented at the Research Planning Conference on Language Development Among Disadvantaged Children, Yeshiva University.

Hymes, D. (1972). Models of the interaction of language and social life. In J.J. Gumperz & D. Hymes (Eds.), *Directions in sociolinguistics: Ethnography of communication* (pp. 37–71). New York: Holt, Rinehart and Winston.

Hymes, D. (1987). Communicative competence. In U. Ammon, N. Dittmar, & K.J. Mattheier (Eds.), *Sociolinguistics: An international handbook of the science of language and society* (pp. 219–229). Berlin: Walter de Gruyter.

Kachru, B.B. (1986). *The alchemy of English: The speech, functions and models of nonnative Englishes.* Oxford: Pergamon Institute of English.

Kachru, B.B., & Nelson, C.L. (1996). World Englishes. In S. McKay & N. Hornberger (Eds.), *Sociolinguistics and language teaching* (pp. 71–102). Cambridge: Cambridge University Press.

Kleifgen, J., & Saville-Troike, M. (1992). Achieving coherence in multilingual interaction. *Discourse Processes, 15,* 183–206.

Labov, W. (1966). *The social stratification of English in New York City.* Washington, DC: Center for Applied Linguistics.

Labov, W. (1972). On the mechanisms of language change. In J.J. Gumperz & D. Hymes (Eds.), *Directions in sociolinguistics: Ethnography of communication* (pp. 512–538). New York: Holt, Rinehart and Winston.

Lyons, J. (Ed). (1970). *New horizons in linguistics.* Harmondsworth: Penguin.

Paulston, C.B. (1974). Linguistic and communicative competence. *TESOL Quarterly, 8,* 347–362.

Pride, J. (Ed). (1985). *Cross-cultural encounters.* Melbourne: River Seine.

Savignon, S. (1971). *A study of the effect of training in communicative skills as part of a beginning college French course on student attitude and achievement in linguistic and communicative competence.* Ph.D. dissertation, University of Illinois, Urbana.

Saville-Troike, M. (1987). Bilingual discourse: Communication without a common language. *Linguistics, 25,* 81–106.

Saville-Troike, M. (1992). Cultural maintenance and "vanishing" languages. In C. Kramsch & S. McConnell-Ginet (Eds.), *Text and context: Cross-disciplinary perspectives on language study* (pp. 145–155). Lexington, MA: D.C. Heath.

Saville-Troike, M. (1996). The ethnography of communication. In S. McKay & N. Hornberger (Eds.), *Sociolinguistics and language teaching* (pp. 351–382). Cambridge: Cambridge University Press.

Saville-Troike, M. (2003). *The ethnography of communication* (3rd ed.). Oxford: Basil Blackwell.

Saville-Troike, M., & Kleifgen, J. (1989). Culture and language in classroom communication. In O. Garcia & R. Otheguy (Eds.), *English across cultures* (pp. 83–102). Berlin: Mouton.

Saville-Troike, M., McClure, E., & Fritz, M. (1984). Communicative tactics in children's second language acquisition. In F. Eckman, L. Bell, & D. Nelson (Eds.), *Universals of second language acquisition* (pp. 60–71). Rowley, MA: Newbury House.

Sherzer, J. (1975). *Ethnography of speaking*. Ms. University of Texas at Austin.

Valdman, A. (1992). Authenticity, variation, and communication in the foreign language classroom. In C. Kramsch & S. McConnell-Ginet (Eds.), *Text and context: Cross-disciplinary perspectives on language study* (pp. 79–97). Lexington, MA: D. C. Heath.

Wieland, M. (1990). *Politeness-based misunderstandings in conversations between native speakers of French and American advanced learners of French.* Ph.D. dissertation, Indiana University, Bloomington.

CHAPTER 2

TEACHING LANGUAGE ALONG THE CULTURAL FAULTLINE

Claire Kramsch

TEACHING CULTURE IN THE 1990s

In the early 1990s, following the successful efforts of the American Council on the Teaching of Foreign Languages to establish guidelines for testing foreign language proficiency in the traditional four skills (speaking, listening, reading, writing), the American Association of Teachers of French appointed a commission to draw up Proficiency Guidelines for the testing of cultural competence, an ambitious enterprise that reflected the growing need to link the teaching of foreign languages more closely to the social and cultural context in which these languages are used.

Three categories of cultural competence were identified for each level: (1) Sociolinguistic ability (verbal and nonverbal behavior patterns); (2) Knowledge of the culture area (France and francophone Europe, Black *francophonie*, French-speaking Canada, and the United States) and methods for observing and analyzing a culture; and, (3) Attitudes (e.g., tolerance to other cultures) (Nostrand, 1991). By assessing a student's ability along

Culture as the Core: Perspectives in Second Language Education, pages 19–35
Copyright © 2003 by Information Age Publishing
All rights of reproduction in any form reserved.

these three dimensions of cultural competence—sociolinguistic competence, knowledge and attitudes—it was hoped that language teachers would better prepare their students to understand and appreciate cultures different from their own. For, as Resnick and Resnick (1991) stated then: "In America, educational reform and testing are intimately linked. Tests are ... widely viewed as instruments for educational improvement ... New tests ... are frequently prescribed, both as a source of information for a concerned public and as a form of 'quality control' and an incentive to better performance by educators and students." After three years of hard work, a draft of the commission's report was published in Steele and Suozzo's (1994) *Teaching French Culture*. It was in part incorporated in what later came to be known as the National Standards in Foreign Language Education Project's *Standards for foreign language learning: Preparing for the 21st century* (1994).

Toward the end of the decade, however, the enthusiasm for the wash back effect of tests on classroom pedagogy had waned. If tests can suggest to teachers *what* they should teach, they don't tell the language teacher *how* to teach it. The procedure through which a competence is tested is not the process through which this competence is taught and acquired; the format of tests is no blueprint for syllabus design and for the achievement of lessons. For example, the Oral Proficiency Interview (OPI) tests a student's ability to respond to an interviewer's questions in a manner that shows mastery of function, content, and accuracy in language use, but teachers don't teach in an OPI format. Rather they conduct lessons through a give-and-take that ideally encourages creative self-expression, critical questioning, and interpretive inquisitiveness. Furthermore, even though tests have to measure individual competence, the knowledge and attitudes that lead to that competence can only be taught and acquired through the interaction of the individual with fellow individuals from the same or from a different culture, in and outside the classroom. What is tested monologically must, in fact, be taught dialogically. Such dialogic teaching is especially true of the development of cultural competence.

The push for the testing of cultural competence, as it is now called in Europe, *cross-cultural* or *intercultural* competence (e.g., Dahl, 1995; Johnstone, 1999; Koole & Thije, 1994; Kramsch, 1999), presents an immediate challenge for the teacher to develop a principled way of dealing with culture in the language class. Up to now, traditional thought in foreign language education has limited the teaching of culture to the transmission of factual information about the people of the target country, and about their general attitudes and world views: social and historical items, that can be retrieved through pencil and paper tests; routine phrases of social etiquette that can be displayed during an oral proficiency interview. It has not dealt with general sociolinguistic competence or with social awareness across cultures. In particular, it has not dealt with the awareness of one's own ways of speaking, reading and writing, and the way one's own discourse is culturally marked as well.

To follow the distinction made by Widdowson (1991), language teaching has traditionally seen the link between language and culture as mainly indexical, i.e., it has seen language as *referring* to the stable, undifferentiated reality of national cultures and identities. It has not paid much attention to the symbolic link between language and culture, i.e., the use of language in discourse as *enacting* social roles and *representing* cultural perceptions and misperceptions (Kramsch, 1990). More specifically, it has not viewed the teaching of culture as a dialogic process of coming to terms with the often conflictive encounter between two or more cultures. At the end of the decade, the need to teach cultural competence as a separate, fifth skill, had given way to an interest in exploring the cross-cultural potential of the language classroom itself.

CULTURE IN DISCOURSE

During the last decade or so, a general rethinking of the role of language as social practice has taken place that suggests new ways of looking at the teaching of language and culture. Four lines of thought emerge in particular.

Gained from sociolinguistics, the first is that the social reality we call culture is reflected in the way we use *language in social contexts*, i.e., it is shaped by the linguistic choices we make. For example, by addressing another French person with *tu* rather than *vous*, a native speaker of French not only makes a choice of singular vs. plural pronoun, but defines his/her social status and current role as showing either more dominance or more solidarity vis-à-vis the interlocutor (Brown & Gilman, 1960; Tannen, 1991). When Napoléon chose to say in an historic speech, *Je suis la révolution*, and not, *la révolution c'est moi*,[1] even as a Corsican he not only knew the dictionary meaning of the unstressed vs. the stressed pronoun in French, but he was also aware of the historic and social significance of the use of these pronouns in the minds of his listeners. *La révolution c'est moi* would have sounded far too despotic for his purposes. By using the unstressed pronoun *je*, Napoléon Bonaparte created a climate of democratic solidarity with the people who had led the French revolution and stressed the continuity between Bonaparte, the revolutionary, and Napoléon, the emperor.

The second insight, gained in recent years through advances made in pragmatics, is that culture is an *interpersonal process of meaning construction.* The meaning of an utterance is neither solely in its reference to the outside world nor only in the intention of its speaker, but, rather, speaker and hearer jointly construct it in their efforts to find a common ground of understanding. If meaning emerges from the negotiation necessary to bring about what Widdowson calls the _convergence of worlds_ (1983, p. 47), then it is not enough for us to teach fixed, normative phenomena of language use. We should also teach the process by which learners can make sense of cross-cultural encounters. We cannot tell them directly: "Do this, say that and I guarantee that you will be liked and accepted by native speakers." Everything depends on the context of use and its perception by the participants. Let us take an example.

Judy, a young American student returning from a stay with a German family, complained recently that, despite her otherwise good command of the language, she never found out how to say, _I'm sorry,_ in German. She would enter the living room where the father was sitting, and he would ask her to close the door. As she would go to close the door, she would feel like saying, _Oh, I'm sorry,_ as she was used to doing from home to show her sensitive attention to another family member's needs. However, the word _Entschuldigung_ seemed inappropriate, _Verzeihung_ seemed too pompous, the phrase, _Es tut mir leid,_ seemed too much of an apology.

Why did the student feel awkward in replicating the text of prior similar situations in her own family? Somehow she sensed that the German situation did not call for sensitive attention to another person's needs. There was neither the fear of draft nor of noise from the outside and the father didn't seem personally inconvenienced by the open door. In fact, the German father was probably teaching the young foreigner a cultural lesson by asking her to close the door (glossed as: "Closing the door behind you when you enter a room is the socially appropriate thing to do in our country"); the father was likely not expressing a personal need. Thus a personal expression of excuse could indeed have been viewed as inappropriate and the father would have interpreted it as a puzzling expression of guilt on the part of a foreigner.

Apology as a speech act has been the object of much research in the field of pragmatics, especially cross-cultural pragmatics (Edmondson, 1981; Fraser, 1981; Holmes, 1989; Olshtain, 1983, 1989). In a study of the way native speakers of English express apology, Borkin and Reinhart (1978) have shown that the expression _I'm sorry,_ by contrast with, _Excuse me,_ is not necessarily used to convey an apology, but, rather, expresses dismay or regret about a situation perceived as unfortunate. The basic concern behind, _Excuse me,_ is "I have broken a social rule" and the basic concern behind, _I'm sorry,_ is, "You are or you may be hurt." Thus the dictionary equivalent of, _I'm sorry,_ may indeed be, _Es tut mir leid,_ in German, but the German expression has quite a different sociopragmatic value in most situations, namely that of an outright apology. Of course Borkin and Reinhart's findings offer the learner no guarantee against personal variations and the always-ambiguous nature of human intentions.

So what should Judy be advised to do? Should she be taught that the social rule in Germany is to, "close the door behind you when you enter a room," and that therefore she should not say, *I'm sorry?* But not only does this behavior go against Judy's whole self-image as a considerate, polite young woman, it means for her accepting as a stable national rule a behavior that might be particular to a specific social class, to a specific family, to the specific relation between an older German male and a young foreign female. Judy certainly should be made aware of the social and cultural conventions of the target society, and of the consequences of flouting these conventions, but she should also be given the tools to understand the larger context in all its diversity. For, ultimately, the decision to behave one way or another will be hers alone (Saville-Troike, 1991; Thomas, 1983).

The third insight we have gained in recent years is that culture is variation and difference. As national identities are being revived and redefined around the world, the temptation is great to view culture only in terms of national traits: The French do this, Germans do that. However, traditional questions such as: What does it mean to be French? To be German? become increasingly difficult to answer considering the growing multiethnicity and multiculturality of French and German societies. Not that national characteristics are unimportant, but they cannot be adduced without further specification of other cultural factors such as age, gender, regional appartenance, ethnic background, social class. National traits are but one of the many aspects of a person's culture (Kramsch, 1998)!

Finally, the fourth insight provided by ethnographers and sociologists is that members of a social group align themselves along invisible faultlines, which in part determine why they say what they say and act the way they do (Carroll, 1987; Zarate, 1986). These *axes of thinking* (Kelly, 1955) become visible in the cross-cultural dialogue of the language class, for they are the cause of misunderstandings or misapprehension of foreign phenomena. For example, the frequent use by American learners of the French term *je suis confus* to express lack of understanding is not only a lexical error (Fr. *confus* = embarrassed; E. *confused* = disoriented), it is also an American euphemism that does not have its equivalent in French. When expressing a lack of comprehension, it is socially much more acceptable in the United States and much less face-threatening for both speaker and hearer to say, *I am confused,* than to have to admit that one just doesn't understand, for this could possibly indicate a lack of wit.[2]

Because of these invisible social attitudes, a teacher's lexical explanations may facilitate comprehension at one level but they can create cultural misperceptions on another. For example, in a first-year German class, the instructor, wanting to clarify the meaning of *Hirschbraten* (venison roast) that figured on the menu the students were reading, improvised a definition: "der Hirsch ist . . . der Vater von Bambi." A linguistically very astute but culturally problematic way of clarifying an item of vocabulary! The class emitted a grunt of disgust at the idea of eating Bambi's father and the students never did understand the high value of game in German cuisine.

CULTURAL REALITY, CULTURAL IMAGINATION

This last example shows that, beyond the referential world of deer and deer stews, culture is a social symbolic construct, the product of self and other perceptions. On the reality of facts and events that constitute a nation's history and culture is superimposed a cultural imagination that is no less real. This cultural imagination or public consciousness has been formed by centuries of discourses of various genres: maps and censuses, works of literature and other artistic productions, as well as by a certain public discourse in the press and other media. All these discourses have helped shape the imagined sense of community that is shared by all native speakers of a language, even though they might not know or have ever set eyes on each other. As Benedict Anderson writes in *Imagined Communities*: "...communities are to be distinguished, not by their falsity/genuineness, but by the style in which they are imagined" (1991, p. 6). American social scientists have analyzed the style of imaginings Americans entertain for example, about the Western frontier (Bellah et al., 1985), the automobile, or modern technology, what Leo Marx calls *the machine in the garden* (Marx, 1964); French sociologists have studied how the French nation was *invented* (Nora, 1986), how stereotypes about regions were constructed over the last two centuries through various forms of public discourse (Bertho, 1980).

The teaching of culture is all the more difficult as imagination and reality both contradict and reinforce one another. The Germans like law and order? For the traveler in Germany, that stereotype has proven to be false again and again, and yet most Germans will be convinced that *Ordnung muss sein* (order is necessary), and so will many foreigners insist that Germans are a very disciplined people. The French, individualists? Any trip to Paris will show the visitor how conformist the French can be in dress and fashion. And yet, everyone believes that, "il n'y a pas plus individualiste que le Francais" (no one is more individualist than the French). That myth is tenacious and will explain the perception many French have of the gregariousness of Americans. Like in a prism, perceptions and counter-perceptions bounce images back and forth. And yet, myths cannot be discarded, for they affect the way learners of a foreign language see others in the mirror of themselves, despite all evidence to the contrary from *objectively* transmitted facts.

Thus, the teacher of culture is faced with a kaleidoscope of at least four different reflections of facts and events. Granted that C1 and C2 are them-

selves aggregates of a multifaceted reality, representing many different subcultures (generational, occupations, educational, regional, age, race or
gender-related), these reflections can be summarized as follows:

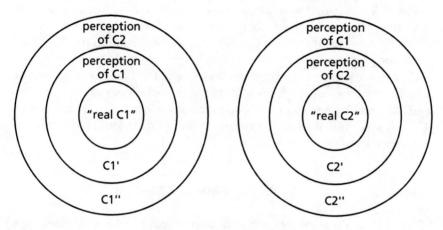

C1' = C1 perception of self

For example, German learners of American English and immersed in a
German C1 carry in their heads an image of the United States that corre-
sponds to the German dream of America, nourished in part by the German
literary imagination of the 19th century, the novels of Karl May, the role of
the American army in Germany since WWII, the new German Cinema
(C1"). This German image of America, of which Americans are unaware,
has deep roots in the way Germans perceive themselves, their hopes and
fears, their dreams and aspirations (C1'). Indeed, it is often an anti-image
of themselves. It has only indirectly and partially to do with American reality (C2).

This German image of America varies across generations and life experiences. For the generation that grew up just after WWII, the enthusiasm for
and the subsequent disillusion with the United States gave rise to a rather
depressing image of the "land of unlimited possibilities" in the late seven-
ties-early eighties. For example, as we can see in Wim Wenders' films like
Paris Texas, The American Friend, or *Stroszek,* German filmmakers featured
the United States as a place of desolation and alienation that most Americans did not recognize as their own. It has certainly little to do with the way
Americans dream of themselves (C2').

On the other hand, the generation born in the late sixties had a different view of the United States. Growing up with a much greater awareness
of the Holocaust than their elders, they viewed the United States through
their own history. Thus, a study conducted by Keller (1987) of self- and

other-stereotypes between German and American high school students found that while 46% of Americans viewed *race-consciousness* as central to their self-image, only 28% of Germans stated *rassenbewußt* as part of their image of Americans, despite the heavy emphasis put by English textbooks in Germany on racial problems in the United States. The terms *race-conscious* and *rassenbewußt* might be semantically equivalent, but they have different social and historical connotations in both countries.

Conversely, German self-perception can be quite different from the way Americans view German reality (C2"). This American perspective on German C1 is partial and filtered through the Americans' view of themselves (C2'). It is often filled with the romantic view of castles and old traditions that they miss in their own culture.

INVISIBLE FAULTLINES

What form do these perceptions and misperceptions take in the language classroom? Most of the time, cultural faultlines (Kramsch, 1993b) remain unidentified, mistaken for lexical errors, glossed over as awkwardness of expression. The following are two cases among the many that can be seen by an attentive observer. (All utterances are given here in their English translation.)

In the first case, 12 students in a third semester German class at a large state university are discussing Dürrenmatt's play *Die Physiker* (1962). Three scientists, Möbius, Newton, and Einstein, patients in a psychiatric hospital, reveal to one another why they each murdered their nurse. These nurses had discovered that the scientists were not insane, but only pretended to be so in order to save humanity from the deadly effects of their scientific discoveries. Newton and Einstein try to convince Möbius to escape with them: Newton, to a Western country, because of the freedom of research there, Einstein to an Eastern bloc country, because of the power of the communist party to use technology only for the good of mankind. Faced with an impossible moral dilemma, Möbius prefers to stay in the insane asylum.

The teacher (Teacher A) leads the discussion on the responsibility of the scientist and writes both Newton's and Einstein's opposing arguments on the board. One student summarizes Newton's argument in his own words: "It is like with a bottle—the scientist makes the bottle, but what the bottle gets filled with, whether with wine or with water, is not the responsibility of the scientist. The same thing with television." The teacher concurs. They then discuss Einstein's position.

T: And what power (*Macht*) does Einstein have?

S1: He wants more power (*Macht*) but he will always be under the government (*die Regierung*).

T: He has relinquished his power (*verzichten*) (writes *verzichten auf*+ acc on the board).

S2: His work makes the government (*die Regierung*) stronger, but he himself remains weak.

S3: Yeah, how can one be free in a position of dependence?

T: That's right. (writes on the board: *die Abhängigkeit* = dependence) Einstein is no more *free* than Newton.

S4: Einstein is in the middle between Newton, who says that the scientist has no responsibility, and Möbius, who says that the scientist carries the full responsibility of his discoveries.

T: Yes, this is the way Möbius sees things too.

Despite the liveliness of the discussion and the obvious linguistic benefits that students derive from it, we have to question the type of cross-cultural communication that is going on. Neither the teacher nor the students are aware that they are discussing in fact two ideological systems, the capitalist and the communist in a period of Cold War; the terms *government* and *responsibility* have quite different connotations for a Soviet communist and for an American capitalist. In addition, the term *government* is inappropriate in a communist context: Einstein specifically makes mention of the *party* and of *political systems*, not of any particular *government*. S1's utterance sounds like the complaint of an American scientist against too much *government interference*, not like a critique of the communist system.

By not exploring any further the ideological context of the students' utterances or not attending to the historical and political context of production of the play, teacher A leaves the students in their native cultural mindsets and fails to engage them in making sense of a reality other than their own.

The second class is a fourth semester German class at the same university. The class has been reading Brecht's *Life of Galilei*. It has discussed the controversial nature of Galilei's discoveries at the time and his problematic attitude vis-à-vis his social responsibility. Students have been asked by their teacher (Teacher B) to bring to class an article from the American or the German press relating to the topic of the play.

S1 brings an article on festivities to honor Francis Crick, the discoverer of the double helix.

T: And what is the name of the other scientist?

S1: I don't know, I am not a biologist.

S4: Watson.

T: Right! Watson and Crick! And why did you choose this article?

S1: Crick is a scientist, just like Galilei.

S2's article deals with the prohibition of perfume in public places. He explains:

S2: Some people are said to be allergic to the fragrance.
 T: How is this relevant to Galilei's theme?
S2: This idea seems as absurd as Galilei's ideas seemed absurd at the time, but later they proved to be the only ones that made sense.

S3 reports on a national center for disease control for doctors with AIDS.

 T: How does it relate to Galilei?
S3: Many people say that AIDS tests have no scientific validity, in the same manner as people didn't believe in Galilei's scientific discoveries. The American Medical Association resembles the scientific establishment at the court of the Medici in Florence.

S4 talks about the recent Oakland fire.

S4: Many people didn't want to believe there could be a danger and they didn't fireproof their houses.
 T: What is the link with Galilei?
S4: Like the old theories of the universe, these houses were destroyed by nature itself.

S5 reports on a survey about suicide in the United States.

S5: Most Americans want to decide themselves about their death, rather than leave the responsibility up to the church or the state.
 T: And what does that have to do with Brecht's Galilei?
S5: Galilei too said that each one has to see, to decide for himself and not believe in obsolete theories.

Teacher B is, at first, impressed by the imagination of his students, then somewhat dismayed at the tenuous links they have established with the Marxist play they have been reading. However, he realizes that the very choice of articles reveals something not only about the personal interests of each of his students, but also about their level of understanding of Brecht's play. So he decides to help them construct a context for the texts they have produced.

He first leads the class to realize how each student has brought his own interest to bear on the task at hand. He lists on the board the names of the students and writes down their field of studies. With the help of the class, he then writes down next to the names a tentative formulation of each student's focus.

S1: A city planner, is interested in the space of the individual in public places.

S2: An engineering major, chose an article that honors a scientific pioneer.

S3: A business major, seems interested in the way academic and professional institutions can impede progress.

S4: A chemistry major, understands the laws of nature.

S5: A humanities major, has obviously chosen an article on the moral responsibility of the individual.

Through their various interests, he adds, the students have resonated to Brecht's play on various levels of meaning. The students seem intrigued and flattered at being interpreted in such a personal manner.

The teacher then asks the students to reorganize the information on the board by linking each focus of interest with the themes of the play. One of the major themes in *Galilei* is indeed the autonomy of the individual against the barriers of conventions, be it fashion (S1), professional guilds (S3), the church or the state (S5). The individual fishmonger on the street was well aware of the social and political consequences of Galilei's discoveries. Brecht also wants to celebrate scientists like Galilei and Watson and Crick for their important influence on science and for their benefit to mankind (S2). Businessmen, like the character of Vanni in the play, had a vested interest in freedom from professional organizations and other impediments to free trade (S3). And finally, Brecht also shows that scientific progress, like laws of nature, cannot be stopped (S4).

S5 has raised the question of responsibility, and this responsibility is not only an individual, but also a social responsibility. Indeed that's where, according to Brecht, Galilei failed, since he recanted and surrendered his power to the Church. So the teacher sums up the discussion by drawing two large circles on the board. The first one, containing the five students' names and their foci of interest, he entitles: "Galilei's responsibility to science." In the other one, that partly overlaps with the first, he writes: "Brecht's *Galilei*" and he entitles it: "Galilei's responsibility to society." The students have obviously grasped the meaning of the first circle, but the meaning of this second circle still remains to be explored. The teacher thus prepares the way for a discussion of the last scene, where Brecht dramatizes Galilei's failure.

It was clear that the students were imposing on a Marxist play their own culturally-determined views of the scientist. In this class, the teacher was able to use the students' input to make visible the cultural faultlines in their understanding of the play. In other words, it was not enough to discuss the Brecht text and to explain its ideological context, the students' texts had to be discussed as well and placed into *their* proper contexts.[3] In the following, I shall try and systematize this approach.

FOUR STEPS TO SOCIAL AWARENESS ACROSS CULTURES

We have seen that the contexts of the native culture (C1) and the target culture (C2) have to be built each on their own terms. The only way to start building a more complete and less partial understanding of both C1 and C2 is to develop a third perspective that can enable learners to take both an insider's and an outsider's view on C1 and C2. As a teaching syllabus, such an awareness across cultures might be developed in four stages at each proficiency level (Kramsch, 1993b).

First, we have to explore *the context of our American students' responses* to the cultural phenomena with which they are confronted. In the discussion of Brecht's *Galilei*, it meant giving breadth and depth to students' utterances. It is certainly not the role of the teacher to impose on the class his/her own interpretation of the text, but it is his/her responsibility to interpret and contextualize the students' responses, what Nyikos calls *stretching students' input* (Nyikos, 1991). Similarly, in the case of Judy mentioned earlier, a teacher would have to first explore what created the difficulty for her, considering the American milieu in which she grew up, her education, her view of herself, the social and cultural myths that shaped her social consciousness? Her head and heart were filled with the American perception of open spaces, individual needs and wants, a typically American view of open doors as a sign of friendliness and sociability. She was not even aware of how uniquely American such views are. As the pedagogical go-between, the teacher has to help students construct their own social and cultural reality.

Second, the learners have to reconstruct *the context of production and reception* of a given text or phenomenon from within the foreign culture itself (C2, C2'). In the German 4 class in the example above, the teacher was trying to show that a Marxist audience might have understood *Galilei* very differently from a German audience attending the play after the atomic bomb fell on Hiroshima. In Judy's example mentioned earlier, the second step might entail understanding the context of open vs. closed doors in bourgeois German tradition (Kramsch, 1983), the value placed on orderliness, the way space is traditionally managed, the significance of the private vs. public spheres, of private life vs. the 9 to 5 public life, the father-daughter relationships in certain German families, attitudes vis-a-vis foreigners (see, e.g., Craig, 1982). Indeed, ethnographic methods of observing and analyzing foreign cultures would come in handy here (e.g., Brooks, 1975; Swaffar, 1991).

The third step involves, beyond understanding each context on its own ground, examining the way in which *C1' and C2' contexts in part determine C1" and C2"*, i.e., the way each culture views the other in the mirror of itself. The links made by the German 4 students between their texts and the Brecht play were influenced by the way their society views science and technology. And, to return to the previous example, Judy was perplexed not because she didn't have the appropriate vocabulary, but because she was interpreting the situation according to her own social values. Not understanding the context, she couldn't know when to use or not to use the vocabulary she knew. Thus the third stage entails understanding how we impose our schemata on the members of other cultures, and how they impose theirs on ours.

Finally, and most important, this approach involves *dialogue and another way of teaching*, for C1 and C2 are not monolithic entities, but a conglomerate of many different perspectives and ways of creating meaning. Rules of meaning are not like rules of grammar. They cannot be generalized across contexts and delivered ready-made, to be comprehended, and/or memorized, and performed. They are up for interpretation and can only be experienced through the cognitive conflicts brought about by dialogic situations. In the examples above, conversational partners have had to engage in the hard and patient attempt, not only to withhold their own and tolerate others' version of events, but also to have their worlds of meaning converge. These *discourse worlds* (Edmondson, 1985) vary with the setting, the participants, the purpose of the interaction, the intentions of the speakers, the tone, the channel of communication, the cultural norms of interaction and interpretation, the type of encounter. They also vary with the perceptions by the participants of each of these dimensions of the context. Between these worlds, boundary phenomena or occurrences of transference should be sought, analyzed and placed into their larger social context. Ultimately, teaching culture or sociopragmatic competence, unlike teaching grammar, requires a mode of interaction that focuses on exploration and description, rather than judgment and evaluation (Thomas, 1983).

CONCLUSION

Despite the recent focus on interactive processes in language learning, many language teachers still think that the meaning of a cultural event, be it a social encounter or a literary text, is either in the event itself or in the individual speaker/reader's perception of that event. The four steps suggested above for the teaching of culture through language are based on the insight that meaning, i.e., culture, is dialogically created through language *in discourse.*

These lines of thought lay the ground for a much richer understanding of the teaching of culture than we have envisaged up to now. We are now much more aware of the extent to which the indexical and the symbolic aspects of language vary with the situation and the context of interaction. Even the concept of a national culture has to be differentiated. An individual's ability to display indexical knowledge about the target culture is no measure of his/her ability to manipulate the symbolic meanings of language in interaction with various interlocutors in a variety of social contexts. And yet, this is precisely the cultural ability which the teacher has to develop in the classroom, irrespective of whether the tests of cultural proficiency will ultimately be able to evaluate it or not.

In two concrete classroom examples, I have shown how teachers cannot only experience the discourse of their classroom but also give it a cultural reading. It is this reading that will enable them to move their students beyond their usual frame of reference and introduce them to other cultures.[4] Our purpose in teaching culture through language is not to make our students into little French or little Germans, but in making them understand why the speakers of two different languages act and react the way they do, whether in fictional texts or in social encounters, and what the consequences of these insights may mean for the learner.

We can ask learners to temporarily play a role that is not theirs, think thoughts that they don't usually think. Ultimately, however, they will have to decide how they wish to shape this culture of the third kind, that is neither the one they grew up with, nor the one they are invited to enter. Social awareness goes hand in hand with social responsibility both vis-à-vis others and vis-à-vis oneself.[5]

NOTES

1.   It would have echoed in part Louis XIV famous statement: *L'état, c'est moi.*

2.   For a discussion of the American proliferation of the word *challenge*, see Kramsch 1993b. See also the current proliferation of the euphemistic *I'm disappointed*, or *This is disappointing* to express frustration, anger, or even rage.

3.   Some teachers might feel that teacher B was unduly manipulative. However, one can also say that he was making visible on the blackboard meanings that were potentially already there in the students' utterances. If, as Halliday says, language is *actualization of meaning potential* (1978), then the teacher was only actualizing one of the many ways of "making sense" of the classroom discourse. And every teacher, implicitly or explicitly, does precisely that, for this is the essence of classroom teaching. Moreover, by interpreting the discourse of the classroom, the teacher provides a model of how to

deal with cultural diversity: comparing, contrasting, searching for further evidence, seeking patterns, challenging hypotheses and responding to challenges.

4. For some recent studies of classroom discussion that foster cross-cultural awareness and a sense of authorship in the classroom, see Kramsch 1993a, 1995, 1996a, 1997, 2000.

5. Since this chapter was written, two aspects of the teaching of language and culture have been given particular prominence: The development of intercultural competence and the use of computer-mediated communication. The concept of intercultural competence, thoroughly researched and operationalized by Michael Byram (e.g., Byram, 1997, Byram et al., 2001), has been investigated from a discourse perspective by Scollon & Scollon (2000) and Kramsch (2002). The interest in the use of the computer to foster communication across cultures has its enthusiastic advocates (e.g., Kern &Warschauer, 2000) and its more cautious proponents (Kramsch & Andersen, 1998; Kramsch, A'Ness & Lam, 2000; Kramsch & Thorne, 2002).

REFERENCES

Anderson, B. (1991). *Imagined communities*. New York: Verso.

Bellah, R. N., Madsen, R., Sullivan, W. M., Swindler, A., & Tiptoe, S. M. (1985). *Habits of the heart: Individualism and commitment in American life*. New York: Harper and Row.

Bertho, C. (1980). L'Invention de la Bretagne: Genèse sociale d'un stéréotype. *Actes de la recherche en sciences sociales: L'Identité (35)*, 45–62.

Borkin, N., & Reinhart, S. M. (1978). 'Excuse me' and 'I'm sorry'. *TESOL Quarterly, 12*, 57–76.

Brooks, N. (1975). The analysis of foreign and familiar cultures. In R. Lafayette (Ed.), *The culture revolution in foreign language teaching* (pp. 19–31). Central States Conference Reports. Skokie, IL: National Textbook Company.

Brown, R., & Gilman, A. (1960). The pronouns and power and solidarity. In T. A. Sebeok (Ed.), *Style in language* (pp. 253–276) Cambridge, MA: MIT Press.

Byram, M. (1997). *Teaching and assessing intercultural communicative comptence*. Clevedon, UK: Multilingual Matters.

Bryan, M, Nichols, A., & Stevens, D. (Eds.) (2001). *Developing intercultural competence in practice*. Clevedon, UK: Multilingual Matters.

Carroll, R. (1987). *Evidences invisibles: Américains et Français au quotidien*. Paris: Seuil. Trsl. by Carol Volk as *Cultural misunderstandings: The French and American experience*. Chicago: University of Chicago Press, 1988.

Craig, G. A. (1982). *The Germans*. New York: Putnam.

Dahl, O. (Ed.) (1995). *Intercultural communication and contact*. Stavanger, Norway: Misjonshogskolens forlag.

Edmondson, W. (1981). On saying 'your sorry.' In F. Coulmas (Ed.), *Conversational routine*. The Hague: Mouton.

Edmondson, W. (1985). Discourse worlds in the classroom and in foreign language learning. *Studies in Second Language Acquisition, 7*, 159–68.

Fraser, B. (1981). On apologising. In F. Coulmas (Ed.), *Conversational routine.* The Hague: Mouton.

Halliday, M. A. K. (1978). *Language as social semiotic: The social interpretation of language and meaning.* London: Arnold.

Holmes, J. (1989). Sex differences and apologies: One aspect of communicative competence. *Applied Linguistics, 10,* 2, 194–213.

Johnstone, B. (1999). Communication in multicultural settings: Resources and strategies for affiliation and identity. In T.Vestergaard (Ed.), *Language, culture and identity* (pp. 23–40). Aalborg, DK: Aalborg University Press.

Keller, G. (1987). Auto- und heterostereotype amerikanischer und deutscher schüler in einer neuen kulturkunde. *Die Neueren Sprachen, 86, 1,* 63–79.

Kelly, G. (1955). *Theory of personal constructs.* New York: W. W. Norton.

Kern, R., & Warschauer, M. (Eds.) (2000). *Network-based language teaching: Concepts and practice.* Cambridge, UK: Cambridge University Press.

Koole, T., & ten Thije, J. D. (1994). *The construction of intercultural discourse: Team discussions of educational advisers.* Amsterdam: Rodopi.

Kramsch, C. (1983). Culture and constructs: Communicating attitudes and values in the foreign language classroom. *Foreign Language Annals, 16,* 437–448.

Kramsch, C. (1990). The order of discourse in language teaching. In B. Freed (Ed.), *Foreign language acquisition research and the classroom* (pp. 191–204). Lexington, MA: D. C. Heath.

Kramsch, C. (1993a). Language study as border study: Experiencing difference. *European Journal of Education, 28,* 349–58.

Kramsch, C. (1993b). *Context and culture in language teaching.* Oxford: Oxford University Press.

Kramsch, C. (1995). Rhetorical models of understanding. In T. Miller (Ed.), *Functional approaches to written texts: Classroom applications* (pp. 61–78). *TESOL France, 2, (2).*

Kramsch, C. (1996a). Stylistic choice and cultural awareness. In L. Bredella & W. Delanoy (Eds.), *Challenges of literary texts in the foreign language classroom* (pp. 162–184). Tübingen: Gunter Narr.

Kramsch, C. (1997). The privilege of the non-native speaker. *PMLA, 112,* 3.

Kramsch, C. (1998). *Language and culture.* Oxford: Oxford University Press.

Kramsch, C. (1999). Thirdness: The intercultural stance. In T. Vestergaard (Ed.), *Language, culture, and identity* (pp. 41–58). Aalborg, DK: Aalborg University Press.

Kramsch, C. (2000). Social discursive construction of self in L2 learning: Vygotskyian perspectives. In J. Lantolf (Ed.), *Sociocultural theory and second language learning* (pp. 133–54). Oxford, UK: Oxford University Press.

Kramsch, C. (2002). In search of the intercultural. Review article. *Journal of Sociolinguistics 6,* 275–85.

Kramsch, C, & Andersen, R. (1998). Teaching text and context through multimedia. *Language alearning and Technology 2,* 2, 31–42.

Kramsch, C., A'Ness, F., & Lam, W-S. E. (2000). Authenticity and authorship in the computer-mediated acquisition of L2 literacy. *Language Learning and Technology 4,* 2, 78–104.

Kramsch, C., & Thorne, S. (2002). Foreign language learning as global communicative practice. In D. Block & D. Cameron (Eds.), *Globalization and language teaching* (pp. 67–82). London: Routledge.

Marx, L. (1964). *The machine in the garden: Technology and the pastoral ideal in America.* Oxford: Oxford Univ. Press.

National Standards In Foreign Language Education Project. (1996). *Standards for foreign language learning: Preparing for the 21st century.* Yonkers, NY: The National Standards Project.

Nora, P. (1986). *Les lieux de mémoire. Vol. II. La nation.* Paris: Gallimard.

Nostrand, H. (1974). Empathy for a second culture: Motivations and techniques. In G. A. Jarvis (Ed.), *Responding to new realities* (pp. 263–328). ACTFL Foreign Language Education Series. Skokie, IL: National Textbook.

Nostrand, H. (1991). Basic intercultural education needs breadth and depth: The role of a second culture. In E. Silber (Ed.), *Critical issues in foreign language instruction.* New York: Garland.

Nyikos, M. (1991). "Teaching as inquiry: New paradigms for language teachers and teacher educators." Presentation at the Annual ACTFL Convention in Washington, D.C. Nov. 23, 1991.

Olshtain, E. (1983). Sociocultural competence and language transfer: The case of apology. In S. Gass & L. Selinker (Eds.), *Language transfer in language learning.* Rowley, MA: Newbury House.

Olshtain, E. (1989). Apologies across languages. In S. Blum-Kulka, J.House & G. Kasper (Eds.), *Cross-cultural pragmatics: Requests and apologies.* Vol.XXXI in the series Advances in Discourse Processes, R. O. Freedle (Ed.). Norwood, N.J.: Ablex.

Resnick, L. B., & Resnick, D. P. (1991). Assessing the thinking curriculum: New tools for educational reform. In B. R. Gifford & M. C. O'Connor (Eds.), *Changing assessments: Alternative views of aptitude, achievement and instruction.* Boston: Kluwer.

Saville-Troike, M. (1991). Cultural maintenance and 'vanishing' languages. In C. Kramsch & S. McConnell-Ginet (Eds.), *Text and context: Cross-disciplinary perspectives on language study* (pp. 148–155). Lexington, MA: D.C. Heath.

Scollon, R, & Scollon, S. W. (2000). *Intercultural communication: A discourse approach.* 2nd ed. Oxford, UK: Blackwell.

Steele, R. & Suozzo, A. (1994). *Teaching French culture: Theory and practice.* Lincolnwood, IL: National Textbook Company.

Swaffar, J. (1991). Written texts and cultural readings. In C. Kramsch & S. McConnell-Ginet (Eds.), *Text and context: Cross-disciplinary perspectives on language study* (pp. 238–250). Lexington, MA: D.C. Heath.

Tannen, D. (1991). Rethinking power and solidarity in gender and dominance. In C. Kramsch & S. McConnell-Ginet (Eds.), *Text and context: Cross-disciplinary perspectives on language study* (pp. 135–147). Lexington, MA: D.C. Heath.

Thomas, J. (1983). Cross-cultural pragmatic failure. *Applied Linguistics, 4, 2,* 91–112.

Widdowson, H. G. (1983). *Learning purpose and language use.* Oxford: Oxford University Press.

Widdowson, H. G. (1991). *Culture and language learning.* Triangle 7 Paris: Didier-Erudition.

Zarate, G. (1986). *Enseigner une culture étrangère.* Paris: Hachette.

CHAPTER 3

A LINGUISTIC ANTHROPOLOGICAL PERSPECTIVE ON LANGUAGE AND CULTURE IN THE SECOND LANGUAGE CURRICULUM[1]

Jill Brody

INTRODUCTION

From the perspective of a linguistic anthropologist considering the role of culture in second language education, it is apparent that although the concept of culture is drawn upon frequently in the second language teaching literature, it is often used in a fairly unconsidered, constrained, and taken-for-granted fashion; the importance of culture is often recognized but seldom analyzed.

It is impossible to deal with second language education without taking culture into account. When the goal of second language learning became communication, culture was inevitably involved. While language is gener-

Culture as the Core: Perspectives in Second Language Education, pages 37–51
Copyright © 2003 by Information Age Publishing
All rights of reproduction in any form reserved.

ally the focus of learning in second language classrooms, culture is very much present in several forms. There is the culture of the language-learner and the culture of the target language. Neither of these two forms of culture is necessarily monolithic, for the students in a second language classroom may be of multiple linguistic and cultural backgrounds, and of course any culture subsumes a broad diversity on many dimensions, including the linguistic dimension. The roles of these two cultures in the classroom setting differ as well: the culture of the language learner is a stepping-stone for comparison with the culture of the target language, while the latter constitutes the knowledge to be imparted in the class. The type of language and culture learning that goes on depends on the type of classroom, whether it is for immigrants, for an auxiliary language, or for minority language speakers; each of these represents an enormously different cultural and classroom situation. Although there are profound differences between foreign language education and second language education in cultural context, some general language and culture issues are common across the distinct situations.

The classroom itself also constitutes a cultural setting. The second language classroom is a first-order authentic locus of second language learning culture; foreign language classrooms may be the unique locus of foreign culture learning. The second language classroom is also a setting for a particular, often highly constrained, sort of culture contact. From this perspective, language teaching and language learning may be observed ethnographically as activities of second language classroom culture.

The proliferation of cultures in the second language classroom carries with it political, pedagogical, and personal implications, and it is useful to be aware of which layer or aspect of culture is pertinent for any given issue. The second language classroom is the locus of culture contact of a particular type with a particular goal—to learn (something of) the target language and (something about) the target culture. At this level the role of culture is problematic—is the goal of second language education to achieve complete bilingualism and biculturalism? While it is possible on some level to have bilingualism without biculturalism (Agar, 1991), culture is nevertheless present at several levels in the second language classroom, notwithstanding the ongoing debates about what it can and should be in that context. Rather than holding out the unrealistic and unreasonable goal of creating biculturalism, the issue of culture in second language education is more a matter of recognizing the particular aspect or level of culture that is pertinent, and making the discussion and treatment of culture overt. Classroom goals may emphasize bilingualism over biculturalism, simply because the latter more apparently requires the apparatus of the larger cultural context, which cannot, in all fairness, ever be replicated within the confines of the average classroom. If the goal is something short of complete bilingualism, how much and what type of culture should be taught?

A linguistic anthropological perspective on these issues can offer illumination in three general areas: (1) expertise regarding the concept of culture, the practice of investigation of culture, and ways in which it can be taught; (2) a close understanding of the relationship between language and culture; and, (3) the methodologies of ethnographic observation and discourse analysis to understand what is really going on in the second language classroom. In order to evaluate what culture is or what it can or should be for second language education, it is crucial to begin with discussion of what anthropological culture constitutes and with a consideration of the relationship between language and culture. I will then expand upon several key aspects of culture as they are viewed by linguistic anthropologists and dealt with by second language education. Throughout the discussion, I will distinguish native culture and language from target culture and language; briefly, native culture is what one is born into and native language is one's first language, both of which are brought into the second language classroom. There the second language and culture are encountered, either exclusively or as part of a cultural immersion.

THE CONCEPT OF CULTURE

The concept of culture is at the core of the discipline of anthropology, especially in North America, and constitutes a hallmark of the discipline. Like any complex, useful concept with a disciplinary home, it not only has technical meanings but also a set of everyday meanings. In addition, the term is frequently borrowed and incorporated by other disciplines, and is altered in that process by the goals and traditions of the borrowers. Culture particularly lends itself to this kind of accommodational lending because it is such a fundamental and complex topic. An update of Kroeber and Kluckhohn's 1952 compilation of definitions of culture would fill an even larger volume. Yet the multiple definitions hover around a core which is important to understand holistically.

There are generally three aspects of culture distinguished: Culture (capitalized) as the highly evaluated products of Civilization (also capitalized); a culture (with the definite or indefinite article) as relating to a particular group of people and their way of life as in *the culture of the Eskimo* (a classically misused example discussed further below); and, culture the anthropological concept. This latter concept of culture subsumes the other two abstractly, and refers to that distinctively human way of organizing, interacting, and understanding each other and the world. An important corollary of the anthropological concept of culture is that of cultural relativity, which means that each culture must be understood in its own terms, without imposing upon it the values and structures of other cultures, or bias from the culture of the observer.

Certainly second language education has traditionally relied heavily on Culture, e.g., great works of art or literature, in teaching language. There are also increasing references to the particular culture held by speakers of a language. However, references to particular cultures tend to assume homogeneity of the target culture and often take a superficial form, e.g., a checklist. This type of approach often focuses on a comparison of cultural particularities, such as table manners, which makes cultural differences in general seem to exist on the order of importance of whether the fork is held in the left or right hand. Besides encouraging trivialization of cultural features and differences, the checklist approach has the danger of portraying cultural differences as a series of peculiarities to be resolved by a simple comparative formula.

As alluded to above, there is a profound danger in the assumption of cultural homogeneity on either side of the teaching equation. No generic notion of *Hispanic culture* can account for the great differences among the many cultural groups speaking Spanish, to take only two examples, in rural Ecuador and Mexico City. The assumption that all Vietnamese immigrants to the United States who are learning English share the same culture is as ludicrous as that of English language speakers representing a homogenous culture. In the case of *the culture of the Eskimo*, the term *Eskimo* has been imposed by outsiders upon a number of different Arctic peoples, such as the Inuit and the Yupik; no *Eskimo* calls herself an *Eskimo*.[2]

The abstract concept of culture emerges within language teaching practices in a much more subtle and diffuse manner, if at all. However, it is this aspect of the culture concept that can result in an integrated and enduring comprehension of not only what culture is, but what particular cultures and their differences are. The anthropological concept of culture provides a holistic understanding of the unique integration of all aspects of human life, which can then be applied to particular encounters.

INTEGRATION OF LANGUAGE AND CULTURE

The following discussion is necessarily highly selective of those interconnected aspects of language and culture that are most applicable to the situation encountered in second language classrooms. Language and culture are inextricably intertwined. Culture is negotiated in large part through language, and language codifies many cultural assumptions and values. This codification is most apparent in the overtly articulated aspects of culture, which, however, are not always as straightforward as they might initially appear to be. Once again, in the case of *the culture of the Eskimo* mentioned above, there is a widely held erroneous belief that the language of the Eskimo has many words for snow because of the snowy environment in which Eskimo people live (see Martin, 1986, for discussion).

Linguistic studies in American anthropology originated as a means of gaining access through the unconscious patterning of language to unconscious cultural patterns (Boas, 1911). The discussion of how language represents culture and how culture is manifested through language has typically been phrased in terms of linguistic relativity. Although linguistic relativity is often referred to as the Sapir-Whorf hypothesis, after two anthropologists who explored the question extensively (Kay & Kempton, 1984), neither Sapir nor Whorf actually articulated their understanding of the relationship between language, culture, and thought as a hypothesis, either in weak or strong form. Linguistic relativity rests on the nature of the relationship between language and culture, which consists of mutual reflection and mutual influence. Friedrich (1986) articulates the central issue of relativity: "a natural language is a different way not only of talking but of thinking and imagining and of emotional life" (p. 16).

Explorations of linguistic relativity have largely concentrated on morphology, as a (grammatically) obligatory part of language structure that is used in an unconscious fashion and that carries cultural meaning. These include fundamental ways of understanding the physical world (e.g., through spatial deixis), time (e.g., tense and aspect), and the social world and the place of the individual in it (e.g., personal pronouns).

As issues of the relationship between language and thought enter into the discussion of second language learning, it is crucial that they be grounded in a detailed understanding of linguistic mechanisms and cultural use. Otherwise, the result may fall short of the standards of either cultural relativism and linguistic accuracy. Both standards are violated in the much cited depiction of *cultural thought patterns* as revealed in written paragraph structure. For instance, in English (the language and culture of reference) the rhetorical structure is claimed to be *linear,* but for other languages and cultural patterns (*Romance, Russian, Semitic, Oriental,* which are in themselves gross generalizations), it is characterized by *digression* and *irrelevant* material (Kaplan, 1966). In fact, most commonplace examples of linguistic relativity are either trivial, wrong, or both.

The challenges of rigorous exploration of the relationships between language, culture, and thought as well as the discouragement engendered by misunderstanding and misappropriation of the Sapir-Whorf hypothesis within and outside of linguistic anthropology resulted in a hiatus of research in the area during the past several decades. Recently, however, linguistic anthropologists have renewed their interest in linguistic relativity and brought new perspectives to its investigation (Gumperz & Levinson,

1996; Lucy, 1992a, b), including expansion into the areas of lexicon (the source of much misunderstanding of the Eskimo words for snow type (Martin, 1986)) and speech community (Gumperz & Levinson, 1996).

In linguistic anthropology, the means for gaining access to cultural modes of appropriate language use in context is the ethnography of speaking, the application of the traditional anthropological qualitative methodology of participant observation to the investigation of language in use (Hymes, 1972b, 1974). Examination of the use of language in ethnographic context allows the recognition of subtle differences across languages and cultures, particularly with regard to turn-taking, appropriate topic or information, silence, argument structure, forms of address, and the meaning of speech acts. Ethnographic approaches to the use of language encompass the participants (who may interact and in what fashion), the setting (what types of language use are appropriate to which locations), as well as the channel, form, content, and genre of the language used; crucial also are the norms of interpretation operative within the community (Hymes, 1972b). The culturally appropriate use of these features is founded in an individual's *communicative competence*, her capabilities for using language appropriately; "competence is dependent upon both (tacit) knowledge and (ability for) use" (Hymes, 1972a, p. 282). As second language curricula have embraced communication as a goal (Brumfit & Johnson, 1979; Widdowson, 1978), teaching some degree of communicative competence has become a primary goal, and the scope of the second language curriculum has been correspondingly altered to include cultural differences in language use. Another way of locating language as a way of seeing the world is through discourse, defined by Brown and Yule (1983) as language in use. Discourse,

> . . . can be oral or written and can be approached in textual or sociocultural and social-interactional terms. And it can be brief like a greeting and thus smaller than a single sentence or lengthy like a novel or narration of personal experience and thus larger than a sentence and constructed out of sentences or sentence-like utterances. (Sherzer, 1987, p. 296)

An approach through discourse allows a rephrasing of the language-culture relationship.

> Instead of asking such questions as does grammar reflect culture or is culture determined by grammar, or are there isomorphisms between grammar and culture, we rather start with discourse, which is the nexus, the actual and concrete expression of the language-culture-society relationship. It is discourse which creates, recreates, modifies, and fine-tunes both culture and language and their intersection. (Sherzer, 1987, p. 296)

Examination of discourse as the use of language in cultural context is impossible without cultural understanding. Second language education has generally embraced an approach using discourse patterns, in contrast to an earlier emphasis on grammar and vocabulary, via greater attention to meaning, especially situated meaning (Smith, 1987). The discourse patterns of the target language, e.g., speech acts, sentence types, coherence and cohesion and rhetorical structure, are identified and taught. Speech acts such as compliments, apologies, invitations and complaints involve rules for speaking that are highly culturally specific (Wolfson & Judd, 1983).

Another sort of approach to understanding another culture that has a lengthy history in anthropology is the examination of cultural themes (Opler, 1945). More recently, anthropologists and linguists have fine-tuned this approach via detailed analyses of culturally significant words in order to understand the semantic and cultural configurations of their meaning and use. Wierzbicka (1991) takes key terms, in this case from Japanese, that express core cultural values and amasses data from many types of sources in order to provide appropriate cultural contextualization: dictionary definitions, cultural commentaries, translations, journalistic, fictional and anthropological accounts. Her ultimate goal is to derive the meaning of the terms from a set of culture-independent universal semantic primitives. Both the process and the goal are revealing of language-culture interactions. Agar (1991) engages in a similar type of comparative analysis, which could be very profitably undertaken in second language education. He identifies key cultural terms as *rich* points in a language, where cultural meaning is attached in a particularly dense fashion. Analysis of rich points,

> ... reveals not only the interpretive wherewithal to properly use the lexical item or to properly engage in speech events that instantiate it. It also reveals a core view of things that ramify into most of the details of everyday life. (Agar, 1991, p. 179)

This kind of analysis is profoundly revealing of culture (within language and also extra-linguistically) and is also adaptable to second language classroom teaching situations. The examples from Wierzbicka and Agar focus on the lexicon as the most accessible area of language for the learner, but it is important to note that other parts of language, such as morphology, can also carry cultural meaning (Sherzer, 1987).

Just as individual terms can carry special cultural associations, so can the relationship between terms have unique cultural meaning. Metaphors as relations between terms are part of the language-culture interface. The cultural meaning of metaphor has been investigated within English as well as within other languages and cultures (the papers in Sapir & Crocker, 1977; see also Freidrich, 1986). The exploration of normal, everyday metaphors, such as "Time is money" for English (Lakoff & Johnson, 1980) or "One paddle leaves early" for Haya (Seitel, 1977) to discover their meanings and appropriate contexts of use rewards analysts with rich information about cultural meaning, values, aesthetics, and associations.

CULTURE IS LEARNED

Linguistic anthropologists recognize that humans are born with a capacity to learn absolutely any culture and any language to which they are exposed. One's native language and culture are learned spontaneously throughout life from experience in a process of enculturation. Different cultures utilize different learning and teaching styles in enculturation. When different cultures come into contact with one another, members learn about the other culture in a process of acculturation. These two modes of learning characterize the fundamental differences between how native culture and language and second language and culture are acquired.

A model for second language learning based on the concept of acculturation emphasizes the influence of social and affective factors on the individual's ability to learn a second language, with the maxim that "the learner will acquire the second language only to the degree that he acculturates" (Schumann, 1978, pp. 28–29). Two types of acculturation are distinguished. One type occurs where the learner is part of or *socially integrated* with the community. Schumann claims that a second type of acculturation takes place when "the learner regards the [target language] speakers as a reference group whose life style and values he consciously or unconsciously wants to adopt" (p. 29). Certainly acculturation, as Schumann defines it, will be necessarily inhibited in situations where the contact between the learner and the language and culture to be learned is limited, as in the foreign language classroom.

An extension of this discussion, often described in terms of types of motivation in second language learning, has been carried out in terms of the learners' receptivity to the language and culture being taught, where significant issues of language and culture differences must be confronted. For example, in discussing the possibility of enhancing receptivity to classroom materials, Allwright and Bailey (1991) suggest that they be designed in a "culturally neutral way so that they reflect the native culture of the learners, rather than that of the target language's native speakers" (p. 159). However, the goal of cultural neutrality is profoundly misguided, representing a lack of understanding of the anthropological concept of culture. If material from the target language is stripped of its culture (even assuming such a possibility) and skewed toward the native language, the result is a conscious separation of language learning from culture learning.

Unfortunately, the *culturally neutral* pedagogy advocated by Allwright and Bailey violates all aspects of cultural learning discussed above. Based on the superficial checklist view of culture, it can never result in anything but the most superficial understanding of cultural differences.

CULTURE IS KNOWLEDGE, BOTH OVERT AND COVERT

One approach often taken by linguistic anthropologists is that culture is what native participants know in order to participate in their culture; knowledge is thus highly specific to culture. Knowledge about what the world consists of and how the world works—some of which is overtly held and some of which is assumed—is shared among members of a culture. Of course, no individual controls all cultural knowledge, and not all participants in a culture share the same range of cultural knowledge; this is vividly the case for complex heterogeneous cultures, as mentioned above. Cultural knowledge is subdivided by subculture, age, region, social group, and a multiplicity of other factors. Second language classrooms exemplify a particularly striking form of cultural diversity when they are composed of native speakers of different languages from a range of cultures.

Cultural knowledge involves, among many other things, knowing how to speak and how to use language appropriately, that is, communicative competence as discussed above. Some cultural knowledge is overt and can be expressed and taught directly. Other kinds of cultural knowledge are not known at the level of consciousness, e.g., the function of sub-phonemic differences, nonverbal behavior, and rhetorical structure. Other commonsense aspects of culture are so utterly taken-for-granted that it seems ridiculous to participants to talk about them, much less to consider alternatives (Geertz, 1983). Fundamental knowledge about the world is highly culture-specific, including such basic factors as what constitutes physical space, temporal existence and social domains, and how they are organized; as mentioned above, much of this information is carried via linguistic structure. What is known at the level of assumptions for native culture may have to be made explicit in order to be taught in the second language classroom.

The view of culture-as-knowledge underscores one of the greatest challenges for the second language classroom. Because it is isolated from the target culture and language, the classroom is thus the sole venue for students of the entire target cultural context. How can cultural knowledge be conveyed when students have only limited access to the everyday contexts of the culture in operation? Culture as knowledge, especially as overt knowledge, is the most accessible mode of culture for second language teaching. Yet the wholesale importation of total cultural knowledge into the classroom is obviously impossible. Aspects of Culture, (e.g., history, geography, art, elements of popular culture, and touristic encounters) typically represent the knowledge of second language education. The importance given to cultural knowledge ranges from *carrier topics* (Allwright & Bailey, 1991) or language classroom type topics: "hors d'oeuvres" such as "holidays," "pets," and "family meals" (Brooks, 1986, pp. 124, 125, 127), through photographs integrated into lessons, to cultural manuals (Althen, 1988; Harrison, 1983).

Alternatively, units covering aspects of overt cultural knowledge are packaged into the curriculum, such as "Language Skills and Cultural Awareness, Pronunciation: Word Stress, Grammar: Levels of Directness, Needs Assessment: Characteristics of a Good Teacher in the United States" in a course for foreign TAs in the United States (Smith, Meyers, & Burkhalter, 1992, p. iii). In either form, culture-as-knowledge is the most overtly recognized and regularly presented version of culture in the second language classroom. The issue of acquiring competence and assumed knowledge confronts second language education with the challenge of teaching in an overt fashion for the second language what is learned tacitly and used unconsciously in the first language. Widdowson (1978) recognizes the problem, but seems to be advocating a similar solution to that of Allwright and Bailey (1991):

> An over-concentration on usage may often have the effect of putting the language being learned at a remove from the learner's own experience of language ... normal communization [in the native language] operates at the level of use and we are not generally aware of the usage aspect of performance. By focusing on usage, therefore, the language teacher directs the attention of the learner to those features of performance which normal use of language requires him to ignore. Thus, the way the foreign language is presented in the classroom does not correspond with the learner's experience of his own language outside the classroom ... On the contrary, the way he is required to learn the foreign language conflicts with the way he knows language actually works ... By effectively denying the learner reference to his own experience the teacher increases the difficulty of the language learning task. (pp. 17–18)

Strevens (1982) identifies circumstances that can interfere with the teaching and learning of a second language. These include "where the purposes for which English is being taught/learned are absent in the learner's culture; ... where rational argument is not revered; ... where ideology outweighs everyday 'reality'; and ... where personal comportment plays a role" (pp. 171–172). However, two of the analytical concepts which Strevens employs—rational argument and ideology vs. everyday 'reality'—are in fact themselves cultural constructs; by privileging them, Strevens is imposing English-speaking Western culture assumptions on his analysis rather than discovering the assumptions of other cultures that might explain successful second language learning.

A largely untapped resource for bringing cultural knowledge and experience directly into foreign language classrooms is the local availability of native speakers for many commonly taught languages. In many U.S. universities, for example, there are native speakers in attendance in the ESL programs. Pairing up native speakers with foreign language students would provide interactions of great mutual benefit.[3]

CULTURE IS A SHARED SYMBOLIC SYSTEM: THE CULTURE OF THE SECOND LANGUAGE CLASSROOM

Culture is more than knowledge. Knowledge is necessarily confined to the individual. While never denying the uniqueness of the individual, culture is understood to be something that is shared among groups of individuals who participate in a way of life. As Geertz (1973) points out,

> ...culture is best seen not as complexes of concrete behavior patterns—customs, usages, traditions, habit clusters ... but as a set of control mechanisms—plans, recipes, rules, instructions ... or the governing of behavior. (p. 44)

Culture does not live in the minds of individuals, but rather in their interactions with one another, as "traffic in ... significant symbols" (p. 45). These symbols include words, gestures, material objects from computers to stones, and nonlanguage sounds. Geertz articulates this semiotic view of culture as "interworked systems of construable signs (symbols)" (p. 14). Kinship, ritual and political structure as well as language are organized symbolically. The enactment of culture in social interaction is its natural environment, or as Geertz states "Culture is public because meaning is" (p. 12).

Participants in the second language classroom—whether it is a foreign language classroom or a second language classroom for immigrants—come to it with varied cultural perspectives and varied ways of understanding the world. While these heterogeneous backgrounds contribute to the particulars of what goes on in the classroom, they are background or *underlife* in the terms set out by Gutierrez, Rymes, and Larson (1995),[4] to the public interaction of the classroom. Within the context of the classroom, a particular type of official interaction is forged and meanings pertinent to the official tasks at hand are publicly invoked. Part of the task at hand is to learn something about the target language and culture, although the class-room is necessarily only a partial representation of the target culture.

The second language classroom itself is a first-order locus of a particular kind of public meaning, where the second-order business of language and culture learning takes place. The participants in classroom interactions are enacting complex cultural behaviors, only some of which can be under-stood in terms of a generalized classroom scenario. In fact, concepts about what a classroom is or should be will by no means necessarily be shared among participants. Knowledge about the target language and culture is imparted in the classroom, at times along with explications of tacit native-culture knowledge. The intercultural nature of the second language class-room does not render it culturally inauthentic, but must be recognized as a distinct and unique situation of cultural contact.

As a cultural phenomenon, the second language classroom can be investigated ethnographically using the anthropological technique of par-ticipant observation mentioned above (Allwright & Bailey, 1991; Green & Wallat, 1981). Ethnographic investigation of the (first-order) culture of the classroom must be undertaken in order to better understand its dynamics with the goal of improving the language and (second-order) cul-ture teaching. Classroom research, however, generally focuses on the teacher, the learner, analysis of errors, and the strategies for communica-tion engaged in by second language speakers (Chaudron, 1988; Tarone & Yule, 1983, 1987).

The anthropologist views the instructor as the anthropological infor-mant, the person serving as cultural broker to the students. Comparing the necessarily constrained classroom cultural setting with culture in all its rich and messy complexity highlights the limitations of the classroom situation. Yet the comparison is useful in another way; it points out that the goals of the student in the second language classroom, especially a foreign lan-guage classroom, are often more closely comparable to those of an anthro-pologist in the field than they are to those of a child learning her first language in a cultural setting. The anthropologist's goal in fieldwork is not to go native, but rather to learn something about the culture she is studying. This typically involves learning to speak the language to some degree and to operate with sufficient communicative competence, in order to behave in culturally appropriate ways, but it does not necessarily include becoming a naturalized part of the culture. The issues differ for foreign language classrooms and second language classroom for immigrants, but they are always present.

Discourse analysis techniques as discussed above can help meet the sub-tle challenges. Discourse analysis has been applied to classroom interac-tions (Gutierrez, Rymes, & Larson 1995; Mehan 1985) and has proven productive in analyzing native-speaker interactions with nonnative speakers (Larsen-Freeman, 1980; Tarone & Yule, 1987, 1989). The methodology of discourse analysis, with its close attention to what is said and the context in which it is uttered, holds the greatest promise for both comprehending the subtleties of language and culture (Brown & Yule, 1983; Sherzer, 1987) and for investigating just what exactly it is that goes on in second language classrooms.

It cannot be overemphasized that the second language classroom situation is not the same everywhere, depending on the particular linguistic and cultural situation, and on the goals of the students and teachers. Furthermore, both culture and language exhibit heterogeneity and undergo constant change, some of which is propelled by contact between members of different cultures and speakers of different languages. For all second language classrooms, the issue presents itself as one of choosing among varieties, and teaching which variety is appropriate to particular cultural contexts.

Cultural differences and cultural relativity are difficult topics to convey, and language teachers are generally not prepared to deal with them in any but the most superficial fashion. Remedies to this situation include education of teachers and students about culture in the largest anthropological sense, as those capacities that all humans share. Then, to ground this understanding within the particular language and culture context of the second language classroom, interaction with native speakers should be promoted. Cultural checklists are inevitably partial and incomplete, but a genuine understanding of the anthropological concept of culture allows its application to any particular situation of culture contact, including in the classroom.

NOTES

1. Many thanks to Gail Chabrán, Laura Martin, Stuart Stewart, and George Yule for directing me to some of the work cited here and commenting on an earlier version. I have gratefully incorporated many of their suggestions, but all errors are my own.
2. This point comes from discussions with Laura Martin.
3. This point comes from discussions with Stuart Stewart.
4. Thanks to Gail Chabrán for bringing this work to my attention.

REFERENCES

Agar, M. (1991). The biculture in bilingual. *Language in Society, 20,* 167–182.
Allwright, D., & Bailey, K.M. (1991). *Focus on the language classroom: An introduction to classroom research for language teachers.* Cambridge: Cambridge University Press.

Althen, G. (1983). *American ways: A guide for foreigners in the United States.* Yarmouth, ME: Intercultural Press, Inc.

Boas, F. (1911). *Handbook of American Indian languages.* Washington, DC: Smithsonian Institution.

Brooks, N. (1986). Culture in the classroom. In J.M. Valdes (Ed.), *Culture bound: Bridging the cultural gap in language teaching* (pp. 123–129). Cambridge: Cambridge University Press.

Brown, G., & Yule, G. (1983). *Discourse analysis.* Cambridge: Cambridge University Press.

Brumfit, C.J., & Johnson, K. (Eds.). (1979). *The communicative approach to language teaching.* Oxford: Oxford University Press.

Chaudron, C. (1988). *Second language classrooms: Research in teaching and learning.* New York: Cambridge University Press.

Friedrich, P. (1986). *The language parallax.* Austin: The University of Texas Press.

Geertz, C. (1973). *The interpretation of cultures.* New York: Basic Books, Inc.

Geertz, C. (1983). *Local knowledge.* New York: Basic Books, Inc.

Green, J.L., & Wallet, C. (Eds.). (1981). *Ethnography and language in educational settings.* Norwood, NJ: Ablex Publishing Corp.

Gumperz, J.J., & Levinson, S.C. (Eds.). (1996). *Rethinking linguistic relativity.* Cambridge: Cambridge University Press.

Gutierrez, K., Rymes, B., & Larson, J. (1995). Script, counterscript, and underlife in the classroom: James Brown versus Brown v. Board of Education. *Harvard Educational Review, 65,* 44–71.

Harrison, P.A. (1983). *Behaving Brazilian: A comparison of Brazilian and North American social behavior.* Rowley, MA: Newbury House Publishers.

Hymes, D. (1972a). On communicative competence. In J.B. Pride & J. Holmes (Eds.), *Sociolinguistics: Selected readings* (pp. 269–293). New York: Penguin.

Hymes, D. (1972b). Models of the interaction of language and social life. In J.J. Gumperz & D. Hymes (Eds.), *Directions in sociolinguistics: The ethnography of communication* (pp. 35–71). New York: Basil Blackwell.

Hymes, D. (1974). *Foundations in sociolinguistics: An ethnographic approach.* Philadelphia: University of Pennsylvania.

Kaplan, R.B. (1966). Cultural thought patterns in intercultural education. *Language Learning, 16,* 1–20.

Kay, P., & Kempton, W. (1984). What is the Sapir-Whorf Hypothesis? *American Anthropologist, 86,* 65–79.

Kroeber, A., & Kluckhohn, C. (1952/1966). *Culture: A critical review of concepts and definitions.* New York: Vintage.

Lakoff, G., & Johnson, M. (1980). *Metaphors we live by.* Chicago: University of Chicago Press.

Larsen-Freeman, D. (Ed.). (1980). *Discourse analysis in second language research.* Rowley, MA: Newbury House Publishers.

Lucy, J. (1992a). *Language diversity and thought: A reformulation of the linguistic relativity hypothesis.* Cambridge: Cambridge University Press.

Lucy, J. (1992b). *Grammatical categories and cognition: A case study of the linguistic relativity hypothesis.* Cambridge: Cambridge University Press.

Martin, L. (1986). Eskimo words for snow: A case study in the genesis and decay of an anthropological example. *American Anthropologist, 88*, 418–19.

Mehan, H. (1985). The structure of classroom discourse. In T.A. van Dijk (Ed.), *Handbook of discourse analysis, volume 3: Discourse and dialogue.* London: Academic Press.

Opler, M. (1945). Themes as dynamic forces in culture. *American Journal of Sociology, 51*, 198–206.

Sapir, J.D., & Crocker, J.C. (Eds.). (1977). *The social use of metaphor: Essays on the anthropology of rhetoric.* Philadelphia: University of Pennsylvania Press.

Schumann, J.H. (1978). The acculturation model for second language acquisition. In R.C. Gingras (Ed.), *Second-language acquisition and foreign language teaching* (pp. 27–50). Washington, DC: Center for Applied Linguistics.

Seitel, P. (1977). Saying Haya sayings: Two categories of proverb use. In J.D. Sapir & J.C. Crocker (Eds.), *The social use of metaphor: Essays on the anthropology of rhetoric* (pp. 75–99). Philadelphia: University of Pennsylvania Press.

Sherzer, J. (1987). A Discourse-centered approach to language and culture. *American Anthropologist, 89*, 295–309.

Smith, J., Meyers, C.M., & Burkhalter, A.J. (1992). *Communicate: Strategies for international teaching assistants.* Englewood Cliffs, NJ: Regents/Prentice-Hall.

Smith, L.E. (Ed.). (1987). *Discourse across cultures: Strategies in world Englishes.* Englewood Cliffs, NJ: Prentice-Hall.

Strevens, P. (1987). Cultural barriers to language learning. In L.E. Smith (Ed.), *Discourse across cultures: Strategies in world Englishes* (pp. 169–178). Englewood Cliffs, NJ: Prentice-Hall.

Tarone, E., & Yule, G. (1987). Communication strategies in East-West interactions. In L.E. Smith (Ed.), *Discourse across cultures: Strategies in world Englishes* (pp. 49–65). Englewood Cliffs, NJ: Prentice-Hall.

Tarone, E., & Yule, G. (1989). *Focus on the language learner.* Oxford: Oxford University Press.

Widdowson, H.G. (1978). *Teaching language as communication.* Oxford: Oxford University Press.

Wierzbicka, A. (1991). Japanese key words and core cultural values. *Language in Society, 20*, 333–386.

Wolfson, N., & Judd, E. (Eds.). (1983). *Sociolinguistics and language acquisition.* Cambridge, MA: Newbury House Publishers.

CHAPTER 4

CULTURE IN SECOND LANGUAGE LEARNING AND TEACHING

Anthropology Revisited

Robert C. Lafayette

INTRODUCTION

Is culture really a central issue in providing students with control of a foreign language, which is, at bottom, the teacher's essential task? Is anything more than incidental encounters with and random reference to cultural matters required in establishing the language skills? Will special emphasis upon culture not be wasteful of precious class time and end up by giving the student less rather than more of what he is entitled to expect from his language course? Should not the language class concern itself with language proper and postpone cultural matters until the student has greater maturity and greater language competence? There are already available many texts with a cultural ingredient in their total content; is it necessary to do more than is already being done? (Brooks, 1968, p. 206)

Culture as the Core: Perspectives in Second Language Education, pages 53–69
Copyright © 2003 by Information Age Publishing

Among the three major components of the curriculum (language, literature, and culture), the greatest amount of time and energy is still devoted to the grammar and vocabulary aspects of language, even though the area of communication has advanced considerably during the last twenty years due to activities surrounding communicative competence, the functional-notional syllabus, and proficiency. Culture, however, remains the weakest component due to its uneven treatment in textbooks and to the lack of familiarity, among teachers, with the culture itself and with the techniques needed to teach it (Lafayette, 1988, p. 47).

Exactly twenty years separate these two citations. The first, dated 1968, is taken from Brooks' celebrated article in the first volume of *Foreign Language Annals* in which he defines culture for the second language classroom. The second, dated 1988, emanates from an article by Lafayette in the Northeast Conference Reports, the sixth in this important collection to be devoted exclusively to the teaching of culture. Although the role of culture in second language learning and teaching has increased during those twenty years, progress has nevertheless been slow and at best erratic. This is in sharp contrast to the significant surge of interest in the areas of reading and writing. Bernhardt (1991) informs us that since 1976 some 350 articles in the area of reading and approximately 200 articles on the topic of writing have appeared in major journals serving the field of second language learning and teaching. Even more important are the facts that about 30% of these are based on empirical research and that the total does not include any of the numerous papers that have appeared in book-length collections on these two topics.

HISTORICAL PERSPECTIVE

Until the advent of audio-lingualism during the fifties and sixties, culture in the second language classroom was for the most part limited to literature, and even that was often confined to textbooks and/or courses beyond the intermediate level. The 90% or more of the student population who never reached the advanced levels had to be content with studying grammar and vocabulary, and analyzing "chock full of meaning" sentences such as "voici les pommes que j'ai mangées." It was actually the now much maligned audio-lingual movement, and its proponents, which opened the door to the two most discussed topics in present-day second language learning and teaching: communication and culture. Communication placed emphasis on oral skills, and culture broadened the definition to include everyday patterns of living. It was Brooks (1968) who implored us to look upon culture not necessarily as geography, history, folklore, sociology, literature, or civilization, even though all of these bore significant value for the classroom, but rather to consider culture in its anthropological sense as patterns for living. He reminded us that the single most important factor in distinguishing culture from other concepts is the fact that we never lose sight of the individual. Culture, he said:

> ... refers to the individual's role in the unending kaleidoscope of life situations of every kind and the rules and models for attitude and conduct in them. By reference to these models, every human being, from infancy onward, justifies the world to himself as best he can, associates with those around him, and relates to the social order to which he is attached. (p. 91)

Later, Brooks (1975) distinguished between culture and civilization using the following words:

> Culture is the distinctive life-way of a people, whether tribesmen, townsmen, or urbanites, who are united by a common language. The dual nature of culture links the thoughts and acts of the individual to the common patterns acceptable to the group. The community provides rules and models for belief and behavior, and these cannot be disregarded by the individual without penalty. The totality of the culture is the pervading medium that gives meaning to each individual's acts, yet his capacity for innovation, choice and rejection is never forgotten.

> Civilization is the flowering of the cultural life-way of a people into varied and refined patterns of thought, belief, action, and aesthetic expression that offer wide scope for the perfecting of individual talent and for involved and highly integrated achievement through joint communal effort. Grafted upon culture, civilization tends to enrich the existence of all members of the community, but it also tends to permit the exploitation of the weak by the strong. (pp. 21–22).

Brooks (1968, 1975) was not alone in suggesting the potential impact of anthropology in the second language classroom especially within the domain of culture. McLeod (1976) published an article entitled "The Relevance of Anthropology to Language Teaching" in which she suggested that three basic tenets of this field may be useful to the ESL/EFL teacher:

1. First of all, there is the concept of culture as the shared value system of the members of a society. As a system, it has discernible patterns which can be understood by an outsider to the particular culture.
2. Secondly, there is the idea of "cultural relativity," a theoretical equality among the cultures of the world; each should be viewed as a complete system having an integrity of its own and as appropriate for its own members.

3. The third point is that the traditional methodology of anthropology, that of comparing two cultures, has proved to be a valuable way of discovering the characteristics of each (McLeod, pp. 211–212).

Upon translation into student textbooks, the efforts of individuals such as Brooks to integrate culture into second language learning did not at first appear to have much success. First and second generation audio-lingual texts included two or three culture-related photographs per chapter; however, they were rarely linked to the language content of the chapter. Beginning in the 1970s, isolated culture notes or capsules began to appear in textbooks, but they too lacked integration and were often accompanied in the teacher's edition by the word *optional* which in reality means *unnecessary* to teachers pressed to cover the material. Short culture-based readings also began to appear at that time as well as expanded cultural explanations in the teachers' editions to help those individuals lacking cultural background due to their almost exclusively literary training. The late 1970s witnessed the introduction of four-color print in the high school textbook market along with a significant increase in the number of culture-laden photographs and an attempt by some publishers to integrate these in language-based activities. As we entered the 1980s, teaching materials were more and more influenced by the prior work of linguists and sociolinguists in the domains of functional-notional and communicative competence. The language of textbooks became more communicative and contextualized. This change, in turn, resulted in increased attempts to explain the cultural context wherein the language was found. In addition, the scope and sequence charts included a column devoted to culture.

At the same time as materials were paying increased attention to communication and culture, new or revised state curriculum guides were urging teachers to include culture as an integral component of second language courses. Wisconsin (1986) identified a set of cultural objectives in its functionally-based curriculum guide. Indiana (1986) developed a guide to proficiency-based instruction that included more than 100 culture-based learning goals.

The generation of materials and textbooks of the mid- and late-eighties, although still grammar driven, maintained all the changes described above and added an array of printed, authentic documents. Also, often included were videotapes that tended to be specifically developed for the classroom rather than being authentic. Probably the most important aspect of these new textbooks was the fact that many made a serious attempt at integrating culture and language. Some even built learning activities and exercises around photographs and illustrations.

In general, teachers of the eighties had at their disposal the materials necessary to include culture as an integral part of second language learn-

ing and teaching. Unfortunately, however, the profession was still dominated by the linear grammar-based syllabus and it remained difficult to
find the time to include culture. Although the material was at hand, many
textbooks still relegated it to secondary or ancillary status. One publisher,
for example, identified its well-researched native language essays on foreign culture and all of its grammar components as essential, but then
turned around and informed the teacher that all application activities that
followed were discretionary. Similarly, many textbooks failed to support
their claim concerning the importance of culture by neglecting to evaluate
it significantly in the tests that accompanied the materials.

Allen's (1985) summary of culture in the eighties proved to be an
insightful one, and one wonders if it might not even be appropriate to foreign language learning and teaching of the mid-nineties:

> Despite the talk of communication and culture, and the desire for their
> attainment, energies are devoted instead to grammar and vocabulary. And
> this is understandable, for grammar offers several advantages over culture: it
> is the concept around which most textbooks and materials are organized; it is
> finite and can be ordered in either a linear, sequential plan of study or else in
> a cyclical one; mastery of it can be easily tested and evaluated; and, finally, it
> is a subject matter the classroom teacher can teach him or herself, if neces-
> sary, using an advanced grammar text, and which, once mastered, is unlikely
> to change. Culture, by contrast, is diffuse, difficult to grasp, translate into
> instructional goals, test, evaluate, and order; prodigious in quantity; and
> ever-evolving (p. 145).

Edwards (1993) explores even further the distinction between the pre-
ciseness, linearity, and security offered by the grammar-based syllabus and
the doubt, uncertainty, and questioning of one's values often present when
studying someone else's culture, or as Edwards describes it, "la rencontre
de l'altérité" (coming face to face with otherness).

PRESENT-DAY SITUATION

The nineties represent the decade of standards, technology, and a renewed
pedagogical interest in the teaching of culture. Thanks to a collaborative
effort of ACTFL, AATF, AATG, and AASTP, the National Standards for Foreign Language Education Project (1996) presented *Standards for foreign language learning: Preparing for the 21st century* to the profession in November of
1995. These standards appeared in print in early 1996. The document lists
five major goal areas referred to as the five C's of foreign language education: Communication, Cultures, Connections, Comparisons, Communities.

Subsumed under these are the eleven national standards of which the following four directly address culture:

- Standard 2.1:   Students demonstrate an understanding of the relationship between the practices and perspectives of the culture studied.
- Standard 2.2:   Students demonstrate an understanding of the relationship between the products and perspectives of the culture studied.
- Standard 3.2:   Students acquire information and recognize the distinctive viewpoints that are only available through the foreign language and its cultures.
- Standard 4.2:   Students demonstrate understanding of the concept of culture through comparisons of the cultures studied and their own.

In addition, the fifth goal, Communities, which calls for participation in multilingual communities at home and around the world, indirectly evokes the importance of culture.

Not long after the appearance of the national standards, the AATF introduced its exhaustive treatment of culture entitled *Acquiring Cross-Cultural Competence* (Singerman, 1996) which defined in detail four stages of competence for students of French: elementary; basic intercultural skills; social competence; socioprofessional capability. For each stage the document lists indicators of competence in seven categories: empathy toward other cultures; ability to observe and analyze a culture; and knowledge of five French-speaking societies (France, North America, Sub-Saharan Africa, Caribbean, North Africa).

The nineties also saw the appearance of several scholarly works devoted to the role of culture in foreign language learning and teaching. Most important among these are the works of Byram (1989), Kramsch (1993), and Steele and Suozzo (1994). Byram (1989) places "cultural studies" at the core of foreign language learning and proposes a model of four related parts: language learning; language awareness; cultural experience; cultural awareness. Similarly, Kramsch (1993) pushes culture beyond a mere component of language learning. Rather, she sees it as an independent aspect of general education. Steele and Suozzo (1994) present a thorough overview of teaching French culture including a chapter on anthropology and the teaching of culture in which they call for teachers to "reach beyond their own educational backgrounds to seek new strategies for imparting cultural knowledge to their students" (p. 68).

Whether or not the above documents eventually impact the actual classroom is still to be determined. The one with the greatest potential is the national standards since virtually all states either have or are completing their own standards and many of them are asking that local school districts create curriculum guides based of the standards. Fortunately, most of the state foreign language standards reflect the national document. Probably the element that will most permit teachers to experiment with recommended changes in the teaching of culture during the nineties is technology, especially the advent of the World Wide Web, which gives students and teachers immediate access to cultures far and wide including presence in real time. This experimentation, however, must be accompanied with shifts of intellectual mindsets especially in the area of assessment and testing and among the university community. Until culture sees its proper place in unit tests, in university placement tests, and in national tests such as the AATF contest, and until university foreign language departments grant culture its proper citizenship, its role in language learning will continue to be subservient, and in some cases still minimal.

CONCEPTS FROM ANTHROPOLOGY

Thirty years ago, the foreign language profession looked to anthropology for assistance in including culture in its language programs. It is time to do so again. Upon revisiting anthropology, we find that the anthropologists' view of culture, like the applied linguists' view of second language learning, has also been subject to evolution, while the latter has evolved due to the impact of functional/notional curriculum, communicative competence and proficiency, emphases, and national and state standards. Culture is no longer seen by many as consisting of behaviors or even patterns of behaviors, but has evolved as a concept to mean shared information or knowledge encoded in systems of symbols. Geertz (1973) defined culture as "an historically transmitted pattern of meanings embodied in symbols, a system of inherited conceptions expressed in symbolic form by means of which men communicate, perpetuate, and develop their knowledge about and attitudes towards life" (p. 89).

The evolution of these ideas, however, is not as simple as one may think. Shweder (1984) informs us that cognitive anthropologists have been in dispute for more than a century over the answers to basic questions. On one side are found the "enlightenment" figures such as Levi-Strauss, Piaget, and Chomsky, who see the mind of man as rational and scientific. On the other side stands the "romantic" rebellion against enlightenment embodied in the writings of individuals such as Whorf and Geertz who maintain the view that ideas and practices emanate neither from logic nor empirical sciences and that they are neither rational nor irrational but rather non-rational.

D'Andrade (1984) maintains that there are three major views about the nature of culture. One is a notion of culture as knowledge, i.e., as the *accumulation of information*. The amount of information in the total cultural pool of knowledge is very large. For each society there may be between several hundred thousand and several million "chunks" of information in the total pool. A second view is that culture consists of *conceptual structures* that create the central reality of a people. According to this view, culture is not just shared, it is intersubjectively shared, so that everyone assumes that others see the same things they see. This culture does not accumulate, any more than the grammar of a language accumulates, and the total size of a culture with respect to information chunks is relatively small. A third view of culture falls between the *culture as knowledge* and the *culture as constructed reality* positions. It treats culture and society as almost the same thing—something made up of institutions, such as family, the market, the farm, the church, the village, and so on, that is, systems or clusters of norms defining the roles attached to various sets of statuses. All three are views of cultural meaning systems. The difference between these views is in the prominence given to the various functions of meaning: to the directive function for the *norms and institutions* view, to the representative function for the *knowledge* view, and to the potential of systems of meaning to create entities for the *constructed reality* view (pp. 115–16).

It is interesting to note that many of these same anthropological principles are reflected in *Acts of Meaning*, a recent work by the psychologist Jerome Bruner (1990).Bruner claims that culture has become the major factor in giving form to the minds of those living under its sway and that culture is not only the world to which we have to adapt but also the tool kit for doing so. He gives three reasons why culture must be a central concept for psychology:

1. The first is a deep methodological point: the constitutive argument. It is man's participation in culture and the realization of his mental powers through culture that makes it impossible to construct a human psychology on the basis of the individual alone.

2. The second reason follows from this and is no less compelling. Given that psychology is so immersed in culture, it must be organized around those meaning-making and meaning-using processes that connect man to culture. By virtue of participation in culture, meaning is rendered public and shared. Our culturally adapted way of life depends upon shared meanings and shared concepts and depends as well upon shared modes of discourse for negotiating differences in meaning and interpretation.

3. The third reason lies in the power of what I shall call "folk psychology," which is a culture's account of what makes human beings tick. It is through folk psychology that people anticipate and judge one another, draw conclusions about the worthwhileness of their lives, and so on. Its power over human mental functioning and human life is that it provides the very means by which culture shapes human beings to its requirements (pp. 12–15).

It is difficult to know whether or not to follow the above principles since Shweder (1984) maintains that cognitive anthropologists draw inferences about the mind of man by studying the ideas and actions of exotic peoples. Virtually none of the cultures whose language is studied in American foreign language classrooms can be said to be exotic. Furthermore, we must not lose sight of the fact that our point of discussion here is not so much the nature of culture in its own theoretical framework, but rather the teaching of culture in the second language classroom. Although the World Wide Web today permits us to visit and communicate live with individuals all over the world, the actual walls of our classrooms are not about to disappear. Working on a classroom activity that calls for consulting the cinema pages of the Parisian newspaper, *Le Figaro*, is not as authentic, nor will it ever be, as consulting *Le Figaro* while drinking a *diabolo menthe* at a café along the Champs Elysées in order to find the film that we wish to see that evening. Similarly, viewing a videotape of Princess Diana's funeral is not the same as having viewed the ceremony on the immense screens set up in Hyde Park in London.

The above constraints notwithstanding, I maintain that culture must continue to become an even more integral part of second language learning and teaching. I see culture as making an impact not merely on language learning within an individual, but rather on the individual himself. As second language teachers, we have a unique opportunity to broaden the horizons of our students, to help them better understand themselves, and in so doing help them understand others. Or maybe it should be the other way around, help them understand others and in so doing help them better understand themselves.

APPLICATION TO SECOND LANGUAGE CLASSROOM

I would like to suggest that in addition to the old concept of culture as patterns of living which now fill the latest generation of textbooks, there are three other ideas or concepts found in anthropology which might help us reorient our teaching of culture while still maintaining a language class: these are *awareness, comparison,* and *other dependent learning.* You will of course note that these same concepts can be found in virtually any other discipline and especially in the field of education. In applying these to the classroom, I am assuming that its objectives are both language and culture, and that the vehicle of instruction is primarily the target language. I do not reject the notion of a culture course in the native language, but then I do not wish to refer to that as a foreign language course.

Awareness is a necessary component in the field of anthropology: awareness of surroundings, awareness of otherness, and awareness of self. It calls for the temporary deconstruction of one's own environment to facilitate the reconstruction of another's environment. Awareness is a difficult characteristic to develop even more so among young adolescents in a structured school environment because it demands keen observation and listening abilities. Unfortunately, beginning with the audio-lingual era up to the present-day communicatively decorated grammar class, the emphasis in second language learning has been on production or performance. Usually the only awareness that this performance creates among students is "the more I participate, the better my chances are for a good grade." We need to place greater emphasis in our classrooms on observation and listening skills, and do so with cultural content in the hope of developing greater awareness of both self and others among our students. And if we believe the work of Postovsky (1982), Winitz (1981), and others in the area of listening comprehension, this might even improve the other language skills.

Authentic video clips, as well as access to the Internet, offer students excellent opportunities to develop observation skills both visual and listening. Many teachers refrain from using authentic video because they claim that the language is impossible to understand. What we need to realize, however, is that activities at all levels of proficiency can be created with virtually any piece of authentic material. For example, a video magazine with clips from Antenne 2 in France includes the story of a small town rural baker who drives his truck from village to village to sell his products. The clip was used in a classroom to create a very simple observation activity without sound for intermediate students. What was he selling, to whom, and where? Then it was replayed with the sound and students were asked to listen for specific words that represented the kinds of breads sold. Finally, students were asked if they knew of any stores in their hometown that delivered food. The obvious answer, which many adults would not think about, was of course pizza.

Another observation and retrospection activity involves a song by Jean-Jacques Goldman entitled, *Quelqu'un, quelque part,* in which the singer lists more than 20 world civilization concepts that happen to be accompanied by numbers such as 10 commandments, 12 apostles, 24 books in the Bible, 6 continents, 5 oceans, 101 Dalmatians, 7 samurai, etc. First, we asked students to listen to the song and simply write down the numbers that they heard. Then, we told them that these numbers were matched to an important concept that they most likely knew and asked them to guess at it. Thirdly, we listened again to the song and let them listen for the numbers and its accompanying noun or phrase such as 10 commandments. Finally, we played the song one more time and gave the students the text with the numbers missing for them to fill out.

Comparison is the second concept to be borrowed from the field of anthropology. Based on the use of written texts, Byrnes (1991) suggests developing cross-cultural communicative competence through one of the most basic ways of dealing with the world, that of comparison. She says that both the uncovering of one's own belief system, as well as the gradual building up of the other, can be achieved by "stimulating students to reflect on their expectations vis-à-vis the C2 culture on the basis of their C1 frame of reference, by seeing these expectations confirmed, disconfirmed, modified as they deal with L2 texts, by having them speculate on what must be true in and for the other culture for certain statements to be possible" (pp. 210–211).

McLeod (1976) also mentions that comparison is a traditional methodology used in anthropology. In her article, she includes questions aimed at discovering the ethnography of a meal. Discussed below, these questions are rather simple linguistically and could constitute an interesting classroom activity. In the description of this activity it is important to note that the notion of comparison is paired with the third anthropological concept, other dependent learning, which D'Andrade (1984) says is the inverse of Piaget's image of self-constructed knowledge. By *other,* D'Andrade means a peer rather than a teacher or someone in a position of power.

The concept of *other dependent learning* is not new to the field of education, which has increasingly promoted the power of cooperative learning, nor is it new to many in the foreign language teaching profession who realize that students can often explain linguistic or cultural concepts better than the teacher. This idea is especially evident in the area of grammar. In addition to advocating a move from self-constructed knowledge to greater dependence on peer consultation, the concept also promotes the use of small groups for *searching* purposes, and most important, as concerns the classroom, it advocates a shift from teacher-centered to learner-centered.

McLeod (1976) suggests that students ascertain the ethnography of a meal in different cultures by asking the following questions:

1. What time of day is the main meal eaten?
2. What kind of food is eaten?
3. What kind of receptacles, utensils are used?
4. How is the food cooked, by whom, where?
5. How is the food served, by whom?
6. Where is the meal eaten?
7. Who eats with whom? Who eats separately? Who eats before or after whom?
8. Does everyone eat the same food, the same amount of food?
9. How long does the meal last?
10. What happens during the meal? Is there talk or silence?

11. Who talks to whom? Who is silent?

12. What are the rules of etiquette, table manners?

Implementing a cooperative learning mode, pairs of students answer these questions about themselves. Then, some pairs answer the same questions making believe that they have recently eaten at McDonalds' or Burger King, while others have been to a "real restaurant." These first two steps represent an attempt using other dependent learning to uncover part of one's own belief system to establish increasing awareness of self and surroundings. The subsequent activities focus on the concept of comparison in order to develop a growing awareness of otherness. These activities include asking the same questions about photographs and readings dealing with restaurants and fast food establishments in the target culture and then comparing the results with those of the initial activities.

RELATIONSHIPS BETWEEN ANTHROPOLOGICAL CONCEPTS AND RECENT CURRICULAR MODELS

Having thus applied the anthropological concepts of awareness, comparison, and other dependent learning to the teaching of culture in the second language classroom, I would like to conclude with a discussion of how these same concepts relate to two recent interpretations of teaching and learning: Edward's (1993) culture teaching model and Lange's (1991) conceptualizations of curriculum.

Not unlike many others who have written about the learning of a second culture in a second language classroom, Edwards (1993) notes that the major obstacle is not only the fact that the learner arrives into the classroom already having absorbed the values and the everyday living patterns of his own culture, but also that he perceives these values and patterns as the proper ones. In short, Edwards sees it as a *we* versus *they* situation, one that will not be altered with token amounts of good will, tolerance, and curiosity. In an attempt to overcome this obstacle, Edwards suggests the following six-step model for the teaching of a second culture:

1. Awareness of one's own non-universal perspective: that which is true on one side of the mountain may be false on the other side;

2. Differentiation: awareness not only that the *other* is different but also that I am different with regards to him.

3. Exploration: an early but tentative desire to pursue knowledge of the *other;*

4. Confrontation: a stage in the dialectic of communication;

5. *Decentration* (changing the center of...): knowing oneself as one is known by others; this constitutes the early stage for integrating *otherness*;

6. Surpassing of oneself: acceptance of the *other.*

One of the most important concepts in Edward's model of second culture learning is the fact that students are not ready to deal with some other culture's ways of living and thinking until they are willing to examine their own. Thus, students must develop both an awareness of self and an awareness that others may be different and valued as well. Arriving at this awareness might very well involve the use of comparison especially if understanding of self necessitates comparison with another. In addition, comparison is mandatory for students to achieve the stages of exploration, confrontation, and decentration since all three stages imply some knowledge of and some relationship with the *other.* Finally, other dependent learning, although primarily defined as peer or cooperative learning, should yield a strong influence in helping students accept the other culture especially if in working with peers, students discover that the view of their own culture differs somewhat from that expressed by members of the same cultural group.

In a generic paper discussing new perspectives and new directions in foreign language education, Lange (1991) describes three different conceptualizations of curriculum:

- Scientific-technical inquiry consists of a group of tendencies that are both analytical and prescriptive. Form and technique drive what is to be learned, while process and values are essentially ignored.
- Practical inquiry embodies the quest for meaning and comprehension of the world as individuals strive to grasp an awareness of their own worth and identification. Knowledge and experience are not thought of only as scientific and rational, but include information from the senses and from intuition.
- Critical or emancipatory inquiry is oriented toward an emancipation of the individual to enable growth and development beyond the accepted social conventions, beliefs, and modes of functioning that operate with the established ideology. As a consequence, people are empowered to question the political, economic, social, and psychological aspects of life and to recreate them. A key ingredient in this inquiry is *praxis,* which is defined as the integration of political and cultural action with critical reflection (pp. 90–93).

Although not specifically related to culture, the awareness mentioned in practical inquiry bears a high resemblance to the awareness described in Edward's (1993) model and consequently to the anthropological concept of awareness. The notion of comparison, on the other hand is easily related to all three types of inquiry described: comparison is an important aspect of analysis in scientific-technical inquiry; it is virtually indispensable in arriving at an awareness of one's own worth in the practical inquiry model; it can serve as a powerful tool in questioning and recreating various political, economic, social, and psychological aspects of life within critical or emancipatory inquiry.

SUMMARY AND CONCLUSION

The basic purpose of this paper was to discuss, from the point of view of a second language specialist, the role that anthropology has played, is playing, and will play in the teaching of culture in the second language classroom.

Although the role of culture in second language classrooms has steadily increased during the past twenty years, culture has yet to achieve the role that it deserves. Nevertheless, more and more individuals within the profession are calling for a broader, more experience-based approach to language learning and teaching, one that goes far beyond the covers of the grammatically sequenced textbook and includes through video and other media the culture and real world of the foreign language. Reflecting upon textbooks in an attempt to bridge the gap between teaching and learning, Schulz (1991) arrives at the following conclusion:

> I argue that second language acquisition theory and research make a convincing case that the traditional textbook—espousing a grammatical syllabus and intended for consecutive, page-by-page coverage in elementary or intermediate language instruction—is an insufficient and deficient medium for language teaching and learning. We need to broaden the palette of instructional materials to include systematically those available media that demonstrate and illustrate language and culture not just via the written word, but also via the ear, via the eye, via smell, taste, and texture, if possible, and via feelings triggered by what the senses perceive. In other words, we need to develop materials which lead the learner to experience the target language and culture(s) as much as it is possible outside the borders of a particular language area (p. 171).

It is difficult to read the above citation and not recall the concepts of awareness, comparison, and other dependent learning. What Schulz calls for requires that students develop not only an awareness of self, but also of other; it necessitates the use of comparison to arrive at a broader understanding of both language and culture; it compels us to call upon other dependent learning to partially replace both the textbook and the teacher. In the end, we must deconstruct and rediscover ourselves. This deconstruction and rediscovery in turn will lay the groundwork for our discovering of others while at the same time permitting us to learn another language.

REFERENCES

Allen, W.W. (1985). Toward cultural proficiency. In A.C. Omaggio (Ed.), *Proficiency, curriculum, articulation: The ties that bind.* Northeast Conference Reports. Middlebury, VT: The Northeast Conference.

Benadava, S. (1993). Enseignement de la civilisation et objectifs linguistiques. In R.C. Lafayette (Ed.), *Culture et enseignement du français: Réflexions théoriques et pédagogiques* (pp. 77–88). Paris: Didier-Erudition.

Bernhardt, E.B. (1991). Developments in second language literacy research: Retrospective and prospective views for the classroom. In B.F. Freed (Ed.), *Foreign language acquisition research and the classroom* (pp. 221–225). Lexington, MA: D.C. Heath and Company.

Brooks, N. (1968). Teaching culture in the foreign language classroom. *Foreign Language Annals, 1,* 204–217.

Brooks, N. (1975). The analysis of language and familiar cultures. In R.C. Lafayette (Ed.), *The culture revolution in foreign language teaching* (pp. 19–31). Central States Conference Reports. Lincolnwood, IL: National Textbook Company.

Bruner, J. (1990). *Acts of meaning.* Cambridge, MA: Harvard University Press.

Byram, M. (1989). *Cultural studies in foreign language education.* Avon: Multilingual Matters.

Byram, M., & Esarte-Sarries, V. (1991). *Investigating cultural studies in foreign language teaching.* Avon: Multilingual Matters.

Byrnes, H. (1991).Reflections on the development of cross-cultural communicative competence in the foreign language classroom. In B.F. Freed (Ed.), *Foreign language acquisition research and the classroom* (pp. 205–218). Lexington, MA: D.C. Heath and Company.

Crawford-Lange, L.M., & Lange, D.L. (1984). Doing the unthinkable in the second-language classroom: A process for the integration of language and culture. In T.F. Higgs (Ed.), *Teaching for proficiency, the organizing principle* (pp. 139–177). The ACTFL Foreign Language Education Series. Lincolnwood, IL: National Textbook Company.

D'Andrade, R.G. (1984). Cultural meaning systems. In R.A. Shweder & R.A. Levine (Eds.), *Culture theory: Essays on mind, self, and emotion* (pp. 88–119). New York: Cambridge University Press.

Damen, L. (1987). *Culture learning: The fifth dimension in the language classroom.* Reading, MA: Addison-Wesley Publishing Company.

Edwards, J.D. (1993). Quelle culture enseigner: Réflexions et pratiques, l'expérience MICEFA/TRIADE. In R.C. Lafayette (Ed.), *Culture et enseignement du français: Réflexions théoriques et pédagogiques* (pp. 89–96). Paris: Didier-Erudition.

Ellis, R. (1988). Investigating language teaching: The case for an educational approach. *System, 16*(1), 1–11.

Erickson, F. (1991). Advantages and disadvantages of qualitative research design in foreign language research. In B.F. Freed (Ed.), *Foreign language acquisition research and the classroom* (pp. 338–353). Lexington, MA: D.C. Heath and Company.

Geertz, C. (1973). *Interpretation of cultures.* New York: Basic Books.

Grittner, F. (1990). Bandwagons revisited: A perspective on movements in foreign language education. In D.W. Birckbichler (Ed.), *New perspectives and new directions in foreign language education* (pp. 9–43). The ACTFL Foreign Language Education Series. Lincolnwood, IL: National Textbook Company.

Kramsch, C. (1988). The cultural discourse of foreign language textbooks. In A. Singerman (Ed.), *Toward a new integration of language and culture* (pp. 63–88). Northeast Conference Reports. Middlebury, VT: Northeast Conference.

Kramsch, C. (1989). Media materials in the language class. In M. Bilezikian & M. Sarde (Eds.), Communication and media in contemporary French culture. *Contemporary French Civilization, 13,* 325–345.

Kramsch, C. (1991). The order of discourse in language teaching. In B.F. Freed (Ed.), *Foreign language acquisition research and the classroom* (pp. 191–204). Lexington, MA: D.C. Heath and Company.

Kramsch, C. (1993). Discours et culture: L'enjeu didactique. In R.C. Lafayette (Ed.), *Culture et enseignement du français: Réflexions théoriques et pédagogiques.* Paris: Didier-Erudition.

Kramsch, C. (1993). *Context and culture in language teaching.* New York: Oxford University Press.

Lafayette, R.C. (1988). Integrating the teaching of culture into the FL classroom. In A. Singerman (Ed.), *Toward a new integration of language and culture* (pp. 47–62). Northeast Conference Reports. Middlebury, VT: Northeast Conference.

Lafayette, R.C. (Ed.). (1993). *Culture et enseignement du français: Réflexions théoriques et pédagogiques.* Paris: Didier-Erudition.

Lambert, W.E. (1991). Pros, cons, and limits to quantitative approaches in foreign language acquisition research. In B.F. Freed (Ed.), *Foreign language acquisition research and the classroom* (pp. 321–337). Lexington, MA: D.C. Heath and Company.

Lange, D.L. (1990). Sketching the crisis and exploring different perspectives in foreign language curriculum. In D.W. Birckbichler (Ed.), *New perspectives and new directions in foreign language education* (pp. 77–109). ACTFL Foreign Language Education Series. Lincolnwood, IL: National Textbook Company.

McLeod, B. (1976). The relevance of anthropology to language teaching. *TESOL Quarterly, 10,* 211–20.

Murphy, J.A. (1991). The graduate teaching assistant in an age of standards. In S. Sieloff Magnan (Ed.), *Challenges in the 1990s for college foreign language programs* (pp. 129–149). AAUSC Issues in Language Program Direction. Boston: Heinle & Heinle Publishers.

National Standards in Foreign Language Education Project. (1996). *Standards for foreign language learning: Preparing for the 21st century.* Yonkers, NY: The National Standards Project.

Porcher, L. (Ed.). (1986). *La civilisation.* Paris: Clé International.

Postovsky, V.A. (1982). Delayed oral practice. In R.W. Blair (Ed.), *Innovative approaches to language teaching* (pp. 67–76). Rowley, MA: Newbury House.

Schulz, R.A. (1991). Bridging the gap between teaching and learning: A critical look at foreign language textbooks. In S. Sieloff Magnan (Ed.), *Challenges in the 1990s for college foreign language programs* (pp. 167–181). AAUSC Issues in Language Program Direction. Boston: Heinle & Heinle Publishers.

Shweder, R.A. (1984). Anthropology's romantic rebellion against the enlightenment, or there's more to thinking than reason and evidence. In R.A. Schweder & R.A. Levine (Eds.), *Culture theory: Essays on mind, self, and emotion* (pp. 27–66). New York: Cambridge University Press.

Singerman, A.J. (Ed.). (1996). *Acquiring cross-cultural competence: Four stages for students of French.* AATF National Commission on Cultural Competence. Lincolnwood, IL: National Textbook Company.

Steele, R., & Suozzo, A. (1994). *Teaching French culture: Theory and practice.* Lincolnwood, IL: National Textbook Company.

Strasheim, L.A., & Bartz, W.H. (Eds.). (1986). *A guide to proficiency-based instruction in modern foreign languages for Indiana schools.* Indianapolis: Indiana Department of Education.

Weidmann Koop, M.-C. (1991). Survey on the teaching of contemporary French culture, Part I: The teachers' perspective. *The French Review, 64,* 463–75.

Weidmann Koop, M-C. (1991). Survey on the teaching of contemporary French culture, Part II: The students' perspective. *The French Review, 64,* 571–587.

Wilczynska, W. (1990). Avez-vous vu la même chose que les Français? *Le Français dans le Monde, 236,* 73–77.

Winitz, H. (Ed.). (1981). *The comprehension approach to foreign language instruction.* Rowley, MA: Newbury House.

CHAPTER 5

CLOSING THE LANGUAGE AND CULTURE GAP

An Intercultural Communication Perspective

Louise Damen

FOREWORD

The following paper was presented at the University of Minnesota in May 1991, at the Cultural Learning in Second Language Conference Symposium. The paper represented a review of the unique approach to culture learning that had been developed in the field of intercultural communication at that time. This historical approach reminds those still struggling with the challenge of incorporating culture learning as an indispensable partner in language learning today that the past is prologue and that a backward look is a map to the future. But, first, where are we now?

LANGUAGE OR CULTURE?

An ESL teacher in France observed in November 1996, in an Email query to fellow teachers that many of his students wanted to learn the language

Culture as the Core: Perspectives in Second Language Education, pages 71–88
Copyright © 2003 by Information Age Publishing
All rights of reproduction in any form reserved.

(English), but had only "a minimal at most interest in the British or American culture." He asked: "Is it possible to learn French cooking without learning the culture?" The writer added: "I think so." His point was that his students just wished to read computer manuals or to use English to communicate with other nonnative English speakers.

First, one might well ask what sort of cooking might result if one were not acquainted with the cultural aura surrounding the French cuisine. Is a *chef* only a cook? Are *les grands plats* simply vittles? Next, can one assume that language use can ever be culture free? Many computer manual readers feel that those who write these guides in English or any other language live in another culture, if not another world.

Because language use involves more than dictionary definitions, one may ask how one communicates in a culture-neutral world. Early exploration in the field of intercultural communication emphasized new definitions of the intertwining concepts of culture, communication, and language. These explorations made clear that those who would set aside the language and culture connection risked missing the message and, thus, perhaps, were doomed to prepare sauces without spices and/or publish incomprehensible manuals. Thus, to ignore the interplay between language and culture is to play the language game without knowing the rules. To explicate a linguistic system without considering how, when, and why the forms are used was to speak to those who could or would not hear.

THE PROBLEM

Contrary to the point of view expressed by the gentleman from France, most language teaching professionals in the United States and abroad have long accepted the propositions that language and culture go together and that language instruction must involve some degree of culture learning, consciously taught or not. These professionals have been much less certain as to the manner and means to effect the desired levels of dual proficiency.

The task is difficult. The complexity of welding the language/culture connection lies in the paradoxical relationship of the dynamic two. Although cultural and linguistic systems are universal to all groups of interacting human beings, the individual systems assume different and distinctive patterns. In human contexts, specific languages and cultures, being mutually interacting and reinforcing, are inextricably bound. Cultural rules and values guide, mold, often control, and nurture the sense of community that defines personal identity and binds disparate individuals into families, villages, cities, and societies. In turn, these cultural givens are transmitted, articulated, and practiced through language.

Because of the recognition of this complex relationship, the problem today lies more in the *hows*, the *whats*, and the *whens* rather than the *whys?* Those who yet question the role of culture learning in language learning contexts may find guidance in the early work of pioneering practitioners and researchers in the field of intercultural communication, a discipline arising largely in the United States at the end of World War II. A review of that development follows.

In this discussion, the term *second language learning* encompasses both learning a foreign language in the student's native culture as well as foreign language learning in the target culture. The term *second language* as widely used in the field of language education is misleading; in this paper, the term is taken to mean an *additional* language.

PEDAGOGICAL IMPERATIVES

Pedagogical problems as to the content, objectives, and methods needed to develop an effective culture/language-sensitive curriculum are all too familiar to the modern language teacher. Those who try to do so are frequently overcome by the enormity of the task they have undertaken; they may even be overcome with guilt as they realize that in spite of their heroic efforts, neither the systems under scrutiny nor their students are being well served by their efforts. These teachers may also realize that their responsibility to culture-language learners is far greater than to those whose instruction is restricted to the quasi-static verbal/vocal code. Cultural competence varies in form and function from linguistic competence. The former is more idiosyncratic and selective, for the culture learner enjoys the luxury of picking and choosing what to accept or reject in the act of culture learning and to internalize the new elements in a highly personal manner (Damen, 1987; Paulston, 1978). Linguistic competence offers far less latitude.

Next is the problem of student preparation. Ross Steele in an article in ERIC/CLL News Bulletin (September 1990) titled, "Culture in the Foreign Language Classroom," defined that damned-if-I-do and damned-if-I-don't dilemma many teachers experience:

> In the case of foreign language learning, the target culture has to be created in the classroom and made real in the minds of the learners. This often involves overcoming stereotypes and preconceived notions about the target culture. Some students may resist learning a foreign culture. Their attachment to their own culture, and a feeling that behavior considered inappropriate in their culture is always "wrong," may cause them to reject the target culture. While they may be willing to learn a new *language* in order to meet educational objectives, they are unwilling to adopt the *cultural* framework

that would allow them to communicate effectively in the target language and culture (p. 4).

Generally, foreign language students in the United States and elsewhere are ill-prepared to acquire the skills to meet the culture-learning requirement. The *process* of culture learning as the key to effective culture learning is often buried beneath a flood of cultural tidbits that may astound but seldom enlighten.

The average foreign language learners in the United States have had little or no in-depth experience in a foreign country; seldom do they speak a second language. Their cross-cultural understanding has been only slightly stirred by ethnic comedies and/or melting pot mythology. They have little understanding as to how languages or cultures work, theirs least of all. Eyes glaze over at the sight and sound of tense and pronoun, not to mention the subjunctive. New cultural information often only reinforces preconceived biases as discussed above. It certainly contributes to the scourge of all teachers: learner deafness. Only rarely do students perceive language study as a means to open the mind or to explore other ways of solving common human problems. The purpose of discovering that some people seem incapable of getting to a party on time or eat snails remains unclear, often even to the teacher.

PAST HISTORY

In general, beginning in the 1980s the format and focus of second language textbooks used to present cultural information was met with varying degrees of success, ranging from disinterest on the part of the learners to outright resentment. Taking a page from the sacred works of Margaret Mead, Franz Boas, and other disciples of the emerging discipline of anthropology, culturally sensitive publications were structured to note similarities and differences between cultures. Early textbook cultural content also often overemphasized innocuous similarities or differences between the target culture and the native culture of the learner. In many cases the only cultural information provided was relegated to a series of neat little boxes at the end of a lesson.

Generally, more recent approaches have been explanatory and often call upon the learner to solve cultural *problems*. Yet, the approach also remains a form of packaging a culture. Overemphasis on cultural generalities was intended to encourage tolerance and positive reactions to the target culture. In some cases, the desire to produce positive feelings toward the target culture resulted in textbook pictures of bevies of happy, well-scrubbed, blue-jeaned folk drinking Coca Cola in scenes that presumably might be found in Dallas, Madrid, or Paris. This homogenization *à l'Améric-aine*, made only slightly legitimate by the obvious facial differences to be noted in scenes depicting Chinese or Japanese, emphasized the Disney version of *it's a small world* differences.

In the desire to foster empathy the individual was lost. Students often perceived the bearers of the target culture as a mysterious lump of people with some strange ways and generalized behaviors. Few lied, cheated, or stole. In following the anthropologists' approach to culture as a group phenomenon, many textbook writers asked students to communicate with an entire country rather than its individual residents. Stereotyping became the name of the game. The real North American, Frenchman, or Japanese were faceless and often upsetting when met face to face.

If this approach was not entirely successful, what then? Solutions to the language learning and culture-learning puzzle seemed to lie in another approach. Curriculum organizers and classroom teachers became aware of the need to expand their approach and address some difficult issues if the language/culture connection was to be made. The challenge lay in deciding how and to what degree to make the language classroom a reflection of the target culture, how to bring this recreated, simulated, or vicariously experienced culture to a useful level of reality in the minds and behavior of the learners, and how to be certain that a little knowledge did not become a dangerous tool that would reinforce cultural prejudice and bias rather than bring understanding. Some felt that equal emphasis should be placed on cultural and linguistic objectives, thus avoiding exercises containing what Robinson (1981) calls *hollow* language which imparted no sociocultural, personal, or motivational meaning to the learner.

As is often the case, possible solutions lay in innovative forces outside the field of traditional language education: research and practice in the relatively new (in 1991), highly practical, fairly amorphous and wholly interdisciplinary field of intercultural communication. The problems these professionals addressed and the new approaches they devised spoke to the problems raised above and provided interesting pedagogical implications.

THE INTERCULTURAL PERSPECTIVE:
ITS HISTORY AND CONCERNS

Polonius' admonition to neither a borrower nor lender be certainly was sensible fatherly advice; some second language teachers might well choose, however, to ignore his advice and take a few lessons from some very unrepentant borrowers and lenders: the professionals in the field of intercultural communication. In borrowing concepts and theories from related social sciences, the interculturalists challenged a few myths and provided new insights into the language/culture conundrum. They drew heavily on the research and practice in the cross-cultural psychology, anthropology, sociolinguistics, and related social sciences in order to develop a unique perspective on the processes of communication and culture learning. In broadening the concept of communication to include more than the traditional definition of language as a verbal/vocal phenomenon, they opened the way to investigating nontraditional definitions of communication. They focused on communication in its cross-cultural diversity and on the overcoming or crossing of these perceived barriers in the development of effective communication.

Briefly, the field developed in the United States during and after World War II when government officials, travelers, consultants, businessmen, and later Peace Corps volunteers in and from the United States found themselves faced with *one world* for which they seemed to be responsible. The establishment of the United Nations on American soil only served to enhance the international mission of the United States.

From their efforts arose the professional and academic field of intercultural communication. The early interculturalists borrowed unashamedly from their source disciplines, but, in so doing, added a few new twists. As Hoopes and Pusch (1979) wrote in an article defining terms used in intercultural and multicultural education:

> Nothing about intercultural or multicultural human relations is really new, but by putting certain ideas about communication, culture, society, education and human psychology together, a different way of looking at and learning about interaction among cultures has emerged. (p. 2)

The new practitioners, who were first mainly communication specialists, but later came to represent all social sciences disciplines, eventually undertook a two-pronged plan of action: the development of cross-cultural awareness of cultural differences and the fostering of effective intercultural sensitivity and behavior as a means of dealing with these differences. The former was the first emphasis because differences and diversity seemed to be stumbling blocks; the latter focused on the ways and means to overcome the differences and so tended to emphasize the process of culture learning, designed to recognize cross-cultural similarities, to foster empathy and flexibility, and even to posit a new social role: the multicultural, mediating man who could cross-cultural boundaries at a single bound and still go home again (Adler, 1976; Bochner, 1973).

Theirs was a bottom-up, problem-solving pragmatic development that dealt with chapter and verse in the real world rather than with paying homage to a set of latter-day Ten Commandments for effective intercultural communication. That language teachers largely ignored their work in the early

1990s was partially caused by the interculturalists themselves, who largely ignored the role of linguistic systems in intercultural contacts. Yet, if the interculturalists can be faulted for not paying attention to language as a system of related cultural meanings as well as the vehicle for the transmission of culture, they may be praised for having removed the focus of culture learning from the confines of specific foreign language instruction. Moreover, they defined the concepts of both culture and communication in very broad strokes, concentrating on shared individual and group behavior rather than on features of what was then called the Culture or Civilization with a capital C; i.e., the art, music, literature and other contributions of a given culture to the benefit of humankind. Those trained under this later approach might well be familiar with the pen of an aunt or have read Racine and Voltaire in French, yet be unable to order a meal or cajole a *concierge*.

Finally, a caveat is in order. Although the field of intercultural communication took on an international perspective almost from its inception, some of the basic tenets and methods were soon called into question as reflecting a Western bias (Smart, 1983). Indeed, this particular aspect was not surprising as most of its founding leaders were North American or European. In time its founding leaders were led to consider the call for revised discovery methods as well as alternative descriptions of the self, learning styles, rhetorical modes, or even profiles of successful language learners. Yet, the widespread use of English as an instrument of international communication continued to reinforce the Western model. The issues raised were not to be ignored if the path of intercultural communication was to remain a two-way street.

In the following discussion some of these new approaches to the basic concepts of communication, culture, and perception, the culture learning process, and roles of both students and teachers in the culture/learning challenge are examined. These insights are then reviewed for their pedagogical implications.

COMMUNICATION: CULTURE AND PERCEPTION

Defining and analyzing the cross-cultural aspects and general nature of the concepts of communication, culture, and perception were the major concerns in the development of the field of intercultural communication. While the end goals of these endeavors lay mainly in their pragmatic application in the fields of international exchange, especially in the business world, the academic pursuits of the interculturalists were focused on revised definitions of these key concepts as they had been delineated in the fields of anthropology, sociology, sociolinguistics, and communication theory as well as their applications in cross-cultural contexts.

COMMUNICATION AND LANGUAGE LEARNING:
SOME REVISIONS

The traditional point of view of language professionals had been that the formal linguistic code defines and limits their discipline, language being regarded as the major means of communication and the foremost purveyor of cultural codes and rules. This premise implies that *learning* a foreign language is all that is needed to open the channels of communication with speakers of other languages.

This was not the full story according to pioneers in the field of intercultural communication and related fields (Barna, 1985; Birdwhistell, 1970; Ekman, 1975; Hall, 1959, 1969, 1977; Stewart, 1972; and others). Communication, they reported, involved the linguistic code as well as an array of alternate or accompanying means of communication including the whole human body from nose to toes. They declared:

- Communication involves more than words; it involves the manner, the purpose, and the intention of the speaker.
- Communication involves nonverbal codes that often carry the major portion of the accompanying social messages, giving credence to the old expression that it is not what you say but the way you say it.
- Communication involves interaction within a social environment (culture).
- Communication occurs between individuals, not cultural systems. Therefore, each communicative act involves the individual cultural *persona* of each communicant.
- Finally, and most importantly: communicative patterns, styles, and purposes vary cross-culturally, even though certain universal patterns can be observed. That is to say that while smiling is a universal human response, the meanings attached to the smile are not.

CULTURE

Culture, on the other hand, was seen as context, or the environment surrounding given communicative acts (Stewart, 1978). Manifested in the behavior and values of an individual, culture was posited to assume the role of an arbiter in determining who says what to whom. In addition, Hall (1977) declared that the major function of culture was to screen confusing stimuli and to provide shortcuts to communication among the *believers*. He stated that *culture is communication and communication is culture* (1959, p. 169), a provocative if somewhat confusing statement.

Clearly, the old definitions of culture were being drastically revised. Hall felt that culture simply defined as the sum total of learned behavior, patterns, attitudes, and material objects was a *muddied concept* (1959, p. 31). His was a revision of the classic anthropological approach to culture as shared ways of living and aggregate patterns, which cast the culture bearers and their individual roles as interpreters of a culture as simply small and largely ineffectual cogs in a very big wheel that churned on endlessly with or without them.

The broadened definition of culture embraced by the interculturalists was reinforced by later interpretive approaches (Geertz, 1973), which defined culture in terms of individual culture bearers and their perception of the cultural reality they encountered in daily life. In this construct a so-called universal subjective culture system which represents "a group's characteristic way of perceiving its social environment" (Triandis et al., 1972, p. 339) set the stage—the players being the individual culture bearers playing their roles as they perceived and conceived them. Those advocating a perceptual approach stated that given cultural systems are internalized by individuals in highly personal patterns (Singer, 1987). Such perceptions would reflect a series of influences, internal and external, such as social group, personal experience, or the health of the individual. Thus, while cultural patterns and rules may filter and color perceptions, it is the individual's perception of the cultural reality that determines what is paid attention to and what is not. Language plays a role, but not the dominant role implied in the strong version of the Sapir-Whorf hypothesis. Singer (1987) concluded that "man behaves as he does because of ways in which he perceives the external world." Gudykunst and Kim (1984), also concentrating on the individual's role, defined communication as largely dialogs between strangers, cultural variations being plotted along a continuum stretching from the shared and familiar to the strange and foreign. The communication process was similar, they wrote, whether it involved people unknown or unfamiliar or people from the native culture (p. v).

Thus, while a cultural score orchestrates communicative acts, individuals who exhibit their own interpretations of that score perform them. Thus, all human communication reflects personal, intracultural, intercultural, and cross-cultural similarities and differences because no two cultures or individuals, as yet, are exactly alike. [See Appendix A for a presentation of the salient points made in the above discussion concerning the nature of culture. This has proved useful as a workshop tool.]

CULTURE LEARNING: A LIFELONG PROCESS

Because interculturalists focused on practical problems as experienced by individuals, they soon moved from simply studying the strange ways of strange folks to analyzing the culture learning process. Driven by the need for international cross-cultural travelers to make their journeys and return intact the focus was: (1) understanding the process of culture learning; (2) providing intervention and/or assistance in the intercultural experience. A main concern was the identification of the symptoms of culture shock (fear of and/or distaste for the new and unknown), its impact, and a possible cure or amelioration. This concern then led to analyses of what was going on in the process of acculturation. This was a major move away from simply emphasizing and/or explicating series of similarities and differences encountered cross-culturally.

Oberg (1958) and others interested in the psychological effects of cross-cultural encounters described the emotional and psychological effects of such episodes in largely negative terms. Later, the experience was plotted as a giant U-shaped learning curve, an emotional roller coaster taking the learner from the joy of the new through a jolting dip into culture shock, followed, it was hoped, by a rising, exhilarating climb to some pinnacle of accommodation. Possible outcomes of the experience could be adjustment, assimilation, or rejection as the learner chose. Poised at the top of the curve, the culture learner was imagined to be ready to undertake another ride.

The need to smooth the passage from one stage of culture learning to the next or even avoid the ravages of culture shock led the interculturalists to center their efforts on experiential, practical training. The training was formulated, often in a workshop format, to heighten individual perception of self and native culture, to recognize cultural values (their own and those of others), to experience culture shock and recovery, to solve cross-cultural riddles, either in make-believe lands or in specific cultures, and, finally, to arrive at a personal response to the new and different.

The major goals of such training were to prepare the cultural traveler to practice the process of culture learning both at home and abroad. New methods were developed. As practice for the coming cross-cultural encounters, trainees were encouraged to experiment in a protected and nonthreatening environment. Techniques were refined to provide this experiential training. Culture capsules (small vignettes of a cultural theme), culture assimilators (practice in discovering appropriate behavior in the target culture), simulation, role play, and other such techniques which provided practice in handling cross-cultural experiences in a protected and nonthreatening environment proved popular and successful. These techniques seem familiar now. They have been borrowed, refined, and used successfully in language texts and training modules (Seelye, 1984). Some of the early training books and collected readings listed in the bibliography provide historical perspective on the development of training modules and preparatory techniques. Among them are the works of Casse (1981), Gaston (1984), Kohls (1981), Pusch (1979), Samovar and Porter (1985), and Smith and Luce (1979).

LESSONS FOR THE TEACHER

The preceding discussion concerning the development of the field of intercultural communication and its particular contribution to the definition of the major concepts of communication and the role of perception, as well as the development of major culture learning methods and techniques, provides some useful road signs for the practicing, culturally-sensitive beleaguered language teacher.

Lesson One: Cultural exploration (home and abroad) should be fashioned as experiential episodes providing students the opportunity to experience the culture learning process (see Appendix B) in a nonthreatening context.

Lesson Two: Culture learning as a process should be included as an ongoing element in the language classroom.

Lesson Three: Patterns of communication and cultural meanings conveyed through body language, silence, smell, taste, time, and space should be explored as culture learning projects. To ignore these channels of communication is to miss much of the message any native speaker may transmit. The teacher, then, must consciously supply experience as to the communicative aspects beyond the verbal code. Insights into these aspects are offered in the early intercultural communication textbooks and articles of Condon and Yousef (1975), Stewart (1972), and others.

Lesson Four: The dangers of stereotyping evidenced in the transmission of generalized statements concerning cultural patterns and mores should be recognized by both teachers and students. This recognition relates to the question of identifying the culture bearer. Is a culture represented only by the whole or by the individuals comprising that whole? Describing cultural similarities and differences in group terms as found in statements such as "North Americans are..." or "Chinese are..." implies that there are no exceptions and effectively hides the individual trees in the forest. As indicated in Appendix A, there are versions of a culture that are constructs of the individual (My Way); there are others that are shared by the group and the individual as part of a group (Our Way) and then there is the contrast culture's view (Their Way).

Which version is most accurate and instructive? The interculturalists would answer: All three. Thus, in guiding culture learning one is constrained to examine general cultural themes, values and beliefs in terms of the groups in question, noting both similarities and differences, but emphasizing that shared traits are only *possible* predictors of behavior; they are not determiners.

Interculturalists have emphasized that each act of communication is to some degree intercultural. Their work has concentrated on individual exchanges and so brings a needed note of caution to cultural exploration. The strangers we meet carry sets of values, beliefs, and customs that may or may not differ from ours. Such meetings are conducted as through a fun house mirror so that distortions and shadows distort the cross-cultural view.

The lesson is clear. Language instructors need to make certain students understand that the traits of the target or foreign culture presented in a textbook may or *may not* be shared by all members of a given cultural group. Recognizing genuine similarities and differences between the target culture and the culture of the language learner as well as individual differences within the target culture will foster productive culture learning. Not every Italian loves pasta.

Lesson Five: Teachers should welcome the next lesson. Testing or evaluation can be made easy through the use of role plays simulation, problem solving, and cultural hypothesizing. Ironically, it is easier to choose the method of evaluating than to assess so-called *progress*. The outcome of culture learning is the choice of the learner so traditional methods fall short. Testing then should be seen as exercises in the art of culture learning. It is a practice of skills rather than solely a review of content. Culture-specific information, of course, lends itself to content review; culture learning should be seen as exercise rather than the digestion of information.

In considering steps in culture learning then, active interchanges with other culture learners as well as cultural informants can be a means to practice culture-learning skills in interaction. Informants from the target culture may provide information for Steps 1 and 2 (See Appendix B). Because it is difficult to perceive one's own cultural givens and biases, it is also essential for a learner to listen to what others have to say about the learner's culture—often a painful experience. For example, the experiences of cultural travelers in the United States in Rodriguez (1981), Tan (1989), and Zongren (1990) provide excellent sources of foreign perceptions of North American culture and origins of conflict or miscommunication. The dinner party described in Tan (pp. 196–206) contrasts Chinese and American approaches to food and manners around a dining table, providing a window on the learner's world as seen through the eyes of outsiders.

Thus, although textbook accounts of nonnative manners and customs are useful in a second language classroom, they should be approached as part of the overall culture learning process, not as an end all and be all.

Lesson Six: The perspective of the interculturalists offers an additional spur to revisit some old, formerly tried, found wanting, and generally banished techniques: using translation and making friends with *faux amis*. Both techniques have been used effectively in cross-cultural research and practice (Brislin, 1976; Osgood et al., 1975). These processes involve active participation of the student and may highlight areas of false attributions. In addition, our students often translate from L1 to L2 and back again and lean on *faux amis*, so why not join what cannot be beaten? Why use translation? It has been generally held that translation slows the process of communication and often leads the translator down a primrose path. While this may be true, there are uses for translation in the second language classroom.

The interculturalists have used translation to establish culture-specific (not dictionary) equivalents. Cultural translation of concepts and lexical items by questioning, back translation (translation from native to the target language and back) allows for the consideration of the emotional affect assigned given lexical items in each language. Teachers may encourage translation as a form of cultural inquiry or interpretation, assessing student reactions and responses as a means of testing the effects of cultural instruction. This is the rationale for the use of the cultural hypotheses testing used in several techniques developed for intercultural training (critical incidents, culture capsules, culture assimilators). Interpretive translation involves understanding context and expressing similar *messages* in two languages.

Is that not what language proficiency is all about?

Also, to test cultural attributions and to explore culture-specific meanings of shared terms or even concepts, teachers would do well to renew their acquaintance with *faux amis*. This could be effected through student questioning and clarification rather than by the transmission of specific knowledge. For example, students need to be aware that the French word for parents means more than mother and father or that *sympathique* has little to do with grief, but much to do with kindness. Both the interpretation and exploration of semantic fields of shared lexical terms or concepts represent tests of culture learning.

Lesson Seven: Finally, the role of the teacher can be redefined in intercultural terms. When asked to define the teacher's role, most would reply, *to teach.* Of course, but because cultures change more rapidly than language, the role of the teacher in cultural inquiry cannot be the traditional one of the all-knowing source of the correct.

Cultures and cultural values are in a constant flux so that no one person can embrace or represent an entire culture. The role of the teacher in the culture learning process must be limited to guidance and support in the student's cultural exploration. Teachers do not have to set culture learning outcomes; they must promote culture learning skills.

Because cultural adjustment is highly idiosyncratic, the teacher's role as cultural mentor must not be as the purveyor of the good, the true, and the believable, but rather as a trainer in the development of sensitivity to cross-cultural differences, of social skills in communicating across cultures, and of personal skills in adapting to the inevitability of change in social and cultural patterns and appropriate behavior as lifetime pursuits.

Some pedagogical roles to be avoided are the heavenly messenger, who brings great but often murky pronouncements from on high; the cultural guru who can expound on all aspects of an entire culture without taking a second breath; or the almighty judge of the culturally correct (Damen, 1988).

CONCLUSION

This discussion has highlighted the insights gained from research and practice in the field of intercultural communication and applicable to the task of incorporating culture learning in language classes. In retrospect, perhaps, we should rephrase the problem. Is not our real task to encourage culture learning skills through and with language learning, the gentleman from France notwithstanding? Because cultures change, do not the culture learning skills achieved far outweigh any skill in the control of the grammatical rules of a given language? Indeed, the specific skill in communicating effectively in Spanish, for example, with an individual Spanish speaker is a far more desirable goal than simply teaching that student to pronounce, ¿*Que dice?* with a Castilian lisp. Indeed, it may be said that the content of culture and language learning in some ways is less important than the experience of communicating across cultures. The latter is far more exportable and less immutable than a series of verbs, nouns, and their exquisite arrangement in a given language. Real culture learning has taken place if the skills used to communicate to Pedro in Spain can be applied to dealing with Hiroki in Japan.

EPILOGUE

The above discussion was presented in early 1991. Its major points seem still valid as the new century begins. The development of worldwide communication via cyberspace only serves to remind us that intercultural communication is still the name of the game. Cultural and linguistic diversity are thriving. As we head to the 21st century, there is little to indicate homogenization. Indeed, anthropologists tell us that lack of diversity is often fatal to a species. A word or warning: If, as the koala, we were fated to eat only eucalyptus leaves, then we would be greatly threatened should those trees disappear. Therefore, because diversity may be a means of survival, we must learn to live in a diverse world. It behooves us to learn to cross linguistic and cultural boundaries and eschew building walls of ethnic distrust. In the modern world, who then can afford to be an inept or indifferent culture learner?

REFERENCES

Adler, P. (1976). Beyond cultural identity: Reflections upon cultural and multicultural man. In L.A. Samovar & R.E. Porter (Eds.), *Intercultural communication: A reader.* 2nd edition. Belmont, CA: Wadsworth.

Barna, L. (1985). Stumbling blocks in intercultural communication. In L. Samovar & R. Porter (Eds.), *Intercultural communication: A reader.* Belmont, CA: Wadsworth Publishing Company.

Birdwhistell, R. (1970). *Kinesics and context: Essays on body motion communication.* Philadelphia: University of Pennsylvania Press.

Bochner, S. (1973). *The mediating man: Cultural interchange and transnational education.* Honolulu, HI: East-West Center, University of Hawaii.

Brislin, R. (Ed.). (1976). *Translation: Applications and research.* New York: Gardner Press, Inc.

Brislin, R. (1977). *Culture learning: Concepts, applications, and research.* Honolulu, HI: East-West Center, University of Hawaii.

Brislin, R. (1986). *Cross-cultural encounters. Face to face interaction.* New York: Pergamon [1981].

Brislin, R. (Ed.). (1990). *Applied cross-cultural psychology.* Newbury Park, CA: Sage Publications, Inc.

Brislin, R., Cushner, K., Cherrie, C., & Yong, M. (1986). *Intercultural interactions: A practical guide.* Volume 9, Cross-cultural research and methodology Series. Beverly Hills, CA: Sage.

Casse, P. (1981). *Training for the cross-cultural mind.* Washington, DC: SIETAR.

Castells, M. (1990). *¡Ya comprendo! A communicative course in Spanish.* New York: Macmillan Publishing Company.

Condon, J., & Yousef, F. (1975). *An introduction to intercultural communication.* Indianapolis, IN: Bobbs-Merrill Educational Publishing.

Cushner, K. (1990). Cross-cultural psychology and the formal classroom. In R. Brislin (Ed.), *Applied cross-cultural psychology* (pp. 98–120).Newbury Park, CA: Sage.

Damen, L. (1983). Reading, writing, and culture shock. *Cross Currents, 2,* 51–70.

Damen, L. (1987). *Culture learning: The fifth dimension in the language classroom.* Reading, MA: Addison-Wesley Publishing Company.

Damen, L. (1988, December). Culture learning: The teacher's role. *TESOL Newsletter.*

Ekman, P. (1975). The universal smile: Face muscles talk every language. *Psychology Today, 9,*(4), 35–39.

Ford, C.K., & Silverman, A. (1981). *American cultural encounters.* San Francisco: The Alemany Press.

Gaston, J. (1984). *Cultural awareness teaching techniques.* Resources Handbook 4. Brattleboro, VT: Pro Lingua Associates.

Geertz, C. (1973). *The interpretation of culture: Selected essays.* New York: Basic Books.

Gudykunst, W., & Kim, Y. (1984). *Communicating with strangers: An approach to intercultural communication.* Reading, MA: Addison-Wesley Publishing Company.

Gullahorn, J.T., & Gullahorn, J.E. (1963). An extension of the U-curve hypothesis. *Journal of Social Issues, 19*(3), 33–47.

Hall, E. (1959). *The silent language.* New York: Doubleday/Fawcett.

Hall, E. (1969). *The hidden dimension.* Garden City, NY: Anchor Books/ Doubleday.

Hall, E. (1977). *Beyond culture.* Garden City, NY: Anchor Press/ Doubleday.

Hoopes, D. (1979). Intercultural communication concepts and the psychology of intercultural experience.In M. Pusch (Ed.), *Multicultural education: A cross-cultural training approach.* Chicago: Intercultural Press.

Hoopes, D., & Pusch, M. (1979).Definition of terms (pp. 2–8). In M. Pusch (Ed.), *Multicultural education: A cross-cultural training approach.* Chicago: Intercultural Press.

Hoopes. D., & Ventura, P. (Eds.). (1979). *Intercultural sourcebook: Cross-cultural training methodologies.* Chicago: Intercultural Press.

Kirk-Greene, C. (1990). *NTC's dictionary of faux amis.* Lincolnwood, IL: National Textbook Company.

Kohls, R. (1981). *Developing intercultural awareness.* Washington, DC: SIETAR.

Levine, D., & Adelman, M. (1982). *Beyond language: Intercultural communication for English as a second language.* Englewood Cliffs, NJ: Prentice-Hall.

Live, A., & Sankowsky, S. (1980). *American mosaic: Intermediate-advanced ESL reader.* Englewood Cliffs, NJ: Prentice-Hall.

Oberg, K. (1958). *Culture shock and the problem of adjustment to new cultural environments.* Washington, DC: Department of State, Foreign Service Institute.

Osgood, C., May, W., & Miron, M. (1975). *Cross-cultural universals of affective meaning.* Urbana: University of Illinois Press.

Ozete, O., & Guillen, S. (1991). *Contigo: Essentials of Spanish* (2nd ed.). Fort Worth, TX: Holt, Rinehart and Winston, Inc.

Paulston, C. (1978). Biculturalism: Some reflections and speculations. *TESOL Quarterly, 12,* 369–380.

Penfield, J. (1987). *The media: Catalysts for communicative language learning.* Reading, MA: Addison-Wesley.

Pusch, M. (Ed.). (1979). *Multicultural education: A cross-cultural training approach.* Chicago: Intercultural Press.

Robinson, G. (1981). *Issues in second language and cross-cultural education: The forest through the trees.* Boston: Heinle & Heinle Publishers, Inc.

Rodriguez, R. (1981). *Hunger of memory: The education of Richard Rodriquez. An autobiography.* Boston:David R. Godine.

Rose, M. (Ed.). (1981). *Translation spectrum: Essays in theory and practice.* Albany: State University of New York Press.

Samovar, L., & Porter, R. (Eds.). (1985). *Intercultural communication: A reader.* Belmont, CA: Wadsworth Publishing Company.

Seelye, H.N. (1984). *Teaching culture: Strategies for intercultural communication.* Lincolnwood, IL: National Textbook Company.

Singer, M. R. (1987). *Intercultural communication: A perceptual approach.* Englewood Cliffs, NJ: Prentice-Hall.

Smart, R. (1983). *Using a Western learning model in Asia: A case study.* Occasional Papers in Intercultural Learning. New York: AFS International/Intercultural Programs.

Smith, E., & Lune, L. (Eds.). (1979). *Toward internationalism: Readings in cross-cultural communication.* Rowley, MA: Newbury House.

Steele, R. (1990). Culture in the foreign language classroom. *ERIC/CLL News Bulletin,* September, 4.

Stewart, E. (1972). *American cultural patterns: A cross-cultural perspective.* Chicago: Intercultural Press.

Tan, A. (1989). *The joy luck club.* New York: Random House.

Triandis, H., Vassiliou, V., Tanaka, Y., & Shanmugam, A. (Eds.). (1972). *The analysis of subjective culture.* New York: Random House.

Zongren, L. (1990). *Two years in the melting pot.* San Francisco: China Books and Periodicals.

APPENDIX A

Culture is Universal

Everybody in the world belongs to one or more cultures or subcultures. It is observed in the ways of behaving, living and believing associated with a given group of human beings. There is no human group or society without culture. Cultural patterns are related to universal problems, but the solutions are culture unique. All human beings need shelter but the forms of shelter vary from an igloo to a penthouse. Family relationships are recognized in every culture but who is considered family and who is not varies from culture to culture.

Culture Makes Living Easy

Social behavior, customs, and even language are designed to avoid your having to make twenty-nine decisions before breakfast. For example, when you got out of bed today did you consider going out without any clothes on? Probably not. It's a cultural no-no except in a nudist camp. Did you drive your car on the left hand side of the road? I hope not for it is not done in the United States. Did you bow to your boss? Probably not unless you are Japanese or working for Nissan. Greetings, road etiquette, or even proper dress are surrounded by cultural maps and sanctions that allow us to avoid pondering these questions daily.

Our Culture and its Patterns Are So Familiar That it is Difficult to Accept Other Ways as Right

Because cultures make life easy they also often filter experience so that we find it difficult to adapt to new ways and embrace different values as valid for those who share them. And keep in mind:

- Cultures are learned just as languages are. New cultural patterns can be taught or acquired.
- Language and culture are closely related and interactive. We learn our culture through language and social communication; cultural patterns and values are reflected in our language.
- Cultures change over time. So culture learning about a culture (mine, ours, and theirs) is a lifelong pursuit.

Our Way, My Way, Their Way

The concept of culture embraces the many ways humankind has devised to cope with life according to a given set of principles, values, and customs deemed correct for a given social group. It is a blueprint for living with accompanying sets of values and beliefs. To those who embrace a given culture it is **Our Way.** Yet each individual culture bearer (you) carries around his/her own personal version of that social blueprint or map because we vary in age, experience, social class, resources, personal attributes, and so his/her version of a culture is **My Way.** While there is certain general agreement that there is an OUR way and a MY way, it's not the same as **Their Way.**

APPENDIX B

Process of Culture Learning

STEP ONE: KNOW YOURSELF AND OTHERS
Information seeking

STEP TWO: COMPARE AND CONTRAST C1 AND C2
Form frames of reference based on information received

STEP THREE: FORM VALID CULTURAL HYPOTHESES AND PERCEPTIONS

STEP FOUR: ADJUST/ADAPT/ASSIMILATE/REJECT

CHAPTER 6

THEORETICAL FOUNDATIONS OF INTERCULTURAL TRAINING AND APPLICATIONS TO THE TEACHING OF CULTURE

Shelley L. Smith, R. Michael Paige, and Inge Steglitz

INTRODUCTION

When originally asked to write about the contributions that intercultural communication theory and pedagogy can bring to the teaching of culture in second language education, we were pleased to take on this task. We have long felt that there was a need to bridge the gap between these two fields; interculturalists and language educators have paid insufficient attention to each other's work, in our view. Damen (1987) and Seelye (1994), for example, are among a handful of language educators who have actually written about the teaching of culture from an intercultural communication perspective. The purpose of this chapter is to address this shortcoming in the literature by presenting ideas about teaching culture, which come from the field of intercultural communication.

Culture as the Core: Perspectives in Second Language Education, pages 89–125
Copyright © 2003 by Information Age Publishing
All rights of reproduction in any form reserved.

Intercultural communication is an academic field. Certainly, the domain of intercultural training has long been considered to be culture as opposed to language. Peace Corps training, for instance, is generally organized into three distinct components: language training, technical training, and intercultural training. In spite of numerous efforts to integrate the language and culture components, it has generally been felt that language preparation, at least in the early stages, is so demanding that the cultural element must become secondary. Moreover, language educators, with rare exception, do not view the teaching of culture as central to their work.

While culture has rarely been the province of language education, it has always been a central objective of the intercultural trainer. Interculturalists discuss in more general and pragmatic terms the issues of language use and style, i.e., how people interact, frame logical arguments, and "get to the point." We explore, in depth, culture learning and adjustment, the forming of intercultural relationships, the role of affect and emotion in intercultural contact, and general intercultural phenomena. Yet anthropology also lays claim to the study and analysis of cultural systems and institutions; sociolinguistics, in turn, has carved for itself a key role in identifying the interdependence of language use and the frameworks of social and cultural meaning; and cross-cultural psychology has explored cultural differences in cognition, perception, and *culture shock* as a problematic phenomenon.

The question remained, "What is specifically ours?" The answer is twofold. First, while our field has incorporated theories from all of these disciplines (including most recently the areas of critical theory, diversity, and multiculturalism), intercultural communication brings a specific perspective to the examination of cultural issues that uniquely frames these phenomena. From an intercultural communication perspective, the focus is not on understanding cultures *per se*, or even on the interface of the individual with a given culture, but on the impact cultural values, beliefs, perceptions, and social relationship patterns have on the relational experience that results from *interaction between people as it occurs within a cultural context*. Second, more than almost any other group, intercultural trainers have examined the multiple ways in which culture can be taught. Faced with the real world problem of preparing people with such diverse needs as Peace Corps volunteers, business professionals, international students, and career diplomats to function quickly and effectively in cultures other than their own, trainers have developed instructional designs which have been tested and become increasingly more refined during the past 30 years. Over the years, intercultural training has incorporated experiential education, cooperative learning, and adult education principles to the teaching of culture and cultural issues. Its focus on culture-general as well as culture-specific knowledge and its strong commitment to developing the skills of *learning how to learn* about culture are two contributions of the field that are particularly well suited to the second language classroom. For example, when asked to teach about *culture*, we suspect that most language instructors experience some degree of confusion. Just which culture does a Spanish instructor teach about? Spain? Mexico? Ecuador? Does a French teacher focus on France? Senegal? Morocco? And beyond the concerns of a general cultural frame, what about issues of regionality? Most of France is proudly un-Parisian, and Brittany and Pays Basques embrace their Celtic and Basque roots respectively. Indigenous groups in Latin America are not only different from one another, but clearly carry cultural patterns quite distinct from those of their Spanish conquerors. Even if one is teaching language to a group planning a specific cultural transition, the concerns are dauntingly complex. What about the issues of class, gender roles, friendship, dating, religious differences, and family relational patterns within any given group? The task remains overwhelming as long as culture is seen as a finite body of knowledge that must be *taught*. If instead, the focus is on the learning to understand how differences in communication, values, perceptions, and relationship patterns can affect our interactions with others, the focus becomes one of appreciating the complexity and diversity of cultural variations and *learning how to learn* about cultural others. This has been the strength of intercultural training.

In this chapter, we suggest that there are specific philosophical, theoretical, and pedagogical lessons interculturalists have learned that are relevant to second languages and cultures education. We will start by presenting brief histories of the evolution of intercultural training and intercultural communication as unique disciplines. We will then present an intercultural communication perspective that represents the philosophical and theoretical frameworks for viewing pedagogical issues and their implications for culture teaching and learning in the second language curriculum. Finally, we will discuss specific intercultural training theories and approaches that we feel are most appropriate to the teaching of culture in second language education.

HISTORICAL BACKGROUND
OF INTERCULTURAL TRAINING

Intercultural training has had a curious history. It was developed in the United States during a post-World War II era characterized by previously unparalleled contact and commerce across nations. As an applied field, it emerged in response to a growing need: the necessity to select and prepare international sojourners—from missionaries to development assistance specialists—for the cultural immersions they would be experiencing. In the beginning, intercultural trainers learned by doing. There was little theory and even less research to guide them. And the pressures and challenges of training were formidable. In the case of the U.S. Peace Corps, for instance, trainers had only three months to prepare trainees to live and work in some of the most geographically remote and culturally distant societies on earth. Trainers had to be pragmatic and flexible, for there were few firm culture teaching principles to follow. They had to try things out first, see what worked, and then formulate their findings in theoretical and pedagogical terms. If training was atheoretical in the early years, it was because no single academic discipline could sufficiently account for the causes and consequences of intercultural interactions, to say nothing of providing a theory-based model for training design. Anthropology came the closest because its field research methodology demanded intensive cultural immersion of its practitioners; yet by the 1960s even anthropologists had not yet formulated an effective training model for preparing fieldworkers.

Harrison and Hopkins' (1967) seminal article critiqued the *university model* and its emphasis on highly analytical, cognitive, and fact-based learning for being woefully inadequate to the task of equipping people for radically different and psychologically intense cultural experiences. Indeed, it took a generation of returning Peace Corps Volunteers, who had been trained at U.S. universities, to indicate exactly how and why such traditional pedagogy was not serving its purposes.

Through those years of trial and error, the domain of intercultural training was, and to this day still is, *culture* as opposed to language. Language education, on the other hand, has rarely emphasized the teaching of culture.

THEORETICAL FOUNDATIONS

The academic discipline of intercultural communication has played a key role in creating an interdisciplinary theoretical model of intercultural interaction, relations, and communication. It can be said that intercultural communication is the disciplinary counterpart of applied intercultural training. There has been an important reciprocity of theory-practice that has strengthened the discipline and intercultural training. Intercultural communication theorists synthesized concepts and theories from other disciplines, most notably interpersonal communication and cross-cultural psychology, secondarily sociology and anthropology, into a holistic explanatory framework.

It is widely accepted that intercultural communication was established both as a term and as a field of study in 1959 with the publication of Edward T. Hall's seminal work, *The Silent Language*. The 40-year evolution of this field has witnessed a synthesis of theories and perspectives from anthropology, sociology, psychology and linguistics with those of speech communication, its present academic home. Some of these theories have their origins in communication theory, some were borrowed from other disciplines, and some were "invented specifically to deal with intercultural phenomena" (Gudykunst & Nishida, 1989, p. 18). All of the theoretical frameworks discussed here generally share the assumption that communication and culture are interdependent and mutually supportive dynamic processes. Just as culture forms the foundation of communication, communication serves as the medium through which culture is created, maintained, and shared among its members.

Because of the introductory nature of this chapter, we have been very selective in choosing the theories, perspectives, concepts, and models we think are most applicable for the task of integrating culture-learning into the language curriculum.

An Intercultural Communication Perspective

A survey of the literature reveals that there is no one agreed upon definition of intercultural communication. Efforts to define it have focused on: (1) the "necessary and sufficient conditions" for a communication event to qualify as intercultural, such as two or more persons from different cultural backgrounds communicating (Samovar & Porter, 1991, p.20); (2) the intrapersonal and interpersonal processes that need to take place in order for effective intercultural communication to occur, for instance, visible adaptive behavior on the part of the communicators reflecting their awareness of the other's *foreignness* (Ellingsworth, 1983); (3) the qualities of the interaction between people from different cultures that define successful intercultural communication, for example, when mutual understanding or *coorientation* has been reached (Szalay, 1981); and (4) the processes that lead to coordination in an encounter between individuals from different cultures (Cronen, Chen, & Pearce, 1988); and on the identity assumptions of the people "who identify themselves as distinct from one another in cultural terms" (Collier & Thomas, 1988, p. 100).

These various definitions do not simply emphasize different aspects of the overall phenomenon of intercultural communication; they reflect profound differences in the way culture, communication, and the culture-communication-communicator relationships are conceptualized. The selection of any given definition informs educational practice and should be based on the requirements of the situation as well as the trainer/educator's personal preference and creativity. We offer a definition of an intercultural communication perspective that brings to the discussion of intercultural training and pedagogy our assumptions about the nature of culture and intercultural communication. These assumptions are central to developing guidelines for understanding the choices educators make in developing their curriculum. This understanding serves as a basis for knowing why certain theoretical perspectives and training strategies are adopted. It also gives educators the guidelines in which to creatively develop their own strategies and curricular designs.

The intercultural perspective is difference-based, face-to-face interactive, processual, holistic, humanistic, phenomenological/socially constructed, developmental, and contextual. A more detailed discussion of each of these elements and their impact on intercultural communication pedagogy follows.

Difference-based communication involves the assumption that people from different cultures will have some marked differences in their communicative behaviors, role perceptions, institutions, basic assumptions about the world, and underlying value systems (Kim, 1988, p. 16). Based on intercultural (Hall, 1959; Singer, 1985; Stewart, 1972) and cognitive development theories (Perry, 1970), Bennett (1993) proposes that the manner in which a person construes, evaluates, and responds to difference is the fundamental factor in the development of intercultural sensitivity. Although all human beings may share similar basic emotions and relationship needs, the reasons for and ways of expressing them may be very different. This carries with it the assumption that communication behaviors are relative not only with regard to an individual's world view, but with regard to the world view of the culture(s) in which they are participants. While there is no question that similarities in communication patterns do exist across cultures, the cultural differences are the sources of intercultural communication problems and misunderstandings. Comprehending these differences can help communicators reach greater levels of empathy and communication effectiveness. The assumption of cultural relativism means that behaviors and values must be understood from a given individual's cultural perspective. As Bennett (1988, p. 25) points out, "Absolute or universal judgments of goodness and badness of behavior and values cannot be made as far as communication is concerned." Differences, when viewed from the intercultural perspective, are more than simply *tolerated.* They are accepted as valid for members of that culture group and are respected as representative of human creativity in seeking solutions to universal problems and concerns.

Face-to-face interactive communication connotes direct, conscious interaction between individuals from different cultural backgrounds, who bring with them their unique, culturally-based perceptions of reality, communication behaviors, and values (Bennett, 1988, 1995). Like all communication, this process involves continuous, multidirectional feedback and "the mutual creation of meaning" that is unique, "irreversible and unrepeatable" (Barnlund, 1962, p. 200). Since "meaning is not in the message, but in the message user" (p. 200), and the participants in an intercultural interaction are using two different cultural (and often linguistic) codes, the potential for misunderstandings is virtually endless. The need for sensitivity, alertness, and openness to the possibility of breakdown in the meaning process (Howell, 1979) is essential if effective communication is to occur. This assumption provides a basis for understanding the difficulties occurring when persons from different cultural systems who have different rules for interaction come together.

With this in mind, intercultural educators need to be prepared to move beyond discussion of *cultural components* (values, language, nonverbal communication, etc.) and to explore in a meaningful way the real issues and implications involved in relationships and interactions as they are affected by cultural differences. They need to understand the tenuous line that divides imparting stereotypes and giving trainees the necessary set of useful, hypothesis-testing tools and baseline information about a culture and its people. Constant vigilance in this area is essential. Awareness of the dynamic nature of communication reminds trainers and trainees alike that we do not interact with cultures *per se*, we form unique and individualized relationships with *people* in whom cultural values and norms are uniquely manifested.

Processual communication views communication and culture as dynamic, ever changing, interdependent, and mutually influential (Barnlund, 1962, p. 202); both creating and emerging from the continual interaction of society's individuals and institutions. This assumes that we will best understand the relationships and events that are involved in intra- and intercultural contact as a function of communication. It is by focusing on the interaction itself, i.e., what is happening *between* communicators (Kim, 1984, p. 16) that we discover the deepest implications of communication as internalized culture (Bennett, 1988, p. 24). This assumption adds a skill-based component that is at the root of the intercultural educator's commitment to experiential learning. Learners need to take their knowledge beyond the abstract and put it into practice. This requires attention to all learning modes—experiential and cognitive.

Holistic communication takes a *holographic* view of culture and communication (Wilber, 1982), which assumes that cultural behaviors, patterns, beliefs, values, and institutions form a *rational* and coherent whole. It further assumes the presence of what may be termed a *cultural map*. It should, therefore, be theoretically possible to determine the structures and values of a culture by mapping its cognitive schemas (Applegate & Sypher, 1983), language, interaction patterns (Carbaugh, 1990) or infer the patterns of social interaction by looking at its values, aesthetics, or institutions (Mansell, 1981).

As a result, the communication between individuals and their greater social and cultural systems is mutually reinforcing and interdependent. Human beings exist within cultural frameworks and those same frameworks exist within the individuals who draw important aspects of their identity and behaviors from them.[1] As a result, ICC educators need to understand the interconnectedness of all elements of culture and culture change. Viewing teachers and learners within a cultural and social context implies that issues of power and oppression cannot be ignored by intercultural educators because "power and power differentials inherent in the social and political context play a critical part in intercultural interaction" (Paige & Martin, 1996, p. 37). Whether these issues are connected to domestic diversity, cultural imperialism, or a colonial history, trainers will inevitably encounter trainees who have deep convictions and emotions connected to them.

Humanistic communication is phenomenological in its assumptions (Bennett, 1988, p. 25). It is based on the belief that human reality is viewed as socially constructed (Berger & Luckman, 1966) and that human beings are "active interpreters of their social environment" (Applegate & Sypher, 1983, p. 64). In addition, it stresses the view of human beings as actors rather than reactors, with the ability to both create and change their conceptual spheres and their environments. It assumes that cultures and their institutions (linguistic, social, religious, and economic), roles, and communication behaviors are created, perpetuated, and changed by people to meet their need for mutual support and predictability. These institutions and behaviors are seen as mutable and nonuniversal in nature, existing only in relationship to their human components. It legitimizes subjective experience. Respect, empathy, and compassion for all aspects of human cultures and conditions, however alien they may seem, are inherent in this assumption.

For intercultural communication educators, the key issues related to a humanistic approach are respect and compassion for all of the individual and cultural perspectives that they may encounter. This means the educator must understand: (1) a wide variety of pedagogical strategies, (2) their usefulness and impact on various learning and cultural styles and stages of cultural sensitivity (M.J. Bennett, 1986), and (3) the limits of their own knowledge and skills. Additionally, they must understand the importance of the learning environment (including physical and emotional climates) and its impact on various learning and cultural styles and the students' sense of safety. This understanding determines to a high degree the choice of training goals and objectives, training strategies, and the sequencing of those strategies.

Phenomenological/socially constructed communication views the nature of reality, the way human beings acquire and interpret knowledge, and the meaning and importance attached to that knowledge as constructed (Paige, 1993; Putnam, 1984). In this perspective, realities are constantly being socially constructed and reconstructed through communication and interaction between the individuals and institutions that share those realities. As a result, all relationships involve the continual negotiation and renegotiation of meaning. Cultural difference, for example, is a function of what we consider to be *different* in the first place. Our constructed categories of difference are then associated with our perceptions of and responses to the *other*.

We believe that a deep exploration and discussion of cultural differences cannot be respectfully or rigorously undertaken without the acceptance of such an assumption. Before we attempt to teach about anyone else, we must first make the effort to achieve a deep sensitivity to differences and some semblance of objective awareness in the face of what must ultimately be our own subjective perspectives. This requires that we recognize our own assumptions and realities and understand how they will color our actions and interpretations. Failure to do this leaves us open to the dangers inherent in making inferences and judgments without an understanding of either our subjects or ourselves. Acceptance of *universals*, therefore, is rare and generally made with regard to our ability to identify transcultural processes that would help to frame, define, and make our cultural differences more understandable.

Developmental communication describes intercultural learning in developmental terms. The most important work during the past 15 years has been Milton Bennett's writings on intercultural sensitivity as a developmental phenomenon (1986, 1993). Bennett proposes that intercultural sensitivity is multifaceted in nature (affective, behavioral, and cognitive), phenomenological (a function of how an individual construes cultural difference), and experiential (related to a person's experiences with difference). Human beings, under certain circumstances, can progress from ethnocentrism (or monoculturalism) to ethnorelativism (or interculturalism), although the former is where most people live their lives. Another way to put this is to say that being intercultural is not the normal condition of human beings. Cultures, somewhat ironically, provide us with the tools for survival within our own community, but do less well in equipping us to venture out beyond it.

Contextual communication means that all human interaction is given meaning by the context (time, place, participants) within which it occurs. Elsewhere (Paige et al., this volume) we discussed context at great length, the purpose being to encourage language teachers to help their students understand language as culture in order to use it more appropriately. There, we argued,

The paper begins with a discussion of the context of culture learning, i.e., the different types of settings and circumstances within which culture learning occurs. The more we read, the more we came to realize that for language and culture learning, context is an overarching concept which subsumes many other variables including: the setting; the teacher; the learner; instructional methods; instructional materials; and assessment approaches.

The major emphasis regarding context has been on defining the term. We were struck by the complexity of the concept and the wide variety of definitions presented in the literature. Eventually, we elected to utilize context as our overall frame of reference for that paper and subsume under it other concepts such as setting, teacher variables, learner variables, curricular materials and instructional methods, and assessment. With respect to these elements, the emphasis in the literature has been on the impact of the setting on culture learning (e.g., immersion in the host culture versus classroom instruction). The classroom-based literature has focused on immersion programs. The next most commonly studied contextual variables have been teacher and learner variables (p. 45).

In review, the adoption of this perspective establishes a set of *givens* in relation to teaching about culture. It requires that educators: (1) understand their own personal and cultural assumptions and their strengths as well as their shortcomings with regard to teaching both culture-general and culture-specific information; (2) be respectful of the personal and cultural assumptions of their students; (3) be keenly aware of a wide variety of cultural possibilities, theoretical frames, and pedagogical strategies; (4) be prepared, since there is no one *right* approach to culture learning (choices made depend on the interface of context, cultures involved, learner needs, resources available, and teacher competencies) to assess the needs, abilities, and level of preparedness of the students to learn cultural information; and (5) be able to implement theory-based strategies and sequencing that are appropriate to both those needs and the cultural and situational contexts in which the learning takes place. This perspective can serve as a template against which those choices are tested.

Communication, Culture, and the Individual

Care needs to be taken in defining both communication and culture because they lie at the root of the discussion of intercultural communication theory. Choosing from the many definitions for communication[2] and culture[3] and the relationship between these phenomena quite literally means taking from all the available options those definitions which are congruent with one's assumptions about the nature of communication and the perspective from which it should be viewed. Barnlund's (1962) definition of communication as *the process of [mutually] creating a meaning* (p. 78) provides a relativistic perspective that has informed much of the work done by intercultural communication scholars. The Zen-like simplicity of this statement has profound implications for the way we view and study human interaction. *Process* implies that our communication behavior is not static and is responsive to and interdependent with the communication behavior of others. *Creation of meaning* assumes that meanings, and therefore social realities, are subjective social commodities that are negotiated/created through communication and are intrinsically tied to one's perceptions of people, contexts, and events. When the idea of *culture as context* and as the *framer of contexts* was introduced into this definition by Hall (1976), it became easier to recognize its potentially powerful relationship to the communication process and the creation of our social realities. Hall went so far as to define communication as *internalized culture* (p. 69).

Culture, then, becomes "a system of symbols and meanings" (Schneider, 1976, p. 198), i.e., "an interpretive system subscribed to by groups of people . . . Communicative constructions of personhood, roles and groups are part of the [cultural] interpretive system" (Thomas, 1991, p. 2). The nature of this systemic view acknowledges the relationship between the internal systems of meanings an individual carries and the external patterns of meaning one may ascribe to a cultural system, *but it does not consider the relationship to be isomorphic.* Instead, it allows for the idea that an individual may subscribe to "multiple systems of meaning and that a given culture is accessible to multiple groups" (p. 3). Further, each individual has internalized those meanings in ways that are to some degree unique. This assumption allows for intercultural interaction to cover a much wider range of contexts and communicators. People cannot be classified merely by nationality, gender or ethnicity. While it recognizes the validity of all those cultural meanings, it allows for variations and combinations that can move an interaction from intracultural to intercultural and back again in a relatively short time. It further assumes that different contextual influences will affect these patterns (Carbaugh, 1990; Hymes, 1962).

The idea that communication and culture are interdependent is not new. Sapir (1931) stated that "every cultural pattern and every single act of social behavior involves communication in either an explicit or an implicit sense" (p. 578). Petersen et al. (1965) echo this view:

> ...communication ... is the carrier of the social processes ... It is the means man has for organizing, stabilizing, and modifying his social life ... The social process depends upon the accumulation and transmission of social knowledge. Knowledge in time depends upon communication (p. 16).

Recently, Agar (1994) argued that the world has moved far past the traditional definition of *culture* as "a closed, coherent system of meanings in which an individual always and only participates" (p. 236). Martin (1993) states that "The notion of culture needs to be extended" and along with that extension, "conceptualizations of [communication] competence should incorporate cultural membership beyond national culture, such as racial, ethnic, or gender groups"—what Singer (1987) defines as *identity groups* (groups that share a common perception, both voluntary and involuntary) (p. 28). This idea is consistent with the views of scholars who believe that each person carries multiple, overlapping cultural frames (nationality, gender, ethnicity, religion, etc.) that are internalized, individuated and emerge in interactions (Collier, 1989; Collier & Thomas, 1988; Kim, 1988). Agar further extends the idea of culture by suggesting that it is essentially identifiable only as it emerges in intercultural interactions:

> ...the discourse that embodies the task [of identifying culture] links to different frames of interpretation ... Find the locations in discourse where the differences occur and [cultures] make the frames that explain the differences explicit (p. 227).

This discussion makes clearer the almost inseparable relationship between culture and communication. Drawing on this relationship, Kim (1988) brings us full circle by defining culture as "the sum of the consensus of the individual communication patterns manifest by the members of a society, giving coherence, continuity and distinctive form to their way of life" (p. 47). She connects this to the concept of identity by further stating that, "The inseparable relationship between these cultural patterns and an individual's internalized conditions are incorporated into a person's *cultural identity* . . . [as] . . . a complex process of continuing interpretive activity internal to individuals as a result of their acculturation experience" (p. 48). These ideas overlap with the key communication theories regarding cultural identity and intercultural communication competence and will be discussed in greater depth in that section.

Theoretical Frameworks of Culture

What are the implications of having a working knowledge of a variety of cultural frameworks for the second languages curriculum? Teaching about cultural difference requires understanding conceptual models of cultural variability. Those summarized here represent some of the most commonly agreed-upon foundations of the culture-communication relationship. While there is an ongoing debate as to the usefulness of searching for cultural universals, models like these provide a place to begin in defining cultural patterns that impact communication. These models seek to identify overriding frameworks, assumptions, or dimensions that can be found to varying degrees in every culture even though they may find different forms of expression.

E.T. Hall's work has centered around the culture-general concepts of proxemics (Hall, 1966/1982), chronemics (Hall, 1984), and the low/high-context continuum (Hall, 1976/1981). At the basis of all of Hall's work are three central ideas: first, culture communicates; second, cultures and the individuals that inhabit them "participate in molding each other" (1966/1982, p. 4); and third, "people from different cultures not only speak different languages but, what is possibly more important, *inhabit different sensory worlds*" (1966/1982, p. 2). That is, people differ with regard to the information they select and interpret from their environment. Hall's (1976/1981) conceptualization of cultures as *high- or low-context* approaches the culture-communication relationship from a slightly different angle. He essentially addresses the question of how important contextual cues are for the communicative meaning of situations. The concept of high- and low-context cultures allows the categorization of cultures into those that tend to derive a great deal of communicative meaning from the context of an encounter (high-context cultures; e.g., Japan) and those where the bulk of communicative meaning is expected to be contained in explicit verbal code (low-context cultures; e.g., the United States).

Implications for interaction within this model are far reaching. Hall (1966/1982) suggests that communication across cultures is often *thwarted* because "neither of the parties was aware that each inhabits a different perceptual world" (p. 5). He believes that in order to understand people with cultural backgrounds different from our own, it is "essential that we learn to read the silent communications as easily as the printed and spoken ones" (p. 6). Understanding what is *said* does not always help you understand what is *meant*. The subtlety of high-context communication is not problematic to another individual with the same cultural assumptions about communication. If a husband knows that the temperature of his tea indicates his wife's mood, the message is clear. To someone from a low-context culture, however, the message would likely to be missed. The result can be escalating misunderstanding and anger and the befuddled cry of the low-context individual, "Why didn't you tell me?!" An excellent application of the high-context/low-context variability is found in Ting-Toomey's (1988) discussion of *facework maintenance* as a mediating variable in the cultural variation in conflict styles. She suggests that high-context cultures tend to use an indirect conflict style, while low-context cultures tend to employ a direct style.

In 1961, Kluckhohn and Strodtbeck published what has become one of the most widely employed frameworks for cultural comparison and analysis of intercultural interaction in the field of intercultural communication. They assume that (1) people in all cultures are faced with common human problems to which they must find solutions, (2) that the possible solutions to these problems are limited within a range of potential solutions, and (3) that all potential solutions are present in every culture even though one solution tends to be preferred by any one culture. Based on these assumptions, the authors posit the existence of five basic value orientations (dimensions) along which each culture can be categorized. Each dimension represents a fundamental question or concern about the nature of the world and suggests three possible "answers" to those questions. The *Human Orientation* asks, "What is the innate character of human nature?" *Human-Nature Orientation* asks, "What is the relationship of humans to the natural world?" *Time Orientation* asks, "What is the temporal focus of human life?" *Activity Orientation* asks, "What is the purpose of human activity?" And finally, *Relational Orientation* asks, "What is the mode of human relationships?" The answers to these questions reveal the bases of a culture's value system and influence both the what and the how of communication within a given culture. Condon and Yousef (1975) expanded the framework to include a wider variety of dimensions. While a more complex conceptualization, the model is ultimately easier to apply to a wider variety of phenomena.

The final dimensions of cultural variability to be discussed here are Hofstede's (1984): individualism-collectivism, uncertainty avoidance, power distance, and masculinity-femininity. These findings are based in his empirical studies of multinational corporations in 53 countries. *Individualism-collectivism* is probably the best known of the four dimensions. This dimension basically deals with how cultures negotiate the "relationship between the individual and the collectivity," with some cultures coming down on the side of the primacy of the individual and others on the side of the superseding importance of the group (Hofstede, 1984, p. 148). In other words, in some cultures "individualism is seen as a blessing and a source of well-being; in others, it is seen as alienating" (p. 148). It is expressed in the various ways people in different cultures live together (e.g., nuclear vs. extended family etc.). Essentially, individualistic cultures emphasize the identity of *I* whereas collectivistic cultures emphasize the identity of *we* (see Gudykunst & Ting-Toomey, 1988). Traindis (1995) identified distinctions between these phenomena at psychological and cultural levels and in vertical and horizontal structures of individualism and collectivism, *per se.* Practical applications of this framework include the identification of specific areas of concern for training persons from individualist and collectivist cultures to interact with one another (Bhawuk & Triandis, 1996; Triandis, Brislin, & Hui, 1988) and cross-cultural psychology (Triandis, 1992). Cultures that are high in *uncertainty-avoidance* are defined as having a lower tolerance for ambiguity and uncertainty, higher levels of anxiety, more formal rules, a need for absolute truth, and low tolerance for societal deviance. According to Hofstede, uncertainty about the future is "a basic fact of life" (p. 110) with which all humans have to cope. Different societies have developed different ways of coping with and adapting to uncertainty, and the roots of these various ways are "non-rational" and "may lead to collective behavior in one society which may seem aberrant and incomprehensible to members of other societies" (p. 111). *Power-distance* is "a measure of the interpersonal power or influence between B [boss] and S [subordinate] as perceived by the least powerful of the two, S" (Hofstede, 1984, pp. 70–71). In other words, it is the degree to which a less powerful person accepts that there is an unequal distribution of power in a society or organization. Cultures with high power distance emphasize coercive power, while low power distance societies tend to believe in the legitimate use of expert power. Like the previous dimensions, a culture's level of power distance is an expression of the solution its members have found to the *basic issue* of human inequality in the various areas of prestige, wealth, status, etc. (p. 65). Hofstede's fourth dimension, finally, is defined in terms of the aspects of cultural life valued by members of a given culture. Cultures high on *femininity* value people, interpersonal relationships, interdependence, quality of life, and open sex-roles, whereas cultures high on *masculinity* value things, differentiated sex roles, achievement, power, and independence. For a critical discussion of Hofstede's work and reports on both theoretical and empirical work on the relationship between Hofstede's dimensions and aspects of interpersonal communication across cultures, see Gudykunst and Ting-Toomey (1988).

One of the criticisms leveled at these and other models of cultural variability is that they reduce culture to a rather static set of variables on which people differ (Cronen, Chen, & Pearce, 1988). However, when properly applied, they can also reveal a tremendous amount about the motivations, perceptions, and world views of culturally different individuals. Proper application is the key here. A great deal has been written and researched with regard to these frameworks that tend to dichotomize cultures into an either/or state, hence the sense of being static. Instead, all of these models were designed as fluid continua within which all cultures have a greater or lesser degree of variability. For instance, even though the United States is widely discussed as a strongly individualist and low-context culture, there is a great deal of regional, religious, and ethnic variability regarding these factors. Further, it does not mean that we have no group-oriented obligations or *understood* meanings. Instead, these frameworks provide a basis for discussing the hierarchies and the relationships between our nested priorities and beliefs in what *ought to be.* The balance between group and individual priorities and concerns, therefore, is situationally and culturally negotiated based on these assumptions and varies a great deal even among cultures that are thought to be highly individualistic (the United States, Germany, England, France, etc.). For the intercultural communication educator, they should serve as tools for analysis of what one discovers about a cultural other, not boxes for cultural stereotypes. Finally, in any discussion of culture, stereotypes are best avoided by providing learners with a careful balance between culture-general frameworks and culture-specific information. This approach gives them skills for analyzing cultural differences as they arise rather than anticipating set patterns of behavior.

Language As Socially Constructed Meaning

A fundamental part of intercultural communication theory is the view that meaning is socially constructed. Communication is seen as the key mechanism through which that is accomplished, and language use and style are significant parts of that process. The culture-communication-individual relationship is represented as a dynamic interrelated process in which individual experience, identity, and cultural meanings are created, shared, and reinforced through communication. The social and personal negotiation of meaning is the key focus; the smallest unit of analysis is *individuals in interaction.* Language is seen in this dynamic as an important part of the process. It is one of the key means through which cultural meanings are shared and revealed.

Linguistic Relativity

The relationship between language, culture, and cognition was most strongly stated by Benjamin Whorf (1952) in his hypothesis of *linguistic relativity*:

> ... the linguistic system (in other words the grammar) of each language is not merely a reproducing instrument for voicing ideas but rather is itself a shaper of ideas, the program and guide for the individual's mental activity, for his analysis of his mental stock in trade (Whorf in Hoijer, 1991, p. 245).

While the deterministic nature of this statement (i.e., language determines thought) has been challenged in the linguistic arena, it is generally accepted by most intercultural scholars that how we think and perceive the world is *reflected in/related to* how we speak about the world (Condon &

Yousef, 1975; Gudykunst & Kim, 1992; Samovar & Porter, 1991; Stewart & Bennett, 1992).Through communication, cultures create social meanings; through language, those meanings become codified/categorized and are further shared. Additionally, the abstract nature of language allows people to share meanings that are philosophical, emotional, and value-laden-constructed realities, which exist for all intents and purposes in the hearts and minds of the community. *How* language is used also carries messages about the deeper culture. Language *style* (whether direct or indirect; how one "gets to the point") and *use* (the colloquial and connotative functions of language), and whether codes are *restricted* (relying heavily on the implicit cues of the social context; prevalent in high-context cultures) or *elaborated* (relying on explicit communication of information; prevalent in low-context cultures) are other frameworks that have been applied to explain the interaction of language and culture (Hall, 1976).

Nonverbal Behavior

A significant part of our communication behavior (60–80%) is considered to be nonverbal. The majority of the rules for nonverbal communication are culture and gender specific and most of that behavior is implicitly learned and out of awareness. The impact of culture on individuals' nonverbal behavior and the effect of those differences on intercultural communication have been discussed by a variety of authors (Brislin, 1981; Brislin et al., 1986; Gudykunst & Ting-Toomey, 1988; Hall, 1959/1981; Jensen, 1985). Nonverbal behavior universally communicates messages about emotion, relationship, power, and attitudes; but its meanings are by no means universal. Differences in the way cultures use space (*proxemics*), touch, (*haptics*), gestures (*kinesics*), eye contact (*occulesics*), time (*chronemics*), vocalics (*paralanguage*), and smell (*olfactics*) have been identified. Hoopes (1979, p. 29) uses the term *cultural code* to refer to this *nonverbal system of communication*. Central to the development of nonverbal theory is Hall's work with regard to space and time. He coined the term *proxemics* (1966) to refer to the biological and physiological foundations of the use of space and to the human experience of space with regard to appropriate interpersonal distance across cultures, public space in cities and buildings (fixed, semi-fixed and moving space) as an expression of culture, and *the language of space*, as witnessed, for example, in literary works. *Chronemics* refers to the variability in the way cultures conceptualize and perceive time. Hall's conceptualization of "time as culture" (Hall, 1984) posits two distinct ways in which cultures influence individuals' experience of time: *monochronic* and *polychronic*. Monochronic cultures view time as linear, extending from the past through the present, into the future. Punctuality and compartmentalization of activities according to clock-time characterize this time concept. One thing is done at one time, and concerns with time tend to supersede interpersonal concerns. Polychronic cultures, on the other hand, view time as a point. The present is primary and a multiplicity of activities can take place simultaneously. Punctuality, according to clock-time, is not a central concern and interpersonal concerns tend to override concerns with time. One of the clear distinctions in this framework is the belief that a community holds with regard to the question, "What is time for?" Is it primarily structured to accomodate people and relationships (polychronic) or is it primarily for reaching prescribed goals or tasks (monochronic)?

The importance of nonverbal communication in the language curriculum should be self-explanatory. How can we teach people to communicate using language alone? The paralinguistic rules of tone, cadence, use of silence, volume, and vocal variation is a key part of any language use. Additionally, a sensitivity to and awareness of facial and body gestures, eye contact, touch, and use of space are at the very heart of an interaction. Finally, the sensitivity to differences in the perception of time is often key to the goodwill one may or may not feel in an interaction or relationship. A person from a polychronic culture may feel rushed or pushed, dehumanized in a monochronic setting. Conversely, the monochronic person often feels stalled, bogged down, and impatient when confronted with polychronic rules of interaction.

The relationship between values, communicative behavior, and relationship dynamics cannot be over-stressed. A body of literature is finally beginning to emerge which directly links cultural values and communication behaviors. Zormeier and Samovar (1997) discuss the values implicit in Mexican-American use of language and proverbs; Andersen (1997) finds deeply value-laden meanings in nonverbal behaviors across cultures; Fong (1997) uses a linguistic framework to discuss the impact of Chinese use and acceptance of compliments on interactions between Chinese and U.S. Americans; and Yum (1997) traces the relationship between Confucian values, relationship formation, and communication patterns. Understanding the implications of values in language use offers limitless opportunity for substantive cultural exploration in the language classroom. What is revealed by the *style* of language use in an interaction (i.e., ornate, simple, direct, indirect)? The choice of words? The presence of words with meanings we can only describe in multiple paragraphs (i.e., the German, *Schaddenfreude*, the Portuguese, *soldage*)?

INTERCULTURAL COMMUNICATION COMPETENCE (ICC)

The exploration of intercultural communication competence (ICC) and/or effectiveness is related to the discussion of intercultural identity, yet has tended to focus more on the requirements of short-term, *overseas* assignments and/or international exchange programs and on the abilities and characteristics individuals bring with them to that experience. Some of these abilities and characteristics are assumed to be *trainable* while others reside in the *personality*. We believe ICC theory to be key to any application of intercultural communication in the language curriculum because it focuses on the management of interaction as a unique personal and interpersonal process. As a result, these phenomena will be discussed in some depth.

A brief overview of the literature on ICC reveals a complex and often contradictory body of work. In a recent review of the literature, Spitzberg and Cupach (1987) found 167 definitions of communication competence specific to the United States alone. If the idea of *good communication* is this variable within a culture, one can imagine that its delineation has been virtually impossible across cultures.

The exploration of ICC began with anecdotal information about *what went wrong*. As Ruben (1989) suggests:

> Much of the impetus for the study of cross-cultural communication competence arose out of efforts to cope with the practical problems of individuals living and working overseas, and by their institutional sponsors (p. 229).

This led to attempts to identify *behaviors* that were indicative of intercultural competence (Guthrie, 1975; Ruben & Kealey, 1979), *individuals* who were best suited to functioning across cultures, and, finally, to establishing criteria for expatriate selection in corporate and academic exchange programs (Kealey & Ruben, 1983; Ruben et al., 1977). These approaches generated endless lists in an attempt to identify an *ideal communicator* who could perform competently across all cultures (Hammer et al., 1978; Hawes & Kealey, 1979; Ruben et al., 1977). These lists of specific personal characteristics and skills were not just contradictory and often poorly defined; they failed to take into account the existence of differing cultural standards for communication competence (Spitzberg, 1989; Wiseman & Abe, 1984). Much of this research has been criticized for a variety of reasons including methodological rigor and lack of theoretical grounding (For a more complete discussion see Spitzberg, 1989). For a decade or more, the composite of the ideal communicator became manifested in Bochner's (1973, 1981) *mediating man/person*, and Adler's (1974) *multicultural man*[sic], and Taft's (1981) mediator as a *cultural bridge*. In his "Toward ethnorelativism: Developmental model of intercultural sensitivity," Bennett (1986) finally framed this multicultural stance as *constructive marginality* and discusses it as the result of a long developmental process of increasing cognitive complexity developing around the concept of the perception of difference. While this is the ultimate synthesis of the trait approach and is *extremely useful for developing training and education programs* in intercultural communication, it defines ultimate competence as *a psychological state* that operates on a broader level of cultural perceptions rather than one-on-one interaction. Additionally, its upper levels, which describe an *ideal* state, essentially exclude the majority of individuals struggling with intercultural communication events.

Ruben (1976) accurately expresses the problem of applying specific standards of communication competence across cultures:

> While one can argue the importance of communication behaviors such as empathy, respect, nonjudgmentalness, etc., transcends cultural boundaries, the way these are expressed and interpreted may vary substantially from one culture (or subculture) to another (p. 344).

Given this caveat, it is necessary to look for a more general, *process-oriented* definition which will allow for unique cultural interpretation and which will give greater insight into the language/competence connection.

The search for a more interactive approach to assessing the issue of ICC requires asking two important questions: (1) What exactly is it we are looking for? and (2) What is the domain of inquiry, i.e., where does it reside: within the person, social context, culture, relationship, or some combination of the above?

The answer to question one is contingent on the basic assumptions about the nature of intercultural communication that have already been outlined. While we may indeed function with the idea of an *ideal* communicator, that ideal will be culturally defined. Further, it is in direct opposition to the assumptions that:

1. Meaning is *mutually created* through the process of communication. Therefore, competence will to some degree be defined within the context of a given relationship and/or interaction;

2. Communicators are socially and culturally contexted with regard to the meanings, perceptions, and realities to which they are predisposed.

3. Culture and communication are inseparable halves of the same whole, existing primarily as internalized patterns and meanings that make up one's cultural identity.

The answer to question two flows naturally from this discussion. ICC within this perspective must be located *within* the dyadic interaction, *related to* the cultural contexts from which the communicators originate and *in which* they find themselves, and involve the negotiation of communicators' *cultural identity* patterns.

Moving away from the trait approach to identifying the *competent communicator* and toward a more *process-oriented* approach leads to a definition of communication competence in an *intercultural* context as a *quality of interaction performance* (Collier, 1988, 1989; Imahori & Lanigan, 1989; Spitzberg, 1989). This perspective sees communicators as making judgments about the *goodness* of oneself and others' communication performance based on the perceived *appropriateness* and *effectiveness*. Communication is appropriate when it meets contextual and relational standards (you did it right given the context); effective when it achieves desired ends or goals or provides satisfaction of both communicators' needs and concerns.

Building on Spitzberg and Cupach's (1984, 1989) work, Imahori and Lanigan (1989) developed a *relational* model of ICC with the dimensions of *knowledge, motivation,* and *skills.* Their assumption is that communicators come to an interaction with a *knowledge* base of appropriate interaction rules: culture specific, culture general, and linguistic. That is they must not only know the language, but also when, where, how, and why it should be used. Communicators are *motivated* by attitudes toward the other's culture, foreign cultures in general, and their partners. Finally, communicators possess a repertoire of *skills* with regard to display of respect, interaction posture, knowledge orientation, empathy, role flexibility, interaction management, tolerance of ambiguity (see Ruben, 1976, 1977), speech accommodation, affinity-seeking behavior, and linguistic facility. These dimensions interact with the communicators' goals and personal, social, and cultural experience in determining the relational outcome of an intercultural interaction. They assume that effective relational outcome (satisfaction/ effectiveness) can only come when a degree of congruence has been achieved between two communicators' competence assumptions and behaviors. Because these issues are relationally defined and negotiated, just how much congruence is necessary, is highly variable and depends on the nature of the relationship.

In this model, Imahori and Lanigan (1989) move beyond the idea that competence involves the "unilateral cultural adaptation of the sojourner to the host" (p. 275) and suggest that a *"highly competent sojourner not only adapts his/her behavior to host nationals but also helps the host nationals adjust to his/her behavior* [italics ours]" (p. 274). Successful interactions result in competent intercultural relationships, e.g., ones that are "mutually satisfying to both partners" (p. 275).

Identity in Intercultural Communication Competence

Collier and Thomas's (1988), "Theory of cultural identity," provides insight into how identity influences the judgment of intercultural communication competence. They suggest that identities are defined through interactions with others, and that *cultural identities* involve identification with and acceptance into groups with shared significant symbols, meanings, and rules for conduct. Culture, therefore, exists only to the degree that it has been internalized and is shared by individuals in a particular group.

Further, people have multiple cultural identities (based on ethnicity, gender, religion, race, occupation, etc.) that can emerge through and in an interaction. Because of this, *communication competence* is a dynamic phenomenon that changes with the identity, which emerges in a particular situation. An interaction becomes *intercultural* if the cultural identities of the people involved differ significantly. *Intercultural communication competence*, therefore is conduct that is appropriate and effective for both individuals.

The intercultural communication competence of dyadic members involves the development of communication skills appropriate to the cultural and relational identities involved. Each person brings a number of such skills to an interaction. Additional skills specific to the needs of the relationship develop over time. ICC influences the speed and effectiveness with which partners move through relationship stages. Because relationship phases are highly interdependent and cyclical, competence develops with and within the relationship. To this end, interactions do not always need to be competent to result in relationship growth. For instance, people in intercultural relationships may inadvertently offend each other by violating the other's cultural rules. However, this *incompetent* behavior can help them identify important concerns that must be met if the relationship is to strengthen (Gupach & Imahori, 1993).

Intercultural Communication Competence and Language

The implications of ICC for the language classroom are many. First, it brings to bear the importance of understanding that communication competence and language proficiency are not the same thing, i.e., being fluent in the host language obviously does not guarantee successful communication with native speakers of that language. It underscores the importance of understanding not just linguistic rules, but also cultural rules and assumptions about interaction, relationship patterns, and communication styles. These cultural factors are critical, not only in terms of communication, but also because they are deeply bound to one's cultural identity. They influence both the native and the nonnative speaker in ways that are

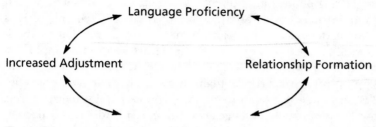

Figure 6.1.

often implicit rather than explicit. A reaction such as "S/he's so rude!" when these rules are broken illustrates how the interpretation of behavior is usually so reflexive and is applied so personally. Language errors are expected; bad behavior is not so easily forgiven. However, there is a critical interface among the three phenomena, which is multidirectional and mutually reinforcing (Figure 6.1). Being proficient in the host language increases one's ability to gain cultural knowledge and form relationships in the host culture. The ability to form successful relationships in a culture is an indicator of competence. Successful relational formation correlates highly with successful adjustment, which is also an indicator of ICC. Through both practice and necessity, forming relationships with host nationals increases language ability. Finally, ICC both facilitates and is improved by relationship interactions.

What this tells us is that language, culture, and intercultural communication competence are significantly intertwined in the reality of intercultural contact. Along with language proficiency, all of the cultural and communicative frameworks we have discussed are a part of the package that makes a student effective in communicating in a second language.

PEDAGOGICAL IMPLICATIONS
OF INTERCULTURAL TRAINING

Up to now, we have primarily discussed the *content* of what intercultural communication has to offer regarding the teaching of culture in the language curriculum. We will now focus on the processes that intercultural trainers and educators have identified with regard to actually teaching that content. Paige (1993) has identified three main factors that characterize the intercultural experience: (1) intensity of emotion, (2) knowledge areas that incorporate cross-cultural differences that sojourners find hard to understand, and (3) cultural differences especially regarding how people think and evaluate information (p. 2).

As Paige (1993) points out, intercultural education is difficult for both teachers and learners for a variety of reasons. First, it requires serious reflection on matters with which learners may have little first hand experience. As a result, a great deal of thought and effort needs to be applied to the development of curriculum so that a balance is achieved between concrete examples and abstract conceptualizations. Second, unlike "more conventional education, which tends to emphasize more depersonalized forms of cognitive learning and knowledge acquisition, it includes highly personalized behavioral and affective learning, self-reflection, and direct experience with cultural difference" (p. 3). Any doubt that changing behavior has highly personal and emotional repercussions, can be dismissed by asking two *typical* American males to walk down the street holding hands. Third, because of the complexity and individual variations that exist within any given culture, it is impossible to teach all there is to know about a specific culture. To attempt to do so does little more than reinforce stereotypes. Therefore, intercultural education stresses *learning how to learn*, a process-oriented pedagogy (Hughes-Weiner, 1986) rather than a product-oriented pedagogy (learning facts) as a major goal. This often involves completely rethinking one's basic assumptions about teaching and learning. Fourth, because the intercultural perspective views human reality as socially constructed, intercultural education involves epistemological explorations regarding alternate ways of knowing and validating what we know (i.e., the meaning of truth and reality). Raising questions about the assumptions that are most basic to our personal and cultural worlds is by its very nature challenging and stressful. The practical application of this knowledge is the realization that cultures are socially developed phenomena that have developed to address complex human needs for social interaction and environmental survival in vastly different ways. Yet "cultures possess their own internal logic and coherence for their members and, hence, their own validity" (Paige, 1993, p.3). As a result, any evaluation of cultural behavior requires a contextual understanding of those behaviors *from the perspective of the culture that is being evaluated.*

If we assume that knowledge is socially constructed, then the lines between teacher and learner are also blurred. Through dialogue and shared experience, instructor and student approach a common understanding that is created within the classroom setting. This is collaborative learning at its best (Mathews, 1994). To create such a climate, students need to feel safe.Accomplishing this goal requires that the instructor be truly nonjudgmental; this means creating an environment where ethnocentrism is accepted as a normal part of everyone's cultural baggage, teacher and student alike. It is not bad, but the place where the dialogue needs to start. Without this understanding, students are not likely to take the necessary risks that are inherent in a truly open dialogue.[4]

Learning and Cognitive Processes

The role of different *cognitive processes* and *learning styles* has found two main areas of focus in intercultural communication theory and research. First is the exploration and explanation of the effect of culture on cognitive processes, definitions of intelligence, and learning styles in order to better understand the conflicts arising in intercultural encounters and international education with regard to issues of rationality, reasoning, and negotiation across cultures (Cole & Scribner, 1974; Glenn & Glenn, 1981; Kaplan, 1966; Lieberman, 1997; Smith, 1987). The second area of focus has been in the application of learning styles, experiential learning theory, and the concept of *learning how to learn* in the planning and implementation of intercultural, diversity, and cross-cultural orientation, training, and education (Bennett, 1986; McCaffery, 1986; Mestenhauser et al., 1988; Rhinesmith & Hoopes, 1972). It is this second area that we will focus on here.

Because the underlying assumptions of adult learning theory appear to match many of the unique requirements posed by intercultural learning situations (e.g., learning is not limited to the formal classroom setting, learners are not necessarily *traditional* students, learning affects the individual on all levels of psychological functioning, learning is not limited to cognitive learning, etc.), many who are interested in the successful facilitation of culture learning and adjustment have adapted elements of adult learning theory in the conceptualization and implementation of cross-cultural training and education (J. Bennett, 1986; McCaffery, 1986; Hughes-Wiener, 1986). One of the most popular theories informing this shift from the classroom to an experiential or learner-centered environment is David A. Kolb's (1984) experiential learning cycle. Kolb defines learning as "the process whereby knowledge is created through the *transformation of experience*" [italics ours] (p.36). He depicts learning as a four-stage process in which students are involved in a new experience (*Concrete Experience*), reflect on this experience (*Reflective Observation*), integrate their observations with theory (*Abstract Conceptualization*), and then build on this knowledge with problem solving in order to adapt more effectively to the same or similar events (*Active Experimentation*). Depending on the needs of the learner and the situation, the cycle can be entered at any point. But, it is only when learners move through the entire cycle that learning becomes integrated. This process is a continuous cycle that involves the learner in an increasing level of knowledge and behavioral sophistication. This theory is at the core of (1) conceptualizing learning as having affective, behavioral, and cognitive dimensions that must all be addressed, and (2) the curricular choices made for the individual courses. While it is clear that not every assignment can cover all four styles of learning, an overall curriculum can and should incorporate the four modes if the students are to truly begin to *own* the knowledge they've acquired.

In addition, the overall assumption is consistent with the idea that the development of international understanding is not something that either *happens* or *does not happen* at the end of the actual exchange experience. Steglitz (1993) has noted that the traditional methodology of lecturing about discrete knowledge areas contradicts the message that intercultural communication is a complex process of negotiating and renegotiating meaning. We would add to this that multiple choice testing of that content is equally antithetical to the principles of cultural learning. It reinforces the idea that there is a finite body of knowledge, which once learned, pronounces the student *interculturally competent*. Instead, the goal of education in this area should be to prepare the student to manage the process of culture learning *while they are engaged in it*. In the second language curriculum, this means finding ways in which students can interact in reasonably realistic cultural settings. Cultural partners, case studies, films, novels, fieldwork, internships, role-plays, and cross-cultural simulations can all be useful in this pursuit.

Additionally, a number of useful perspectives have been proposed to specifically describe the process of effective culture learning and offer guidelines for educational sequencing that will assist in its development. Milton Bennett (1993) has proposed a developmental model that describes the process of culture learning by defining the stages of intercultural sensitivity a person undergoes in processing and adapting to cultural differences. The individual moves from stages of *ethnocentrism* (denial of difference, defense against difference, and minimization of difference) to stages of *ethnorelativism* (acceptance of difference, adaptation to difference, and integration of difference into the definition of self). As a person accepts the principle that cultures differ fundamentally in the way their members organize and interpret reality, they become more adept at interpreting events within the appropriate cultural framework. As a result, intercultural sensitivity and awareness should increase, leading to an increased competence in intercultural communication, culture analysis, and decision-making skills. Ethnorelativism, Bennett argues, does not occur automatically with intercultural contact. Careful educational sequencing can, however, produce smoother transitions to more ethnorelative states. Exposure to differences in behaviors (nonverbal, linguistic, relational, institutional) should precede exposure to differences in values.

Janet Bennett (1986) made important distinctions between *orientation*, *training, and education*. In this taxonomy, she defines orientation as giving the minimal survival information needed while answering the questions of "Who, what, when, and where?" Training goes beyond the limits of orientation by also addressing the *how* of the sojourn: how individuals can increase their intercultural communication effectiveness, cope adequately with the adjustment, and maximize learning in the new culture. This is most often carried out on a *skills level.* Education adds to this a theoretical framework that addresses the *Why?* question and lays the most solid structure on which the student can continue to *learn how to learn* and "can creatively apply the information they've gained in new environments, acquiring new frames of reference with which to continue inquiry" (p. 118). This view of education as providing the student with *the cognitive tools necessary to manage their own continued learning* is what sets education in general and ICC education in particular apart from other forms of culture learning. To be truly proactive, the student must be prepared to continue their culture learning experience long after the classroom experience has ended.

Rhinesmith and Hoopes (1972) discussed the issue of *learning how to learn* by applying Lewin's (1972) model of learning as a process of *Unfreezing-moving-refreezing.* They claim that because cultural vision and identity are highly resistant to change, or *frozen,* great care must be taken in implementing the process of culture learning. The conditions for optimal learning must be created. Willingness to give and receive feedback, confront issues squarely, honesty and openness are essential so that the student can develop a *cognitive map* for analysis of experience. The process must be explicit, attending to affective, cognitive, and behavioral dimensions of learning so that the individual leaves knowing how to learn about her/himself and how to manage behavioral change. During refreezing, the individual locks into place the new perceptions. Once completed, regression into the previous mode of behavior will not readily occur.

Gudykunst, Guzley, and Hammer (1996) synthesized many of these approaches when they identified two central issues that need to be considered in developing intercultural training programs: *approaches* (didactic or cognitive vs. experiential) and *content* (culture specific vs. culture general). They also identify a wide variety of strategies and exercises that can be used under each category (Figure 6.2) and offer sample illustrations of theory-based training designs.We have included a list of resources at the end of this chapter that will provide more explicit information about all of these issues.

Experiential learning assists learners in practicing the skills they will need. To implement it, an intercultural educator needs to be knowledgeable about when and how to undertake the inherent risks of that format; a badly or incompletely facilitated cross-cultural simulation or encounter can be devastating to learners. Good facilitation skills require a deep knowledge base that can be applied to (1) guiding the *process* by allowing for a balancing of structure and spontaneous discovery and (2) making *content* responsive to the needs and concerns of the trainees as they emerge in response to the activities (Paige & Martin, 1996, p. 38).

	Didactic	Experiential
Culture General	• Lecture/Discussion about culture-general frameworks • Culture-General Assimilators • Videotapes about culture-general issues and concerns	• Intercultural Workshops (open discussion with multiple cultures represented) • Culture-general simulations (BAFA, Ecotonos, Albatross, Barnga, etc.) • Instruments for self-assessment of intercultural communication competence
Culture Specific	• Culture-specific lecture • Language training • Culture-specific assimilators • Culture-specific readings	• Bicultural Intercultural Workshops • Culture-specific simulations • Culture-specific role plays

Figure 6.2.

CONCLUSION

Intercultural trainers have struggled with the culture-teaching dilemma for a long time. First through trial and error, later through a more theory- and research-based pedagogy, they have acquired many insights into culture teaching and learning. Their methods have been tested in real world applications where the consequences of poor training quickly become obvious. Their methods have been measured against observable criteria for success: how well the learners function on the job in the field; how comfortably they interact with and are received by host country counterparts; the degree to which they become overwhelmed by the negative aspects of cultural immersion and come home early, experience stress in the family, etc.; how effectively they can transfer ideas, technology, or management practices; how enjoyable the cross-cultural experience is for them. Experienced intercultural trainers also understand the limitations of training, what it can and cannot accomplish.

This paper has suggested that what intercultural trainers have learned, from theory and practice, can inform the teaching of culture with language. Conversely, language educators have a great deal to offer interculturalists regarding the phenomenon of language and culture: how language influences the construction of social reality, the role language plays in maintaining and transmitting culture, and the importance of language in the acquisition of second culture competence.

NOTES

1. The implication here is *not* that culture is the thing that makes us all the same, but that it is *the processes, which organize our diversity*. This definition allows for the uniqueness of the individuals within a cultural framework while recognizing their connection to it.
2. Dance and Larson (1976) identified 126 different definitions of communication.
3. In 1952, Kroeber and Kluckholn had already identified over 200 definitions of culture. Definitions have continued to multiply ever since.
4. Paige (1993) identifies six risk factors that are inherent in teaching intercultural communication: (1) risk of personal disclosure, (2) risk of failure, (3) risk of embarrassment, (4) risk of threat to one's cultural identity, (5) risk of becoming culturally marginal or culturally alientated, and (6) risk of self-awareness (p. 13).

REFERENCES

Adler, P. S. (1974). Beyond cultural identity: Reflections upon cultural and multi-cultural man. *Topics in Culture Learning, 2*, 23–41.

Agar, M. (1994). The intercultural frame. *International Journal of Intercultural Relations, 18*, 221–238.

Andersen, P. (1997). Cues of culture: The basis if intercultural differences in nonverbal communication. In L.A. Samovar & R.E. Porter (Eds.), *Intercultural communication: A reader* (8th ed., pp. 244–255). Belmont, CA: Wadsworth.

Applegate, J.L., & Sypher, H.E. (1983). A constructivist outline. In W.B. Gudykunst (Ed.), *Intercultural communication theory: Current perspectives* (pp. 63–78). Beverly Hills, CA: Sage.

Barnlund, D.M. (1962).Toward a meaning-centered philosophy of communication. *Journal of Communication, 12*, 197–211.

Bhawuk, D.P.S., & Triandis, H.C. (1996). The role of culture theory in the study of culture and intercultural training. In D. Landis & R.S. Bhagat (Eds.), *Handbook of intercultural training* (2nd ed., pp. 17–34). Thousand Oaks, CA: Sage.

Bennett, J.M. (1986). Modes of cross-cultural training: Conceptualizing cross-cultural training as education. *International Journal of Intercultural Relations, 10*, 117–134.

Bennett, M.J. (1986). A developmental model of cultural sensitivity. *International Journal of Intercultural Relations, 10*, 179–196.

Bennett, M.J. (1988). Foundations of knowledge in international educational exchange: Intercultural communication. In J. Reid (Ed.), *Building the professional dimension of educational exchange* (pp. 121–139). Washington, DC: NAFSA.

Bennett, M.J. (1993). Toward ethnorelativism: A developmental model of cultural sensitivity. In R.M. Paige (Ed.), *Education for the intercultural experience* (pp. 21–72). Yarmouth, ME: Intercultural Press.

Bennett, M.J. (1995).An intercultural perspective. In M.J. Bennett (Ed.), *Basic concepts of intercultural communication: A reader.* Yarmouth, ME: Intercultural Press.

Berger, P.L., & Luckmann, T. (1966). *The social construction of reality.* Garden City, NY: Doubleday Anchor.

Bochner, S. (1973). The mediating man and cultural diversity. *Topics in Culture Learning, 1,* 23–37.

Bochner, S. (1981). *The mediating person: Bridges between cultures.* Cambridge, MA: Shenkman.

Brislin, R. (1981). *Cross-cultural encounters.* New York: Pergamon Press.

Brislin, R.W., Cushner, K., Cherrie, C., & Yong, M. (1986). *Intercultural interactions: A practical guide.* Newbury Park, CA: Sage.

Burleson, B.R. (1987). Cognitive complexity. In J.C. McCroskey & J.A. Daly (Eds.), *Personality and interpersonal communication* (pp. 305–349). Newbury Park, CA: Sage.

Carbaugh, D. (1990). Intercultural communication. In D. Carbaugh (Ed.), *Cultural communication and intercultural contact* (pp. 151–175). Hillsdale, NJ: Lawrence Erlbaum.

Cole, M., & Scribner, S. (1974). *Culture and thought: A psychological introduction.* New York: Wiley.

Collier, M.J. (1989). Cultural and intercultural communication competence: Current approaches and directions for research. *International Journal of Intercultural Relations, 13,* 287–302.

Collier, M.J. (1988). Conversation comparison among domestic cultures: How intra- and intercultural competencies vary. *Communication Quarterly, 36*(2), 122–144.

Collier, M.J., & Thomas, M. (1988). Cultural identity: An interpretive perspective. In Y.Y. Kim & W.B. Gudykunst (Eds.), *Theories in intercultural communication* (pp. 99–120).Newbury Park, CA: Sage.

Condon, J.C., & Yousef, F. (1975). *An introduction to intercultural communication.* New York: Macmillan.

Cronen, V., Chen, V., & Pearce, W.B. (1988). Coordinated management of meaning: A critical theory. In W.B. Gudykunst & Y.Y. Kim (Eds.), *Theories in intercultural communication* (pp. 66–98). Beverly Hills, CA: Sage.

Cupach, W.R., & Imahori, T.T. (1993). Identity management theory: Communicationcompetence in intercultural episodes and relationships. In R. Wiseman & J. Koester (Eds.), *Intercultural communication competence* (pp. 112–131). Newbury Park, CA: Sage.

Damen, L. (1987). *Culture learning: The fifth dimension in the classroom.* Reading, MA : Addison-Wesley.

Ellingsworth, H.W. (1983). Adaptive intercultural communication. In W.B. Gudykunst (Ed.), *Intercultural communication theory: Current perspectives (Vol. 7, International and intercultural communication annual)*. Beverly Hills, CA: Sage.

Fong, M. (1997). The crossroads of language and culture. In L.A. Samovar & R.E. Porter (Eds.), *Intercultural communication: A reader* (8th ed., pp. 207–212). Belmont, CA: Wadsworth.

Glenn, E.S., & Glenn, C. (1981). *Man and mankind: Conflict and communication between cultures*. Norwood, NJ: ABLEX.

Gudykunst, W.B., Guzley, R.M., & Hammer, M.R. (1996). Designing intercultural training. In D. Landis & R.S. Bhagat (Eds.), *Handbook of intercultural training* (2nd ed., pp. 61–80). Thousand Oaks, CA: Sage.

Gudykunst, W.B., & Kim, Y.Y. (1992). *Communicating with strangers: An approach to intercultural communication* (2nd ed.). New York: McGraw-Hill.

Gudykunst, W.B., & Nishida, T. (1989). Theoretical perspectives for studying intercultural communication. In M.K. Asante & W.B. Gudykunst (Eds.) (with E. Newmark), *Handbook of international and intercultural communication* (pp. 17–46). Newbury Park, CA: Sage.

Gudykunst, W.B., & Ting-Toomey, S. (1988). *Culture and interpersonal communication*. Newbury Park, CA: Sage.

Guthrie, G. (1975). A behavioral analysis of culture learning. In. R.W. Brislin, S. Bochner, & W.J. Lonner, *Cross-cultural perspectives on learning*. New York: Wiley/Halsted.

Hall, E.T. (1981/1959). *The silent language*. Garden City, NY: Anchor Books.

Hall, E.T. (1981/1976). *Beyond culture*. Garden City, NY: Anchor Books.

Hall, E.T. (1982/1966). *The hidden dimension*. Garden City, NY: Anchor Books.

Hall, E.T. (1984). *The dance of life*. Garden City, NY: Anchor Books.

Hammer, M.R., Gudykunst, W.B., & Wiseman, R.L. (1978). Dimensions of intercultural effectiveness: An exploratory study. *International Journal of Intercultural Relations, 2*, 382–393.

Harrison, R., & Hopkins, R. (1967). The design of cross-cultural training: An alternative to the university model. *Journal of Applied Behavioral Sciences, 3*, 341–60.

Hawes, F., & Kealey, D. J. (1979). *Canadians in development: An empirical study of adaptation and effectiveness on overseas assignment* (Technical report). Ottawa, Canada: Canadian International Development Agency.

Hofstede, G. (1984). *Culture's consequences: International differences in work-related values* (Abridged ed.). Beverly Hills, CA: Sage.

Hoijer, H. (1991). The Sapir-Whorf hypothesis. In L.A. Samovar & R.E. Porter, *Intercultural communication: A reader* (6th ed., pp. 244–250). Belmont, CA: Wadsworth.

Hoopes, D.S. (1979). Intercultural communication concepts and the psychology of the intercultural experience. In M.D. Pusch (Ed.), *Multicultural education: A cross-cultural training approach* (pp. 10–38). Yarmouth, ME: Intercultural Press.

Howell, W.S. (1979). Theoretical directions for intercultural communication. In M.K. Asante, E. Newark, & C.A. Blake (Eds.), *Handbook of intercultural communication* (23–41).Beverly Hills, CA: Sage.

Hughes-Wiener, G. (1986). The *learning how to learn* approach to cross-cultural orientation. *International Journal of Intercultural Relations, 10*, 485–505.

Hymes, D. (1962). The ethnography of speaking. In T. Gladwin & W. Sturtevant (Eds.), *Anthropology and human behavior* (pp. 13–53).Washington, DC: Anthropological Society of Washington.

Imahori, T.T., & Lanigan, M.L. (1989). A relational model of intercultural communication competence. *International Journal of Intercultural Relations, 13,* 269–285.

Jensen, J.V. (1985). Perspective on noverbal intercultural communication. In L.A. Samovar & R.E. Porter (Eds.), *Intercultural communication: A reader* (4th ed., pp. 260–276).Belmont, CA: Wadsworth.

Kaplan, R. (1966). Cultural thought patterns in intercultural education. *Language Learning, 16*(1 & 2), 1–20.

Kealey, D.J., & Ruben, B.D. (1983). Cross-cultural personnel selection criteria, issues, and methods. In D. Landis & R.W. Brislin (Eds.), *Handbook of intercultural training* (Vol. 1, pp. 155–175). New York: Pergamon.

Kim, Y.Y. (1984). Searching for creative integration. In W.B. Gudykunst & Y.Y. Kim (Eds.), *Methods for intercultural communication research* (pp. 13–30). Beverly Hills, CA: Sage Publications.

Kim, Y.Y. (1988). *Communication and cross-cultural adaptation.* Philadelphia: Multilingual Matters Ltd.

Kim, Y.Y. (1992). Facilitating immigrant adjustment: The role of communication. In W.B. Gudykunst & Y.Y. Kim (Eds.), *Readings on communicating with strangers: An approach to intercultural communication* (pp. 345–356). New York: McGraw-Hill.

Kluckhohn, F., & Strodtbeck, F.L. (1961). *Variations in value orientations.* Evanston, IL: Row, Peterson.

Kolb, D.A. (1984). *Experiential learning.* Englewood Cliffs, NJ: Prentice-Hall.

Lewin, K. (1972). Quasi-stationary social equilibria and the problem of personal change. In N. Margulies & A.P. Paia (Eds.), *Organizational development: Values, process andtechnology.* New York: McGraw-Hill.

Lieberman, D.A. (1997). Culture, problem-solving, and pedagogical style. In L.A. Samovar & R.E. Porter (Eds.), *Intercultural communication: A reader* (8th ed., pp. 191–206).Belmont, CA: Wadsworth.

Mansell, M. (1981). Transcultural experience and expressive response. *Communication Education, 30,* 93–108.

Martin, J.N. (1993) Intercultural communication competence: A review. In R. Wiseman & J. Koester (Eds.), *Intercultural communication competence* (pp. 16–29). Newbury Park, CA: Sage.

Mathews, R.S. (1994). Collaborative learning: Creating knowledge with students. In R.J Menges, E. Weimer, & Assoc. (Eds.), *Teaching on solid ground: Using scholarship to improve practice* (pp. 100–124). San Francisco: Jossey-Bass.

McCaffery, J.A. (1986). Independent effectiveness: A reconsideration of cross-cultural training. *International Journal of Intercultural Relations, 10,* 159–177.

Mestenhauser, J.A., Marty, G., & Steglitz, I. (1988). *Culture, learning, and the disciplines: Theory and practice in cross-cultural orientation.* Washington, DC: NAFSA.

Paige, R.M. (1993). On the nature of intercultural experiences and intercultural education. In R.M. Paige (Ed.), *Education for the intercultural experience* (pp. 1–19). Yarmouth, ME: Intercultural Press.

Paige, R.M. (1996). Intercultural trainer competencies. In D. Landis & R.S. Bhagat (Eds.), *Handbook of intercultural training* (pp. 148–164). Thousand Oaks, CA: Sage.

Paige, R.M., & Martin, J.N. (1996). Ethics in intercultural training. In D. Landis & R.S. Bhagat (Eds.), *Handbook of intercultural training* (2nd ed., pp. 35–62). Thousand Oaks, CA: Sage.

Perry, W.L., Jr. (1970). *Forms of intellectual and ethical development in the college years.* New York: Holt, Rinehart and Winston.

Petersen, T., Jensen, J.W., & Rivers, W. L. (1965). *The mass media and modern society.* New York: Holt, Rinehart, & Wilson.

Putnam, L.L. (1984). The interpretive perspective: An lternative to functionalism. In *Traditional communication perspectives* (pp. 31–54).Beverly Hills, CA: Sage.

Rhinesmith, S.H., &Hoopes, D.S. (1972). The learning process in an intercultural setting. In D.S. Hoopes (Ed.), *Readings in intercultural communication.* Pittsburgh, PA: RCIE.

Ruben, B.D. (1976). Assessing communication competency for intercultural adaptation. *Group and Organizational Studies, 1,* 334–354.

Ruben, B.D. (1983). A system-theoretic view. In W.B. Gudykunst (Ed.), *Intercultural communication theory: Current perspectives* (pp. 131–145). Beverly Hills, CA: Sage.

Ruben, B.D. (1989). The study of cross-cultural competence: Traditions and contemporary issues. *International Journal of Intercultural Relations, 13,* 223–240.

Ruben, B.D., & Kealey, D.J. (1979). Behavioral assessment of communication competency and the prediction of cross-cultural adjustment. *International Journal of Intercultural Relations, 3,* 15–48.

Ruben, B.D., Askling, L.R., & Kealey, D.J.(1997). Cross-cultural effectiveness. In D.S. Hoopes, P.B. Pederson, & G.W. Renwick (Eds.), *Overview of intercultural education, training, and research, Vol. 1: Theory.* Pittsburgh, PA: SIETAR.

Samovar, L.A., & Porter, R.E. (1991). *Communication between cultures.* Belmont, CA: Wadsworth.

Sapir, E. (1981). Conceptual categories of primitive languages. *Science, 74,* 78.

Schneider, D. (1976). Notes toward a theory of culture. In K. Basso & H. Selby (Eds.), *Meaning in anthropology* (pp. 197–220). Albuquerque: University of New Mexico Press.

Seelye, H.N. (1994). *Teaching culture: Strategies for intercultural communication* (3rd ed.). Lincolnwood, IL: National Textbook Company.

Singer, M.R. (1987). Culture: A perceptual approach. In L.A. Samovar & R.E. Porter (Eds.), *Intercultural communication: A reader* (pp. 62–70). Belmont, CA: Wadsworth.

Smith, S.L. (1987). *Cognitive learning styles of international students.* Unpublished Master's thesis, Portland State University, Portland, OR.

Spitzberg, B. (1989). Issues in the development of a theory of interpersonal communication competence and intercultural context. *International Journal of Intercultural Relations, 13,* 241–268.

Spitzberg, B.H., & Cupach, W.R. (1984). *Interpersonal communication competence.* Beverly Hills, CA: Sage.

Spitzberg, B.H., & Cupach, W.R. (1987, November). *The model of relational competence:A review of assumptions and evidence.* Paper presented at the Speech Communication Association Conference, Boston.

Spitzberg, B.H., & Cupach, W.R. (1989). *Handbook of interpersonal competence research.* New York:Springer-Verlag.

Steglitz, I. (1993). *Intercultural perspective-taking: The impact of study abroad.* Unpublished doctoral dissertation, University of Minnesota, Minneapolis.

Stewart, E.C. (1972). *American cultural patterns: A cross-cultural perspective.* Pittsburgh, PA: Intercultural Communication Network.

Stewart, E.C., & Bennett, M.J. (1992). *American cultural patterns* (rev. ed.). Yarmouth, ME: Intercultural Press.

Szalay, L.B. (1981). Intercultural communication—a process model. *International Journal of Intercultural Relations, 5,* 133–146.

Taft, R. (1981). The role and personality of the mediator. In S. Bochner (Ed.), *The mediating person: Bridges between culture.* Cambridge, MA: Shenkman.

Ting-Toomey, S. (1988). Intercultural conflict styles: A face-negotiation theory. In Y.Y. Kim & W.B. Gudykunst (Eds.), *Theories in intercultural communication* (pp. 213–135).Newbury Park, CA: Sage.

Thomas, M. (1991). *Cultural versus intercultural ethnography: The third culture revisited.* Unpublished paper presented at the Central States Communication Association Annual Conference, Chicago.

Triandis, H.C. (1975). Culture training, cognitive complexity, and interpersonal attitudes. In R. Brislin, S. Bochner, & W. Lonner (Eds.), *Cross-cultural perspectives on learning.* Beverly Hills, CA: Sage.

Triandis, H.C. (1992). Collectivism and individualism: A reconceptualization of a basic concept in cross-cultural psychology. In W.B. Gudykunst & Y.Y. Kim (Eds.), *Readings on communicating with strangers: An approach to intercultural communication* (pp. 71–81).New York: McGraw-Hill.

Triandis, H.C. (1995). *Individualism and collectivism.* Boulder, CO: Westview.

Triandis, H.C., Brislin, R, & Hui, C.H. (1988). Cross-cultural training across the individualism-collectivism divide. *International Journal of Intercultural Relations, 12,* 269–289.

Werkman, S.L. (1983, Spring). Coming home: Adjustment problems of Americans to the U.S. after living abroad. *The International Schools Journal,* 49–64.

Whorf, B.L. (1952). *Collected papers on metalinguistics.* Washington, D.C.: Foreign Service Institute.

Wilber, K. (Ed.). (1982). *The holographic paradigm and other paradoxes.* Boulder, CO: Shambala.

Wiseman, R.L., & Abe, H. (1984). Finding and explaining differences: A reply to Gudykunst and Hammer. *International Journal of Intercultural Relations, 11,* 11–16.

Yum, J.O. (1997). Impact of Confucianism on interpersonal relationships and communication patterns in East Asia. In L.A. Samovar & R.E. Porter (Eds.), *Intercultural communication: A reader* (8th ed., pp. 78–88). Belmont, CA: Wadsworth.

Zormeier, S.M., & Samovar, L.A. (1997). Language as a mirror of reality. In L.A. Samovar & R.E. Porter (Eds.), *Intercultural communication: A reader* (8th ed., pp. 235–239).Belmont, CA: Wadsworth.

APPENDIX A

List of Resources

1. Culture General Simulations

Gouchenour, T. (Ed.). (1993). *Beyond experience: An experiential approach to cross-cultural education.* 2nd ed. Yarmouth, ME: Intercultural Press. [See chapter 12: Simulations for building intercultural skills (includes Albatross and the Owl).]

Nipporica Associates, & Saphiere, D. H. (1997). *Ecotonos: A multicultural problem-solving simulation.* 2nd ed. Yarmouth, ME: Intercultural Press.

Simulation Training Systems. (nd). *Bafa Bafa: A diversity/cross-cultural simulation.* Del Mar, CA: Simulation Training Systems.

Thiagarajan, S., & Steinwachs, B. (1990). *BARNGA: A simulation game on cultural clashes.* Yarmouth, ME: Intercultural Press.

2. Cultural General Assimilator

Cushner, K, & Brislin, R.W. (1996). *Intercultural interactions: A practical guide.* Thousand Oaks, CA: Sage.

3. Culture General Readings

Baumeister, R.F. (1986). *Identity: Cultural change and the struggle for self.* New York: Oxford University Press.

Condon, J.C., & Yousef, F. (1975). *An introduction to intercultural communication.* New York: Macmillan.

Gudykunst, W.B., & Kim, Y.Y. (1992). *Communicating with strangers: An approach to intercultural communication* (2nd ed.). New York: Random House.

Gudykunst, W.B., & Kim, Y.Y. (Eds.). (1992). *Readings on communicating with strangers: An approach to intercultural communication.* New York: McGraw-Hill.

Hofstede, G. (1984). *Culture's consequences: International differences in work-related values* (Abridged ed.). Beverly Hills: Sage.

Hall, E.T. (1981/1959). *The silent language.* Garden City, NY: Anchor Books.

Hall, E.T. (1981/1976). *Beyond culture.* Garden City, NY: Anchor Books.

Hall, E.T. (1982/1966). *The hidden dimension.* Garden City, NY: Anchor Books.

Hall, E.T. (1984). *The dance of life.* Garden City, NY: Anchor Books.

Gudykunst, W.B., &Kim, Y.Y. (Eds.). *Readings on communicating with strangers: An approach to intercultural communication.* New York: McGraw-Hill.

Kim, Y.Y., & Gudykunst, W.B. (Eds.). (1993). *Theories in intercultural communication.*Newbury Park, CA: Sage.

Kohls, L.R. (1979). *Survival kit for overseas living: for Americans planning to live and work abroad.* Yarmouth, ME: Intercultural Press, Inc.

Lustig, M.W., & Koester, J.(1994). *Intercultural communication competence* (2nd ed.). New York: HarperCollins.

Samovar, L.A., & Porter, R.E. (1997). *Intercultural communication: A reader.* Belmont, CA: Wadsworth.

Triandis, H.C. (1995). *Individualism and collectivism.* Boulder, CO: Westview.

4. Culture Specific Readings

Albert, R. (1996). A framework and model for understanding Latin American and Latino/Hispanic cultural patterns. In D. Landis &R.S. Bhagat (Eds.), *Handbook of intercultural training* (2nd ed.). Thousand Oaks, CA: Sage.

Althen, G. (1988). *American ways.* Yarmouth, ME: Intercultural Press, Inc.

Anderson, J.W. (1997). A comparison of Arab and American conceptions of effective persuasion. In L.A. Samovar & R.E. Porter (Eds.), *Intercultural communication: A reader* (8th ed., pp. 98–106). Belmont, CA: Wadsworth.

Barnlund, D.C. (1975). *Public and private self in Japan and the United States: Communicative styles of two cultures.* Tokyo: The Simul Press, Inc.

Barnlund, D.C. (1989). *Communicative styles of Japanese and Americans: Images and realities.* Belmont, CA: Wadsworth.

Broome, B.J. (1997). Palevome: Foundations of struggle and conflict in Greek interpersonal communication. In L.A. Samovar & R.E. Porter (Eds.), *Intercultural communication: A reader* (8th ed., pp. 98–106). Belmont, CA: Wadsworth.

Condon, J.C. (1980). *With respect to the Japanese.* Yarmouth, ME. Intercultural Press.

Condon, J.C. (1985). *Good neighbors: Communicating with the Mexicans.* Yarmouth, ME: Intercultural Press, Inc.

Fieg, J.P., & Mortlock, E. (1989). *A common core: Thais and Americans.* Yarmouth, ME: Intercultural Press, Inc.

Hall, E.T., & Hall, M.R. (1989). *Understanding cultural differences: Germans, French, and Americans.* Yarmouth, ME: Intercultural Press, Inc.

Hill, R. (1995). *We Europeans.* Europublic SA/NV.

Hong-Kingston, M. (1976). *The woman warrior.* New York: Vintage Books.

Jamieson, N. (1993). *Understanding Vietnam.* Berkeley: University of California Press.

Kapp, R.A. (1983). *Communicating with China.* Chicago: Intercultural Press, Inc.

Kleffner Nydell, M. (1987). *Understanding Arabs: A guide for Westerners.* Yarmouth, ME: Intercultural Press, Inc.

Mura, D. (1991). *Becoming Japanese.* New York: Anchor Press.

Pye, L. (1985). *Asian power and politics.* Cambridge, MA: Belknap of Harvard University Press.

Renwick, G.W. (1991). *A fair go for all: Australian/American interactions.* Yarmouth, ME: Intercultural Press, Inc.

Richmond, Y. (1992). *From nyet to da: Understanding the Russians.* Yarmouth, ME: Intercultural Press, Inc.

Richmond, Y. (1995). *From da to yes: Understanding the East Europeans.* Yarmouth, ME: Intercultural Press, Inc.

Stewart, E.C., & Bennett, M.J. (1992). *American cultural patterns* (rev. ed.). Yarmouth, ME: Intercultural Press.

Tan, A. (1989). *The joy luck club.* Thorndike, ME: Thorndike Press.

Tantranon-Saur, A. (1992). What's behind the "Asian mask?" In R. Holeton (Ed.), *Encountering cultures: Reading and writing in a changing world.* Englewood Cliffs, NJ: Blair Press.

Wenzhong, H., & Grove, C.L. (1991). *Encountering the Chinese: A guide for Americans.* Yarmouth, ME: Intercultural Press.

Yoshikawa, M. (1978). Some Japanese and American characteristics. In M. Prosser (Ed.), *The cultural dialogue* (pp. 220–230). Palo Alto, CA: Houghton-Mifflin.

5. Training Resources

Brislin, R.W., & Yoshida, T. (Eds.). (1994a). *Improving intercultural interactions: Modules for cross-cultural training.* Thousand Oaks, CA: Sage

Brislin, R.W., & Yoshida, T. (1994b). *Intercultural communication training: An introduction.*Thousand Oaks, CA: Sage.

Landis, D., & Brislin, R.W. (Eds.).(1983). *Handbook of intercultural training, Vols. I, II, & III.*Elmsford, NY: Pergamon.

Landis, D., & Bhagat, R.S. (Eds.). (1996). *Handbook of intercultural training* (2nd ed.).Thousand Oaks, CA: Sage.

Hoopes, D., & Ventura P. (1979). *Intercultural communication sourcebook: Cross-cultural training methodologies.* Washington DC: Society for Intercultural Education, Training, and Research.

Paige, R.M. (1993). On the nature of intercultural experiences and intercultural education. In R.M. Paige (Ed.), *Education for the intercultural experience* (1–19). Yarmouth, ME: Intercultural Press.

Pusch, M.D. (Ed.). (1981). *Multicultural education: A cross-cultural training approach* (pp. 10–38). Yarmouth, ME: Intercultural Press.

Storti, C. (1990). *The art of crossing cultures.* Yarmouth, ME: Intercultural Press.

Triandis, H.C. (1975). Culture training, cognitive complexity, and interpersonal attitudes. In R. Brislin, S. Bochner, & W. Lonner (Eds.), *Cross-cultural perspectives on learning.* Beverly Hills, CA: Sage.

Triandis, H.C., Brislin, R, & Hui, C.H. (1988). Cross-cultural training across the individualism-collectivism divide. *International Journal of Intercultural Relations, 12,* 269–289.

CHAPTER 7

A CRITICAL PERSPECTIVE ON CULTURE IN THE SECOND LANGUAGE CLASSROOM

Linda M. Crawford and Peter McLaren

INTRODUCTION

The content taught in contemporary public schools in the United States is under siege. On the one hand, conservative critics of education such as Bloom (1987), Hirsch (1987), and Ravitch (1985) call for an articulation of knowledge aligned to the dominant culture. On the other hand, critical educational theorists argue for a pedagogy which subjects taken-for-granted knowledge not only to critical review but also to re-creation (Aronowitz & Giroux, 1985; Giroux, 1983; McLaren, 1989). The former approach encourages students to accept the prevailing distribution of power in the world while the later approach invites students to assume power for the purpose of transforming power/knowledge relations. Within the neoconservative view, school curricula, including the second-language curriculum, are grounded in a concept of homogeneous and monumentalized master culture predominating over diverse subordinate cultures. Certain strands of critical pedagogy, on the other hand, situate school

Culture as the Core: Perspectives in Second Language Education, pages 127–157
Copyright © 2003 by Information Age Publishing
All rights of reproduction in any form reserved.

curricula within a postmodernist view of culture (Aronowitz & Giroux, 1991; Giroux, 1990; McLaren, 1990, in press).

This tension between the neoconservative and postmodernist views of culture has important implications for rethinking second language curriculum. Language instructors have long accepted that the teaching of language and culture are essentially inseparable (Brooks, 1964, 1968; Seelye, 1984). Further, they came to understand culture in its anthropological sense as a proper domain of instruction in language classes (Brooks, 1968; Nostrand, 1967; Seelye, 1984).However, the study of culture and its relationship to language not only remains peripheral in the language classroom, but also, when it occurs, it generally adopts a model of cultural transmission in the neoconservative vein rather than assuming the postmodernist posture (Crawford-Lange & Lange, 1984).

This paper challenges the neoconservative agenda by rethinking culture from a postmodernist perspective. Implications for the second language curriculum and classroom are explored in the context of each selected aspect of a postmodernist and post-colonialist definition of culture. With Aronowitz and Giroux (1991), we interpret postmodernism in the broadest sense to refer "to an intellectual position, a form of cultural criticism, as well as to an emerging set of social, cultural, and economic conditions that have come to characterize the age of global capitalism and industrialism" (p. 62). In terms of curriculum, postmodernism postulates that "the curriculum can best inspire learning only when school knowledge builds upon the tacit knowledge derived from the cultural resources that students already possess" (Aronowitz & Giroux, 1991, p. 15).

The term *postmodernism*, in fact, straddles several definitional boundaries. It refers at once to a sensibility, a political perspective, a state of mind and a mode of social analysis. Taking these boundaries as an amalgam we may speak of the postmodern age: an era wherein democratic imperatives have become subverted, values simulated, and emancipatory symbols and their affective power commodified. It is an age in which the modernist quest for certainty and meaning, as well as the liberal humanist notion of the individual as a unified and coherent essence/agency, are being forcefully challenged.

Much of the discourse of postmodernism has been criticized because it tends to betray a dry cynicism in which irony and pastiche become politic's last recourse at social change. It is a discourse that often reveals an uncompromising distaste for the masses, adopts a form of highbrow anti-bourgeois posing, and occasionally assumes the role of a self-congratulatory vanguardism that resonates dutifully with the *high-seriousness* of the academy, at times appearing as dressed-up restatements of Nietzche and Heidegger. Attendant characteristics of the postmodern turn in social theory also include the rejection of truth claims that have a grounding in a transcendent reality independent of collective human struggle and an abandonment of the teleology of science, the construction of lifestyles out of consumer products and cultural *bricolage*, and cultural forms of communication and social relations that have evolved from the disorganization of capitalism.

However, there are enabling aspects to the postmodern turn in critical social theory.Within postmodernism, disciplinary conventions collapse and high status knowledge becomes more accessible to a plurality of recipients outside the province of experts. Postmodernism signals changed configurations of knowledge—the advent of a new series of hybrid genres and a fusion of rationalities. Knowledge is no longer disembodied within separate spheres of formal, intrinsic properties, but is coterminous with the sensuous aspects of everyday life. Some educators have attempted to reveal how certain postmodern insights into language and culture can be appropriated by teachers in a pedagogy of liberation (Aronowitz & Giroux, 1991; McLaren, in press;McLaren & Hamer, 1989).

Our use of the term *postcolonialism* refers here to the importance of problematizing pedagogical discourses in light of the current trajectory toward global capitalism, while admitting its disorganized and disjunctive character, and the narratives and cultural logic associated with and resulting from the breaking up of old imperialisms, based on nation-states. Postcolonial pedagogy, as we are using it, is a pedagogy of anti-imperialism that attempts to challenge the very categories through which the history and narratives of the colonized have been written. Explicit in this form of pedagogy is a challenge to the way situated knowledges are produced within the larger context of the social formation as well to global transnational capitalism as a Euro-American tale of progress, and specifically, the way that Anglo-European discourses have banished or romanticized difference in politically and ethnically disabling ways. Of course, the term *postcolonial* is always to be understood in situated and context-specific ways, and we do not seek to sketch out its possible contours without placing it into contradiction with its possible universalistic assumptions. In this regard, we see postcolonial pedagogy as a temporary suspension of the colonial moment, a liminal space that, while still containing traces of colonial and neo-colonial discourses, effectively allows or a community of resistance to develop.

The term, *poststructural*, as used in this paper, may best be understood as a perspective that is not attached to fixed meanings. Rather, it accepts that systematized knowledge is not possible (Culler, 1984) and it explores the situatedness and constructedness of meanings by asking questions as to their origin, their manner of production, and the root of their authority (Cherryholmes, 1988; Lankshear & McLaren, 1993; McLaren, 1987). Poststructuralism can be distinguished from its structuralist predecessor. Structuralists typically conceive of language as an arbitrary system of differences in which meaning is guaranteed by the linguistic system itself and the values given to signifying practices within particular linguistic communities.In other words, given the signs and linguistic practices, meanings follow. For structuralists, discovering or cracking the code that explains how elements of a social text function together uncovers meaning. Often, these codes are granted a transcendental status, serving as privileged referents around which other meanings are positioned.

Poststructuralism is less deterministic; we are using it as a postmodern mode of locating culture as an arena of contested discourses. Poststructuralism places much more emphasis on meaning as a contested event, a terrain of struggle in which individuals take up often conflicting subject positions in relation to signifying practices. Poststructuralists acknowledge explicitly that meaning consists of more than signs operating or being operated in a context. Rather, there is a struggle over signifying practices. This struggle is eminently political and must include the relationship among discourse, power, and difference. Poststructuralists put much more emphasis on discourse and the contradictions involved in subjective formation. They regard transcendental signifieds as discursive fictions. In addition, poststructuralism draws attention to the significant danger of assuming that concepts can exist independently of its signifying systems or language itself, or that meaning can exist as a pure idea, independently of its contextual embeddedness in the materiality of speech gesture, writing, etc. Poststructuralism does not locate the human subject within the structure of language that is within the rules of signification. Rather the subject is a constitutive aspect of the structure of language and the signifying system.

By *critical pedagogy* we refer to an approach to curricular, instructional, and evaluative practices that empowers students to perceive contradictions present in their lived experience and both to interrogate and transform those contradictions for the improvement of life conditions (Freire, 1970; Giroux, 1988; Livingstone, 1987; McLaren, 1988, 1989, 1995a, 1995b).

RETHINKING CULTURE

An important new debate over culture is currently surfacing in the social sciences with respect to how contemporary social life is to be understood and the various roles individuals play in it, both wittingly and unwittingly. In the United States, this debate has spilled beyond the borders of mainstream sociology and anthropology to include poststructuralist approaches, largely European in origin and formed within a radical political framework. This debate has profound implications for the manner in which schooling in general is understood and transformed as well as for the construction of second language curriculum in particular.

This essay draws on poststructuralist perspectives in order to advance the argument that culture does not consist simply of isolated, bounded, and cohesive meaning systems, but rather reflects and is constitutive of a multiplicity of voices reflecting a wide array of conflicting and competing discourses. As systems of meaning, cultures can never be ontologically separated from economies of privilege and politics. For teachers, this means that cultures do not exist as metaphysical entities that impose themselves on schools or on societies under study. Neither do they occur as uniform standards of behavior and beliefs that can be delineated and described in topic outlines. Nor are they superficial entities such as setting the table or eating with the left hand. Cultures occur as students and teachers and societies live them in the world.

Culture is not some *grand hotel* reflective of a grand design and central authority. Collins (1989) realizes that our postmodern culture is discourse-sensitive; what we consider to be our culture and what speakers of other languages consider to be theirs depends on the frameworks used to conceptualize the world. Distinctions made within Western enlightenment and colonialist systems of rationality between higher and lower, inside and outside, are no longer tenable. We are now in the realm of transborder identity and ways of understanding cultural memory in a popular cultural world in which signs are not anchored the way they are in museums. We can never have access to the past, present, or future of our or other's cultures except through expressed representations that never escape the realm of politics and ideology.

Given the language of efficiency that has colonized the domain of education in recent years, as well as the stress on management techniques and accountability schemes, it is hardly surprising that this debate over culture has only just begun to seep beyond the bounds of mainstream educational research. In particular, white Anglo-Saxon educators have been generally incautious about their pretenses to occupy a privileged cultural vantage point with respect to other cultures; they have, for the most part, remained loyal to a view of culture which permits them to secure their meanings in a bedrock of their own prejudices and in so doing have failed to disturb the popular assurance of received orthodoxies about the cultural fields that inform the classrooms where they teach. This condition is particularly dangerous for second language educators because not only must they reconceive their native culture on their students' terms, they must also conceive of and explore with students the target cultures of study as multivariate processes rather than entities for transmission.

CULTURE AND THE AGE OF POSTMODERNISM

Within contemporary research on schooling, one of the central strands of the debate over culture centers on the question of the role of schools in shaping student identity. This strand of the debate has generated a great deal of concern with respect to the increasing alienation of our youth. The postmodern condition signals the undecidability, plurality, and *throwness* of culture rather than its homogeneity or consensual nature. Some students are *thrown away* or *pushed out*, although the blame is put on them since it is they who drop out. In schools, separating students brings this alienation to an extreme, even from each other, through a tracking system that reinforces students positioning themselves in oppositional class cultures (Oakes, 1985).

This alienation benefits from a culture of exclusion rather than inclusion, of which departments of second language are guilty. Exclusion occurs when entry-level language courses use prior academic performance as a gate-keeping prerequisite or when *high status* knowledge is favored over the *low status* knowledge of popular cultural forms. Inclusion occurs when courses are open to all students wishing to attempt them and when their own class, ethnic, and gender location does not become a barrier to self and social empowerment. It also occurs when language courses are designed, marketed, and taught to meet the communicative needs of all students in a global society, empowering those most marginalized by the social order. Exclusion occurs when language teachers assume that certain groups of students are incapable of learning a second language; inclusion occurs when teachers assume that all students can learn language and accept the instructional challenge of assisting them—all of them.

An exclusionary stance subjects students to the *throwness* that marks postmodern culture. By critically examining and changing practices that contribute to an exclusionary posture, second language departments can contribute to the transmutation of the educational system into one that not merely develops each student's potential to fit into the social order, but one that invites students to cultivate the vision, skills, and democratic imperatives for transforming existing asymmetrical relations of power and privilege within the larger arena of postindustrial capitalist society.

CULTURE AS DISCOURSE

A significant contribution of postmodernist social theorists is the insight that culture is a construction that is not always immediately present to itself. A radical reconceptualization of culture as a field of discourse or text (cf. Clifford & Marcus, 1986) has helped to make our common understanding of culture quite uncommon, allowing us to explore the complexity of meaning of this term and the process to which it refers. By discourse, we follow Kaplan's (1987) definition of "any social relation involving language or other sign systems as a form of exchange between participants, real or imaginary, particular or collective . . . which defines the terms of what can or cannot be said and extends beyond verbal language to a range of fields in which meaning is culturally organized" (p. 187).

Discourses in this sense are necessarily competitive and as such embody particular interests, "establish paradigms, set limits and construct [human] subjects" (Collins, 1989, p. 12). To speak of culture, as discourse, is to situate it in what Foucault (1890) calls *a discursive field*. Weedon (1987) describes discursive fields as "competing ways of giving meaning to the world and organizing social institutions and processes . . . [offering] . . . the individual a range of modes of subjectivity" (p. 35).

When surveying any discursive field, it is important to recognize that not all discourses will carry equal weight or power. For instance, in education there are competing discourses, which influence how teachers plan curricula, organize classroom space, undertake disciplinary measures, grade papers, evaluate student progress, etc. Some of these competing discourses are drawn from educational psychology, critical social theory, learning theory, and the like. Discourses which contest the organization and selective interests of dominant forms of pedagogy, such as Marxist social theory, are likely to be marginal and generally dismissed by most teachers, whereas others are drawn from competing discourses within the educational environment itself. Discourses of students, parents, building and district office administrators, school boards, institutes of higher education, and state departments of education each differ in degree of accessibility, social power, and the political strengths of the interests they represent.

In other words, culture within the postmodernist perspective is always being constructed and is always being produced within a multiplicity of contexts of unequal power. The perspective of culture as human construction, however, is generally underemphasized or absent in second language classrooms. Instead, a perspective of culture as information to be transmitted predominates.

Crawford-Lange and Lange (1984) explain that when the acquisition and dissemination of elements of cultural information remain the predominant teaching strategy, severe limitations are imposed on the learning of culture. An information-centered, culture-teaching strategy implies that the culture under study is closed, final, and complete, in contradiction to the view of culture as under continual construction. While such a strategy may correctly identify cultural characteristics that are valid at some particular time, it does not adequately prepare students to recognize and understand cultural change over time. This deficit in understanding proves particularly problematic for the person who studies a second culture in high school, but does not actually confront the target culture until many years later.

Not only does information-focused culture education inadequately treat cultural changes over time, but it also neglects consideration of individual and regional variations within the target culture. This neglect eliminates consideration of culture at the personal level where the individual interacts with and acts upon the culture. Instead, culture is viewed as a static abstraction and attribution of its construction and reconstruction is either ignored or assigned to a few elite. Further, although most second language teachers intend to diminish stereotypes and biases, an information-only culture-learning strategy may actually establish stereotypes, since it provides no means of accounting for cultural variation across individuals or regions at the same point in time.

Learning culture by amassing bits of information leaves the student stranded when facing a cultural situation not previously studied. The student has acquired no tools to facilitate understanding of an unknown cultural circumstance. This situation occurs not only within a culture; it arises across cultures as well. For example, students with much information about the culture of France may behave inappropriately in French-speaking Africa if they do not possess the skills for understanding and learning the new culture.

Although culture contains knowable facts, these facts are in constant flux. More important to an understanding of culture than the collection of facts is an appreciation of culture as a constellation of phenomena in a continual process of change, brought about by the participants in the culture as they live and work. Culture is continually in the process of becoming and therefore should be taught as process. To study culture as a body of facts is to study the characteristics of culture; to study culture as a process is to study its essence.

Second language educators have generated a number of proposals contributing significantly to progress in promoting the systematic inclusion of culture-as-process in language courses (Damen, 1987; Jorstad, 1981; Lange, 1979; Nostrand, 1967, 1974; Seelye, 1984; Singerman, 1988). Crawford-Lange and Lange (1984) offer an integrative language/culture learning process that: treats culture as in-construction rather than as a static entity; provides students with skills to form and re-form perceptions of culture; develops students' ability to interact successfully in novel cultural situations; and exemplifies that participants in the culture are the authors of the culture.

Teaching culture as grounded in material struggle over competing discourses and social practices permits teachers to move beyond the prevailing conception of culture as simply a storehouse of information and inserts them into the fray among competing school interest groups. Who decides the perspective from which culture is taught when textbooks generally become rather than contribute to the curriculum? Who decides this question when state evaluation systems predominantly use multiple-choice items with one right answer rather than engagement of students in situations intended to reveal comprehension of process and cultural construction? Whose voices are heard when some students want a culturally factual, linguistically grammatical course that they consider necessary for college while other students want to learn to communicate with, understand, and work with other people in a common project of social change? Responses to these questions challenge the very heart of education and are complicated by the realization that culture is not only under constant construction from a variety of power centers, but is also polyphonic rather than unitary.

CULTURE AS PLURIVOCAL

Postmodern social theory has given us a differentiated view of culture as distinct from the unitary one that informs most mainstream discourses of teaching. Culture has come to be understood as more distinctly multiplex and political than its usual conception as the proliferation of historically produced artifacts forged within a neutral arena of social relations. Culture is conceived from the postmodernist perspective as both the medium and the outcome of discourses which "establish the limits of the sayable" (Frow, 1986, p. 78) and a constituent aspect of subjectivity forged within asymmetrical relations of power and privilege.

Quantz (1989) summarizes some of the prevailing conceptions of culture in order to set the stage for a drastic rethinking of the concept. He argues that traditional scholarship has defined culture as a social construction created by an interrelated network of people, a consensual entity created in the inter-subjective reality of an identifiably bordered group. Whether researchers or educators happen to be speaking about the *culture of poverty* or *Appalachian culture*, or the culture of a particular school, these cultures are usually understood as relatively homogeneous entities consisting of shared patterns of symbols and cultural practices. Quantz argues that this traditional conception of culture as shared patterns of beliefs and customs is wrong because it fails to take into account how such beliefs, values, and customs are historically and ideologically constituted.

Drawing from work done at the Birmingham Centre for Contemporary Cultural Studies, Quantz (1989) argues that culture needs to be understood with reference to the level at which social groups develop distinct patterns of life and also the meanings and expressive forms which these groups give to those structures of lived experience. But, of course, as Giroux (1988),

Quantz (1989), and others within the critical educational tradition have pointed out, this emphasis on shared meanings and understandings will not suffice because culture is fundamentally a struggle over meanings and about meanings. Furthermore, it is a struggle over events, representations, and interpretations. From this perspective, it is important to recognize that there is not simply one monolithic, unitary, seamless culture, but a multiplicity of cultures, subcultures, oppositional cultures, and alternative cultures.

Similar to the Soviet sociolinguist Bakhtin, Quantz (1989) believes that culture must be understood as *multivoiced* or *polyphonic.* He warns against the expression of polyphonic cultures as monophonic entities, which tends to misrepresent the concrete and lived experience of subordinate groups. For example, by presenting black teenage parents as a monophonic culture, as many news reports have done in the U.S. media, the ideological illusion is created that these teenagers frequently choose to uniformly victimize themselves by making selfish choices at inopportune moments in their lives. Blacks are presented as willfully negligent and irresponsible parents, a view which can only be un-problematically asserted by those who choose to ignore the complexity and specificity of material constraints and ideological apparatuses which position black women and men at an extreme disadvantage within the larger social order.

Second language educators are impacted by the polyphony of culture along three dimensions. *First,* polyphony prevails within the native culture. Students vary along a variety of factors affecting school life, for example, hours of employment, involvement in extracurricular activities, and career and educational goals. Curricular and instructional planning must take these differences into account. *Second,* there is polyphony of cultures within which the target language is spoken as well as polyphony within each of those cultures. In traditional second language courses, cultural study is associated with a single linguistic unit. For instance, French courses tend to concentrate on the culture of France, Spanish courses on Spain, German courses on Germany. Further, in studying the culture of France, the focus is generally limited to either mainstream, middle-class culture or to classical and artistic accomplishments. The myriad voices of subordinate groups often are not represented. *Third,* there is a polyphony between native and target cultures, which tends to be explored in terms of grossly defined and rather superficial similarities and differences.

The complexity of respecting these polyphonies within the second language classroom would be clearly evident in a three-dimensional drawing. However, a postmodernist view of culture disallows avoidance due to complexity. Possibilities for addressing these voices do exist. For example, during the initial stages of study of a cultural topic or theme, student dialog could be directed to examination of the topic within the native culture, attending to experiences of subordinate as well as mainstream groups in relation to the topic. Also, instead of studying, for instance, home life in Spain, some students could explore home life in Spain, some focus on the same in Central America, some in Puerto Rico, and some in Spanish Harlem. Bringing these perspectives together for joint dialog would reveal to students the multiplicity and multiplexity of culture, as well as the asymmetrical relations of power that help situate select groups in relations of domination over other groups. Further, dialog could be conducted in terms of the interrelationships among native and target cultures. The limitation of classroom resources to support such exploration is admittedly real. Crawford-Lange and Lange (1987) have collated some suggestions for overcoming this limitation.

CULTURE AND TRADITION

Ryan (1989), who offers a politically enabling poststructuralist account of culture, articulates the perspective of culture that comes closest to our own. According to Ryan, culture is not "a secondary representation or embodiment of a group life substance that is assumed to be prior and that is expressed through culture" (p. 21). Rather, culture "as shape, form, representation, embodiment, and objectification play[s] a more constitutive role in the making of group life" (p. 21). That is, "people don't live materially and then add culture, they live and have culture at the same time" (p. 21). In this view, social reality and social rhetoric are mutually informing. It is within such a perspective that we can agree with Ryan when he writes that "[t]he lives of working class kids are given shape and narrative form by the discourse in which they live, one whose privileged metaphor is the freedom of the white capitalist and whose most prevalent synecdoche is the part-for-whole lives to which the majority are reduced" (p. 24).

Such an agreement does not lead us, however, to consider the whole of culture as something to be irrevocably condemned. Certainly you can overcome tradition without breaking all contact with it. We do not object to tradition itself. What we do object to is the concealment of cultural uncertainties in the way that tradition gets ideologically produced. And, we object to the dishonest equation of some defenders of culture on the New Right that culture equals truth. That is, we do not reject tradition in an a priori sense, but rather the immutable construction of heritage. In our view, it is important to understand the limits of various traditions so one can enter into dialog with them. Culture needs to be analyzed in terms of its presences and absences, in terms of both its lived and semiotic constitution and in light of its diverse readings, social codes, and vocabularies of cultural experiences.

As educators, we need to analyze the relationship between culture and power, as well as the role that culture plays in enabling or disabling people to speak and to reproduce systematic mismatches between subjective states and inter-subjective identity structures. While this focus may not be the only possible one on the issue of culture, it simply cannot be ignored. It is certainly true that culture constitutes more than forms of domination and emancipation. The question we would like to raise for educators is: Why shouldn't all aspects of culture be problematized? To problematize culture does not guarantee that everything *traditional* will be condemned or rejected.The contexts in which dominant interests become articulated through popular cultural forms (e.g., popular music, entertainment genres, television shows, leisure activities, sports) need to be analyzed, both in terms of how these interests are either neutralized or else compounded in the sense that their contradictions become resolved and remain operative, though hidden, in our daily engagements in the politics of living. As Laclau (1990) notes: "the relation with tradition should not be one of submission and repetition, but of transformation and critique. One must construct one's discourse as difference in relation to that tradition and this implies at the same time continuities and discontinuities. If a tradition ceases to be the cultural terrain where creativity and the inscription of new problems take place, and becomes instead a hindrance to that creativity and inscription, it will gradually and silently be abandoned. No one claims that social and cultural transformation is an easy task" (p. 12).

Educators need to make the effort to strip the term *culture* from its accumulated theoretical paraphernalia. Educators need to be able to uncover and to allow students to uncover the social contradictions that are ideologically resolved or harmonized to preserve existing relations of power, relations that have debilitating effects on specific groups. Here it becomes useful to employ Barthes' (1973) concept of *mythologies* to illustrate how cultural narratives, which often bear a structural affinity to traditional myths, frequently celebrate dominant values and power structures by providing the symbolic constructs which suppress social contradictions in order to naturalize and idealize relations of oppression that exist within the cultural infrastructure. Educators need to acquire a more critical grasp of the way in which culture becomes encapsulated by a corporatist perspective that structures individual intent and shapes the direction of students' desiring.

One of the ways in which culture becomes encapsulated by a corporatist perspective is in the production of textbooks, which may be interpreted as the construction of a national curriculum. The view of culture, which subjects tradition to critical problematization, underscores the folly of any national curriculum that claims to represent the values, knowledge, and interests of all groups in a society. Since textbooks are subject to obvious limitations of, for example, space and dimension, it is the uncritical assumption that the content selected for textbook presentation is sociolog-ically and culturally accurate and complete, which is as damaging as the reality that content is indeed selected on the basis of androcentric, patriar-chal, and Eurocentric assumptions.

Kramsch (1988) demonstrates that the influence of tradition on the production of second language textbooks, if accepted uncritically, serves the interests of the dominant native culture, minimizing the interests of subordinate native cultures and both dominant and subordinate target cul-tures. Supported by her review of actual textbooks, she identifies a major problem: lack of attention to logic of presentation, i.e., whether patterns of thought and cultural phenomena are presented from a native or target cul-ture perspective. The implications she draws force a reconceptualization of concepts and culture, authentic materials, contextualized learning, person-alized learning, and the inclusion of native culture. Her problematization of second language textbooks needs to be continued into the classroom and performed with students.

In addition to the problematization of textbooks, the problematization of culture itself, rather than simple transmission of tradition, is essential to the conduct of second culture learning from a poststructuralist per-spective. Making a distinction between a cultural topic and a cultural theme may prove useful to problematizing culture in the second language classroom (Crawford-Lange & Lange, 1984, 1987). A topic may be taken to identify cultural content, for example, geography, mealtime, occupa-tions, school, soccer. A theme focus on issues, values, and/or problems related to the topic. For example, themes related to the topic of employ-ment may be: What is the availability of employment for adolescents in a depressed area? For what reasons do adolescents work? To what use do adolescents put their earned income? Themes related to the topic of school may be: Who is disciplined in school and for what offenses? How are grades determined? How are extracurricular activities structured; who participates in them and why?

Cultural themes, therefore, are provocative and perhaps emotionally charged concerns or issues that motivate the culture learner's conduct, engage critically the values of the culture (Crawford, 1979; Freire, 1970; Nostrand, 1974), and that reveal cultural contradictions. The stronger the relationship of the theme to the lives of the students, the more powerful the theme will be for language/culture learning. For example, for a school in a depressed area with high adolescent unemployment, the theme of availability of employment for adolescents would be more powerful than in a wealthy suburb. In a wealthy suburb, a more powerful theme may be what adolescents do with disposable income. In both cases, exploration of the theme should reveal contradictions. For example, what contradictions are contained in varying rates of employment for different socioeconomic classes of adolescents, in varying levels of and uses for disposable income? Further, powerful themes for second language classrooms promote cross-cultural investigation. What differences in grading and evaluation might an exchange student to this country experience? Do schools in France and Chicago discipline students the same way for the same offenses?

Textbooks and course syllabi, however, generally assist only in defining topics, not cultural themes. Massaging topics into themes requires listening to the textbook and to the students. What do my students talk about before class starts, in the hallway, at lunch? What is contained in the text material that holds promise as a theme? What human problem is present in or implied by the topic presented in the text? What questions do my students and I have about this topic? In what way(s) does the topic relate to my students? In what way(s) does the topic present opportunities for students to historicize and analyze the power structure of society?

By problematizing the topics contained in second language texts, tradition, which is valued as immutable and permanent by the dominant societal voice, undergoes critical analysis. This critical analysis does not deny tradition, but does subject it to the lived experience of the present humans who are responsible for the making of their own cultural world, of those groups whose voices have been marginalized or silenced by the regimes of truth constructed under the cover of such tradition.

CULTURE AND RESISTANCE

Passive, compliant individuals or groups do not control the making of cultures. Individuals and groups resist. Most notably Giroux has taken up the importance of the concept of resistance over the last decade. Giroux (1983) points out that: "...the idea that people do make history, including its constraints, has been neglected" (p. 259). Schools are seen as *sites* for ideological struggle and class conflict, in which subordinate cultures partake of moments of self-production as well as reproduction. In reference to the classroom, Giroux maintains that students do not constantly submit to the dictates of the legitimation and socialization of the educational systems. In Giroux's (1983) view, "schools represent contested terrains marked not only by structural and ideological contradictions, but also by collectively informed student resistance" (p. 268). There are numerous examples of alternative pedagogies being practiced by politically informed teachers, such as the work being done at Dr. Pedro Albizu Campos Puerto Rican High School in Chicago. In addition, Kathleen Weiler's book, *Women Teaching for Change* (1988), documents some important work being done by feminist teachers to counter the expansive hegemony of dominant social and cultural arrangements.

Departments of second languages often deal with student resistance in a self-serving manner. Entrance to courses is frequently restricted by high prerequisites in terms of prior academic performance (Arendt, Lange, & Wakefield, 1986; Crawford-Lange, 1985; Lange, 1987). This elitism is curious when one considers that it operates under the assumption that some students cannot learn a second language when virtually all students have achieved proficiency in a first language. The job of teachers is not to select out and identify those who cannot learn a language, but rather to provide effective language and culture learning opportunities, and find ways to teach language and culture to those students whom they had assumed to be unteachable.

Students who fail a term of second language instruction are merely dismissed, removed to a study hall or placed into another elective course. However, school failure is an insidious concept. Prior to and outside of school, failure is considered part of learning rather than non-learning. When watching a toddler first negotiate a flight of stairs, adults applaud awkward, unsuccessful attempts. In school, those attempts would likely have been graded as *F.* Prior to and outside of school, youth pursue personal and group interests that engage them joyfully and successfully. In school, youth of all classes and ethnicities are pursued by a curriculum determined by adults of the dominant class. Resisting that curriculum relegates the student to a non-legitimated status in society—no high school diploma.

Research on resistance in schools and its uncovering of cultural struggle in the classroom presents educators with data that could assist teachers in politicizing their own understanding of the school system (Giroux & McLaren, 1989). As teachers, we would do well to use resistance theory as a means of understanding how to transform classroom resistance into an emancipatory struggle toward empowerment.

CULTURE AND THE CONSTRUCTION OF THE INDIVIDUAL SUBJECT

It is now commonplace in critical educational studies, which attempt to move beyond some of the theoretical parameters of resistance theory, to give serious consideration to the relationship among schooling, culture, and subjectivity. We are using the term *subjectivity* after Weedon (1987) to refer to "the conscious and unconscious thoughts and emotions of the individual, her sense of herself and her ways of understanding her relations to the world" (p. 32). In recent years, radical educators have paid close attention to the semiotic basis of cultural activity, in particular the social and cultural production of student subjectivity with respect to race, class, and gender. In so doing they have employed the term *subjectivity* rather than *identity* in order to highlight the decentered or multiply organized aspect of the self which poststructuralist theorists argue is more fluid, plural, discontinuous, and contingent than the model of the self bequeathed by the Cartesian or humanistic tradition most often associated with conservative and liberal conceptions of the subject. Much of the recent work in feminist versions of postmodern social theory has also taken up the idea that subjectivity is contradictory and multiplex, a view which runs counter to various traditions of humanist social theory. Within this perspective, the subject is always partial and often defined in contradictory ways as the effects of multiple determinations that may be affective, ideological, material, or gendered. A theory of articulation suggests that there are always multiplicities of subject positions to be occupied and ways in which different experiences, meanings, and identities can be articulated together. Individuals can act against particular historical tendencies since the structural totality can never be guaranteed in advance; yet individuals are always constituted by their location within already inscribed systems of difference (Grossberg, 1988, p. 137).

Feminist poststructuralists have made the important observation that human subjects are constantly traversed by contradiction within their respective discursive fields. To a certain degree, individuals are always already installed by available discourses into contexts that have been historically constructed and therefore position individuals ideologically. Yet, it is important to emphasize that the positioning of social agents, e.g., teachers and students, within the cultural field, e.g., classroom and school, is always relational, as students enter the struggle over subjectivity from different historically given levels of material, social, and cultural endowments. It is also important to view the subject as never irrevocably determined but also determining, i.e., making culture and not just the product of it. We are not suspended *placelessly* outside of history, nor lodged immovably within discursive positions. The human agent can never indeterminately float outside of historical and cultural determinations, antiseptically removed or extracted from the larger social formation. At the same time, it is true that the human agent is never irrevocably determined by the social structures out of which it has been formed.

Human agents exist as a tangle of discourses, crossed by dialectical lines of force, often with no central narrative to coordinate the play of differences of every competing human text (Collins, 1989). The different contexts in which various discourses intersect will largely determine which discourses will prevail in providing the subject with his or her primary subject position. For instance, a teacher may reflect a *contradictory* subjectivity in the sense that he or she takes a pro-life stand with respect to the issue of abortion, yet at the same time maintain an aggressive stance in favor of the death penalty. Or, he or she may work with students using a student-centered pedagogy, yet, as a parent, adopt a strict and perhaps even abusive disciplinarian approach to child rearing. It is the context of the specific situation, the discourses available, as well as the individual's own history, race, gender, and socioeconomic status that will shed some determinative light on the subject positions which are taken up on a daily basis. A progressive teacher may, for instance, hold radical views on issues related to race, gender, and class, and yet assume a pedagogical discourse that exhibits forms of racism, sexism, and classism. In this case, personal and pedagogical discourses may contradict each other.

By now it should be relatively clear that ideological struggle often consists of attempting to *win* some new sets of meanings, some new discourses from which we can position ourselves as subjects. Thus, it should be more evident how culture functions not as a frozen set of meanings and practices, but rather as a field of discourses in a decentered power struggle in which, through the materiality of social struggle, they make appeals to decidedly heterogeneous audiences and groups (Collins, 1989).

In this sense, the position of the teacher and the students in the second language classroom can never be considered as politically or personally neutral. School people have inherited an unfortunate legacy from empiricism, the pretension to objectivity and the rejection of the partial and the contingent. However, as described above, culture and individual subjectivity are intertwined. If, in teaching culture, one pretends to impart an objective description of a presumably objective reality, one denies the teacher's own politics of location, the multiple selves of the cultural participants, and the selves of the students. On the other hand, subjectivity could be recognized by solicitation of personal, reflective statements including not only perceptions of the cultural phenomena under study but also reactions to the phenomena (Crawford-Lange & Lange, 1984). With such statements as the basis for dialog in the context of culture taught as process rather than information transmission, a transformational richness will develop from the overlay and interaction of cultural understandings.

While all students possess some form of subjectivity, not all students possess historical agency. Historical agency is the ability to self-reflectively strategize the decentered and disarticulated aspects of subjectivity such that the individual is able to assume the kind of agency that situates him or her as an active agent of and in history rather than its passive recipient. Finding little solace in the concept of the fractured or decentered subject, Grossberg (1992) claims that there is no solution to the paradox of subjectivity since it is built on a conceptual model that identifies individuals as both the subjects and agents of history. Grossberg attempts to escape from this paradox "by distinguishing subjectivity (the site of experience and of the attribution of responsibility), agency (the active forces struggling within and over history, and agent-hood (actors operating as subject, whether knowingly or unknowingly, on behalf of particular agencies)." Agency in this case not only refers to the location of individuals in systems of discourse and difference but also to historical agency. Historical agency deals not so much with social identity as with historical effectivity or what Gramsci (1971) called "tendential forces" (e.g., capitalism, industrialism, technology, democracy, nationalism, religion). Such forces "map out the long term directions and investments which have already been so deeply inscribed upon the shape of history that they seem to play themselves out in a constantly indeterminate future" (p.23). However, agency requires historical and cultural agents to accomplish specific activities. Agents may be individuals or nominal groups such as organizations and political parties that, admittedly, may have their own political agendas. But such agendas ultimately depend on the apparatuses of agency.

CULTURAL POLITICS AS THE DISCOURSE OF THE OTHER

We have been arguing that it is important to understand culture as articulation. Articulation, as we are using the term, involves both the disjunctive patterning of identities and the mutual constitution of the political and the pedagogical. According to Grossberg (1988), articulation relates texts to meanings and therefore involves practices and structures as well as the production of contexts and the repositioning of practices within those contexts. Thus, texts and contexts are articulated to each other, not added to each other. Consequently, it is difficult if not impossible to offer any definition of culture that allows culture to maintain an immunity to politics; that is, a definition that allows it to remain un-implicated in the process of ideological production. This is the case because any cultural discourse, as both a linguistic creation and a social and material practice, is always historically and socially contingent. In other words, any discourse of culture is bounded by the historical, cultural, and political conditions and also the epistemological resources available to articulate its meaning.

Rosaldo (1989) draws attention to the way in which the discourse of culture reproduces itself through ideological constructs of the *Other*, that is, with respect to its fictions of the marginal, the deviant, the disaffected, and the underclass.The questions that we must raise as analysts of the discourse of culture in our classrooms and in society at large are: What is left out? What is unsaid? Whose voices are silenced in our classrooms through exclusion? Whose voices are barbarized and demonized through our fictions of what constitutes cultural difference?

For example, during the Reagan administration some teachers unconsciously embodied in their teaching practices discourses supported by that administration's policies toward minority groups, a perspective in which Blacks, Latinos, and other groups were essentialized as either biologically or culturally deficient and treated as a species of inferior vertebrates. Let us also not forget that the presidential campaign run by George Bush played on the public's fear of the stereotyped version of the Black male in its notorious Willie Horton television campaign spot. Blacks are also stereotyped in the remonstrations of liberals most often as occupying a *culture of poverty* which is frequently portrayed as a seamless jumble of pathology. We are taught to forget that the relations of power and privilege at play in the formation of such a culture are largely determined by the dominant, white Anglo culture.

Rosaldo (1989) points out that *zones of cultural visibility and invisibility* play a distinct part in the location of these groups in the social hierarchy in which "full citizenship and cultural visibility appear to be inversely related" (p. 198). Here, Rosaldo is introducing the important idea of precultural, cultural, and postcultural identities. He suggests that within the dominant social order certain groups are classified into those who have culture and those who are civilized. For instance, within the nation-state, cultural distinctiveness "derives from a lengthy historical process of colonial domination" (p. 199). Rosaldo is quick to point out that cultural differences are "relative to the cultural practices of ethnographers and their readers" (p. 202). This common form of ethnographic practice sees difference generally from the North American upper-middle-class professional perspective, in which "the *other* becomes more culturally visible [as] the *self* becomes correspondingly less so" (p. 202).

Cultural visibility, or having more culture, is associated with being less rational or civilized than the white citizen who is considered *postcultural.* Viewed from this perspective, the process of schooling is geared to creating a postcultural citizenry and often involves what Rosaldo calls a form of *cultural stripping.* Cultural stripping takes place when individuals are stripped of their former cultures, enabling them to become transparent, just like you and me, people without culture, part of the culturally invisible mainstream (Rosaldo, 1989). White culture loses its ethnicity and passes unobserved into the rhythms of daily life. Being white is an entitlement, not to preferred racial attributes, but to a raceless subjectivity. That is, being white becomes the invisible norm for how the dominant culture measures its own civility.

Blacks are stereotypically portrayed as more physical and emotional (less rational) and therefore betraying more culture. The same is true of the French Canadians in Canada. In both cases, these cultural minorities are denied full participation in the economic, social, and political life of the nation-state. To be cultural, in Rosaldo's terms, is to be more visible and to get less. Educators must be wary, therefore, of labeling certain minority groups as those in possession of a surplus of *authentic* culture because such a perspective tends to celebrate the distance middle-class whites have evolved, i.e., have become more rational and less cultural.

Educators, like ethnographers, often err by regarding *authentic* culture as something frozen and static, if it exists at all. Rosaldo (1989) claims that such a position has, in fact, become a "useful fiction" in developing research strategies "that exclude social struggles revolving around issues of class, race, gender and sexual orientation" (p. 220). The *other*, in this case, becomes a cultural fiction that allows educators and researchers to ignore the partiality of their own perspectives that assign culture and *otherness* to certain groups. The process of constructing the *other* also helps to conceal how the pedagogies used by teachers who work with visible minorities are sometimes an unwitting exercise in forms of cultural repression and ideological violence as well as a means of indulging in the will to dominate. Furthermore, such pedagogical practices conceal the possibilities for democratic and empowering social relations available through assuming multiple cultural positions from which individuals are able to speak, act, and contribute to pluralistic society.

We are arguing that the culture of authenticity as we have been describing it is discriminatory in both senses of the word; it discriminates in the sense of distinguishing the *other* from the mainstream and in marginalizing certain groups on the basis of a selective perception of cultural endowment.

Unfortunately, the manner in which many second language educators conduct instruction about culture reinforces a definition of the *other* as lesser by just the means described above, cultural visibility. Sincere and well-meaning teachers present cultural differences as *cute, quaint*, and *interesting*. When cultural similarities are explored, *they* are seen to be *just like us*, rather than *us* being *just like them*. The cultures become dichotomized in reference to each other with superiority granted to an invisible norm linked to the dominant language and social practices. We ogle the peculiarities of cultures different from our own and subsume their equivalencies.

Such pedagogical practices persist in second language classrooms in part because the curricular design identifies and presents the culture of the other as the object of study and exempts the dominant native culture from critical examination, allowing it to remain invisible. This invisibility was highlighted for one of the authors during a summer study program for language teachers in France. During an international evening for students from all programs of summer study, students from each country were to present some aspect of their culture. In discussing what to present, the group from the United States, all white, middle-class language teachers, thought that it would be easy for the other groups to present their cultures because they had a lot of culture. However, the group from the United States stated that they could identify no cultural aspect to present; they understood themselves as cultureless. This scenario reinforces the comments from Rosaldo cited earlier.

A curricular design with possibilities for overcoming this visible/invisible cultural definition of self and other would incorporate elements such as those suggested in the integrative language/culture learning process (Crawford-Lange & Lange, 1984). Such a curriculum includes dialogic and investigative stages addressing both native and target cultures. Once a cultural theme, as explained above, has been selected, dialog focuses initially on description and analysis of thematic features. For example, for a theme related to school discipline: What offenses are listed in the discipline code? What punishments are given? In what ways do the punishments relate to the offenses? How are parents involved? Is there evidence of student input into the discipline code? Then dialog centers on reactions in terms of one's own cultural patterns, for example: How does the target culture discipline code relate to the native culture discipline code in terms of offenses and punishments? How well do consequences relate to offenses in each? Which do you feel is the more severe? The more effective? Which would you rather live under? Why? What problems are inherent in both? What advantages?

Investigation of the cultural theme is conducted from both target and native culture perspectives. By examining as many resources as are available to them, print, visual, and human, different students may pursue different aspects of the theme depending on interest. The investigation is a parallel one in which resources from both target and native cultures are examined and observations drawn. The various observations from both cultural arenas are brought together and described, analyzed, and compared to original perceptions. Within this dialogic opportunity, changes in the perceptions of both the target and native cultures are specifically noted and described, as are positive and negative reactions. Dialog is extended to examine issues related to understanding culture as articulation: Why are there cultural similarities/differences? What effects have geography, time, and people had on cultural evolution? Are there different cultural patterns in different regions? How has the pattern existed in the native culture? Are there differences in patterns within the native/target cultures? Are there any influences of the target culture on the native culture? Has the native culture influenced the target culture in any way? How do phenomena studied in the target culture interact with other systems in the same culture? How are cultural patterns and systems geopolitically constituted? If your cultural perceptions changed during this unit, what caused them to change? How is the very dichotomy of *target/native* culture constructed and what are the strengths and limitations of such a characterization? In other words, where are the teacher and students standing sociopolitically when defining some cultures as native and others as target? This last question enables the teacher and students to explore the ideological situatedness of the unit of study as well as their own centeredness in the discourses of their own self-formation.

By problematizing the native as well as the target culture in the second language classroom, as well as the cultural embeddedness of the unit and pedagogy employed, students may begin to see their own culture become visible to themselves. The opportunity arises for exposure to the plurality of and embeddedness in one's own culture, for understanding the self as a creator of history and culture, and for diminishment of the elitism achieved through the assignment of cultural *otherness*.

CULTURE AND THE DISCOURSE OF LIBERATION

Teachers must attempt to recognize their own subjective cultural status and in so doing refrain from reserving a noncultural status, a status that creates subject positions, which carry civic power and self-interest, for those most like *them*, that is for educators from the dominant, patriarchal, and middle-class culture. The importance of this insight for educators lies in the recognition that by defining groups as differentially endowed with culture, the gatekeepers of the status quo are able to erase the normative interests which inform their own cultural politics. By remaining unreflective about the interests, which inform their own cultural politics, teachers fail to notice how their pedagogies, curricula, and research practices may be employed at the expense of the *other*. In other words, our pedagogies often produce and represent difference as *other* by hiding, or naturalizing, the interests that inform them. That is, the cult of postcultural rationality that undergirds the discourse of cultural authenticity renders these interests invisible. We would additionally argue that this conceptualization has obvious implications for curriculum in respect to what is put in and left out and the grounds upon which this is justified or rationalized.

Another way of putting this would be to argue that critical pedagogy must always be directed against the indissolubility of the self, that is, against a concept of the self that is static, unchanging, and unified. The postcultural self to whom white culture adheres must therefore be recognized as only one reality within a multiplicity of realities. These, though, are not free-floating realities; they exist with hierarchies of possibility and restraint. In this way, educators can avoid the privileging of patriarchal and bourgeois assumptions, which inform the postcultural self and a subjugation of all other interests to them. The postcultural self must not assume a definitive ascendance as a privileged position from which to construct the *other* (Rosaldo, 1989). The *other* is constructed by systems of meanings which have been durably installed and which become *other*-destructive when they remain buried by tradition and transformed into weapons of stigmatization.

Cottom (1989) offers a way of avoiding both the identity-in-difference of cultural relativism and the identification with a monolithic culture by "working to identify the differences between the imaginary law of culture and the life that escapes it" (p. 100). The pedantic rationality of assuming a *proper* cultural decorum and possessing the requisite cultural *facts* turns culture into a mausoleum of dead historical relics and history into a junkyard. Educators need to reject the monologic view that education simply involves the unilinear transmission of collected information in favor of the more critical and postcolonial practice of disentangling the codes, ideologies, and social practices that make social life meaningful, understanding how these meanings have been constructed, and recognizing how they remain implicated with domains of power.

In other words, teachers should avoid both the authoritarianism that accompanies an ethnocentric perspective of culture and the relativism that goes hand-in-hand with the concept of a liberal cultural pluralism. A critical pedagogy should speak against the notion that all cultural realities need to follow one dominant narrative or that all diverse culture realities need to be given voice, since it is obvious that many of these realities harbor racist, classist, and sexist assumptions. The key here is not to insist simply on cultural diversity, transforming culture into a living museum of contemporary choices, but a critical diversity.

A critical diversity means that choices need to be seen as social practices which are themselves historically and socially constructed, and teachers need to distinguish cultural choices in terms of the degree to which they are liberating or oppressive, as well as in what contexts they function as such. "Choices under the name of democracy or totalitarianism can serve as totalizing abstractions 'divorced' from the group affiliations and commitments that constitute their identities and give them a perspective on social life" (Young, 1990, p. 114). Choices are never impartial; they all occupy specifiable locations in relations of power. In her book, *Justice and the Politics of Difference*, Young (1990) argues convincingly that impartiality in moral theory expresses a logic of identity that seeks to reduce differences to unity. She writes that the attributes of *detachment* and *dispassion* that claim to produce impartiality are achieved "only by abstracting the particularities of situation, feeling, affiliation, and point of view" (p. 97). Particularities always operate in the context of action. The ideal of impartiality not only creates a dichotomy between the universal and particular, public and private, reason and passion, but also serves debilitating ideological functions by masking the ways in which dominant perspectives claim universality and justify forms of domination. As Young (1990) writes:

> Insistence on the ideal of impartiality in the face of its impossibility functions to mask the inevitable partiality of perspective from which moral deliberation actually takes place. The situated assumptions and commitments that derive from particular histories, experiences, and affiliations rush to fill the vacuum created by counterfactual abstraction; but now they are asserted as *objective* assumptions about human nature of moral psychology. The ideal of impartiality generates a propensity to universalize the particular (pp. 115–116).

Where social group differences exist, and some groups are privileged while others are oppressed, this propensity to universalize the particular reinforces that oppression.

Young's argument can be read productively in the context of second language teaching as a form of cultural politics. She is saying that when differences are reduced to a universal category, totality of unity, that reduction actually results in the dichotomizing of reason between self-legislation and self-regarding empirical facts mediated by the private desires of the researcher. Ethnographers must stress the partiality and contingencies of their own analyses. They must acknowledge their abjected *other*, that is, their fear and loathing of the possibility that the border between self and other will dissolve and thus destroy the self.

Not only does the cultural imperialism of the researcher provide and insist on only one subject position, that of unified, disembodied reason identified with white bourgeois men, it promotes members of culturally imperialized groups to devalue themselves and other oppressed groups. Young (1990) is worth quoting at length on this issue:

> Within the unifying logic of modern reason and respectability, the subjectivity of members of culturally imperialized groups tends to stand in the same position as that of the privileged groups. From that supposedly neutral subject position all these despised and deviant groups are experienced as the abjected Other (p. 147).

In other words, members of culturally imperialized groups themselves often devalue members of their own groups and other oppressed groups by internalizing the cultural knowledge that dominant groups *fear and loathe them*. However, oppressed and marginalized groups do not simply assume the dominant subjectivity toward themselves and other members of the groups with which they identify, they also live a subjectivity different from the dominant subject position that they have derived from their positive identification and social networks with others in their group. The dialectical relationship between these two subjectivities, "the point of view of the dominant culture which defines them as ugly and fearsome, and the point of view of the oppressed who experience themselves as ordinary, companionate, and humorous" (Young, 1990, p. 148), represents what Young calls *double consciousness.*

Young (1990) also points out that it is important to stress the positivity of the value and specificity of the culture and attributes of oppressed groups because this serves to relativize the dominant culture:

> In a political struggle where oppressed groups insist on the positive value of their specific culture and experience, it becomes increasingly difficult for dominant groups to parade their norms as neutral and universal, and to construct the values and behavior of the oppressed as deviant, perverted, or inferior. By puncturing the universalistic claim to unity that expels some groups and turns them into the Other, the assertion of positive group specificity introduces the possibility of understanding the relation between groups as merely difference, instead of exclusion, opposition or dominance (p. 166).

Second language teachers would benefit from following Young's way out of culturally defined forms of oppression and *double consciousness* by helping all subjects to understand themselves as plural, shifting, and heterogeneous. In other words, teachers can help students confront "the very desire to have an orderly identity and the dependence of such a unified identity on the construction of a border that excludes aspects of subjectivity one refuses to face"(Young, 1990, p. 155).

This perspective of culture slices up its presumed uniformity into diverse pieces of shifting perspectives and untold possibilities. This understanding should signal the importance of redefining the educator's role as the authority. As Chock and Wyman (1986) remark: "An ambiguous and multivocal world demands an interpreter, a translator, a reader, or chronicler to replace the realist and the monophonic voice . . . It is in this spirit that we must ask who has access to and power over the discourses which define, order and classify the social world for students" (p. 11).

If we follow Rosaldo (1989) in understanding culture as *multiple border zones* and as an *inter-textual arena* in which social practices do not have or possess norms but continually remake cultural norms, then one of the challenges of a postcolonial pedagogy becomes clear. It is softening the certainty and in some cases rupturing the discursive authority of social texts that circumscribe and command both the classroom and the larger arena of social life.

The lesson here is that, if reality does not exist as a social fact, it need not exist the way it presently does. We must remember that just as there are multiple forms of power, there are also multiple forms of resistance. Students living in subordinate social positions need not accept those positions and consequently they often struggle against the dominant articulations of groups in power. Teachers and students must together decide which discourses are to be hacked out from a thicket of possibilities, and which are to be discarded, which discourses need to be denaturalized and democratized, and which need to be opened up as potential points of resistance and political struggle. Established knowledge and social relations can be revised. New pedagogical discourses can be constructed which allow women, minorities, and working-class students to struggle for voice, for new subject positions which will allow them to speak and act both in and on the world.In this way educators and students can play a part in the regenerative processes of cultural change.

Teachers would profit from recognizing that too often in classroom practices the *other* (blacks, women, Latinos, working-class groups) have been demonized as a result of a monogamous identification between the self of discourse and the rules, strictures, codes, and social practices that normatively ground the surrounding culture (Lankshear, 1987). What is needed is an informed resistance to such monological identification, a commitment to the sounding of multiple voices, and participation in a dialog with self and other, while always recognizing our divided selves, realizing the alien voice ringing in discourse itself and how such a voice has been worked and traversed by contradictions.

The challenge for postmodern teachers who seek the creation of a postcolonial pedagogy of transformation is to identify within curricular forms and pedagogical practices the centralizing principles of power at work with respect to race, class, gender, self, nation, and aesthetic form "...in order to determine what these centres push to their silent or invisible peripheries" (Connor, 1989, p. 227). Teachers might ask themselves what effects of race, class, and gender arrangements lie beneath the naturalizing facades that make up various forms of schooling. How do the curriculum forms, institutional practices and pedagogical processes at work in schooling silence those whom they address in their regimes of representation? We are suggesting that critical pedagogy must seek to simultaneously release and explore the multiplicity of *otherness* which those who are served by the dominant discourses regard as threatening and thus act to delegitimize and marginalize. This thought means that we must become aware of the ideological conflicts concealed and carried out in our pedagogical agendas. A truly critical pedagogy for the postmodern age must constantly unveil reality in such a way as to serve both as a delegitimization of the oppressive hegemonic discourses of the dominant cultural order and a liberation of classroom knowledge which the discourses of schooling has purified by systematically concealing and repressing oppositional voices and practices. Alternatively put, how can we, as postcolonialist educators, both unlearn our privileged positions as narrators of other people's lives and still be able to exercise moral and political leadership in the struggle for social change and political transformation?

The second language teacher who wishes to address this question seriously will revise the classroom role of both teacher and students. Presumably, the teacher possesses more expert and systematized linguistic knowledge than the students. Possession of this systematized knowledge, in fact, identifies the teacher as teacher, should not be denied, and is to be shared with the students (Freire & Shor, 1987). From the point of view of critical pedagogy, however, the selection of linguistic knowledge to be shared, for example, grammar and vocabulary, is subject more to the communicative needs identified by the students, the meanings emanating from themselves, than to the distribution of topics in course syllabi or textbook tables of contents. For example, within the integrative language/culture learning process (Crawford-Lange & Lange, 1984), linguistic content is identified and organized in relation to communicative needs, named by the students, surrounding the cultural themes under study. Teacher and students examine language needed in order to proceed with the cultural investigation: functions, notions, structure, syntax, registers, and general vocabulary. The textbook, then, serves as one resource for the language material to be presented and practiced. In this way, power of defining the curriculum is invested with the students and disinvested from the text publishers.

In concert with the understanding of culture developed in this paper, the teacher cannot be the distributor of assumed cultural knowledge but rather must participate with the students in cultural exploration. While teachers might have an understanding of culture as a concept and the processes of becoming acquainted with a second culture, within a critical pedagogical framework they are required neither to possess a catalog of cultural information nor to be the ultimate cultural expert. Teachers learn about culture along with the students. Any cultural knowledge and skills possessed by teachers are not parceled out to the learning group for ingestion; they are utilized by the group in investigating cultural themes from both native and target culture perspectives and from a multiplicity of voices within each of these cultures (Crawford-Lange, 1981).

While adopting the stance of critical pedagogy is clearly liberating for and empowering of students, the effect is the same for teachers. Despite acceptance of the importance of learning about culture, second language teachers continue to push an exploration of culture to the periphery of their classroom pedagogies, relegated perhaps to a Friday afternoon or end-of-unit activity rather than centrally located as the core of instruction. Two explanations may account for this second-class status accorded to understanding culture. First, teachers feel inadequate in their knowledge of the foreign culture. Second, teachers may not have been adequately trained in the teaching of culture. They are familiar with a variety of culture-teaching strategies, such as culture capsules, culture clusters, cultural assimilators, and cultural mini-dramas, but they do not know how to integrate the strategies into a systematic study of culture or how to integrate culture study with language learning (Crawford-Lange & Lange, 1984).

Accepting the role of teacher as co-investigator of cultures constantly under construction by groups of people located in a multiplicity of power bases and rejecting the role of teacher as cultural expert dispensing finished descriptors of a closed cultural field yields relief and freedom for those educators open to the voices of their students.

The second language educator who adopts the stance of critical pedagogy also adopts a behavior not always rewarded for North American teachers, listening: listening to the students reveal their perceptions of native and target cultural entities; listening to students identify the meanings they wish to communicate and providing linguistic tools on that basis rather than on the basis of predefined syllabi; listening to students naming their own world rather than adult, white, middle-class educators naming their world for them. By truly listening, teachers become challenged. In whose name is the curriculum constructed? Whose culture is represented? Who is included? Excluded? Why are second languages and cultures included in the curriculum? Who subscribes to them? Who avoids them and why?

Answering such questions humbles the teacher and unites both teacher and students in active educational and social transformation, in the production of culture and history. Answering them acknowledges that knowledge and learning is not disseminated and received but engaged in, created, struggled over, and contested. The power educators believe they own is a mythological, arrogant nonentity when placed in relief against the dignity of all people making their own society, culture, world.

In summary, this paper has reconceptualized culture as a postmodern construct in a postcolonialist context. Examination of culture in relation to discourse, plurivocalism, tradition, resistance, individual subjectivity, discourse of the other, and the discourse of liberation has yielded insights of importance to educators in general. In particular, culture reconceived along each of the dimensions listed above has been examined in terms of second languages and cultures education. The postmodern world can no longer accept education as we have known it; postmodern educators need to adapt, grow, and change, coming to terms with culture and history.The domain of second language education, reconceived as integrated language and culture education, is ripe for the transformation.

REFERENCES

Arendt, J.D., Lange, D.L., & Wakefield, R. (1986). Strengthening the language requirement at the University of Minnesota: An initial report. *Foreign Language Annals, 19,* 149–156.

Aronowitz, S., & Giroux, H.A. (1985). *Education under siege: The conservative liberal and radical debate over schooling.* So. Hadley, MA: Bergin & Garvey.

Aronowitz, S., & Giroux, H.A. (1991). *Postmodern education: Politics, culture, and social criticism.* Minneapolis: University of Minnesota Press.

Barthes, R. (1973). *Mythologies.* (A. Lauers, Trans.). London: Granada.

Bloom, A. (1987). *The closing of the American mind.* New York: Simon and Schuster.

Brooks, N. (1964). *Language and language learning: Theory and practice* (2nd ed.). New York: Harcourt, Brace & World.

Brooks, N. (1968). Teaching culture in the foreign language classroom. *Foreign Language Annals, 1,* 204–217.

Cherryholmes, C.H. (1988). *Power and criticism: Poststructural investigations in education.* New York: Teachers College Press.

Chock, P., & Wyman, J.R. (1986). Introduction: Discourse and the social life of meaning. In P. Chock & J.R. Wyman (Eds.), *Discourse and the social life of meaning* (pp. 1–20). Washington, DC: Smithsonian Institution Press.

Clifford, J., & Marcus, G. (1986). *Writing culture: The poetics and politics of ethnography.* Berkeley: University of California Press.

Collins, J. (1989). *Uncommon cultures.* London: Routledge & Kegan Paul.

Connor, S. (1989). *Postmodern culture.* Oxford: Basil Blackwell.

Cottom, D. (1989). *Text and culture.* Minneapolis: University of Minnesota Press.

Crawford, L.M. (1979). Paulo Freire's philosophy: Derivation of curricular principles and their application to second language curriculum design. *Dissertation Abstracts International, 39,* 7130A.

Crawford-Lange, L.M. (1981). Redirecting second language curricula: Paulo Freire's contribution. *Foreign Language Annals, 14,* 257–268.

Crawford-Lange, L.M. (1985). Foreign language enrollments: Why are they declining? What can be done? *NAACP Bulletin, 69* (478), 14–21.

Crawford-Lange, L.M., & Lange, D.L. (1984). Doing the unthinkable in the second-language classroom: A process for the integration of language and culture. In T.V. Higgs (Ed.), *Teaching for proficiency, the organizing principle* (pp. 139–177). The ACTFL Foreign Language Education Series. Lincolnwood, IL: National Textbook.

Crawford-Lange, L.M., & Lange, D.L. (1987). Integrating language and culture: How to do it. *Theory into Practice, 26,* 258–266.

Culler, J. (1984). *On deconstruction: Theory and criticism after structuralism.* Ithaca, NY: Cornell University Press.

Damen, L. (1987). *Culture learning: The fifth dimension in the language classroom.* Reading, MA: Addison-Wesley.

Freire, P. (1970). *Pedagogy of the oppressed.* (M.B. Ramos, Trans.). New York: The Seabury Press.

Freire, P., & Shor, I. (1987). *A pedagogy for liberation: Dialogues on transforming education.* So. Hadley, MA: Bergin & Garvey.

Frow, J. (1986). *Marxism and literary history.* Cambridge, MA: Harvard University Press.

Giroux, H.A. (1983). *Theory & resistance in education: A pedagogy for the opposition.* London: Heinemann Education Books.

Giroux, H.A. (1988). *Schooling and the struggle for public life.* Minneapolis: University of Minnesota Press.

Giroux, H.A. (Ed). (1990). *Postmodernism, feminism and cultural politics*. Albany: SUNY Press.

Giroux, H.A., & McLaren, P. (Eds.). (1989). *Critical pedagogy, the state, and cultural struggle*. Albany: SUNY Press.

Gordon, C. (Ed.). (1980). *Power/knowledge: Selected interviews and other writings*. New York: Pantheon.

Gramsci, A. (1971). *Selections from the prison notebooks*. (Q. Hoare, & G.M. Smith, Eds. and Trans.). New York: International Publishers.

Grossberg, L. (1988). The formations of cultural studies: An American in Birmingham. *Strategies, 2,* 114–146.

Grossberg, L. (1992). *We've got to get out of this place: Popular conservatism and postmodern culture*. London: Routledge.

Hirsch, E.D., Jr. (1987). *Cultural literacy: What every American needs to know*. Boston: Houghton Mifflin.

Jorstad, H.L. (1981). Inservice teacher education: Content and process. In D.L. Lange & C. Linder (Eds.), *Proceedings of the national conference on professional priorities* (pp. 81–85). Hastings-on-Hudson, NY: ACTFL Materials Center.

Kaplan, E.A. (1987). *Rocking around the clock: Music television, postmodernism, and consumer culture*. New York: Methuen.

Kramsch, C. (1988). The cultural discourse of foreign language textbooks. In A.J. Singerman (Ed.), *Toward a new integration of language and culture* (pp. 63–88). Northeast Conference Reports. Middlebury, VT: Northeast Conference on Teaching of Foreign Languages.

Laclau, E. (1990). *New reflections on the revolution of our time*. London: Verso.

Lange, D.L. (1979). Suggestions for the continuing development of pre- and in-service programs for teachers of second languages. In J.G. Arendt, D.L. Lange, & P.J. Myers (Eds.), *Foreign language learning, today and tomorrow: Essays in honor of Emma M. Birkmaier* (pp. 169–192). New York: Pergamon Press.

Lange, D.L. (1987). Developing and implementing proficiency oriented tests for a new language requirement at the University of Minnesota: Issues and problems for implementing the ACTFL/ETS/ILR proficiency guidelines. In A.Valdman (Ed.), *Proceedings of the symposium on the evaluation of foreign language proficiency* (pp. 275–290). Bloomington: Indiana University Press.

Lankshear, C. (1987). *Literacy schooling and revolution*. Philadelphia: Falmer Press.

Lankshear, C., & McLaren, P. (Eds.). (1993). *Critical literacy: Radical and postmodernist perspectives*. Albany: SUNY Press.

Livingstone, D.W. (1987). Introduction. In D.W. Livingstone & Contributors, *Critical pedagogy & cultural power* (pp. 1–12). So. Hadley, MA: Bergin & Garvey.

McLaren, P. (1987). Postmodernity and the death of politics: A Brazilian reprieve. *Educational Theory, 36,* 389–401.

McLaren, P. (1988). Culture or canon: Critical pedagogy and the politics of literacy. *Harvard Educational Review, 58,* 213–234.

McLaren, P. (1989). *Life in schools*. New York: Longman.

McLaren, P. (1990). Schooling the postmodern body. In H.A. Giroux (Ed.), *Postmodernism, feminism and cultural politics* (pp. 144–173). Albany: SUNY Press.

McLaren, P. (1995b). *Critical pedagogy and predatory culture: Oppositional politics in a postmodern era*. London: Routledge.

McLaren, P. (Ed.). (1995a). *Postmodernism, postcolonialism, and pedagogy.* Albert Park, Australia: James Nicholas Publishers.

McLaren, P., & Leonard, P. (Eds.) (forthcoming). *Paulo Freire: A critical encounter.* London: Routledge & Kegan Paul.

Nostrand, H.L. (Ed.). (1967). *Background data for the teaching of French.* Seattle: University of Washington Press.

Nostrand, H.L. (1974). Empathy for a second culture: Motivations and techniques. In G.A. Jarvis (Ed.), *Responding to new realities* (pp. 263–327). The ACTFL Foreign Language Education Series. Lincolnwood, IL: National Textbook.

Oakes, J. (1985). *Keeping Track: How schools structure inequality.* New Haven: Yale University Press.

Quantz, R. (1989, November). *Culture: A critical perspective.* Paper presented at the American Educational Studies Association, Toronto, Canada.

Ravitch, D. (1985). *The schools we deserve: Reflections on the educational crises of our time.* New York: Basic Books.

Rosaldo, R. (1989). *Culture and truth: The remaking of social analysis.* Boston: Beacon Press.

Ryan, M. (1989). *Politics and culture: Working hypotheses for a post-revolutionary society.* Baltimore: Johns Hopkins University Press.

Seelye, H.N. (1984). *Teaching culture: Strategies for intercultural communication.* Lincolnwood, IL: National Textbook.

Singerman, A.J. (Ed.). (1988). *Toward a new integration of language and culture.* Northeast Conference Reports. Middlebury, VT: Northeast Conference on the Teaching of Foreign Languages.

Weedon, C. (1987). *Feminist practice and poststructuralist theory.* London: Basil Blackwell.

Weiler, K. (1988). *Women teaching for change: Gender, class & power.* New York: Bergin & Garvey.

Young, I.M. (1990). *Justice and the politics of difference.* Princeton, NJ: Princeton University Press.

Part II

CULTURE AS THE CORE:
INTEGRATION CULTURE IN THE
SECOND LANGUAGE CURRICULUM

CHAPTER 8

NATIONAL STANDARDS FOR FOREIGN LANGUAGE LEARNING

Culture, the Driving Force

June K. Phillips

INTRODUCTION

By doing the video and the research we did find out about different cultures and how and why people immigrated, the culture down there that causes them to immigrate. We learned what their connection with us was through immigration, and why they wanted to come here. And we also learned the similarities and differences between the two cultures. —9th grade, Spanish III student, Frederick, MD. (Schwartz & Kavanaugh, 1997, p. 125)

The insights expressed by the student quoted above did not arise, never would have arisen, from studying culture in the capsule form or as boxed in notes in a textbook. The perspectives gained by this student after a three-week video-based unit on Guatemalan immigration demonstrate a

Culture as the Core: Perspectives in Second Language Education, pages 161–171
Copyright © 2003 by Information Age Publishing

thoughtfulness and a reflectiveness that goes deeper than adolescent language reveals. The comments were certainly rewarding to the collaborators, a university professor and a high school teacher, who had undertaken the challenge to develop a unit premised on the cultural framework proposed in the foreign language standards (National Standards, 1996). That framework emphasizes the interactions between products and practices of cultures with the perspectives that render cultures distinct.

The Minnesota Culture Conferences were taking place during the time that the Standards Task Force was gathering information from the research and comments from the profession. It is not accidental that the framework in the National Standards document (1996) resonates with similar interdisciplinary thinking, especially from the social sciences, and intercultural connections, for those represent the direction and central focus that place culture learning at the forefront of language instruction.

AN EVOLUTION TOWARD STANDARDS

Historically, culture has played a number of roles in second language classrooms, but it has never dominated in terms of methodology or approach. It has been appended to the language learning modalities, as in *four skills and culture*. It has even been pulled in slightly more to the center referred to by some as a fifth skill. At the upper division in colleges and universities, a culture or culture/civilization course has usually been a part of the sequence for majors/minors; frequently, it has been geared to coverage of history and fine arts as a background necessary for courses in literature. In terms of content, an emphasis on either the patterns of life or civilization have been reflected through designations such as little *c* and big *C* culture. The inadequacy of this division meant that instruction in little *c* topics often became trivialized or over generalized in ways that perpetuated stereotypes, while the big *C* remained on the level of facts, such as names, places, and historical periods. Neither a cultural dichotomy, nor culture as an aside had ever been the intent of those who spoke most eloquently for culture as an essential component of second language learning. Brooks (1968) argued for an anthropological orientation that focused on the interaction of social patterns with the individual, but his vision of overlapping spheres of formal and deep culture gave way to the temptation of classroom practice to categorize the pieces and lose the tableau. Allen's (1985) excellent review of the many models for teaching culture in classrooms captures the theoretical premises of several models and the solid analysis that formed the basis for instructional materials. Unfortunately, over the years, little of this information seems to have filtered to the level of classroom practice or materials.

Will the influence of the national standards and the commitment to culture contained therein change this situation? That remains unknown, but we do have an opportunity to once more impart the message of Hall (1973) that *culture is communication* (p. 97) and Fantini's (1997) addendum that *communication is culture.* (p. 3). The Standards Task Force intended from the beginning of the project to expand the cultural experiences in which learners would engage, but it was the completed publication and subsequent classroom applications that demonstrated that culture had indeed become the driving force of the standards. Culture ended up permeating every goal area. As noted by Lange (Lange & Wieczorek, 1997), when commenting upon a series of classroom case studies, "the focus of the projects is always on the interaction of the learner with some aspect of culture. I would say that the projects stay away from the dichotomy of large *C* and small *c* culture. I think that is a plus because it's really culture that is important and the broad array of elements which that includes . . . all the projects are working toward the same basic goal, which is culture undivided into traditional categories of large and small" (p. 245). The standards, then, do not propose anything radically new in terms of culture; they do attempt to refocus teachers' attention upon culture as the core so that it may become the central outcome of student learning, long espoused but seldom achieved.

THE CULTURAL FRAMEWORK IN THE STANDARDS

The dominant role of culture in the standards can be seen by the multiple ways in which it is incorporated in sections of the document; two of these strands are explicit and one is implicit: Culture is one of the Five Cs along with Communication, Connections, Comparisons, and Communities. The Culture goal area generates two standards, but a culture standard is also one of the Comparisons that learners are encouraged to make. Culture as content is identified as part of the curricular weave that supports learning in all the goal areas (National Standards, p. 29). Furthermore, as classroom applications of standards are being developed, it becomes apparent that culture forms the context in which all the other goal areas play out. What is communication in a second language if it does not reflect in language and in social behaviors the culture in which discourse occurs? As interdisciplinary connections are forged, the perspectives of the target cultures are conveyed through the focus of the disciplines. Using language in communities at home and abroad requires attention to and further learning about the society of action. In every way, culture becomes integrated with and integral to language learning.

CULTURE AS GOAL AREA AND STANDARDS

Visually the goals are portrayed as interlocking circles to illustrate their interdependence and an absence of hierarchical relationship (see Figure 1). Specific standards are derived for each goal area, so that instruction and assessment can focus on one area even as the dynamic of learning tasks and of the learning environment encourages various elements to be integrated.

The full rubric for the Culture Goal states that students "will gain knowledge and understandings of other cultures." The two standards for Culture are:

- Students demonstrate an understanding of the relationship between the practices and perspectives of the cultures studied;
- Students demonstrate an understanding of the relationship between the products and perspectives of the cultures studied.

Understanding perspectives, that is the meanings, attitudes, values, and ideas of cultures studied, is the ultimate goal for learners of the world's

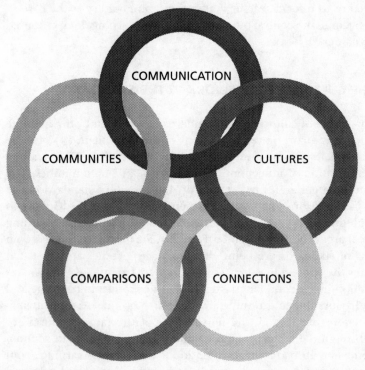

Figure 8.1.   The five c's of foreign language education (*National Standards*, 1996, p. 28).

languages. Perspectives are the common thread in the two standards that fashion the culture goal. The profession recognizes that for both pragmatic and humanistic reasons the standards needed to feature prominently the study of many diverse cultures. Many members of the business and government community who support the study of other languages and cultures do so out of a desire for students to become citizens who can live and work in a world with fewer cultural misunderstandings. Likewise in the academic community, those who place priority on culture for humanistic, aesthetic, or personal development reasons find the framework to be an effective organizer. At the same time, the task force had to attend to the philosophical and political turmoil currently surrounding cross-cultural issues in U.S. education. Strident voices from various educational watchdog groups stood ready to attack any intrusion of values (at least those of others) into the curriculum. The decision was taken to set standards that challenged students to understand the perspectives that generated practices and products and the transmutation the latter has on the former. This decision should result in in-depth and meaningful study without necessarily promoting the endorsement or assimilation of those values by students. (Figure 2 illustrates the interaction among perspectives, practices, and products.)

In reality, an observation of a cultural phenomenon usually merges all three elements of the triangle. For classroom purposes, it is thought that practices and products are distinctive enough to enable a curricular focus and analytical observations by students of all ages. Yet, in order to understand the whole, students and teachers are encouraged to think triangularly and let the angles interact. As the standards become more widespread in practice, it will be important to monitor whether these divisions create the categorizations common in the past or whether the gestalt holds.

The standards framework avoids adopting any one model for culture learning to the exclusion of others. The construct behind the labels does

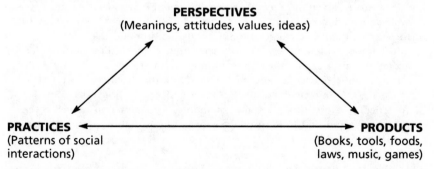

Figure 8.2.   Interaction among perspectives, practices, and products (*National Standards*, 1996, p. 43).

seem to be compatible with a great many contemporary theories or models, most of which share a basis in anthropology or social sciences. For example, Fantini and Fantini (1997) in their work in cross-cultural training propose a model that has students look at artifacts (things people make), sociofacts (how people come together and for what purpose), and mentifacts (what people think or believe). At one time, the American Council on the Teaching of Foreign Languages (1983) attempted to include culture guidelines with its proficiency guidelines, but soon acknowledged that culture did not fit the hierarchical model of the skills. Allen (1985) and Lafayette (1988) both provide extensive illustration of how the profession has sought to accommodate the learning of culture into various models that often mixed information about the culture with approaches to student learning. The standards task force built upon extant research and instructional models, but looked at culture (and the other goal areas) through the prism of student performances. Now that the Minnesota Culture Conferences have gathered together a number of models and processes based upon current research, it will be informative to align those with the standards framework to assess the degrees of compatibility.

THE INTERACTION OF PERSPECTIVES, PRODUCTS, AND PRACTICES

For many years, teachers have used artifacts from target cultures so that students might see, touch, or experiment with a product. Increased availability of video and authentic text permits learners to observe behaviors and, more important, to investigate whether conclusions drawn from their observations are idiosyncratic or generalizable to a culture.

An example of perspectives, practices, and products drawn from the standards document illustrates the interaction:

> ... in some Asian cultures members are positioned (a perspective) on a hierarchical scale based on age, social status, education, or similar variables. In those cultures, the exchange of business cards (a product) that provides key information is a helpful practice. Because these cards facilitate social interaction and are treated with respect in those cultures, one should not scribble another name or telephone number on the business card (taboo practice). The information on the card also affects the nonverbal behavior (practice) of those involved in the communicative interaction, as well as the choice of linguistic forms (products) that indicate status. (National Standards, 1996, p. 46)

Under this paradigm, students of language/culture acquire insights from a larger context, which allow them to see the complexity inherent in all peoples. The hope is that they realize few absolutes exist, that they must often suspend judgments and seek expanded observations. To accomplish this hope, teachers, textbook writers, seminar leaders on cultural topics are urged to explore the construct to determine its effectiveness. As one peruses the literature, it is not unusual to see a match with the standards framework even though the author had not so intended. Nostrand (1996) describes how a film (product), based upon a piece of literature (product), was used in a beginning college class to develop student awareness of some of the values held in French culture (perspectives). The film/literary text was Marcel Pagnol's *Le château de ma mère* which students watched with sub-titles. Nostrand describes scenes from the film that permitted students to observe products and practices as they discussed with the instructor the perspectives represented. For example, a dinner table scene illustrated the elegant presentation of dishes (products) in a preordained succession (practice). The family conversation around the dinner table and the obvious intimacy of the discussion evoked student insights into the line that separates *la famille et les amis* from *les autres* (p. 23). Even as this chapter is being written, summer institutes and workshops are providing teachers with opportunities to design lessons around the standards framework and to assess units they have done in terms of the model.

CULTURE AS CONTENT IN THE CURRICULAR WEAVE

The standards task force was charged with creating content standards and was responsive to the question: What should students know and be able to do? The *doing* is specified in the standards themselves, whereas the *knowing* is delineated as the myriad curricular experiences in which learners are involved. The interaction between *knowing* and *doing* is illustrated in the standards document as a weave where curricular elements support all the standards (National Standards, p. 29). The strands represented are not finite nor are they parallel; they include content and process. For example, subject matter includes the language system, cultural content, and a vast array of content from other disciplines of interest or import to learners. Processes such as communication strategies, critical thinking skills, learning strategies become vital for successful language learning as students are challenged to work with authentic text, to engage in interpersonal communication with peers, and to surf the Web for information on topics of interest. One element of the weave, technology, addresses the importance of student control over delivery systems and resources that bring language and culture to today's learners.

In this weave, cultural content forms part of the knowledge base for virtually all the standards, not just the cultural ones discussed above. This configuration is what infuses a standards-driven curriculum with culture so that it can never again be treated as an aside. The Communication standards are divided into modes of interpersonal, interpretive, and presentational communication. In the Framework of Communicative Modes, the underlying cultural knowledge is explicated for each of these categories (National Standards, 1996, p. 33). Interpersonal communication is predicated upon the capacity for direct negotiation of meaning to take place between interlocutors. The interpersonal standard requires that students demonstrate in the negotiation "knowledge of cultural perspectives governing interactions between individuals of different ages, statuses, and backgrounds." The framework also calls for learners to develop the "ability to recognize that languages use different practices to communicate" and the "ability to recognize that cultures use different patterns of communication." Experts in specific languages/cultures will need to help teachers acquire that knowledge initially and continue to update themselves as practices and patterns change. By focusing on traditions, conventional approaches to culture frequently failed to track changes occurring in all modern societies. A basic example that impacts interpersonal communication might be the rules governing formal and informal second person pronouns in many European languages. Today's students, negotiating meaning on the Internet with peers, quickly discover that textbook conventions do not necessarily hold true, nor do the societal rules that their teachers experienced in other times and places.

The Interpretive standard requires students to show their "knowledge of how cultural perspectives are embedded in products (literary and artistic), knowledge of how meaning is encoded in products." Learners must also develop the "ability to analyze content, compare it to information available in [one's] own language and assess linguistic and cultural differences" and the "ability to analyze and compare content in one culture to interpret U.S. culture." Within the interpretive mode, the listener/reader/viewer, unable to negotiate meaning with the creator of the text, achieves success by processing language, visual cues, intonation, background knowledge, and the like. The deeper the understanding of the cultural context, the greater the understanding of the total discourse! For example, in a French class taught by the author in spring 1996, students were working with a continuing news feature on *Antenne 2* (via SCOLA). Daily stories were broadcast about immigrants in France and the effect of new laws on those *sans papiers*. The words in the journalistic report were comprehended on a literal level, but students discovered quickly that a lack of adequate background information prevented their fully digesting what was happening. They undertook further research in the language to discern the roots of the problem in former French colonialism, to identify the reasons immigrants had come to France, and to reflect upon concepts of assimilation from the perspective of the newly arrived and the French. They also found themselves reconsidering their own views on immigration and paying more attention to political discussion and social ramifications of current U.S. immigration policy (Cultural Comparisons standard). As they progressed toward competency in the interpretive mode, they were acquiring new cultural perspectives from observations and knowledge of current and past practices and products (new laws).

The Presentational standard describes the "knowledge of cultural perspectives governing interactions between a speaker and his/her audience and a writer and his/her reader" inherent in this mode. Additionally, students should develop the "ability to present cross-cultural information based on background of the audience" and the "ability to recognize that cultures use different patterns of interaction." Concepts from first language instruction, such as a process approach to writing, when adapted for second languages, can be powerful tools toward achieving this standard. The focus on audience requires attending to cultural expectations and norms for oral and written presentations. The language of an e-mail message or of an interpersonal dialogue, for example, would be inappropriate for a more formal situation. Those differences go well beyond the communicative tasks, or functions, common to today's curriculum, even that based upon a communicative approach. For example, the function of "complaining about a product" is a familiar task in textbooks. Under the standards communicative framework, that could be played out under the interpersonal standard as among acquaintances in a relatively neutral cultural stance. The student might complain through an e-mail exchange about a CD program recently purchased from an international vendor. The interchange may entail minimal cultural references. As the student is encouraged to document that complaint to the vendor with a request for reimbursement or exchange, then appropriate protocols for formal letters (a tilt toward the presentational standard) become prominent. The student writer will need information about exchange policies in the target country. An additional presentational performance might be a newsletter or magazine article that critiques the product, a task that would require attention to the target audience and its culture, as well as explaining the cultural context of the complainant's world. Thus, a common function plays out quite differently depending upon the communicative mode required; one of the parameters will be cultural contexts and practices (All of the preceding quotes are from National Standards, 1996, p. 33.).

The cultural weave is a strong strand throughout the standards in the areas of Connections, Comparisons, and Communities. One of the two Connections standards describes a unique outcome of the study of world languages and cultures:

- Students acquire information and recognize the distinctive view-points that are only available through the foreign language and its cultures (Standard 3.2, p. 52).

This standard underscores the cultural insights gained only through the study of a culture's language and constitutes a powerful reason for second-language study.

The Comparisons goal looks at how students "develop insight into the nature of language and culture." Many of our students have little idea about aspects of their lives definitive of their own culture. As they discern the perspectives of others through study of practices and products, insights into their own culture should spring up along with a broader and more generic view of *culture* as a concept. In the view of many, the Communities goal comprises the ultimate basis for and is the culmination of all experiences in the study of another language. When our students are asked to "Participate in multilingual communities at home and around the world," that is the conclusive test of their linguistic and cultural achievements.

CULTURE-DRIVEN CURRICULA

Should, could, would culture drive the curriculum in an environment where standards act as a powerful directional force for learning the world's languages? Early indications are that as content and as goal, culture increasingly dominates standards implementation. Of the thirty-four learning scenarios in National Standards (1996), twenty-two target directly a *culture* standard. In the collaborative case studies in the 1997 *Northeast Conference Reports* (Phillips, 1997), each focused most directly on a different goal area, yet the cultural message was the most vibrant one sent from each classroom. If there is an impediment to a culture-driven curriculum, it might be the unease with which teachers confront culture, for their own experiential and knowledge base may be least firmly rooted there. A stated goal of teaching culture in the standards is that students have "opportunities for many different kinds of interaction with members of other cultures, so that students draw informed conclusions and develop sensitivity to the perspectives, practices, and products of others" (p. 45). This goal means that teachers have to do it right in order not to perpetuate the stereotypes. They have to be lifelong learners themselves; they have to have confidence that it is not essential that they have all the answers but that they know how to investigate the issues with their students, how to observe cultures, how to analyze them, and how to suspend judgments until the insights can be confirmed. An important charge lies ahead for teacher educators, for faculty with expertise in language, literature, and cultural studies, as well as for material developers, to assist teachers and learners in using an effective framework for the acquisition of cultural knowledge and the understandings that accompany it.

REFERENCES

Allen, W.W. (1985). Toward cultural proficiency. In A.C. Omaggio (Ed.), *Proficiency curriculum, articulation: The ties that bind* (pp. 137–166). Northeast Conference Reports. Middlebury, VT: Northeast Conference.

American Council on the Teaching of Foreign Languages. (1983). *ACTFL provisional proficiency guidelines.* Hastings-on-Hudson, NY: Author.

Brooks, N. (1968). Teaching culture in the foreign language classroom. *Foreign Language Annals, 1*, 204–217.

Fantini, A.E. (1997). Language: Its cultural and intercultural dimension. In A.E. Fantini (Ed), *New ways in teaching culture* (pp. 3–15). Arlington, VA: TESOL.

Fantini, B.C. de, & Fantini, A.E. (1997). Artifacts, sociofacts and mentifacts: A sociocultural framework. In A.E. Fantini (Ed.), *New ways in teaching culture* (pp. 57–61). Arlington, VA: TESOL.

Hall, E.T. (1973). *The silent language.* New York: Doubleday.

Lafayettte, R.C. (1988). Integrating the teaching of culture into the foreign language classroom. In A.J. Singerman (Ed.), *Toward a new integration of language and culture* (pp. 47–62). Northeast Conference Reports. Middlebury, VT: Northeast Conference.

Lange, D.L., & Wieczorek, J. (1997). Reflections on the collaborative projects: Two perspectives, two professionals. In J.K. Phillips (Ed.), *Collaborations: Meeting New Goals, New Realities* (pp. 97–139). Northeast Conference Reports. Lincolnwood, IL: National Textbook Company.

National Standards in Foreign Language Education Project. *Standards for foreign language learning: Preparing for the 21st Century.* (1996). Yonkers, NY: National Standards Project.

Nostrand, H.L. (1996). How to discover a culture in its literature. *Foreign Language Annals, 29*, 19–26.

Phillips, J.K. (Ed.). (1997). *Collaborations: Meeting new goals, new realities.* Northeast Conference Reports. Lincolnwood, IL: National Textbook Company.

Schwartz, A.M., & Kavanaugh, M.S. (1997). Addressing the culture goal with authentic video. In J.K. Phillips (Ed.), *Collaborations: Meeting new goals, new realities* (pp. 97–139). Northeast Conference Reports. Lincolnwood, IL: National Textbook Company.

CHAPTER 9

CULTURE LEARNING IN LANGUAGE EDUCATION

A Review of the Literature

R. Michael Paige, Helen L. Jorstad (Emerita), Laura Siaya,
Francine Klein, and Jeanette Colby

INTRODUCTION

This paper examines the theoretical and research literatures pertaining to culture learning in language education programs. The topic of teaching and learning culture has been a matter of considerable interest to language educators and much has been written about the role of culture in foreign language instruction over the past four decades. For insightful analyses see Morain (1983), Grittner (1990), Bragaw (1991), Moore (1991), and Byram and Morgan (1994). Most important, in recent years various professional associations have made significant efforts to establish culture-learning standards (*Standards*, 1996; AATF, 1995). Yet, to date, there have been few critical reviews of the literature. In certain respects this is not surprising because culture learning is not exclusively the domain of language educators. On the contrary, the field is highly interdisciplinary in nature; contributions to the knowledge base have come from psychology, linguistics, anthropology, education, intercultural communication, and elsewhere. Moreover, anthropologists, intercultural communication scholars, and psychologists, in particular, have studied cultural phenomena quite apart from their relationship to language learning. The review confirmed what we expected: a substantial amount of important writing on culture learning exists, much of which is completely unrelated to language education.

The rationale for conducting this review of the literature was to determine if studies existed which could:

1. Support and/or challenge current language education practices regarding the teaching of culture;
2. Provide guidance to language educators on effective culture teaching methods;
3. Suggest ways to conceptualize culture in the language education context;
4. Suggest ways to assess culture learning; and,
5. Indicate which instructional methods are most effective for various types of culture learning objectives.

We have organized this article into six sections pertaining to the major topics we discovered in the theoretical and research literatures. These include:

1. Research and theory on the setting;
2. Research and theory on teacher variables;
3. Research and theory on learner variables;
4. Research and theory on instructional methods;
5. Research and theory on curricular materials (e.g., textbooks); and,
6. Research and theory on measuring and assessing culture learning.

We begin the paper by providing a brief history of the Intercultural Studies Project and follow that with a discussion of the philosophical and conceptual frames of reference that informed our literature review. We then present an overarching conceptual structure based on the multifaceted concept of *context*. At that point, we enter into the discussion of our literature review in these six aforementioned areas.

HISTORY OF THE PROJECT

The staff of the Intercultural Studies Project (ISP) undertook this study, which is one of several projects operated by the Center for Advanced

Research in Language Acquisition (CARLA). In part, CARLA is funded by the U.S. Department of Education and is located at the University of Minnesota, Twin Cities campus. The five-person ISP team included Professors Helen Jorstad and R. Michael Paige (co-principal investigators); Laura Siaya (senior research associate), Francine Klein, and Jeanette Colby (research associates). The central purpose of the ISP has been to advance culture teaching in the language education profession. At its first conference held in November 1994, language and culture education scholars met with language teachers to discuss the major issues regarding culture teaching and learning. The conferees agreed that there were significant gaps in the literature that should be addressed in future writings and conferences. This confirmed the intention of the ISP to convene a second conference in 1996 and to commission the writing of three complementary state-of-the-art papers on culture learning to be discussed at that conference and then published. The papers included: (1) a review of the literature on culture learning, (2) a theoretical work conceptualizing culture learning, and (3) an applied paper presenting the implications of theory and research for culture teaching. This is the first of the three papers.

Work on the literature review began in 1994 with the identification of relevant databases and the conducting of initial searches. The process was exceptionally time consuming as we had to search a large number of databases and constantly cross-reference them for duplications of citations. The initial literature search generated more than 3000 citations. Eventually, we narrowed it down to 1228 citations, primarily journal articles, and reviewed the abstract for each of those references. The first determination to be made was whether the reference was relevant or not for our purposes based on the information provided in the abstract. As it turned out, many were not. The use of the term *culture* as a descriptor had generated many citations where the discussion of culture was far removed from our concerns. Eventually, 289 references were placed into one of three categories: application (descriptions of teaching methods and materials), theory (conceptualizations of culture teaching and learning), and research (empirical studies). The final count from that search included 158 application, 66 theory, and 65 research references.

In September 1995, the team began the process of reading and analyzing the literature. The research articles, for instance, were read by two of the team members and their observations were recorded on a data sheet, which included the following information: the research focus; the research orientation (primarily qualitative or quantitative); methodology (the specific research methods utilized for data gathering and data analysis, the subjects/respondents); the language education setting/context; how culture was defined; the major results and their implications for language pedagogy. The theoretical pieces were shared among the team members and reviewed for the central concepts and propositions regarding culture learning.

THEORETICAL FRAMEWORK FOR CULTURE TEACHING AND LEARNING

At the outset of this paper, we want the reader to note that we brought our own understandings of culture, culture teaching, and culture learning to this task. Our views have been strongly influenced by the writings of Jorstad (1981), Seelye (1981, 1994), Crawford-Lange and Lange (1984), Byram (1988), and Kramsch (1993), all of whom have proposed models for integrating culture and language teaching. These works share a common conceptual core and set of intricately related assumptions regarding the teaching and learning of culture. Due to the fact that our model of culture learning served as the benchmark for evaluating the literature, we feel it is essential to present it to the reader.

A Conceptual Model of Culture Learning

Earlier models (Brooks, 1975; Nostrand, 1974) tended to view culture as a relatively invariate and static entity made up of accumulated, classifiable, observable, thus eminently teachable and learnable *facts*. This perspective focused on surface level behavior, but did not look at the underlying value orientations, nor did it recognize the variability of behavior within the target cultural community, the participative role of the individual in the creation of culture, or the interaction of language and culture in the making of meaning (Moore, 1991). By contrast, the more recent models mentioned above see culture as dynamic and variable, i.e., it is constantly changing; its members display a great range of behaviors and different levels of attention to the guiding value orientations; and, meaning is continuously being constructed through human interaction and communication. This major transformation in perspective has also been characterized by conceptual shifts from culture-specific to culture-general models of intercultural competence, cultural stereotypes to cultural generalizations, cultural absolutes to cultural variations (within and across cultures), and culture as distinct from language to culture as integral to language. Language in this process plays a fascinating and complex double role: it is a medium for as well as shaper of culture.

Definition of culture learning.   For the purposes of this chapter, our general definition of culture learning is as follows:

Culture learning is the process of acquiring the culture-specific and culture-general knowledge, skills, and attitudes required for effective communication and interaction with individuals from other cultures. It is a dynamic, developmental, and ongoing process which engages the learner cognitively, behaviorally, and affectively.

Culture learning goals and outcomes.   In this newer perspective, the learning goals shift from the memorization of cultural facts (including sociolinguistic conventions for language use) to higher order learning outcomes including: the acquisition of *interactional competence* (a term suggested by Allen and Moore at the 1996 culture conference in Minneapolis) and learning how to learn about culture. According to Paige (1997), such learning would include:

1. Learning about the self as a cultural being;
2. Learning about culture and its impact on human communication, behavior, and identity;
3. Culture-general learning, i.e., learning about universal, cross-cultural phenomena such as cultural adjustment;
4. Culture-specific learning, i.e., learning about a particular culture, including its language; and,
5. Learning how to learn, i.e., becoming an effective language and culture learner.

Item five in our model is a point which we feel deserves special mention, in part because it is often overlooked and also because we consider it to be extremely important. Culture and language learning involve a dynamic relationship between the situation and the actors in which cultural context, prior experience, and other factors come into play (Street, 1993). Putting culture at the core of language education means preparing students to be culture learners. Thus, it is never enough to find and accept someone else's static definitions of the culture. Words and their meaning are linked to a cultural context, and language and cultural patterns change over time and vary according to the situation. To become effective culture learners, students must develop a variety of learning strategies ranging from reflective observation to active experimentation or what Kolb (1984) refers to as *experiential learning* style. Most importantly it is knowing how to learn from the context while immersed in it, or what Hughes (1986) refers to as *learning how to learn.*

These culture-general learning outcomes do not replace culture-specific learning objectives, but they constitute the larger learning framework within which target culture learning occurs.

Conceptual model of culture learning.   Figure 9.1 presents our more detailed model of culture learning. One of the major conceptual distinctions to be noted is between what is commonly referred to as the culture-specific versus culture-general domains of learning. Culture-specific learning refers to the acquisition of knowledge and skills relevant to a given *target culture,* i.e., a particular culture group or community. Culture-general learning, on the other hand, refers to knowledge and skills that are more generalizable in nature and transferable across cultures. This body of knowledge includes, among other things, the concept of culture, the nature of cultural adjustment and learning, the impact of culture on communication and interaction between individuals or groups, the stress associated with intense culture and language immersions (culture and language fatigue), coping

A. Knowledge
   1. Culture-General: Intercultural Phenomena
      cultural adjustment stages
      culture shock
      intercultural development
      culture learning
      cultural identity
      cultural marginality

   2. Culture Specific
      "little c" target culture knowledge
      "Big C" target culture knowledge
      pragmatics
      sociolinguistic competence

B. Behavior
   1. Culture General: Intercultural Skills
      culture learning strategies
      coping and stress management strategies
      intercultural communicative competence
      intercultural perspective-taking skills
      cultural adaptability
      transcultural competence

   2. Culture Specific: Target Culture Skills
      "little c" culture—appropriate everyday behavior
      "Big C" culture—appropriate contextual behavior

C. Attitudes
   1. Culture General
      positive attitude toward different cultures
      positive attitude toward culture learning
      ethnorelative attitude regarding cultural differences

   2. Culture Specific
      positive attitude toward target culture
      positive attitude toward target culture persons

Figure 9.1.   A conceptual model of culture learning.

strategies for dealing with stress, the role of emotions in cross-cultural, cross-linguistic interactions, and so forth. Culture-general skills include the capacity to display respect for and interest in the culture, the ability to be a self-sustaining culture learner and to draw on a variety of resources for that learning, tolerance and patience in cross-cultural situations, control of emotions and emotional resilience, and the like (cf. Lustig & Koester, 1996: Kelley & Myers, 1997).

The second point to be noted is the distinction between attitudes, behavior, and knowledge, i.e., the affective, behavioral, and cognitive domains of learning. This is a distinction based on the pioneering work of psychologists such as Bloom (1964) and interculturalists (see Damen, 1987, for a extensive review of culture learning models). It is a conceptual perspective finding increased recognition among foreign language educators (Buttjes & Byram, 1991; Byram & Morgan, 1994; Seelye, 1981, 1995).

Teaching Methodology When Culture is at the Core

The methodology suggested by Crawford-Lange and Lange (1984), Kramsch (1993), Seelye (1994), and, particularly, Byram (1988) is congruent with Paige's definition of culture learning in that it is anchored in three fundamental learning processes: (1) the learners' exploration of their own culture; (2) the discovery of the relationship between language and culture, and (3) the learning of the heuristics for analyzing and comparing cultures. Meta-awareness and cross-cultural comparison lie at the heart of such a culture pedagogy. This implies providing opportunities for interaction such that "members of the host culture can impart their own epistemology, their own way of seeing things" (Jurasek, 1995, p.228) on the learner. Twenty years ago, Robinson (1978) already pointed out that means are defined by their goal; if the goal is empathetic understanding of the people, it implies an "affective personal response" to real people (quoted in Robinson-Stuart & Nocon, 1996, p. 435).

A recent response by the language teaching profession has been to turn to anthropology and intercultural education to explore the systematic use of ethnographic techniques in and outside of the classroom, whereby, as Jurasek (1995) explains, the "product" of the ethnography is considered less important than "the process of observing, participating, describing, analyzing, and interpreting" (p. 225). (For a more complete description of the ethnographic method and suggestions for its integration into foreign language instruction, see Byram, 1989; Jurasek, 1995; Robinson, 1985; Robinson-Stuart & Nocon, 1996). Starting with the recognition that we "can never see through another's eyes; we must see through our own" (Robinson, 1981, p.150), the overall goal for the learner is to progress toward the development of intercultural competence by addressing the affective component of such a competence (see M. Bennett, 1993). Jurasek (1995) suggests that such an outcome has two general facets: (1) consciousness-raising in regard to perception and perspective, and (2) "an ever-increasing ability to recognize at least in a limited way what things might look like from the viewpoint of members of another culture" (p. 228). It is worth remarking that the gradual development of such a competence is at the heart of the recently published National Standards for Foreign Language Learning (see Phillips, in this volume).

Let us conclude this introduction with the observation that the dimensions of culture learning suggested above became important road markers for the team. We screened the studies for their (1) underlying concept of culture, (2) implicit and subconscious culture learning goals, and (3) application of innovative pedagogical principles such as hypothesis refinement (Crawford-Lange & Lange, 1984) and cross-cultural training methods (Damen, 1987). Ultimately, we were interested in finding conceptual frames of reference and research evidence regarding (1) the degree to which a paradigm shift was occurring in language education with respect to the teaching of culture, and (2) the impact of alternative pedagogies on culture learning.

THE CONTEXT OF CULTURE LEARNING: AN OVERALL FRAME OF REFERENCE

The paper begins with a discussion of the *context* of culture learning, i.e., the different types of settings and circumstances within which culture learning occurs. The more we read, the more we came to realize that for language and culture learning, context is an overarching concept which subsumes many other variables including: the setting; the teacher; the learner; instructional methods; instructional materials; and assessment approaches. This paper has sections pertaining to each of these categories. We begin with a discussion of the larger concept and the literature associated with it.

The Concept of Context

Byram (1988) asserts that language has no function independent of the context in which it is used, thus language always refers to something beyond itself: the cultural context. This cultural context defines the language patterns being used when particular persons come together under certain circumstances at a particular time and place. This combination of elements always has a cultural meaning that influences language use. Indeed, Heath (1986) states that most human interaction is based not so much on people having shared intimate knowledge of each other, but rather on their having an understanding of the context in which the communication is taking place. Understanding the context means the persons know these cultural meanings associated with time, place, person, and circumstance. This understanding, in turn, prescribes language behavior appropriate to those circumstances. In essence, one does not need to be familiar with the other person in order to communicate, but one does need to understand the context. This, of course, becomes far more problematical in cross-cultural encounters.

A central and recurring theme in discussions of context is the idea of the meaning structures associated with time, place, person, and circumstance. Gudykunst and Kim (1992) assert that there are two types of contexts that are important in intercultural encounters. *External context* refers to the various locations or settings where interactions occur and the meanings society attaches to them. For example, two people might address each other more formally in an office setting than if they were to meet outside on the street because the culture views the workplace as a more formal and professional, rather than social, setting. External context, then, is about social meaning on the grand scale, i.e., the ways in which a particular culture group construes the various settings for human interaction and communication. *Internal context,* on the other hand, refers to the cultural meanings that people themselves bring into an encounter. It is the internal context that creates the conditions for understanding or misunderstanding among people from different cultures because, as Hall (1976) points out, there are many cultural variations that influence how people perceive situations and each other; these range, for example, from how far they stand apart during a conversation to how much time they are willing to spend communicating.

In order to illustrate these concepts, let us take the language classroom as a setting and explore the ways that setting influences target language use. A primary external factor is societal attitudes toward education, in general, and what constitutes appropriate classroom behavior. For example, is education about memorization and written examinations? Or is it about verbal production? To what degree is the classroom a setting for cognitive learning as opposed to the development of behavioral skills? To what degree is the classroom expected to be a setting for experiential learning? Another external factor is the way second language education is viewed by society. Is it primarily about reading target language literature? Or is language education about actual communication competence? Is second language learning accorded any real importance in the culture (e.g., viewed as a practical necessity) or is it considered irrelevant? The answer to these

questions will have a strong influence on teaching practices and, ultimately, on the type of language use being encouraged in the second language classroom. Internal contextual factors refer to such things as the
motivations, interests, and understanding the students and teachers themselves bring to the classroom about appropriate classroom behavior, in general, and second language use, in particular.

The concept of context takes additional forms in sociolinguistic analysis.
Hymes (1974) lists eight factors that he believes make up context in interpersonal communication and he uses the acronym SPEAKING to identify
them. They include: setting, participants, end (or purpose), act sequence
(form and content of an utterance), key (verbal and nonverbal manner),
instrumentalities (choice of channel and code), norms of interaction and
interpretation, and genre. Another type of context less frequently mentioned is the context created by the interaction itself. Ellis and Roberts
(1987) claim that, along with the internal and external dimensions of context which are set before the encounter, the two interactants will continuously be scanning each other's verbal and nonverbal communication
(contextualization cues) for insights into the meaning of their encounter;
communication is altered is meaning as construed and reconstrued.
Related to this is what Halliday (1989) terms the *intertextual context*, that is,
the historical dimension or the accumulation of all other contexts. For
instance, if a teacher has had previous experiences with a particular type of
student such as a newly arrived immigrant, those experiences will then
help shape that teacher's current communication with what is perceived to
be a similar type of student. The past and the present experiences come
together to shape the intertextual context.

Culture is central to all of the types of context mentioned by these
authors and researchers. It is not the context itself that alters language use
or how the interactants behave, it is the meaning associated with that context, and that meaning is determined by the culture. It is essential, therefore, for language learners to also be effective culture learners. They must
know how to *read* the context. This suggests that language instruction must
provide opportunities for students to be exposed to, or better yet,
immersed in the target culture in order to gain skills in ascertaining the
cultural meanings of time, place, person, and circumstances.

Trends in Language Education Associated with Context

During the past 40 years, there have been important shifts in how language educators have viewed context. The enduring issue has been the
search for settings that could best promote language and culture learning.
The central questions have been around the classroom as a learning set-

ting as opposed to the *field*, i.e., real world settings where the target language and culture is used. In the 1960s, many researchers and language educators believed that an understanding of context was crucial to language study, thus a lot of support was generated for experience-based learning such as study abroad programs and culture simulations in the classroom. The 1970s saw a shift toward cognitively-focused instruction with much less attention given to the role of context and experience in the learning process (Edwards & Rehorick, 1990). From the 1980s to the present time, language educators have directed much attention to context. Immersion schools, for example, represent an attempt to *contextualize* (i.e., create opportunities to study meaning in) the learning environment (Edwards & Rehorick, 1990; Moos & Trickett, 1987). Study abroad programs, which have grown in popularity, constitute efforts to locate the language learner in the actual cultural context.

THE SETTINGS FOR CULTURE LEARNING

In the remainder of this article, we focus on what the literature tells us about culture learning with respect to the different contextual factors mentioned above. It is important to note, however, that in the limited body of extant research, many of the studies listed here have examined these cultural variables only as secondary factors or have simply theorized about them as possible influences in the learning of language and culture. Accordingly, we often found ourselves talking about language as well as culture learning and this is reflected on our writing; the reader will find occasional references to language learning even though that was not the purpose of this review article.

We anticipated at the outset that there would not be a great deal in the research literature to guide language educators interested in culture learning and we were correct. For example, only a few qualitative studies (in the form of classroom ethnographies) exist which shed light on how culture is actually presented in the foreign language classroom and none of those deal with the secondary classroom. Moreover, evidence from methods courses, conference sessions and workshops, and theoretical writings in the field indicate that foreign language and culture pedagogy is extremely eclectic and largely dependent on the individual teacher's definition of culture. A recurrent finding is that the actual practice of teaching a second language seems to have changed little over the past half century, and is still dominated by grammar instruction (Kramsch, 1993). In other words, culture, taught either in more common culture-specific terms or as more generalizable culture-general (e.g., intercultural communication) skills, does not appear to figure prominently in language instruction.

We now turn to the two principal settings for language programs: the naturalistic setting of the field and the formal, structured setting of the classroom.

Naturalistic Settings: Culture Learning in the Field

The study abroad literature yields the most abundant research on the importance of context on culture learning. This is due in part to the fact that these language programs have been of interest to researchers in several disciplines including education, psychology, and linguistics. It is also due to the growing interest in international education and the large international flow of students. Recent figures indicate that close to half a million international students come to the United States to study each year and, in 1994–1995, approximately 71,000 U.S. undergraduates participated in study abroad programs (Freed, 1995). The experiences of these students and the impact of their educational sojourns abroad have intrigued researchers. It is important to note that much of the literature is focused on language learning; far fewer studies have researched culture learning as the primary focus. We report on both sets of findings in this section.

What is the impact of study abroad on language and culture learning? First, the research generally supports the hypothesis that second language proficiency is enhanced by the study abroad experience (Carlson et al., 1991; Diller & Markert, 1983; Dyson, 1988), but it also shows that the process is more complex than previously thought. In an early and large-scale study, Carroll (1967) examined the effects of a study abroad experience on 2,782 college seniors from various campuses around the United States. He found that the amount of time studying abroad and the age of the student were the two strongest predictors of language listening skills. More recently, DeKeyser (1991) researched two groups of students who were studying in Spain, one for six months and the other for one year. He found a large difference between the two groups in terms of their vocabulary gains, but that the study abroad context did not enhance language ability to a large extent in other ways such as reading and writing. He attributed the vocabulary gains to three factors: (1) availability of native speakers, (2) enhanced motivation for learning new words, and (3) a large number of possible settings in which to practice with new vocabulary. Moehle (1984) and Raupach (1987) researched groups of students who went to study at various universities abroad. They both found that after several months abroad the rate of the students' speech was faster, but their grammatical proficiency and the complexity of their sentence structures had not changed. In Meara's (1994) study, students did not feel that their reading and writing skills improved during their study abroad experience, but half felt that their oral-aural skills had improved. Freed (1995), in a replication of an earlier study by Spada (1987), found that the benefit derived from an overseas experience hinged on the type of contact students had during their overseas stay and their language level. In general, those individuals who had *interactive encounters* (i.e., socializing with host culture persons) gained more than those who engaged in *non-interactive behaviors* (i.e., watching TV or reading in the second language). However, the author also found that non-interactive contact was more beneficial to upper level students.

The research findings show that the effects of a study abroad experience on culture learning are complex in nature. In general, study abroad appears to enhance feelings of self-confidence and self-esteem as well as positive attitudes toward language and culture learning. Armstrong (1984) and Hansel (1985) showed that a study abroad experience positively influences later language study, promotes favorable attitudes toward other cultures, and brings about a greater level of cultural awareness. Armstrong (1984) studied 126 high-school students participating in a seven-week language study and homestay program in Mexico. He found that study abroad impacted career choices and positively influenced attitudes toward the host culture. In addition, students said that they acquired independence, self-confidence, and maturity through the study-abroad and home-stay experiences. He cautions that the homestay element was crucial to these results, but did not offer evidence from the study of how this conclusion was reached.

Hannigan (1990) found a strong relationship between successful intercultural communication and certain personal traits such as: cultural empathy, flexibility, organizational skills, and superior linguistic skills. But his study, like many others, could not demonstrate a causal relationship between the intercultural experience and the development of these qualities. Carlson et al. (1991) conducted a longitudinal study of the long term effects of the undergraduate study abroad experience involving 400 U.S. and European students as well as a control group. They found, in addition to the language gains correlated with length of stay, that (1) students who chose to study abroad differ in predictable ways from non study-abroad students by show greater *cultural interest* and a lower *domestic orientation*; (2) social and personal development are important parts of the international experience; and, (3) participants in the study abroad program scored higher than the comparison group on cultural interest and *peace and cooperation* indicators.

There are certain interesting problems associated with researching the study abroad experience, one being timing of the assessment to assure an accurate measure of learning. Hashimota (1993) found many of the benefits are not even realized until well after the person has returned. For instance, one student who was studying in Japan did learn the more complex linguistic and cultural features of the Japanese language while in Japan, but it was not until her return home to Australia that she began to incorporate these more complex variables into her speech. Another issue has been the reliance on quantitative measures, such as test scores to assess benefits. In the often-cited Carroll (1967) study, test scores were relied upon exclusively to measure language improvement and many critics charge that this does not provide a complete picture of the ability of the sojourner in terms of verbal or cultural skills. Mauranen (1994) investigated a group of Finnish students studying in the United Kingdom. The author's qualitative study revealed that the students felt secure about their ability to use English as a second language, but insecure about their knowledge of how to participate in the different discourse environments due to cultural factors, such as when is it appropriate to ask a question or interrupt someone. In a review of the literature, Mauranen (1994) noted the problems of small sample size and research programs too short in duration to adequately reflect the actual changes that occur over a longer period of time. In addition, the author found that control groups were frequently absent in the research design and multiple methods, which would increase the rigor and validity of the study, were rarely used.

To summarize, the evidence is consistent that study abroad promotes language learning in certain ways. The research findings are much less clear on the impact of study abroad on culture learning, although certain outcomes—greater self-confidence, an increase in global awareness, enhanced cultural self-awareness (Barnlund, 1988), and positive attitudes toward other culture groups—are consistently found to be associated with overseas learning experiences. However, the research also suggests that one negative experience abroad can also dominate a person's perspective about the new culture, impede language acquisition and culture learning (DeKeyser, 1991; Freed, 1991; Spada, 1987), or reinforce negative generalizations (Byram et al., 1991).

Structured Settings: Culture Learning in the Classroom

The formal classroom as a venue for culture learning provides a very different setting than the study abroad environment and there has been much theorizing about language and culture learning in this more formal and structured setting. Unfortunately, there is a remarkable scarcity of empirical or descriptive studies dealing with the real world of the classroom (Boutin, 1993). Chaudron (1986), arguing for an interaction of quantitative and qualitative approaches to classroom research, points out that up to 1983, less than 7% of the combined quantitative and qualitative research articles published in two major linguistic journals dealt with measures of classroom learning. The author deplores the fact that despite many years of qualitative observational studies that should have generated hypotheses about effective teaching and learning behaviors, we have today only a small selection of classroom process variables that can be agreed upon as potentially influential for learning. He attributes this problem to the lack of consistency in descriptive categories that renders a comparison between the results of both kinds of research almost impossible (p. 711). Equally strong calls for more classroom research have come from the immersion education professionals. Salomone (1991) points out that even in the well-researched area of French immersion, there is an absence of empirical, classroom data.

The theoretical literature on the role of the classroom in language and culture learning reveals a variety of perspectives regarding its contribution to culture learning. Distinguishing between learning and acquisition, Krashen (1982) suggests that the classroom setting is not conducive to language or culture acquisition, only to the learning of rules. Others argue that there may be little difference between learning in the classroom versus learning in a natural setting because introductory level students cannot communicate sufficiently well to take advantage of the naturalistic environment (Van Lier, 1988). Most researchers though, fall somewhere in between and consider that there are both disadvantages and advantages to language and culture learning in the classroom.

There are several key theoretical criticisms of the classroom as an environment for culture learning. Damen (1987), for example, argues that classroom-based learning is cognitive and deductive in nature, relying far too much on rule-ordered pedagogy. Accordingly, learning becomes superficial; students simply memorize the material without reflecting or integrating it into a larger cultural knowledge base. Likewise, based on a review of studies done on classroom interaction, Ellis (1992) asserts that the discourse in the average classroom is rigidly controlled by the teacher, who determines who speaks, how long they speak, and when they start and stop. This type of setting provides little opportunity for students to learn how to appropriately engage or disengage the communication process (Sacks, Schegloff, & Jefferson, 1974). Similarly, Pica (1983) found that the formal classroom emphasizes rules, sequence, and predictable error correction by the teacher. Naturalistic settings do not function this way. There is no clear articulation of rules, the meaning is more important than the form, and error correction rarely occurs. Along these lines, Jurasek (1995), Robinson-Stuart and Nocon (1996) have recently argued that without direct experience of the culture, culture learning is only *cognitive boundary crossing* (Robinson-Stuart & Nocon, 1996, p. 434), the acquisition of a *scholarly skill* which leaves unexamined and unchallenged the learners' previous beliefs and attitudes. On the other hand, there is only so much foreign culture that can be brought into the classroom, and preserving authenticity under these conditions is a challenge in itself (Baumgratz-Gangl, 1991; Kramsch, 1993).

Other authors have theorized that the classroom as an artificial community can provide some unexpected benefits for language and culture learning (Damen, 1987; Kramsch, 1993; Mitchell, 1988). In particular, they hypothesize that the classroom is a protective environment where students can feel free to make mistakes without any lasting repercussions, in contrast to a student who is studying abroad and makes a mistake that can have enduring consequences. This protective setting enables students to safely experiment with the language and thus encourages them to make sense of the language and culture for themselves.

Ellis (1992) argues that, although there are many differences between learning environments, the discourse and learning produced depend on the roles employed by the teacher and learner, the tasks that are utilized in the classroom, and the purpose (i.e., outcome or process) of the learning. Freed (1991) reiterates this by noting that the crucial variables do not seem to be the external environment, but the internal one created by factors such as the type of instruction, the level of the class, and the individual differences associated with the teacher and the students. This does not mean that the external context is unimportant, as each type brings different potentials and problems, but it is the interaction between external and internal context that dictates the type of learning that will occur (Freed, 1991). Breen (1985) suggests that we look at classrooms themselves as living cultures that are interactive, differentiated, collective, highly normative, asymmetrical, inherently conservative, jointly constructed and immediately significant. Rejecting two previous metaphors (the classroom as *experimental laboratory* and the classroom as *discourse*) for neglecting the "the social reality of language learning as it is experienced and created by teachers and learners" (p. 141). Breen argues that the metaphor of the classroom as *culture* or as *coral gardens* (p. 142) allows us to perceive the psychological change and social events characteristic of the classroom as "irrevocably linked and mutually engaged" (p. 151). Such a perspective on classroom can help explain more fully the relationship between classroom input and learning outcomes, and is particularly relevant in the culture-learning situation.

Immersion programs.   The immersion approach is based in theory on the notion that instruction conducted in the target language will enable students to effectively learn the language. Moreover, by using the target language across the curriculum in courses other than language, the student will have *real experiences* with the language (Edwards & Rehorick, 1990). Research suggests that the reality is more complex. Swain (1991) discusses the finding in immersion programs that students acquire native-like comprehension, but their productive skills often lag behind. The author hypothesizes that the reason for this may be that students experience a *ceiling effect*, a level beyond which they cannot easily move but where they can understand each other and the teacher. This level then becomes the goal rather than a stage in an ongoing learning process. Some researchers have found that immersion language learning is negatively influenced by the competitiveness of the academic environment. Loughrin-Sacco (1992), who had noticed this problem in an earlier ethnographic study, reports on an alternative intensive two-week summer immersion class designed to alleviate the anxiety students experienced in a regular school year immersion program. In the summer session class, taken outside of the regular school year context, students felt reduced anxiety about the target language and less competitiveness toward other students. In addition, students' perception of the foreign language showed a positive increase, they developed more effective learning strategies, and they were more focused on their course. This small body of research shows that the researchers have a nearly exclusive focus on linguistic gains. The section on attitudes and motivation below will address further more complex learning outcomes.

Foreign language classrooms versus second language classrooms. Kramsch (1993) posits that the second language classroom and the foreign language classroom are becoming more similar. The foreign language secondary school classroom in the United States has traditionally been viewed as relatively homogeneous in terms of the students (mostly White, college bound and high achievers), a view which has recently prompted Bernhardt (1995) to express her suspicion that the foreign language profession may still be considering itself "a profession of the elite" (p.17). In any case, with student populations becoming more diverse, the FL classroom is likely to become more like the SL classroom with students representing a variety of nationalities and cultures.

However, the second language classroom such as the ESL classroom in the United States or the FLE (Français Langue Etrangère) in France does create a unique learning environment that differs from the foreign language classroom not only in terms of student composition, but also with regard to motivation and perspective. While foreign language students are more likely to take the course voluntarily, second language students may be required to take the class (e.g., new immigrants or international students who are provisionally admitted pending successful completion of the ESL course). While the foreign language teacher is generally from the same culture as the students, the second language teacher, generally a native speaker of the language being taught, is likely to be of a different culture than the students. And the students themselves are likely to be culturally diverse. One important consequence of the cultural homogeneity between teacher and student in FL classrooms is that neither educator nor pupil need consciously attend to the ways in which they are engaged in *cultural transmission* (Ferdman, 1990, p. 189), an omission that can hinder the culture learning process. In second language classrooms, other problematical dynamics occur such as fear of being assimilated into the target culture and anxiety about the teacher, who is a representative of that culture. Both are compounded by the fact that these students are experiencing cultural dislocations and culture shock in their own daily lives. In theoretical terms, the foreign language classroom can easily downplay culture or ignore it altogether. On the contrary, second language classrooms exemplify Breen's (1985) *classroom as culture* metaphor.

The limited research that exists confirms some of these theoretical ideas. In the study of ESL classes in South Asia, Canagarjah (1993) found that the students felt alienated and negative toward the target language and culture. They discovered that this was due to the implicit Western bias of the materials and of the instructor, reinforced by the fact that the cultural context was never explicitly discussed. Consequently, the students felt anxious about and disconnected from the target language and culture. Because of the circumstances, these students indicated that they favored the more traditional approach of memorizing the grammar and vocabulary, presumably because it was a process that allowed them to keep a certain distance from the language and the culture. The second language students' fear of being absorbed by the culture of the language they are studying is repeatedly brought up by researchers in the United States and abroad (see Hoffman, 1989, for Iranian ESL students; Ryan, 1994, for students of English in Mexico; Bex, 1994, for ESL students in Europe). In another study, McGinnis (1994), found that differences between teacher and student expectations concerning what is *good teaching* entailed conflicting assumptions about what should be included in a language learning context, assumptions which greatly interfered with the learning process by obstructing student-teacher communication.

The above discussion illustrates the crucial role played by the teacher, whether in the ESL or the foreign language classroom, in bridging languages and cultures. We will now turn to a closer examination of teacher variables that impact culture learning.

TEACHER VARIABLES IN CULTURE LEARNING

Although there have been numerous calls to conduct classroom-based research, the reality is that we still know little as to what really goes on in the foreign language classroom, and even less about the knowledge and beliefs that inform the teachers' instructional decisions, particularly with respect to culture instruction (Bernhardt & Hammadou, 1987). Salomone

(1991) points out that while student performance has been studied extensively for more than 20 years in the French immersion classroom, immersion teachers' practices and beliefs have not been similarly scrutinized (p. 57). This is somewhat surprising because teachers are viewed theoretically as major agents in successful immersion programs (Boutin, 1993).

This state of affairs is partly due to the strong influence of the American Council on the Teaching of Foreign Languages-led language proficiency movement of the 1980s, which resulted in a research agenda dominated by proficiency studies for the past decade and a half. It may also be speculated that less research has been directed toward the study of other goals, such as culture learning, because such goals are more elusive. It is difficult to measure something as complex as "the ability to understand, respect and accept people of a different sex, race, cultural heritage, national origin, religion, and political, economic and social background as well as their values, beliefs and attitudes," which is New York's statement on foreign language learning outcomes (cited in Kramsch, 1991a, p. 226).

It is important to point out that much of the literature is methodological and theoretical in nature. It is also inconsistent in how it views the culture teaching process. Murphy (1988), for instance, observes, "In some approaches culture is presented as being homogeneous . . . In others it is presented as incorporating intra- and inter-cultural variations" (p. 147). Baumgratz-Gangl (1991) speculates that, "If pupils are to leave this stage of intercultural guessing, explicit comparisons need to be encouraged; this can be done by asking questions from the vantage point of the foreign reality" (p. 234). Bex (1994) suggests, "Awareness of cultural diversity can be introduced into the classroom gradually, first by developing the pupils' perceptions of the grosser differences between their own culture and that of the target language, and then by comparing linguistic variation within their own culture with linguistic variation within the target culture" (p. 60).

The theoretical literature identifies many teacher roles and qualities hypothesized to be central to promoting culture learning in language education. Hughes (1986) states that a teacher should be a philosopher, geographer, historian, philologist, and literary critic. To Altman (1981), the teacher functions as a "skillful developer of communicative competence in the classroom," "dialectologist," "value clarifier," and "communications analyst" (pp. 11–13). The teacher role is to be an educational sociologist according to Kleinsasser (1993). And with reference to Kane's (1991) impressive "Taxonomy of Cultural Studies Objectives" (pp. 245–247), the teacher needs to be anthropologist and ethnographer, intercultural educator, and, of course, comparative sociolinguist mastering the ins and outs of culturally-determined linguistic variation. How the teachers themselves perceive language education, culture teaching and learning, and their role

as culture educators have been questions posed by a number of researchers. We now turn to that empirical literature.

The Empirical Literature on Teacher Variables

The role of the teacher.   The research suggests that it is critically
important for the teacher, within or outside of the classroom, to explicitly
take on the role of culture educator and deliberately assist students with
their process of cultural analysis. Byram et al. (1991) reported that trips
abroad for 10 to 12 year olds more often than not resulted in negative stereotyping, after only one encounter with members of the host culture,
when the students were left to themselves and when they lacked previous
knowledge to use in interpreting intercultural encounters. Without the
teacher's active involvement, students become more rather than less ethnocentric in their attitudes toward the target culture. Robinson (1981) concurs with this view when she suggests that mere exposure to a foreign
language will not automatically promote favorable attitudes toward the culture, nor will positive attitudes toward a culture necessarily facilitate the
acquisition of the language. She found that the goals, attitudes, and priorities of the foreign language teacher are important considerations.

Teachers' views regarding the goals of language education.   Robinson
(1981) was the first to attempt a large-scale investigation of the perceptions
held by teachers, students, and parents regarding the sociocultural goals of
foreign language study, particularly in the elementary grades. Her investigation was set in Australia, but many of her findings apply to the situation
in the United States today. Regarding the value of foreign language study,
she found a remarkable agreement among the three groups that language
study was first and foremost for "understanding the people," "general
enjoyment" and "language enrichment" (p. 22). These reasons, she points
out, reflect the "collective justification for including foreign language
study in the school curriculum at primary, secondary and tertiary levels" (p.
33). When she pressed for explanation regarding the sociocultural benefits, she found them justified in terms that "foreign language study will give
one the key to another culture, will lead to an awareness, understanding
and sensitivity toward other people and their way of life" (p. 24).

Similar opinions were expressed by British teachers of French participating in the Durham project, a massive international research program carried out at the university of Durham between 1985 and 1988. The goal of
the project was to investigate "the effects of language teaching on young
people's perception of other cultures" (Byram et al., 1991, p. 103). Two
groups of about 200 pupils, beginning at age 11, were followed in their language study for three years. The researchers used a mixed research meth-

odology consisting of nonparticipant observation of teaching (eight months), semi-structured interviews, questionnaires, case study analysis, and pre-post tests at the beginning and end of school year. The researchers assessed students' knowledge of French culture and pupils' level of ethnocentrism with respect to French people (measured via semantic differential tests). The major findings regarding teachers were, first, that teachers have similar objectives for and beliefs about the value of foreign language. In particular, they feel that it promotes gains in personal development in the form of learning about others as well as becoming open and more tolerant. Second, there is great variation in *styles* or approaches to teaching about the foreign culture and teachers frequently use culture as a pedagogic device for capturing student interest, or for contextualizing language teaching. Third, teachers generally have limited experience with the target culture. Finally, instruction is dominated by the textbook, which is used extensively and determines the topics as well as the sequence of instruction. But unlike Robinson's teachers, the teachers interviewed by Byram and his colleagues reveal an emerging awareness of culture in the curriculum. In the authors' words, "teachers talked about how it is important for children to know about other ways of living which may or may not be better than their own. Through such knowledge, they may become more tolerant of other peoples and less restricted in their own lifestyle" (p. 111). Nonetheless, the researchers concluded from their extensive classroom observations that the teaching of "culture remains didactic, oriented toward the transmission of information" (p. 118).

Several studies have been conducted in the past decade in the United States regarding foreign language teachers' goals, priorities, and concerns. In a survey of foreign language teachers, supervisors, and consultants, Cooper (1985) found that *culture learning* ranked only eighth among the respondents' top ten priorities. Testing, promoting interest in foreign language, language learning theory, and developing the oral proficiency of students all ranked higher. More recently, Wolf and Riordan (1991) found a similar pattern in the prioritizing of needs by U.S. language teachers, but here culture teaching did not even get listed among the top ten priorities. While this listing of priorities could be attributed partly to the domination of proficiency concerns, it also may be indicative of fundamental uneasiness with the vagueness of the notion of teaching for cultural understanding or culture learning.

In light of such results regarding the lower priority status of culture learning among teachers, it should come as no surprise that what students want and what teachers provide do not match. For instance, Davis and Markham's (1991) nation wide study on student attitudes toward foreign language at historically black institutions revealed just such a discrepancy. Although 87% of the faculty reported feeling strongly "about comparing and contrasting issues related to culture," 54% of students thought that this area was neglected and said that they wanted more emphasis on culture. Although such surveys do not allow us to probe for deeper representation of culture concepts in teachers' and students' minds, they hint at unclarity and confusion regarding the nature and teaching of culture.

Teacher perspectives on culture. Knox's (1984) *Report on the teaching of French civilization* contains responses given by French secondary and university teachers to an 18-item survey which included questions on how they came to be teaching civilization, how and what they teach, the problems they encounter in their courses, and, finally, their perceived needs regarding the teaching of French civilization. In both settings, the primary areas of interest for French civilization are: current events; history; literature and the fine arts; cultural values and customs; and French-American contrasts. But these two institutional contexts differ slightly with regard to instructional content. College courses tend to emphasize small *c* (daily life) culture, while secondary teachers report more frequent instruction on the topics of current events, history, and geography. This difference in emphasis could be due to the fact that college teachers may have a more extensive experience with the target culture, which, in turn, would increase their level of comfort dealing with the topics of daily living. In answer to the question of whether they teach what students are most interested in, 38 of the 65 teachers said they did. The author also found that one of the top four concerns expressed by the teachers lack of support by the profession for the teaching of culture and civilization. Their top needs were updating teacher knowledge, better instructional materials, and better teacher training.

Teacher perspectives of their subject matter. There is important evidence to suggest that teacher perspectives of their subject matter influence teaching practice. Pajares (1992) conducted a review of the research literature and found that an individual teacher's beliefs strongly correlate with behavior, particularly with respect to choices and decisions about instructional practice. Stodolsky and Grossman (1995) conducted a large-scale study of math, foreign language, social studies, English, and science teachers' perceptions of the nature of knowledge in their field. *Defined* knowledge was conceptualized as a body of knowledge and skills on which teachers agree. *Sequential* knowledge involved the belief that certain prerequisites are necessary and that there is a necessary order of coverage in their subject matter instruction. *Static* knowledge was defined as the enduring, relatively unchanging knowledge in the subject area. According to the authors, the most remarkable finding was that foreign language teachers shared with math teachers the view that their respective subject matters were strongly characterized by defined and static knowledge. This perception of an enduring and agreed upon body of knowledge is primarily linguistic in nature and our concern is that it seems to leave little room for the inclusion of complex cultural variables in the instructional process.

Cultural conflict between teachers and students. Sociolinguistic research has brought forth evidence that, when a clash between teacher culture and learner culture occurs, it is likely to prevent learning. In the language education context, there is a strong possibility of this phenomenon occurring because the teacher is acting as a transmitter of another language and culture (Spindler, 1974), even when the teacher and the students come from culturally similar backgrounds. In second language classrooms, problems of this nature are even more likely because the students are often the newcomers to the country, having arrived as immigrant or refugees. Pajares' (1992) conclusion that teachers' beliefs are mirrored in their teaching practices is particularly relevant in the U.S. context of second language education, since a teacher's attitude toward cultural diversity in general, and the students' cultures in particular, may result in the sending of unconscious messages of intolerance or ethnocentrism.

This is precisely what Gougeon (1993) discovered when he set out to explore the sociocultural context of ESL from the teachers' perspective. He interviewed 27 senior high school teachers in Alberta, Canada, and concluded that, in spite of official statements to the contrary, school systems are fundamentally ethnocentric, supporting the "English language Anglo-Saxon culture," and they are uncommitted to providing equal service to ESL students. In the foreign language classroom, the teacher transmits the target culture, thus by definition engages the students in discussions of cultural difference, contrast, and conflict. As Kramsch (1994) points out, even the most basic engagement of a reader with a textbook generates opposition, what she refers to as "oppositional practice" (p. 29).

Dirksen (1990), investigating whether the learning styles of ESL Chinese students matched traditional Confucian, or western, teaching methods, observed that Chinese students increase their rejection of western methods as they spend more time in a western style classroom. The author attributes this rejection to the fact that the more students learn about the target culture, as they are experiencing it in the classroom, the more they encounter culture contrast that trouble them. In a similar study, Reid (1987) found that ESL students show a preference for the kinesthetic and tactile learning style, but that great variations also occurred according to culture groups, field, gender, and academic level (graduates or undergraduates). Interestingly, Reid found that (1) the learning styles of students with higher TOEFL scores more closely resembles the learning styles of native speakers; and (2) the longer ESL students stayed in the United States, the more auditory their preferences became. Investigating the potential for culture clash between the culture of instruction of Chinese TAs and the culture of learning of U.S. students, McGinnis (1994) found confirmation of his culture clash hypothesis in three areas: (1) accuracy of language vs. creativity; (2) perceived importance of interaction with native speakers; and (3) perspectives on the role of authentic materials.

Falsgraf (1994) looked at language and culture at a Japanese immersion school, in particular whether teachers' speech, especially ways of expressing status and formality, socializes U.S. children to the norms of the Japanese classroom. He found that Japanese immersion teachers' speech displays implicit culture (for example, they used more imperatives and a certain level of formality when dealing with the whole class) and that U.S. children's interlanguage reflects their having acquired the ability to discern those implicit cultural cues. The researcher concludes that metacultural and metalinguistic instruction is not necessary at this early age since teaching through language provides sufficient input for the acquisition of implicit culture. Although these findings may not hold true for older students, they show how much culture the native teacher carries into the classroom.

According to Arvizu, Snyder, and Espinosa (1981), teachers respond in very different ways to the conflict associated with the teaching and learning of culture. The first approach is to minimize the threat by avoiding culture and by rigidly holding to the traditional (presumably shared) values of classroom behavior. A second and very different approach is to display the "adaptive response of overcompensation in the direction of the new system." In the third approach, teachers vacillate between the alternative cultural systems by unsystematically integrating various parts of them into classroom life. The fourth approach, which the author refers to as the "ideal adaptive response," is characterized by the treatment of cultural conflict "openly and directly in a comparative cross-cultural manner" (p. 32). Which response the teacher engages in will depend greatly on his or her attitudes toward the target culture and perspectives on the teaching of culture in the language classroom.

Several recent studies have looked at teachers' perspectives regarding cultural diversity. Haberman and Post (1990) studied 227 teachers attending a summer workshop at the University of Wisconsin-Milwaukee. They were asked to choose what they considered to be the most important culture teaching goal, from a list of five (based on Sleeter and Grant's (1994) typology of multicultural education). Eighty-three percent of the respondents chose either "all people are individuals" or "cooperation and tolerance are vital," answers, which the authors interpreted as reflecting the teachers' commitment to tolerating differences, but also their suspicion "that anything positive will come from their continued existence" (p. 33). In Minnesota, a small replication study was done involving 30 foreign language teachers of French, German, and Spanish who were participating in a statewide articulation project. They were asked the same question, but the pattern of responses is quite different. Only 43% of the foreign language teachers (vs. 83% of Haberman and Post's teachers) chose the two goals described above. Conversely, 27% of the Minnesota sample (vs. 4%) selected the "America is a melting pot" response, twice as many Minnesota teachers (30% vs. 14%) selected the goals of "Subgroups should be maintained and enhanced," and 20% (vs. 5%) chose "Equity for subgroups is common responsibility." According to Haberman and Post, the last two positions not only "actively seek to maintain and enhance subgroups," but also "see some danger to subgroups from individuals and the general society" (p. 33). One could argue that the set of beliefs underlying the latter two choices would appear to be more conducive to the kind of cross-cultural instruction and interaction that lead to the development of intercultural competence.

Relationship between teachers' beliefs and their instructional practice. Some recent studies have attempted to show the association between teachers' beliefs and instructional practice. The comprehensive Durham project (Byram et al., 1991) is an example of such an effort. On the basis of their extensive classroom observations and interviews with teachers and students, the researchers found that methodological approach appeared to have a causal relationship with teachers' beliefs. The largest number of respondents indicated that the teaching of culture was a *pedagogic device* that makes lessons more interesting, contextualizes language teaching, and fills in "lessons where language-learning ability is believed to be limited" (p. 111). This set of beliefs was reflected in the way culture was found to enter language teaching, namely through the teacher's use of cultural anecdotes, culture facts, and cultural artifacts. In their reflections of the teacher's role, students said that the teacher "supplements the textbook . . . but also improves on the textbook" and "can provide experience which the textbook cannot" (p. 113). Cook (1996), in her investigation of how first year university students develop cultural understanding, found indeed that older students hold more differentiated, but still quite similar, views of the role of the teacher. She concludes that the teachers who possessed French language and culture expertise were valued more highly by students than those who did not. When such expertise was granted to them, the students considered their teachers to be an important source of cultural information.

Ryan's (1994) is the first study to directly explore the relationship between foreign language teachers' perceptions of culture and their instructional behavior. In an initial interview study conducted in Mexico of 30 teachers of English at a major university, Ryan first looked at how teachers talk about culture and then categorized their *culture filters* into six basic beliefs in accordance with Keesing's categories of meaning: (1) culture is knowledge gained through reading; (2) culture is institutions which should be analyzed; (3) culture is the daily way of life; (4) culture is transmitted from one generation to another; (5) culture means having a critical attitude toward the world; and, (6) culture is lived and experienced. She then conducted six case studies based on those categories, using participant observation and interviews. During the observation part, the teachers' episodic and spontaneous cultural inserts provided a way of analyzing how teachers handled information about English-speaking cultures.

Ryan (1994) found that linguistic analysis and practice dominated instruction, and that teachers carefully distinguished between linguistic practice and cultural aspects (p. 230). She reports that insertion of information about the target culture was done in several ways. In addition to the three ways reported in the Byram study (teacher anecdotes, facts and artifacts), she identified two additional forms: cross-cultural comparisons between C1 and C2; and, "brief, encapsulated cultural statements frequently seen as talking off the subject" (p. 231). She concluded that there was "some degree of relation between teachers filters" and the corresponding teacher behavior (p. 231). For instance, the teacher whose culture filter was that "culture is the daily life of people" would begin class by asking her students about current events and frequently provided cultural anecdotes based on her own personal experiences. Ryan also concludes that in general teachers are teaching culture as facts, rather than for cultural understanding and intercultural competence. Although there is some controversy surrounding the interpretation of the findings (see Fang, 1996), Ryan's research is important in shedding light on how teachers are teaching about culture.

A different kind of impact of teacher beliefs and behavior on student learning is suggested by Hall and Ramirez (1993). In order to explore the notions of identity held by high school learners of Spanish and how these change as a result of increased study of Spanish, Hall and Ramirez asked 180 students of Spanish to first come up with descriptors or dimensions that describe Spanish speakers, and then to estimate the *distance* from the eight most frequently cited characteristics of Spanish speakers of themselves, English speakers and Spanish speakers. Puzzled by the lack of complexity and cultural specificity of the dimensions offered by the students (e.g., dark, fast talking, interesting, poor, good-looking, intelligent, weird dressers), the authors suggest that this may be due to the way foreign language educators address cultural identity in the classroom. Using Ferdman's (1990) model, they discuss two main views on the treatment of cultural identities in the classroom: (1) the pluralist view which consists in celebrating differences between groups while ignoring group membership of individuals; and (2) the melting pot view, which, by emphasizing sameness, may tend to overlook possible differences in the name of equal treatment. Hall and Ramirez argue that, in the melting pot view, individual differences are explained primarily in psychological terms, because "to think beyond the individual could introduce an unwanted level of difference," i.e., stereotyping (p. 616). Thus, if a teacher subscribes to this view and does not make group characteristics explicit for fear of a negative outcome, students may simply not come to possess the words needed to discuss the characteristics of another culture. On the other hand, Hall and Ramirez reason that if the teacher subscribes to a pluralist view of ethnic differences, students may entirely lack a framework for discussing cultural identity as group membership. Given that recent models of intercultural competence require a methodology based on cross-cultural analysis (e.g., Damen, 1987), Hall and Ramirez' conclusion brings us back to Kramsch's (1987) question of whether teachers possess enough meta-awareness of their own culture to be able to engage with their students in more than superficial comparisons across cultures.

Cooper (1990) also suggests a causal relation between teacher attitudes and teacher behavior. His intent was to investigate the connection between student teachers' cross-cultural experience, attitudes, and further action. He gave the Self Assessment in Multicultural Education (SAME) instrument to two groups of teachers, 18 of whom had gone to teach in Texas, the remaining five staying to teach in Minnesota. Cooper found that although both groups had similar ideas as to what should be, the teachers with cross-cultural experience were able to manifest those ideals into reality. He found the teachers with experience in Texas to be more culturally sensitive than the Minnesota teachers. They were more comfortable talking about controversial issues, more likely to encourage different viewpoints in class, and held higher expectations of students from diverse backgrounds. Texas teachers also had more contact with students and helped them acquire the skills needed in a White society without denying the students' other values. Cooper hypothesized that there was an _ecological impact_, i.e., that the Texas setting aided teachers in changing their attitudes, practices, and beliefs. What is not known is if the teachers who decided to take a job in Texas had different beliefs about the value of cultural diversity in the first place.

Impact of learning environments on teaching and learning. Kleinsasser (1993) conducted a study meant to investigate the _technical cultures_ of 37 high school foreign language teachers. He defines technical culture as something that "encompasses the nature of activities to be carried out . . . and embodies the procedures, knowledge and skills related to attaining organizational goals" (p. 2). Most important, a technical culture manifests itself in a teacher's belief system. Through interviews and micro-ethnographic observations, Kleinsasser was able to document the existence of two distinct technical cultures that he labeled "certain/non-routine" and "uncertain/routine" (p. 3). The uncertain/routine culture is characterized by a view of teaching as a solitary individual task, an emphasis on accuracy and correctness, a teacher's belief that some students are doomed to never learn the subject, little use of the language by teachers in or out of class, lack of opportunities for the teacher to develop professionally, and a textbook which "became the nucleus of classroom experience by default" (p. 5). By contrast, the certain/non-routine teachers collaborated with their colleagues, took pride in their work, and had great certainty about their instructional practice. These teachers believed that all their students could learn the language and provided learning experiences accordingly. They recognized language as a dynamic process, and language learning as being made up of grammatical, sociolinguistic, discourse, and strategic competencies. Although Kleinsasser never explicitly mentions cultural learning, we may assume that his underlying definition of sociolinguistic competence includes at least a basic knowledge of how different cultures shape the communicative context. Kleinsasser, unfortunately, did not venture a guess as to how prevalent each of the two models is. We can assume, however, that teaching for culture learning hardly seems compatible with the norms reflected in the uncertain/routine technical culture as described above, which treats language—and by extension, culture—as a series of discrete items that can be manipulated and memorized (Moore, 1991). Kleinsasser concludes with some optimism that the traditional paradigm of foreign language instruction is "a paradigm shifting but not yet shifted" (p. 5).

   Loughrin-Sacco's (1992) ethnography of an elementary French class at Michigan Technological University revealed further constraints on teaching and learning in the foreign language classroom, some institutional and some social. The institutional constraints he identifies include: the competitiveness of the institution; the fact that French, being an elective, was given low priority by students; a lack of courses to enable students to actually reach proficiency; and, interestingly, the students' acculturation in term of their past school habits such as set expectations regarding foreign language study, the wrong mindset (fear of making mistakes), and a sense that risk taking is not rewarded. The primary social constraint was the unfortunate mixing of real beginners with more experienced learners, a situation which polarized the classroom environment and led to bad feelings in both groups. Like other qualitative researchers and classroom observers before and after him (e.g., Byram et al., 1991; Kleinsasser, 1993; Ryan, 1994), Loughrin-Sacco encountered learning conditions characterized by grammar overload and a textbook-syllabus organized by grammar points. In addition, he found that the emphasis on early oral production caused great anxiety among the students. Most of his findings dealt with linguistic learning. For instance, he found that the students' rankings of skill difficulty (from least to most difficult: reading, writing, listening, speaking)

were confirmed by test scores, that students liked creative writing the best, and that true beginners performed similarly to false beginners on those kinds of tasks.

Regarding culture learning, this otherwise compelling and thorough investigation exhibits an unfortunate omission. The only explicit reference to culture appears in the author's statement that "our profession's goal of developing Foreign language and intercultural proficiency would come to realization sooner if false beginners proceeded to a higher level instead of retaking elementary French" (p. 98). Apparently, Loughrin-Sacco regards intercultural proficiency as a major goal/outcome of foreign language instruction but seems to be adhering to the old *skill before content* theory, which requires mastery of the language before cultural content can be introduced. Yet, the interesting finding about beginning students' ability and interest in engaging in creative writing tasks suggests that content and skill do go hand in hand and that "language exists to exert meaning" (Patrikis, 1995, p. 301). We also acknowledge, as do Robinson and Nocon (1996), that a limited proficiency places certain restrictions on intercultural communication.

Teachers' knowledge base to teach for cultural learning. The importance of the role of the teacher in the culture learning process should now be manifestly obvious. Thus, it is somewhat surprising to learn, as Bernhardt and Hammadou (1987) discovered in their review of the teacher education literature, that there is very little empirical research on the preparation of language teachers. Since that time, several investigations have added to our knowledge base. Byram et al. (1991) identified three idiosyncratic orientations that determine the teachers' contributions: (1) individual philosophy regarding language pedagogy in general; (2) the nature of personal experience with the foreign culture; and, (3) expectations regarding the learning potential of a class (p. 63). Byram and his colleagues single out the intercultural experience as the most important factor of the three. If a teacher's personal experience with the target culture is limited, this restricts the teacher's ability to teach culture, leads students to question the credibility of the teacher to serve as a cultural informant, and thus constrains the teacher's ability to help students bridge the home and target cultures. Intercultural experience is ultimately indispensable for the development of Bennett's (in this volume) form of authentic intercultural competence, which involves knowledge, attitudes, and behavior.

Kramsch (1993) reports on a small-scale experiment involving 12 teachers, from three different language and cultures, who were participating in a three-day training seminar in France. The purpose of this seminar was for teachers to explore the complexity of culture, culture teaching, and culture learning. The teachers perceived their greatest difficulty to be doing justice to the diversity of perspectives and values that exist among natives within the same national culture. Kramsch points out that not one single national group was able to achieve consensus on what version of American or French or German culture should be taught abroad. This inescapable diversity of perspectives in turn made teachers "realize their own, subjective perspective in their choice of pedagogical materials" (p. 355). The second pedagogical challenge was making the target culture "attractive enough to be worthwhile studying, yet casting enough of a critical eye on it to make believable" (p. 356). Among the insights gained during the seminar, the participants mentioned (1) the notion of cultural relativity; (2) a heightened linguistic vigilance and distrust of lexical equivalencies; and, (3) an awareness of the importance of personal contact and dialogue when trying to understand another culture, what Kramsch calls an "essential reality check against stereotypical visions of the other" (p. 356). Kramsch concludes with a four-stage model for the process of cross-cultural understanding which would include an initial misunderstanding of intent, a subsequent misunderstanding of the source of the misunderstanding, attempts to explain the problem within one's own frame of reference, and, finally, a (necessary) switch to the other person's frame of reference. According to Kramsch, two implications follow from such a model for the development of a language pedagogy. First, it must present authentic documents together with their contexts of production and reception, i.e., the different readings given to these texts by various native and nonnative readers from a variety of cultural backgrounds. Second, learners and teachers must be given the opportunity to reflect upon the *cultural fault lines* that underlie their classroom discourse. From her own classroom observations, Kramsch (1993) concludes that the reflective component is most sorely missing as "Too many opportunities for cross-cultural reflection are brushed aside in the name of communicative practice" (p. 357). Her statement underscores once more the urgent need for classroom-based research that would help identify the ways in which cross-cultural reflection can be encouraged.

LEARNER VARIABLES

For many foreign language educators, an important reason for bringing culture into the classroom has been the hope that the study of culture will increase student motivation and improve attitudes toward language learning. Yet, our understanding of attitude formation is still far from complete (for a review of past debates, see Byram & Morgan, 1994, pp. 31–39). In the past, culture entered the classroom via literature, which was considered to be the ideal carrier of culture and a strong motivator for the study of language. Such an approach neglected the many students who dropped the study of language before they had reached the proficiency level required in a literature course. The introduction of little *c* culture (culture as daily life) at earlier stages of language learning was intended to address the needs of these learners, by making the lessons more interesting, and therefore motivate them to continue language study.

Motivation and interest are not easy to identify and study. We must look within the learner to find the often-subtle indicators of personal and classroom motivation. When there are 25 or more learners in a classroom, learner background variables become very complex. We must then add to that mix the atmosphere or culture of the classroom itself, which is known to affect the behavior of these particular students at this particular time (Cook, 1996). With these caveats in mind, we can examine the major research findings on motivation, attitudes, and other learner variables.

Motivation

The early work of Gardner and Lambert (1972), posited two major clusters of motivation indices: instrumental and integrative. Integrative motivation, the desire by the student to be liked by people in the target culture, is the major motivational influence on language learning in the school setting. Byram and Morgan (1994) after reviewing work by McDonough (1981) and Bley-Vroman (1989) point to the difficulty of inferring the causal relationship between language learning and motivation, arguing that high motivation may be a *result* of success in learning rather than the *cause* of that success. Burstall et al. (1974), Backman (1976), and others have argued that high achievement causes positive attitudes and high motivation, while the Gardner (1985) model explicitly suggests reciprocity between these variables.

Schumann's acculturation model (1978a, 1978b, 1986) examined the effects of personal variables such as relative status, congruence, attitude, integration, closed or open attitudes, amount of time in the culture, size of the learning group, and cohesiveness of the group on adult language learning. Schumann suggested three strategies taken by adult learners: total adoption of the target culture (assimilation), preservation of the home culture (total rejection of the target culture), and acculturation, which he defines as learning to function in the new culture while maintaining one's own identity. In the foreign—unlike the second—language classroom, the situation is slightly different in that the need for assimilation or acculturation is practically nonexistent, especially at beginning levels and in languages such as French or German where, as Byram and Morgan (1994) suggest, "understanding the target culture is appreciated . . . but generally only as a support to linguistic proficiency" (p. 7). In Spanish, by contrast, where the cultural reality is readily encountered, a different set of responses to culture learning may occur, ranging from a desire to getting to know one's neighbor to a deliberate effort to keep members of the other culture at a safe distance (Robinson-Stuart & Nocon, 1996). Regarding the role of language in culture learning, Marin and Sabogal (1987) created an acculturation scale for Hispanics and found that 55% of the variance in the scale was accounted for by language.

Crookes and Schmidt (1991) suggest that the limiting nature of second-language studies of motivation makes imperative the examination of the construct from other areas of social and educational psychology. They also suggest that researchers consider factors such as student interest, feedback effects, effects of student self-perceptions, and materials/syllabus design, in order to better understand and then improve language learning in the classroom. More recently, Gardner and MacIntyre (1993), Gardner and Tremblay (1994), Crookes and Schmidt (1991), Dornyei (1994), and Oxford and Shearin (1994), among others, have returned to the basic task of defining motivation, seeking to strengthen the theoretical basis for further study from inside or outside the second-language acquisition field.

An additional problem is the difficulty of generalizing findings on motivation across languages because, as foreign language teachers well know, each language seems to carry its own *motivational baggage*. Furthermore, the identification of factors making up motivation and its definition may still not be useful to teachers at all levels. What motivates students to begin L2 may be different from the factors leading them to continue language study, or to begin a third or fourth language when it is not required. Momber (1979) and Myers (1978) both found that students need high motivation to continue, but that motivation as a trait is highly unstable. In addition, they suggest that any research findings on motivation and continued language study are problematic due to the unreliability of self-report measures that are so common in this type of research. The same student, for instance, may exhibit different motivations in different classrooms as a function of the particular characteristics (e.g., student composition, classroom climate, the teacher) that exist in each classroom.

Motivation can also change over time and vary by age. For instance, a student who begins studying Spanish initially because a friend is studying it, may continue into the second year due to family pressure to develop proficiency in the language, and may go on to a third year in order to travel in Latin America. Burstall et al. (1974) studying children, adolescents, and adults found age, in addition to experience and other personal variables, to be a significant factor in predicting differences in motivation. Gardner and MacIntyre (1992, 1993) summarize the complex effects of student factors involved in second-language learning.

Crookes and Schmidt (1991) suggest that one of the reasons why work on motivation in second language learning has been inconclusive is because motivation has been limited to social-psychological conceptualizations of the construct and also has been frequently confused with attitudes toward the target culture (see also Glicksman, 1981, above). This view has been contradicted by Gardner and Tremblay (1994), however, who feel it is based in part "on a misunderstanding and resulting misrepresentation of the *Gardnerian* model and research (p. 360). Crookes and Schmidt (1991) recommend that research move away from self-report and correlational studies toward survey instruments, observational measures, ethnographic work, action research, and introspective measures, in addition to "true experimental studies" (p. 502). We may believe that a systematic inclusion of cultural components in language courses will increase motivation to study the language or support adaptation to the culture of the people who speak that language, but there is only limited evidence to support this claim. Two recent studies (Martin & Laurie, 1993; Robinson & Nocon, 1996) have attempted to improve the state of the art by systematically investigating student motivation for language and culture study.

Martin and Laurie (1993) investigated the views of 45 students, enrolled in an intermediate level French course at Flinders University in South Australia, about the contribution of literary and cultural content to language learning. They found that the students' reasons for studying French "were more related to linguistic than cultural interests" (p. 190), with practical reasons such as oral proficiency, travel plans, and employment opportunities dominating the list. When asked specifically about the role of literature and culture as motivating factors, the "desire to study the French way of life" motivated nearly 90% of students, while "hegemonal aspects of the culture motivated rather less than half (p. 195). These findings are consistent with previous research conducted in Australia. After discussing possible reasons for the students' "fear of literature" (p. 205), Martin and Laurie advance the hypothesis of *culture anxiety* caused by the perceived lack of "cultural background to relate to a foreign literature" (p. 205) and propose a methodology for presenting literature.

Robinson-Stuart and Nocon (1996) report on an ethnographic experiment in a 3rd semester Spanish course at San Diego State University. They investigated the hypothesis that training in ethnographic techniques and a commitment to face-to-face contact would have a positive effect on students desire to study the language and use it to communicate. They started from three key assumptions: (1) students have a tendency to "separate the language from the culture of the people who use it and, by extension, from the people" (p. 434), a conclusion already arrived at by Hall and Ramirez (1993); (2) one should not assume that language students have an intrinsic motivation or desire to communicate (Robinson, 1981); and, (3) that salience and exaggeration form a general frame of perception that even resists counter-evidence (supported by findings in person-perception psychology). Robinson-Stuart and Nocon used a threefold methodology of in-classroom training, in-the-field interviews, and pre- and post-surveys of the students. They found that the project had initiated "positive perceptual, affective and cognitive changes" for the students (p. 443) as evidenced by students' enhanced attitudes toward the study of Spanish and increased desire to communicate with local Spanish speakers, and by students' better understanding of their own culture and the lived culture of local Spanish speakers. Regarding motivation, the authors refer to the controversy in psychology surrounding motivational theory which consists of two competing sets of beliefs: (1) that by first changing the attitude a behavioral change will follow, or (2) that by changing the behavior an attitudinal transformation will follow. They point out that the value of the ethnographic approach lies in its ability to satisfy both criteria by "structuring the environment to change both behavior and attitude" (p. 444). Their findings are promising.

Attitudes

While motivation generally can be defined as the factor which impels the student to study a target language in the first place and to continue or to stop studying it, attitudes can be generally defined as the positive or negative feelings that students have toward the language, the language teacher, the language class, the culture(s) of people who speak that language, and the study of the language. While the concepts of motivation and attitudes are closely related, they appear to be different constructs in certain respects. By way of example, a student might be highly motivated to study a language and culture for instrumental reasons, which would not necessarily entail the development of positive attitudes toward the target culture. Beyond these conceptual distinctions lies a set of research questions regarding the complex relationship between motivation, attitudes, language learning, and behavior (specifically, behavior that is appropriate and effective in the target culture).

The theoretical possibility that linguistic experience and proficiency do not automatically lead to improved attitudes toward members of the target culture has been documented repeatedly since Tucker and D'Anglejan's (1974) well-known report on the Canadian St. Lambert immersion project. Massey (1986) also found that attitudes became more negative and motivation decreased the longer students studied the target language. He studied 236 sixth and seventh grade students in three schools who were currently studying French 40 minutes daily, but who had studied it only 20 minutes per day for the three years prior to the investigation. He administered the

Gardner Attitude and Motivation Test Battery at the end of one academic year and again four weeks into the following year; the scores became more negative over time in all the settings. Hamers (1984) inquired as to whether 5th, 6th, 9th, and 10th-grade students would improve attitudes and motivation if exposed to exchanges with French or English-speaking Québécois students. She studied 24 classes (*n* = 439) evenly divided between francophones and anglophones. Her two main findings were that interregional exchange affected students most positively at the secondary level, and that children from urban areas seemed to benefit less from any exchanges than children from rural areas. In the Durham study (Byram et al., 1991), researchers found that girls tended to be more positive in their attitudes toward the French, that the *better* classes had more positive attitudes, and that younger students seemed more prejudiced toward specific cultural groups than older students.

Stelly (1991), reporting on "the effects of whole language approach using authentic French texts on student comprehension and attitude," found that the students' attitudes toward French culture did not significantly improve after a course which exposed them to authentic materials in a learner-centered, communicative environment. Surprisingly, attitudes did significantly improve in the control group, a supposedly traditional classroom that had followed a regular syllabus. In fact, the control was preparing for an upcoming trip to France, many class members were going to go on the trip, and the teacher was using her own videos, photographs, and cultural artifacts as a complement to text-based classroom activities. The findings, therefore, must be interpreted with great caution. Nocon (1991) found that while attitudes toward Spanish speakers did not usually change over the time, the existence of a foreign language requirement was correlated with negative attitudes toward the language and speakers of the language (quoted in Robinson-Stuart & Nocon, 1996, pp. 432–34).

Contact with people from the target culture, either in the school setting or in the target culture, has been found to have a positive influence and improve attitudes under certain circumstances (see discussion of study abroad programs). Porebski and McInnis (1988), like Robinson and Nocon, submit that increased contact leads to positive attitudes rather than the reverse. They followed almost 2,500 children for three years (1975–78) and found that middle-school-age children who had daily contact with French peers in an *animator* program had a highly significant increase in contact with French peers outside the classroom from grade to grade, as well as higher listening and reading proficiency in French. The instruments used, a sociometric friendship-pattern scale and IEA French language achievement scales, are quite different from the usual self-report scales for measuring attitudes. The researchers operationalized *positive attitudes* as the willingness of students to seek out speakers of the target culture for pleasure. Similarly, Park (1995) used as the measure of attitudes and motivation of adult learners their voluntary current and past contact with native speakers of the language being studied (Japanese or Korean), as recorded in journals kept over two years, reported in interviews, and noted on a contact questionnaire.

A number of other learner factors have been examined, among them learning style (Dirksen, 1990; Reid, 1987), intelligence, previous language background, language aptitude, and strategy use. Gardner and MacIntyre (1993) detail a *Socioeducation model* of second-language acquisition, which suggests that all of these factors, and perhaps many others, influence linguistic and nonlinguistic (presumably cultural) outcomes in formal and informal language acquisition contexts. The research on motivation and attitude seems to gravitate around the notion of 'contact' and its role in the embryonic stage of intercultural development. While causality is far from being unidirectional, more studies point to contact improving attitudes than vice-versa. It appears that favorable contact leads to the discovery of cultural similarities and of our common humanity (cf. Robinson and Nocon's approach). The question then becomes how to help learners move beyond this still ethnocentric stage of intercultural development and into the intercultural stages where acceptance of cultural differences is the norm (see J. & M. Bennett, this volume).

CURRICULAR MATERIALS

Textbooks

No longer thought to be value-neutral, textbooks and other materials used in language learning generally present a certain way of looking at the world, that is, through the cultural lens of the author. Prior to the 1940s, many textbooks were written from a monocultural perspective according to Kramsch and McConnell-Ginet (1992). The multiple realities that make up culture were not included. The underlying belief was that a homogeneous and relatively static national culture could be identified. It could be described. And its facts could be memorized. Cultural elements were selected for study on the basis of their comparable importance in the home culture of the authors. Cultural artifacts, the more visible elements of culture, were studied at the exclusion of cultural values. With the advent of the functional and communicative proficiency approaches in the 1970s, and all through the 1980s, teachers moved away from relying solely on textbooks to teach language. The textbook became viewed as a snapshot, and only one of many, through which the culture could be explored and understood (Kramsch & McConnell-Ginet, 1992). The target culture was now entering the classroom via authentic cultural materials. Nonetheless, the main finding about today's textbooks is that they are still central to language educators as the main source of culture learning and, in many respects, they are still problematical.

The Durham researchers (Byram et al., 1991) found that the textbook was used extensively, functioned as instructional guide, and determined themes and sequence of material. Furthermore, extensive and frequent interviews with their young learners led the authors to conclude that the textbook influenced most of the internalized knowledge the students had of French culture. They found this particularly problematic because the textbook topics were frequently poorly chosen and represented a distorted view of reality by taking a tourist's perspective (e.g., focusing on topics such as restaurant meals or public transportation). The authors emphasize that the influence of the textbook on the range and depth of the cultural information should be cause for concern to all foreign language educators.

The conclusion arrived at by Byram and his colleagues regarding the influence of the textbook also holds true for the language classroom in the United States (Loughrin-Sacco, 1992; Ryan, 1994). Kramsch (1987) compared eight first-year German textbooks to examine how culture was taught through the pictures, dialogues, and exercises. To gain insight into the way cultural facts are conceptualized, presented, and validated, she examined chapters on sports in textbooks widely used in the US. While she found that the authors made a serious attempt to teach culture through the dialogues, readings, and language exercises presented, she was concerned about the factual nature of the understandings conveyed, and by the German textbooks' tendency to rely on contrasts with American culture to *construct* a view of German culture. Learners are asked to contrast their subjective views of U.S. culture with generalities presented about German culture. But because readers rarely have sufficient understanding of their own culture, they are unable to critically assess the concepts being presented and they reduce the comparative process to a low-level comparison of facts. Kramsch also found that the texts tended to stress similarities between cultures to minimize potentially threatening differences instead of helping the learner construct an understanding of German culture based on higher-level contrastive relational analyses. Furthermore, the textbook authors' frequently biased perspective on the target culture becomes reality and truth for the learner because the culture contrasts are based on low-level concepts and the textbook authors' viewpoint is not presented. Kramsch concluded from her study that much of the content of these textbooks and their use could actually impede the development of positive cultural understanding.

Moore (1991), in her thorough analysis of the cultural content of Spanish textbooks, reached a similar conclusion. She meticulously analyzed the cultural readings, and their related comprehension questions, in the six most commonly used Spanish textbooks for first-year, college-level students. She found that while 92% of the selections contained some cultural information and that this information was generally comprised of *factual fragments* or highly generalized information intended to indicate the norms of behavior in the Spanish-speaking world. There was little or no explanation of how patterns of behaviors develop to fit in with a complex cultural system, and only few indications that any of the norms or values presented might differ among people of different ages, genders, religions, socioeconomic levels, regions or political orientations. Both Byram and Moore point out how, in the absence of knowledge about *cultural antecedents* (Triandis, 1972) learners are left to interpret the text on the basis of a priori assumptions, and, as a result, tend to assimilate the culture under study to their own.

Other researchers have documented the lack of complexity in the cultural information presented in textbooks (Ueber & Grosse, 1991). Ueber and Grosse (1991) studied business French and Spanish texts, and found the cultural content to be *extremely limited* and *basic*. In the French texts, in particular, the instructional goals of the text were found to be "deliberately well-focused and narrow." Wieczorek (1994), surveying the content of twelve French textbooks, found that the texts were limited not only in the depth of cultural information, but also in the range of French-speaking cultures depicted. In the 12 books that were examined, information about countries other than France averaged only about 5.13% of the total content and, even then, much of this information was taken out of its cultural context. These studies point out that French texts often construct a hierarchical representation of the francophone world, with the views from *la métropole* (capital city) serving as the ultimate point of reference for our understanding of French culture. Wieczorek worries that such biased and simplistic cultural presentations, i.e., texts lacking in cultural and linguistic complexity, are likely to reinforce preexisting assumptions and stereotypes.

Authentic Materials

While there is a large and growing body of theoretical writing concerned with promoting the use of authentic materials, proposing ways of incorporating these materials into the curriculum, and discussing the concept of authenticity (Baumgratz-Gangl, 1991; Kane, 1991; Kramsch, 1993; Robinson, 1981), there is very little actual research that has attempted to study the effects of authentic materials on either linguistic or cultural competency. As reported earlier, Stelly (1991) found no effects attributable to authentic materials, but the design of the study is highly problematical. We found only one other research study on this topic by Kienbaum, Russell and Welty (1986), who used a quasi-experimental design to compare traditional textbook-based classrooms with those using only authentic materials for second year college courses. Although they found no statistically significant difference between experimental and control groups in terms of language gain or attitudes toward the target language (a finding they attribute to their small number of subjects), they did find that, (1) all students responded favorably to the absence of a traditional text and applauded the use of authentic materials; (2) students appreciated the view of the target country's cultural and social reality offered through the instructors' personal slides and interviews with citizens; and, (3) students responded favorably to the current events selections and, through articles and editorials related to the United States, gained a better understanding of their own cultural assumptions and values.

Computer-assisted instruction.   One of the most intriguing developments in language and culture education, computer-assisted instruction (CAI), is just emerging on the scene. Some computer-assisted learning programs that are process-oriented and interactive have been successfully developed (e.g., *A la rencontre de Philippe*, a French program). Although computers are still an artificial means of learning, proponents of CAI argue that the added visual dimension gives students more contextual and linguistic information than a standard textbook can provide. An early study by Halliday (1978) found that students often felt that they did not have enough information about a situation to act it out appropriately in a role-play or to respond to questions about it. A computer scenario can provide added contextual cues while involving the student as one of the characters in the scene. The learners can stop, ask questions, get more information along the way, and even change the outcome of the interaction. In any case, getting immediate feedback allows negotiation of meaning and communication to go forward.

To conclude this section on curricular materials, the small research literature supports the use of authentic materials in culture instruction. Kramsch (1991b) and Robinson (1981) remind us, however, that the use of authentic materials needs to be accompanied by an understanding of how one derives meaning from them. The danger of inaccurate or monocultural interpretations of the materials is always present.

THE ASSESSMENT OF CULTURE LEARNING

Introduction

It is axiomatic among educators that what is tested is what is taught, and what is taught is what is tested. As we have observed throughout this chapter, much of what passes for culture instruction is inadequate, so it is not surprising that the assessment of culture learning has also been problematical. Placing culture learning at the core of language education is challenging because: (1) assessment, in general, emphasizes the use of objective, paper and pencil instruments which are easy to administer and grade; (2) culture is seen as difficult to teach and assess; (3) culture instruction has been primarily and narrowly focused on culture-specific information; and, (4) up until fairly recently, language teachers have not received much help from the profession in terms of conceptualizing, teaching, and assessing culture learning. All of these factors have interacted with each other to inhibit culture teaching and learning.

A Brief History of Assessment in Second Language Education

In the 1950s, foreign language teaching centered on a knowledge of grammar, vocabulary, and reading in the target language. Consequently, assessment took the form of translation exercises, vocabulary lists, dictations, and fill in the blank type exercises whose purpose was to measure linguistic gains. The emphasis was on cognitive understanding and rote reproduction of language rules rather than on communicative and sociolinguistic competence. Culture learning, even though ambitiously conceptualized as "a more enlightened Americanism through adjustments to the concept of differences between cultures" (MLA 1956 steering committee, quoted in Paquette, p. 381) was an expected by-product resulting from the study of literature, geography, and other factual and tangible elements of the target culture referred to as Big *C* culture.

The audiolingual movement of the 1960s generated assessment techniques, which paralleled language-teaching methods, namely the discrete testing in each of the four skills of listening, reading, speaking and writing. Examples of this new trend were the MLA Cooperative Foreign Language Tests and the Pimsleur Proficiency Tests, which are divided into skill-specific sections. Although this approach incorporated some behavioral components, it too relied primarily on memorization of small, discrete language units rather than on the integration of knowledge with communicative skills demonstrating understanding of language usage in its cultural context. Such assessment differed from earlier practices only in that culture had by now been expanded to include what became referred to as small *c* culture, or what Brooks as early as 1954 had called "culture as everything in human life" and "culture as the best in human life" (1975, pp. 20–21). Both Brooks' model of culture as a network of nodes and parameters and Nostrand's *Emergent Model* (1974) introduced culture as *social patterns of living* (Steele, 1989) and postulated a strong interrelation between language and culture. However, while they may have provided a useful matrix for a systematic analysis of a foreign culture by helping teachers pose appropriate questions, (Brooks, 1975), these models did not significantly alter extant assessment practices which emphasized objective types of knowledge.

The two sociolinguistic decades of the 1970s and 1980s brought along a new culture teaching and learning focus. Culture became fully recognized as the context without which a word has no meaning, to paraphrase Seelye's famous statement, and was deemed necessary to achieve a working knowledge of the language (Lessard-Clouston, 1992). Saville-Troike (1983), for example, stated that "interpreting the meaning of linguistic behavior means knowing the cultural meaning of the context within which it occurs" (pp. 131–132). Lessard-Clouston (1992) added that not assessing culture learning sends out a message that culture is not important. Valdes (1990) noted that assessment of culture learning also provides feedback to students as to the validity of their cultural understanding and informs teachers about the nature of the cultural understanding gained by the students.

The debate in the United States over assessment had begun in the early 1970s with the President's Commission on Foreign Languages and International Studies, which reported that foreign language study was a "national scandal of ignorance and ineptitude" (Patrikis, 1987, p. 26). In the 1980s, several states and professional organizations such as ACTFL issued new guidelines to expand the language education to explicitly include culture learning (ACTFL, 1984; Kramsch, 1991a). But the wave of criticism encountered by the culture section in the 1984 *Provisional Guidelines* and their subsequent elimination from the final version (ACTFL, 1986) marked a setback for the assessment of culture learning. To this day, according to Kramsch (1991a), culture learning remains a murky issue.

Although progress has been slow, there are encouraging new developments in the assessment of culture learning. As Philips (this volume) points out, the new culture learning standards articulated by the language education profession provides a clearer sense of direction than anything to date. Moreover, the curriculum is being broadened to include distinct cultural studies components including both culture-specific and more generalizable intercultural communication materials (Murphy, 1988). The assessment of culture learning is also becoming more sophisticated, shifting from over reliance on pre- and post-tests to assessment that is done throughout the learning experience and uses alternative materials (e.g., portfolios, dialogue journals, and ongoing performance evaluations).

The Nature of Assessment

It is our view that the assessment of learning, in much of the western world, is carried out primarily by means of so-called objective testing of knowledge, the most common instrument of which is paper and pencil examinations. There are important reasons for this, for example, the concern in the United States with being a *world class* nation, not falling behind other countries, and maintaining a position of economic prominence in the world (Berube, 1996; Kean, 1995). These concerns lead to the desire of politicians to assert more control over education and to have convenient ways (objective tests) to benchmark education's accomplishments and shortcomings. Assessment is also connected to the cultural values of a country, such as efficiency, objectivity, and fairness in many Western nations. In the language and culture classroom, these cultural traits have profound implications for teaching and learning. For example, students are encouraged to study the target culture *objectively*, like a set of facts, as opposed to "experiencing culture as a process of producing meaning regarding each other's way of being in the world," (Robinson-Stuart and Nocon, 1996, p. 444). Objective tests are then used to measure the degree to which they have learned those culture facts.

Assessment, to us, means far more than objective tests of how much information the student has learned in a given period of time. It should be formative (i.e., ongoing), behavioral and affective as well as cognitive, and expanded with respect to the ways in which assessments are conducted.

Issues in the Assessment of Culture Learning

While the possibilities of what can be assessed are many, Seelye (1994) found that there were actually only five main components that were regularly being tested: historical facts, trivia items, toponyms, vocabulary, and familiarity with the arts (i.e., big *C* culture). He also discovered that the content generally focused on matters of interest to the majority group in the home culture. For instance, students would be graded on how well they could accurately reflect how an average middle-class male from the target culture would answer the question rather than the possible divergent points of view minority persons in the host culture. Damen (1987) points to the difficulty often felt by teachers of choosing which culture to teach. Many countries, for example, have more than one culture and language within their borders. In addition to racial and ethnic differences, there is diversity due to age, gender, socioeconomic class, religion, and other variables. Moreover, different countries often speak the same language and share a similar cultural heritage. Thus, how would a French teacher represent or talk about French culture? What about the French spoken in East Africa, the customs of Martinique or francophone Canada? Crawford-Lange and Lange (1984) suggest a process for culture learning which is exploratory in nature, builds upon but does not restrict the learners to initial stereotypes, and utilizes observable cultural facts as just one of many inputs into the learning process.

Partly to avoid the uncertainty that comes with taking into account the cultural diversity of the target culture, teachers often choose to focus their tests on the Big *C* culture (e.g., architecture, geography, and artistic traditions) associated with the presumed center of the target culture. Hughes (1986) calls test questions relating to these cultural artifacts *institutional questions* as they are largely factual in nature and can be easily looked up and memorized by students. Likewise, Kramsch (1991a) found that many foreign language textbooks in the United States encourage this type of learning and testing by including a disproportionate number of topics on literature, art, and statistical facts. Valette (1986) argues that many teachers for practical reasons prefer the focus on discrete elements of cultural knowledge: they are easy to prepare, test, and score.

Furthermore, as Byram and Morgan (1994) convincingly argue, testing for the other two components of intercultural competence, attitudes, and behaviors, is extremely complex and fraught with many pitfalls. For instance, there is a difference between assessing the application of an attitude, and its existence. The ability to act appropriately in a new cultural context does not necessarily mean the acceptance of a new world view; indeed, as Byram and Morgan (1994) note, it is not easy to assess the meaning of behaviors. In addition, testing for something beyond factual knowledge such as the presence of positive attitudes, also raises ethical issues since testing should match what has been deliberately taught and consciously learned (Byram & Morgan, 1994). Byram questions how much control a learner has over the development of an attitude such as openness or empathy, or of flexibility of mind, or the ability to decenter? It should come, therefore as no surprise that testing for cultural knowledge seems more attractive than testing for aspects of intercultural competence.

One could ask whether testing/assessment of learning other than knowledge has a place in the instructional setting? Kramsch, looking at the different goals put forth by state education offices, found a wide range of justifications for assessing culture learning, from concrete political goals such as meeting the challenge of international competition to broader and less tangible reasons such as fostering cross-cultural awareness and understanding. She points out the vast discrepancy that exists today between the cultural goals and assessment procedures; the suggested assessment approaches often bear no resemblance to the expected learning outcomes proposed by state education departments (Kramsch, 1991a, pp. 225–26). Kramsch believes that the confusion between guidelines and assessment comes from not knowing ultimately why the tests are being used.

Assessment Models

One of the first assessment models found in the literature, the social distance scale, was developed by Bogardus (1933). This test set out to measure peoples' reaction to other cultures. Other cultures were grouped by racial and linguistic features. Respondents were asked to indicate if they accept a person from that group in different situations. For example, the question would ask if the respondent would mind if a person from group x married his/her sister. Respondents would indicate their level of acceptance on a seven-point scale. The use this type of scale has been popular in terms of measuring cultural attitudes and understandings (see Cadd, 1994, for recent use of this type of scale). A similar model was used by Osgood, Suci, and Tannenbaum (1957) with their semantic differential approach. Their scale was developed to measure how a person evaluates another culture in terms of bipolar traits using a multipoint Likert scale. For instance, the question would ask if the respondent thinks whether persons in group x are good or bad. Grice (1934) developed a test, still used today (Seelye, 1994), which asks respondents to agree or disagree with statements about a specific culture group (e.g., The French are emotional). These early assessment models have a tendency to use binary constructions and, thus, run the risk of encouraging dualistic thinking or stereotyping of other cultures.

More recent assessment techniques have expanded significantly upon the earlier models. The culture assimilator model, for example, incorporates contextual factors by presenting short, intercultural episodes that place the reader in real life situations. Brislin, Cushner, Cherrie, and Yong (1986), for example, have published a *culture-general* assimilator which includes 100 such episodes or critical incidents. In their version, each episode is followed by three to four specific answers from which the students are asked to select what they think is the best explanation of that particular cross-cultural situation. Here, the assessment is culture-specific; the student either does or does not pick the most appropriate answer. The promising *Intercultural Perspective-Taking Scale* developed by Steglitz (1993) demonstrates another use of the critical incident, one, which leads to more culture-general assessment. Here, the students read the story and then write an essay explaining their interpretation of what is occurring in the cross-cultural encounter. The teacher or coder rates the essay on the degree to which the student (1) incorporates cultural variables into the analysis and (2) reflects upon how the culturally different person in the story might be construing events.

King (1990) developed a cultural awareness test similar to the assimilator called cultural mini-dramas. These dramas incorporate the performance of linguistic as well as small *c* culture practices, which can be observed by the teacher. Other interesting assessment techniques include the use of videotaping of cultural role plays (Falsgraf, 1994) and interactive computer programs that prompt students with various verbal and nonverbal cues (Baugh, 1994). Some European educators and researchers (Kordes, 1991; Meyer, 1991) have argued for the use of cross-cultural mediation tasks that would enable the teacher to assess a learner's culture-general skills such as empathy, tolerance, the ability to suspend judgment, and the adoption of someone else's point of view. For the purpose of assessing such intangible learning (e.g., the development of empathy), Byram and Morgan (1994) propose the following five-level scale: (1) rejection of the foreign culture; (2) explanation provided but "from the outside"; (3) explanation "from the inside"; (4) "genuine attempt to recreate an alien world view"; and, (5) "recognition of how one's own world view is culturally conditioned" (p. 150). They also suggest new and flexible criteria for assessing cultural knowledge such as accuracy, detail, relevance of the factual material, recognition of diversity, and avoidance of stereotyping. Damen (1987) diagrams out four types of evaluation techniques for culture learning: self-report, enactments (such as role-plays or simulations), productions of materials (essays or letters), and observation by the teacher or other peers when the student is demonstrating specific cultural skills.

Two more instruments deserve mention here: the Cross-Cultural Adaptability Inventory (CCAI) (Kelley & Meyers, 1995) and the Intercultural Development Inventory (Hammer & Bennett, in press). The CCAI is a 36-item paper and pencil, culture-general assessment instrument which measures four qualities hypothesized by the authors to be associated with intercultural competence: emotional resilience, flexibility and openness, perceptual acuity (the ability to read verbal and nonverbal cues), and personal autonomy. The CCAI has been used in at least one study of an education abroad program, a six-month language and culture immersion program in Senegal (Paulson, 1995), where the author found that the learners improved in these areas during their time abroad.

The Intercultural Development Inventory (IDI) (Hammer & Bennett, in press) is a 70-item paper and pencil instrument intended to measure the respondent's degree of *intercultural sensitivity* along an eight-stage developmental continuum. The IDI is based on the work of M. Bennett (1986, 1993, this volume with J. Bennett), who has conceptualized intercultural competence as a developmental phenomenon characterized by the affective, behavioral, and cognitive ways in which a person construes and responds to cultural differences. We consider this model to be one of the most important in the literature in terms of both its theoretical contributions to our understanding of culture learning, but also with respect to its practical implications for language and culture educators. The IDI presents learner profiles which show which stage they identify most strongly with at the moment, one of the four ethnocentric (monocultural) stages, or one of the four ethnorelative (intercultural) stages. The first author of this chapter has two studies underway in which the IDI is being used to assess the intercultural sensitivity of high school and university language students.

We were pleased to find that many teachers have experimented with new ideas such as these to assess their students' culture learning. Royer (1996) called her approach to assessing culture learning in her French class *summative authentic assessment*, by which she defines as the ability to communicate in the new language and culture, not just the ability to use correct grammar. In addition, she developed ways to regularly assess the students' progress in the areas of "social and life skills of listening, sharing, group problem solving, handling confrontation, and negotiation" (Royer, 1996, p. 174). Her assessment techniques took many forms including audio recordings, performances, written essays, observation of group work, and group projects. This allowed her to assess a variety of learning goals as they work together rather than as discrete skills.

The Challenges of Assessment

Content and criteria. Kordes (1991), Meyer (1991), and Byram and Morgan (1994) have identified the enormous challenges associated with the assessment of culture learning. As a result, some educators feel like giving up the idea altogether. For instance, Byram (1988) points out that in England, the Minister for Education left out criteria associated with cultural understanding because it was felt that only *practical communication* could be listed as a criteria for learning. Other researchers conclude that culture learning can only be assessed through informal means, and only "by the learners themselves" (Damen, 1987, p. 291).

Cultural (mis)interpretations. Another problem associated with the assessment of culture learning in the foreign language classroom is a reliance by teachers on their own personal experiences when they create an assessment instrument. Seelye (1994) tells a story about a Spanish exam he and other teachers were involved in creating. Each teacher took one chapter of the material and wrote ten multiple-choice questions. These questions were then presented to a group of native Spanish speakers for evaluation of the exam. The native Spanish speakers answered each question in at least two different ways for 90% of the questions; in 20% of the cases the question was answered in four different ways. All of the native Spanish speakers introduced variations on what the question meant and wrapped slightly different contextual factors around the questions so that it had meaning for them, but different meaning in each case. Seelye's story is strongly reminiscent of the experience of teachers unable to agree on a core culture as reported by Kramsch (1993). The difficulty of cultural interpretation is a serious challenge to the whole notion of assessment. Lessard-Clouston (1992) argues that valid assessment needs to mirror classroom instruction (see also Byram & Morgan, above) and if one student interprets the culture differently from others, there needs to be some flexibility for adjustment. Such a possibility strongly undermines the myth of objective, reliable testing.

A positivistic tradition. There is a tendency for assessment to be embedded in a positivistic tradition of research (e.g., Ferguson & Huebner, 1991), one that emphasizes scholarly objectivity. Kramsch, however, argues that objectivity is not possible when dealing with culture because it is subjectively experienced and construed. As Seelye's story of the Spanish examination so aptly demonstrated, intracultural variation itself will always generate a plethora of different meanings for different observers of the same events. Zeidner (1986) also suggests that even without the cultural component, language aptitude tests are biased depending on the respondent's cultural identity, age, sex, and social class. Similarly, Dirksen (1990) asserts that differences in learning styles also play into the process. Most assessment methods are of the timed pencil and paper variety, although many students feel that this does not allow them to adequately demonstrate what they know. In a study by Reid (1987), it was found that many ESL students preferred and performed better using kinesthetic/tactile methods, rather than the more passive methods that were being used in the classroom.

There are indications that change in assessment practices would be welcomed by students. In one study (Warren, 1987b) in which small groups of students in three large universities were interviewed, the students found the traditional methods of assessment greatly lacking in their ability to accurately assess the actual learning that took place during the course. The students expressed their distaste for tests that assessed only their ability to remember fragments of information. In addition, when the test did not provide the opportunity for them to show all that they had learned, the students felt betrayed, as their grade reflected neither their learning nor their work. Ultimately, the instructors were blamed for creating bad tests, a criticism which reflects the teachers own concern that they do not feel competent enough to create their own tests (Warren, 1987a). On the other hand, the students could recount instances where assessment procedures used during instruction were integrated as learning exercises, rather than an exercise in memorization at the end of the course. They all stated a preference for this type of assessment.

Academic insularity. Some authors and researchers find that the source of many assessment problems stems from the inability of the various professions, which are concerned with this issue, to work cooperatively together (Ferguson & Huebner, 1991; Freed, 1991). Many departments such as intercultural communication and foreign languages are compartmentalized to the extent that interdisciplinary research and collaboration is very difficult. Likewise, the segregation between academic departments and practicing professionals generates few qualified researchers able to conduct the type of research and to create the assessment tools appropriate for a pedagogy based on an integration of language and culture (Seelye, 1994).

Intercultural competence and the teacher.   Finally, for many teachers, culture teaching and learning is a relatively new and unfamiliar venture, especially in the framework of our model of culture learning. The problem is compounded by a lack of concrete examples of how to teach for intercultural competence (for an exception, see Crawford-Lange & Lange, 1987) and by teachers' mistaken belief that they need to be culture experts. Rather, we hope teachers will come to share the view so perceptively expressed by Kane (1991) that, "By being the one invested with the knowledge and authority, the teacher's responsibility is to invite—and join—the students in challenging unexamined beliefs and stereotypes" (p. 245). In our view, teachers can become guides and partners in a process of culture learning and discovery with their students, rather than culture experts upon whom their students exclusively rely for cultural knowledge.

Our work here will by no means bring closure to the debate over why, how, and what to test, but hopefully it will underscore how many creative possibilities there are for assessing culture learning. Byram (1988) expresses the fear that due to the difficulty of assessment, culture learning will retain a second-class status. We share this concern, but hope that the ideas presented in this paper regarding the conceptualization and assessment of culture learning, will help elevate this topic to the position of prominence in the field that many foreign language educators feel it deserves.

CONCLUSIONS

In this closing section, we present the major points that we extracted from the theoretical and research literatures. For each of the previous sections of the paper, we attempted to indicate the following: what the major emphases in the literature were; what the research does and does not tell us; how culture is presented in the literature; how culture is assessed; and, our recommendations for future research.

Context

The major emphasis regarding context has been on defining the term. We were struck by the complexity of the concept and the wide variety of definitions presented in the literature. Eventually, we elected to utilize context as our overall frame of reference for this paper and subsume under it other concepts such as setting, teacher variables, learner variables, curricular materials and instructional methods, and assessment. With respect to these elements, the emphasis in the literature has been on the impact of the setting on culture learning (e.g., immersion in the host culture versus classroom instruction). The classroom-based literature has focused on immersion programs. The next most commonly studied contextual variables have been teacher and learner variables.

- The actual research literature on context as a broader variable is virtually nonexistent. The vast majority of the research deals with specific elements of context such as settings or curricular materials.
- In the context literature, context is culture. Understanding the context means understanding the culture-general dynamics of human interaction and communication, as well as the specific culture in question (target culture). For example, creating a context for culture learning in the classroom means finding ways to approximate the target culture in the classroom.
- With respect to the assessment of context, we found no literature that provided models for contextual assessment in the holistic sense. There is a growing literature that informs us about culture-general and culture-specific assessment.
- What we feel is most strongly needed is research which integrates the various elements of context into a total research program where the interaction of these contextual variables could be examined.

Setting

- The emphasis in the research literature regarding settings for culture learning has been on naturalistic settings as represented by study abroad programs. With respect to the classroom as the setting, the research literature has emphasized immersion programs.
- We have learned from the research on setting that immersion in the target culture makes a difference; it can promote accelerated language and culture learning. But there appear to be two major conditions. First, the impact of study abroad depends on the individual learner's motivation and previous language background. Second, it is important for the experience in the target culture to be positive. The naturalistic setting, of and by itself, does not guarantee increases in either language or culture learning beyond what can be provided by the classroom. But if the study abroad cultural immersion experience is positive and the learner has the proper motivation and background, study abroad can significantly enhance culture learning.
- What we do not know from the literature is very much about classroom settings that attempt to replicate or approximate the target culture. There is also a gap in the literature on how naturalistic and classroom settings might interact to promote culture learning. Many questions thus remain. When is the best time to study abroad? What level of existing language proficiency is needed to derive the greatest benefit from a study abroad program?
- Culture in this literature has been defined mostly in terms of *facts* about the target culture. The emphasis has been on culture-specific knowledge and that knowledge has been primarily about surface-level, visible culture (e.g., food, clothing) rather than deep culture (e.g., values, beliefs). There has been little written on culture defined in more culture-general, intercultural competence terms.
- Regarding assessment of settings, there has been very little in the research literature that deals with this issue.
- Our recommendations for future research include: (1) studies of classrooms that attempt to create a target culture environment which can show us how this might be done and what the impact of such classroom settings might be on culture learning; (2) studies of the relative impact of different settings on the acquisition of the deeper elements of culture, and, (3) studies of immersion classrooms that pay specific attention to the way culture is taught. The assumption appears to have been that immersion programs teach culture.

Teacher Variables

- The research examined under the heading of teacher variables reveals two underlying emphases: the struggle to understand the nature of cultural instruction in the foreign language classroom and the crucial role played by the teacher in the process of cultural learning.
- The research tells us that teachers consider language study to be more than just learning a language: they see it as discovering and learning about other ways of living, and about understanding other peoples. Research also tells us that teachers are an essential component in culture learning, that students consider teachers to be their most important resource, and that there are discrepancies between what students want and what teachers provide. Furthermore, as members of the educational system, teachers may have to work in an ethnocentric environment, or under institutional and societal constraints, that can defeat their best intentions.

Research also hints at the fact that teachers' knowledge, attitudes, and beliefs about the nature of culture and cultural diversity may profoundly impact their instructional and methodological choices. We also know that teachers often feel insufficiently prepared for the task of teaching for cultural teaching, i.e., teaching toward objectives other than linguistic.

Finally, in spite of some apparent confusion regarding the nature of culture/culture teaching, foreign language teachers view their field as composed of a well-defined body of knowledge on which they can agree.

- The research reviewed raises more questions than it answers and many gaps remain. Among the more salient questions are the following: (a) how do teachers translate their objectives for cultural learning into practice? (b) in what ways do teachers' knowledge and beliefs actually inform their practice; and, (c) what is the nature of the relationship between teachers' teaching of culture in the foreign language classroom and students' development of intercultural competence? And, finally, some nagging questions remain: given how challenging the goal of teaching for intercultural awareness is perceived to be, why isn't there a greater demand for help on how to do it? And conversely, if the goal is perceived to be so important, why isn't there more effort put into helping teachers learn ways to achieve it?
- These are the questions we feel should frame the research agenda for the coming years. There is some sense of urgency, particularly for more classroom-based research, the kind that will help us recreate the holistic context for teaching and learning, language and culture.

Learner Variables

- Motivation and attitudes, though elusive and difficult to identify, are major factors within individual learners, which affect their study of a second language as well as the manner and depth of their attention while they study it. Research on these factors began in the early 1970s, and was strongly influenced by Gardner and Lambert's (1972) finding that learners who desire to become like people in a target culture are the most successful in language study. This idea dominated the field and led to numerous follow-up studies based on their work, although even Gardner and Lambert now suggest that their findings were sometimes misinterpreted (Gardner & MacIntyre, 1993). Byram (1994) suggests that this work has been limited by the fact that linguistic gains were seen as the major benefits of increased motivation and positive attitudes, and other types of gains are not as frequently examined. It is also not possible to assess cause and effect in the investigations. The problems associated with the study of attitudes and motivations have been the difficulties of definition, measurement, and interpretation of findings.
- Recent work which examines voluntary contact with native speakers of the language by students who are studying that language may lead to more interesting and useful findings, as suggested by studies of Porebski and McInnes (1988) and Park (1995).
- Future studies of voluntary contact by students with native speakers and authentic materials should focus on affective gains as well as linguistic competence. A wide variety of qualitative means for studying affect should be tried, in order to discover the more elusive aspects of affective factors within individual students and between students both in classrooms and in other language-acquisition settings.

Curricular Materials and Instructional Methods

- The research literature on curricular materials and instructional methods emphasizes the primacy of the textbook in the classroom. Alternative materials and methods often appear to teachers to be more time consuming, less efficient, and more difficult to use. The literature also demonstrates that the culture-specific aspect of culture learning is emphasized in the research studies. This is not surprising given that the majority of textbooks approach culture learning as the learning of target culture facts.
- The research findings make it clear that the current materials, mainly textbooks, are shallow and superficial with respect to their

treatment of culture. They are therefore inadequate to the task of teaching culture specifics in the deeper sense (values, norms, beliefs, etc.) or culture-general skills. The literature also indicates that shallow presentation of culture can reinforce inaccurate stereotypes, both positive and negative in nature. There is a serious absence of impact studies that examine the effects of different types of materials and methods on culture learning.

- Culture in this literature is defined in culture-specific terms. The cultural information that is provided is rather basic (e.g., food, dress, holidays). There is little or no research on the assessment of culture in this literature. To the degree that it exists, assessment means testing for culture facts.

- What is sorely needed is research on alternative textbooks (cf. Allen & Foutllier-Smith, 1994), which incorporate a far wider range of cultural elements and involve the learner more actively in the culture learning process. Studies of authentic materials, especially in terms of their place in the curriculum and their relationship to other methods, would also be very helpful.

Assessment

- There are a number of points that stand out in the assessment literature. The first is that assessment, viewed in methodological terms, most commonly means objective testing in the manner that reflects western cultural biases. The most commonly used assessment techniques are often chosen for the sake of efficiency and ease of interpretation; a single score tells us the extent of the learner's knowledge and ability. Due in part to this methodological bias, assessment has often been focused on demonstrating cognitive knowledge, but ignoring behavioral and affective learning gains. This focus on cognitive learning is reflected by the frequent use of paper and pencil questionnaires, which ask about factual cultural knowledge. What has been routinely assessed, though, has been the more superficial aspects of cultural understanding (i.e., geography, food, and festivals). There are several new assessment methods such as the Intercultural Development Inventory (Hammer and Bennett, in press), which attempt to look at deeper cultural knowledge and different aspects of culture learning. In our view, they are quite promising.

- The literature suggests that the nature of assessment, as described above, represents confusion over what else to test. While we have articulated a multidimensional model of culture learning in this paper that represents the advanced state of the theoretical literature, this model is not yet well known to teachers in the field. Moreover, the literature suggests that teachers already do not feel adequately prepared to construct tests, whether of the traditional type or the alternative measurements that have recently been used.

Changes in assessment are occurring, however. Alternative methods of assessment are increasingly being used. These include: portfolios, self-reports of progress; journaling of culture learning; simulations, role-plays and other experiential techniques; critical incidents and case studies; culture immersions; and new, more conceptually sophisticated paper and pencil instruments.

- These have shown to be promising methods, but there is scant research on how well they work and how they can be integrated into the instructional process. In addition, the literature hints that alternative assessment can also alter the dynamics of the classroom. For example, it could change the motivation for learning (i.e., learning for the test versus for learning for competence) and the relationships between the teacher and the learner (i.e., the learner has more voice in the ways in which she or he is assessed). More research needs to been done in these areas.

REFERENCES

Allen, W., & Fouletier-Smith, N. (1994). *Parallels.* Boston, MA: Heinle & Heinle.

Altman, H.B. (1981). What is second language teaching? In J.E. Alatis, H.B. Altman, & P.M.Alatis (Eds.), *The second language classroom: Direction for the '80s* (pp. 5–19). New York: Oxford University Press.

American Association of Teachers of French (1995, January). AATF framework for cultural competence. *AATF National Bulletin.*

American Council on the Teaching of Foreign Languages (1983). *ACTFL Provisional Proficiency Guidelines.* Hastings-on-Hudson, NY: Author.

Armstrong, G.K. (1984.). Life after study abroad: A survey of undergraduate academic and career choices. *The Modern Language Journal, 68,* 1–6.

Arvizu, S.F., Snyder, W.A., & Espinosa, P.T. (1980). *Demystifying the concept of culture: Theoretical and conceptual tools* (Vol. III, No. 11). Bilingual Education Paper Series. Los Angeles: California State University, National Dissemination and Assessment Center.

Backman, N. (1976.). Two measures of affective factors as they relate to progress in adult second-language learning. *Working papers on Bilingualism, 10,* 100–122.

Barnlund, D.C. (1988). Communication in a global village. In L.A. Samovar & R.E. Porter (Eds.), *Intercultural communication: A reader* (6th ed., pp. 22–32). Belmont, CA: Wadsworth Publishing Company.

Baugh, I.W. (1994). Hypermedia as a performance-based assessment tool. *The Computing Teacher, 22,* 14–17.

Baumgratz-Gangl, G. (1991). Relating experience, culture and language: A French video project for language teaching. In D. Buttjes & M. Byram (Eds.), *Mediating languages and cultures* (pp. 228–239). Clevedon, Avon: Multilingual Matters.

Bennett, J.M. (1993). Cultural marginality: Identity issues in intercultural training. In R.M. Paige (Ed.), *Education for the intercultural experience* (pp. 109–135). Yarmouth, ME: Intercultural Press.

Bennett, M.J. (1986). Towards ethnorelativism: A development model of intercultural sensitivity. In R.M. Paige (Ed.), *Cross-cultural orientation: New conceptualizations and applications* (pp. 27–69). Lanham, MD: University Press of America.

Bennett, M.J. (1993). Towards ethnorelativism: A developmental model of intercultural sensitivity. In R.M. Paige (Ed.), *Education for the intercultural experience* (pp. 21–71). Yarmouth, ME: Intercultural Press.

Bernhardt, E. (1995). Teaching literature or teaching students. *ADFL Bulletin, 26*(2), 5–6.

Bernhardt, E., & Hammadou, J. (1987). Research in foreign language teacher education. *Foreign Language Annals, 71,* 289–298.

Berube, M.R. (1996). The politics of national standards. *The Clearing House, 69*(3), 151–153.

Bex, A.R. (1994). The problem of culture and English language teaching in Europe. *International Review of Applied Linguistics in Language Teaching, 32*(1), 57–67.

Bley-Vroman, R. (1989). What is the logical problem of foreign language learning. In S. Gass & J. Schachter (Eds.), *Linguistic perspectives on second language acquisition* (pp. 41–68). Cambridge: Cambridge University Press.

Bloom, B. (1964). *Stability and change in human characteristics.* New York: John Wiley.

Bogardus, E.S. (1933). A social distance scale. *Sociology and Social Research* (January–February), 265–71.

Boutin, F. (1993). A study of early French immersion teachers as generators of knowledge. *Foreign Language Annals, 26,* 511–525.

Bragaw, D. (1991). Priority Curriculum: The global imperative and its metalanguage. *Foreign Language Annals, 24,* 115–124.

Breen, M.P. (1985). The social context for language learning: A neglected situation? *Studies in Second Language Acquisition, 7,* 135–158.

Brislin, R.W., Cushner, K., Cherrie, C., & Yong, M. (1986). *Intercultural interactions: A practical guide.* New York: Sage Publications.

Brooks, N. (1975). The analysis of language and familiar cultures. In R. Lafayette (Ed.), *The cultural revolution in foreign language teaching* (pp. 19–31). Northeast Conference Reports. Lincolnwood, IL: National Textbook.

Burstall, C., et al. (1974). *Primary French in the balance.* Windsor, Ontario: NFER Publishing Co.

Buttjes., D. & Byram, M. (Eds.) (1991). *Mediating languages and cultures: Towards an intercultural theory of foreign language education.* Clevedon, Avon: Multilingual Matters.

Byram, M. (1988). Foreign language education and cultural studies. *Language, Culture, and Curriculum, 1*(1), 15–31.

Byram, M. (1989). A school visit to France: Ethnographic explorations. *British Journal of Language Teaching, 27*(2), 99–103.

Byram, M., Esarte-Sarries, V., Taylor, S., & Allatt, P. (1991). Young people's perception of other cultures. In D. Buttjes & M. Byram (Eds.) (1991). *Mediating languages and cultures: Towards an intercultural theory of foreign language education* (pp. 103–119). Clevedon, Avon: Multilingual Matters.

Byram, M., & Morgan, C. (1994). *Teaching-and-learning language-and-culture.* Clevedon, Avon: Multilingual Matters.

Cadd, M. (1994). An attempt to reduce ethnocentrism in the foreign language classroom. *Foreign Language Annals, 27,* 143–160.

Canagarajah, A.S. (1993). Critical ethnography of a Sri Lankan classroom: Ambiguities in student opposition to reproduction through ESOL. *TESOL Quarterly, 27,* 601–626.

Carlson, J., et al. (1991). Study abroad: The experience of American undergraduates in Western Europe and the United States. *Occasional Papers on International Education Exchange Research Series.* (ERIC Document Reproduction Service No. ED 340322.)

Carroll, J.B. (1967). Foreign language proficiency levels attained by language majors near graduation from college. *Foreign Language Annals, 1,* 131–151.

Chaudron, C. (1986). The interaction of quantitative and qualitative approach to research: A view of the second language classroom. *TESOL Quarterly, 20,* 709–715.

Cook, S. (1996, April 10). *College students' perspectives on culture learning in a required French course.* Paper presented at the American Educational Research Association, New York.

Cooper, T.C. (1990). Preparing teachers for diversity: A comparison of student teaching experience in Minnesota and South Texas. *Action in Teacher Education, 12*(3), 1–4.

Cooper, T.C. (1985). A survey of teacher concerns. *Foreign Language Annals, 18,* 21–24.

Crawford-Lange, L.M., & Lange, D.L. (1984). Doing the unthinkable in the second-language classroom: A process for integration of language and culture. In T.V. Higgs (Ed.), *Proficiency: The organizing principle* (pp. 139–177). The ACTFL Foreign Language Education Series. Lincolnwood, IL: National Textbook.

Crawford-Lange, L.M., & Lange, D.L. (1987). Integrating language and culture: How to do it. *Theory into Practice, 26,* 258–266.

Crookes, G., & Schmidt, R.W. (1991). Motivation: Reopening the research agenda. *Language Learning, 41,* 469–512.

Damen, L. (1987). *Culture learning: The fifth dimension in the language classroom.* Reading, MA: Addision-Wesley.

Davis, J.J., & Markham, P.L. (1991). Student attitudes towards foreign language study at historically and predominantly black institutions. *Foreign Language Annals, 24,* 227–236.

DeKeyser, R.M. (1991). Foreign language development during a semester abroad. In B.F. Freed (Ed.), *Foreign language acquisition research and the classroom* (pp. 104–119). Lexington, MA: D.C. Heath.

Diller, E., & Markert, A. (1983). The telescope curriculum. *Unterrichtspraxis, 16,* 223–229.

Dirksen, C. (1990). Learning styles of mainland Chinese students of English. *IDEAL, 5,* 29–38.

Dörnyei, Z. (1994). Motivation and motivating in the foreign language classroom. *The Modern Language Journal, 78,* 273–84.

Dyson, P. (1988). *The year abroad.* Report for the Central Bureau for Educational Visits and Exchanges. Oxford, England: Oxford University Language Teaching Centre.

Edwards, V., & Rehorick, S. (1990). Learning environments in immersion and non-immersion classrooms: Are they different? *The Canadian Modern Language Review, 46,* 469–493.

Ellis, R. (1992). The classroom context: An acquisition-rich or an acquisition-poor environment? In C. Kramsch & S. McConnell-Ginet (Eds.), *Text and context* (pp. 171–186). Lexington, MA: D.C. Heath.

Ellis, R., & Roberts, C. (1987). Two approaches for investigating second language acquisition in context. In R. Ellis (Ed.), *Second language acquisition in context* (pp. 3–30). Englewood Cliffs, NJ: Prentice-Hall.

Falsgraf, C.D. (1994). *Language and culture at a Japanese immersion school.* Unpublished doctoral dissertation, University of Oregon, Eugene.

Fang, Z. (1996). A review of research on teacher beliefs and practices. *Educational Research, 38*(1), 47–65.

Ferdman, B. (1990). Literacy and cultural identity. *Harvard Educational Review, 60,* 181–204.

Ferguson, C.A., & Huebner, T. (1991). Foreign language instruction and second language acquisition research in the United States. In K. de Bot., R.B. Ginsberg, & C. Kramsch (Eds.), *Foreign language research in cross-cultural perspective* (pp. 3–20). Amsterdam: John Benjamins Publishing Company.

Freed, B.F. (Ed.). (1991). *Foreign language acquisition research and the classroom.* Lexington, MA: D.C. Heath.

Freed, B.F. (1995). *Second language acquisition in a study abroad context.* Philadelphia, PA: John Benjamins Publishing Company.

Gardner, R.C. (1985). *Social psychology and second language learning: The role of attitudes and motivation.* London: Edward Arnold.

Gardner, R.C., & Lambert, W.E. (1972). *Attitudes and motivation in second language learning.* Rowley, MA: Newbury House.

Gardner, R.C., & MacIntyre, P.D. (1992). A student's contributions to second-language learning. Part I: Cognitive variables. *Language Teaching, 25,* 211–20.

Gardner, R.C., & MacIntyre, P.D. (1993). A student's contributions to second-language learning. Part II: Affective variables. *Language Teaching, 26,* 1–11.

Gardner, R.C., & Tremblay, P.F. (1994). On motivation, research agendas, and theoretical frameworks. *The Modern Language Journal, 78,* 359–68.

Gliksman, L. (1981). *Improving the prediction of behaviours associated with second language acquisition.* Unpublished doctoral dissertation, University of Western Ontario, London, Ontario, Canada.

Gougeon, T.D. (1993). Urban schools and immigrant families. *The Urban Review, 25,* 251–287.

Grice, H.H. (1934). The construction and validation of a generalized scale to measure attitudes toward defined groups. *Purdue University Bulletin, 25,* 37–46.

Grittner, F. (1990). Bandwagons revisited: A perspective on movements in foreign language education. In D.W. Birckbichler (Ed.), *New perspectives and new directions in foreign language education* (pp. 9–43). The ACTFL Foreign Language Education Series. Lincolnwood, IL: National Textbook.

Gudykunst, W.B., & Kim, Y.Y. (Eds.). (1992). *Readings on communicating with strangers: An approach to intercultural communication.* New York: McGraw-Hill.

Guidelines for teacher education programs in modern foreign languages. (1966). Originally published in *The Modern Language Journal, 50.* Menasha, WI: The National Federation of Modern Language Teachers Associations.

Haberman, M., & Post, L. (1990). Cooperating teachers' perceptions of the goals of multicultural education. *Action in Teacher Education, 12*(3), 31–35.

Hall, E.T. (1976). *Beyond culture.* New York: Doubleday.

Hall, J.K., & Ramírez, A. (1993). How a group of high school learners of Spanish perceives the cultural identities of speakers, English speakers, and themselves. *Hispania, 76,* 613–20.

Halliday, M.A.K. (1978). *Language as a social semiotic.* London: Edward Arnold.

Halliday, M.A.K. (1989). Context of situation. In M.A.K. Halliday & R. Hasan (Eds.), *Language, context, and text* (pp. 3–12). Oxford: Oxford University Press.

Hamers, J.F. (1984). L'évolution des attitudes envers la langue seconde et l'identité culturelle chez les jeunes Quebecois francophones et anglophones. *Canadian Modern Language Review, 41,* 283–307.

Hammer, M.R. (1999). A measure of intercultural sensitivity: The intercultural development inventory. In S.M. Fowler & M.G. Mumford (Eds.), *The intercultural sourcebook: Cross-cultural training methods* (Vol. II, pp. 61–72). Yarmouth, ME: Intercultural Press.

Hannigan, T.P. (1990). Traits, attitudes and skills that are related to intercultural effectiveness and their implications for cross-cultural training: A review of the literature. *International Journal of Intercultural Relations, 14,* 89–111.

Hansel, B.G. (1985). *The impact of a sojourn abroad: A study of secondary school students participating in a foreign exchange program (culture learning, contact travel, educational).* Unpublished doctoral dissertation, Syracuse University, Syracuse, New York.

Hashimota, H. (1993). Language acquisition of an exchange student within the homestay environment. *Journal of Asian Pacific Communication, 4,* 209–224.

Heath, S.B. (1986). *Beyond language: Social and cultural factors in schooling language minority students.* Sacramento: California State Department of Education.

Hoffman, D. (1989). Language and culture acquisition among Iranians in the United States. *Anthropology and Education Quarterly, 20,* 118–132.

Hughes, G.H. (1986). An argument for culture analysis in the second language classroom. In J.M. Valdes (Ed.), *Culture bound: Bridging the cultural gap in language teaching* (pp. 162–169). New York: Cambridge University Press.

Hymes, D.H. (1974). *Foundations in sociolinguistics: An ethnographic approach.* Philadelphia: University of Pennsylvania Press.

Jaworski, A. (1994). Pragmatic failure in a second language: Greeting responses in English by Polish students. *International Review of Applied Linguistics in Language Teaching, 32*(1), 41–55.

Jorstad, H.L. (1981). Inservice teacher education: Content and process. In D.L. Lange & C. Linder (Eds.), *Proceedings of the National Conference on Professional Priorities* (pp. 81–85). Hastings-on-Hudson, NY: ACTFL Material Center.

Jurasek, R. (1995). Using ethnography to bridge the gap between study abroad and the on-campus language and culture curriculum. In C. Kramsch (Ed.), *Redefining the boundaries of language study* (pp. 221–251). Boston: Heinle & Heinle.

Kane, L. (1991). The acquisition of cultural competence: An ethnographic framework for cultural studies curricula. In D. Buttjes & M. Byram (Eds.), *Mediating languages and cultures* (pp. 239–247). Clevedon, Avon, England: Multilingual Matters.

Kean, M.H. (1995). The national testing movement, redux. *The Clearing House, 68,* 201–204.

Kelley, C., & Meyers, J. (1999). The Cross-Cultural Adaptability Inventory. In S.M. Fowler & M. Mumford (Eds.). *Intercultural sourcebook: Cross-cultural training methods. Volume 2* (pp. 53–60). Yarmouth, ME: Intercultural Press.

Kienbaum, B.E., Russel, A.J., & Welty, S. (1986). *Communicative competence in foreign language learning with authentic materials: Final project report.* (ERIC Document Reproduction Service No. ED 275200).

King, C.P. (1990). A linguistic and a cultural competence: Can they live happily together? *Foreign Language Annals, 23,* 65–70.

Kleinsasser, A.M. (1995). Assessment, culture, and national testing. *The Clearing House, 68,* 205–210.

Kleinsasser, R.C. (1993). A tale of two technical cultures. *Teaching and Teacher Education, 9,* 373–83.

Knox, E. (1984). Report of the teaching of French civilization. *French Review, 56,* 369–378.

Kolb, D.A. (1984). *Experiencial learning: Experience as the source of learning and development.* Englewood Cliffs, NJ: Prentice-Hall.

Kordes, H. (1991). Intercultural learning at school: Limits and possibilities. In D. Buttjes & M. Byram (Eds.), *Mediating languages and cultures* (pp. 17–30). Clevedon, Avon: Multilingual Matters.

Kramsch, C.J. (1987). Foreign language textbooks' construction of foreign reality. *The Canadian Modern Language Review, 44,* 95–119.

Kramsch, C. (1991a). Culture in language learning: A view from the United States. In K. de Bot, R. B. Ginsberg, & C. Kramsch (Eds.), *Foreign language research in cross-cultural perspective* (pp. 217–240). Amsterdam: John Benjamins Publishing Company.

Kramsch, C. (1991b). The order of discourse in language teaching. In B.F. Freed (Ed.), *Foreign language acquisition research and the classroom* (pp. 191–204). Lexington, MA: D.C. Heath.

Kramsch, C. (1993). *Context and culture in language teaching.* New York: Oxford University Press.

Kramsch, C. (1994). Redefining literacy in a foreign language. *Unterrichtspraxis* 27(1), 28–38.

Kramsch, C., & McConnell-Ginet, S. (Eds.). (1992). *Text and context.* Lexington, MA: D.C. Heath.

Krashen, S. (1982). *Principles and practice in second language acquisition.* Oxford: Pergamon Press.

Lessard-Clouston, M. (1992). Assessing culture learning: Issues and suggestions. *The Canadian Modern Language Review, 48,* 326–341.

Loughrin-Sacco, S.J. (1992). More than meets the eye: An ethnography of an elementary French class. *The Canadian Modern Language Review, 49,* 80–101.

Lustig, M.W., & Koester, J. (1996). *Intercultural competence: Intercultural communication across cultures* (2nd ed.). New York: Harper-Collins.

Marin, G., &. Sabogal, F. (1987). Development of a short acculturation scale for Hispanics. *Hispanic Journal of Behavioral Sciences, 9,* 183–205.

Martin, A.L., & Laurie, I. (1993). Student views about contributions of literary and cultural content to language learning at intermediate level. *Foreign Language Annals, 26,* 188–207.

Massey, D.A. (1986). Variations in attitudes and motivation of adolescent learners of French as a second language. *Canadian Modern Language Review, 42,* 607–618.

Mauranen, A. (1994). Two discourse worlds. *Finlance, 13,* 1–40.

McDonough, S. (1981). *Psychology in foreign language teaching.* London: Allen and Unwin.

McGinnis, S. (1994). Cultures of instruction: Identifying and resolving conflicts. *Theory into Practice, 33,* 16–22.

Meara, P. (1994). The year abroad and its effects. *Language Learning Journal, 10,* 32–38.

Meyer, M. (1991). Developing transcultural competence: Case studies of advanced language learners. In D. Buttjes & M. Byram (Eds.), *Mediating languages and cultures* (pp. 136–158). Clevedon, Avon, England: Multilingual Matters.

Mitchell, R. (1988). *Communicative language teaching in practice.* London: Centre for Information on Language Teaching.

Moehle, D. (1984). A comparison of the second language speech of different native speakers. In H. Dechert et al. (Eds.), *Second language productions* (pp. 26–49). Tubingen: Gunter.

Momber, H.E. (1979). *An examination of secondary school student and teacher variables related to student discontinuance in second language study after the first year.* Unpublished doctoral dissertation, University of Minnesota, Minneapolis, Minnesota.

Moore, J. (1991). *An analysis of the cultural content of post-secondary textbooks for Spanish: Evidence of information processing strategies and types of learning in reading selections and post-reading adjunct questions.* Unpublished doctoral dissertation, University of Minnesota, Minneapolis, Minnesota.

Moos, R.H., & Trickett, E. (1987). *Classroom environment scale manual.* Palo Alto, CA: Consulting Psychologists Press.

Morain, G. (1983). Commitment to the teaching of foreign languages. *The Modern Language Journal, 67,* 402–412.

Murphy, E. (1988). The cultural dimension in foreign language teaching: Four models. *Language, Culture and Curriculum, 1,* 147–163.

Myers, P.J. (1978). *Student factors as indicators of continuation in secondary school study of French/German/Spanish as a second language.* Unpublished doctoral dissertation, University of Minnesota, Minneapolis.

Nostrand, H.L. (1974). Empathy for a second culture: Motivations and techniques. In G.A. Jarvis (Ed.), *Responding to new realities* (pp. 263–327). The ACTFL Foreign Language Education Series. Skokie, IL: National Textbook.

Osgood, C.E., Suci, G., & Tannenbaum, P.H. (1957). *The measurement of meaning.* Urbana: University of Illinois Press.

Oxford, R., & Shearin, J. (1994). Language learning motivation: Expanding the theoretical framework. *The Modern Language Journal, 78,* 12–28.

Paige, R.M., & Stringer, D. (1997). *Training design for international and multicultural programs.* Portland, OR: Intercultural Communication Institute.

Pajares, F.M. (1992). Teachers' beliefs and educational research: Cleaning up a messy construct. *Review of Educational Research, 62,* 307–322.

Paquette, F.A., comp. (1966). Guidelines for teacher education programs in modern foreign languages: An exposition. *The Modern Language Journal, 50,* 323–425.

Park, J.J. (1995). *Adult learners' motivation in learning a non-cognate foreign language (second language).* Unpublished doctoral dissertation, University of Minnesota, Minneapolis.

Patrikis, P.C. (1987). Assessing foreign language learning. *Liberal Education, 73*(3), 26–28.

Patrikis, P.C. (1995). Where is computer technology taking us? *ADFL Bulletin, 26*(2), 36–39.

Paulson, L.M. (1995). *Gender orientation, the cross-cultural adjustment process, and education: An exploratory study.* Unpublished master's thesis, University of Minnesota, Minneapolis.

Pica, T. (1983). The role of language context in second language acquisition. *Interlanguage Studies Bulletin, 7,* 101–123.

Porebski, O.R., & McInnis, C.E. (1988). Changes in the friendship pattern and proficiency level of FSL students as a result of the French animator program. *Canadian Modern Language Review, 44,* 285–294.

Raupach, M. (1987). *Procedural learning in advanced learners of a foreign language.* Duisberg: Universität Gesamthochschule Duisburg.

Reid, J.M. (1987). The learning style preferences of ESL students. *TESOL Quarterly, 21,* 87–111.

Robinson, G. (1978). The magic-carpet-ride-to-another-culture syndrome: An international perspective. *Foreign Language Annals, 11,* 135–146.

Robinson, G.L. (1981). *Issues in second language and cross-cultural education: The forest through the trees.* Boston: Heinle & Heinle.

Robinson, G.L (1985). *Cross-cultural understanding: Processes and approaches for foreign language, English as a second language and bilingual educators.* Oxford: Pergamon.

Robinson-Stuart, G. & Nocon, H. (1996). Second culture acquisition: Ethnography in the foreign language classroom. *The Modern Language Journal, 80,* 431–449.

Royer, K. (1996). Summative authentic assessment in the French classroom. *The Clearing House, 69,* 174–176.

Ryan, P.M. (1994). *Foreign language teachers' perceptions of culture and the classroom: A case study.* Unpublished doctoral dissertation, University of Utah, Salt Lake City, Utah.

Sacks, H., Schegloff, E., & Jefferson, G. (1974). A simplest systematics for the organization of turntaking for conversation. *Language, 50,* 696–735.

Salomone, A.M. (1991). Immersion teachers: What can we learn from them? *Foreign Language Annals, 24,* 57–63.

Saville-Troike, M. (1983). An anthropological linguistic perspective on uses of ethnography in bilingual language proficiency assessment. In C. Rivera (Ed.), *An ethnographic/sociolinguistic approach to language proficiency assessment* (pp. 131–136). Clevedon, Avon: Multilingual Matters.

Schumann, J.H. (1978a). The acculturation model for second language acquisition. In R.C. Gingras (Ed.), *Second language acquisition and foreign language teaching* (pp. 27–50).Washington, DC: Center for Applied Linguistics.

Schumann, J.H. (1978b). *The pidginization process: A model for second language acquisition.* Rowley, MA: Newbury House.

Schumann, J.H. (1986.). Research on the acculturation model for second language acquisition. *Journal of Multilingual and Multicultural Development, 7,* 379–92.

Seelye, N. (1981). *Teaching culture: Strategies for foreign language educators* (2nd ed.). Skokie, IL: National Textbook Company.

Seelye, N. (1994). *Teaching culture: Strategies for intercultural communication* (3rd ed.). Lincolnwood, IL: National Textbook Company.

Sleeter, C.E., & Grant, C.A. (1994). *Making choices for multicultural education: Five approaches to race, class and gender* (2nd ed.). New York: Macmillan.

Spada, N. (1987). Relationships between instructional differences and learning outcomes: A process-product study of communicative language teaching. *Applied Linguistics, 8,* 137–155.

Spindler, G. 1974. Beth Anne—A case study of culturally defined adjustment and teacher perceptions. In G.D. Spindler (Ed.), *Education and cultural process.* New York: Holt Rinehart and Winston.

Steele, R. (1989). Teaching language and culture: Old problems and new approaches. In J.E. Alatis (Ed.), *Georgetown University Roundtable on Languages and Linguistics: Language Teaching* (pp. 153–162). Washington, DC: Georgetown University Press.

Steglitz, I. (1993). *Intercultural perspective-taking: The impact of study abroad.* Unpublished doctoral dissertation, University of Minnesota, Minneapolis.

Stelly, C.H. (1991). *Effects of a whole language approach using authentic French texts on student comprehension and attitude.* Unpublished doctoral dissertation, Louisiana State University and Agricultural and Mechanical College, Baton Rouge, Louisiana.

Stodolsky, S.S, & Grossman, P.L. (1995). The impact of subject matter on curricular activity: An analysis of five academic subjects. *American Educational Research Journal, 32,* 227–249.

Street, B.V. (1993). Culture is a verb. In D. Graddol et al. (Eds.), *Language and culture* (pp. 23–42). U.K.: BAAL and Multilingual Matters.

Swain, M. (1991). French immersion and its offshoots: Getting two for one. In B.F. Freed (Ed.), *Foreign language acquisition research and the classroom* (pp. 91–103). Lexington, MA: D.C. Heath.

Thompson, L. (1995). *K–8 foreign language assessment: A bibliography.* Washington, DC: National K–12 Foreign Language Resource Center. (ERIC Document Reproduction Service No. Ed 385 265).

Triandis, H.C. (1972). *The analysis of subjective culture.* New York: Wiley.

Tucker, R.G., & d'Anglejean, A. (1974). Cognitive and attitudinal consequences of bilingual schooling: The St. Lambert project through grade five. *Journal of Educational Psychology, 65,* 141–159.

Ueber, D.M., & Grosse, C.U. (1991). The cultural content of business French texts. *The French Review, 65,* 247–255.

Valdes, J.M. (1990). The inevitability of teaching and learning culture in a foreign language course. In B. Harrison (Ed.), *Culture and the language classroom* (pp. 20–30). Oxford: Modern English Publications/British Council.

Valette, R.M. (1986). The culture test. In J.M. Valdes (Ed.), *Culture bound: Bridging the cultural gap in language teaching* (pp. 179–197). New York: Cambridge University Press.

Van Lier, L. (1988). *The classroom and the language learner.* London: Longman.

Warren, J. (1987a). Assessment at the source. *Liberal Education, 73*(3), 2–6.

Warren, J. (1987b). What students say about assessment. *Liberal Education, 73*(3), 22–25.

Wieczorek, J.A. (1994). The concept of *French* in foreign language texts. *Foreign Language Annals, 27,* 487–97.

Wolf, W.C., & Riordan, K.M. (1991). Foreign language teachers' demographic characteristics, in-service training needs, and attitudes towards teaching. *Foreign Language Annals, 24,* 471–478.

Zeidner, M. (1987). Are English language aptitude tests biased towards culturally different minority groups? Some Israeli data. *Language Testing, 3,* 80–98.

SUGGESTIONS FOR FURTHER READINGS

Alatis, J.E. (Ed.). (1989). *Language teaching, testing, and technology: Lessons for the past with a view toward the future.* Georgetown University Round Table on Languages and Linguistics. Washington, D.C: Georgetown University Press.

Alatis, J.E., Straehle, C.A., & Gallenberger, B. (Eds.). (1995). *Linguistics and the education of language teachers: Ethnolinguistic, psycholinguistic, and sociolinguistic aspects.* Georgetown University Round Table on Languages and Linguistics. Washington, DC: Georgetown University Press.

Allen, W.W. (1985). Toward cultural proficiency. In A. Omaggio (Ed.), *Proficiency, curriculum, articulation: The ties that bind.* (pp. 137–165). Northeast Conference Reports. Middlebury, VT: Northeast Conference on the Teaching of Foreign Languages.

Bailey, K.M., Omaggio, A.H., Magnan, S.M. & Swaffar, J. (1991). Priority: Research. *Foreign Language Annals, 24,* 89–107.

Byram, M. (1989). *Cultural studies in foreign language education.* Philadelphia: Multilingual Matters.

Crockett, M. (1996). Reculturing American education. *The Clearing House, 69,* 183–187.

Ellis, R. (Ed.). (1987). *Second language acquisition in context.* Englewood Cliffs, NJ: Prentice-Hall.

Ferdman, B., Weber, R.M., & Ramirez, A.G. (Eds.). (1994). *Literacy across languages and cultures.* Albany: SUNY Press.

Goodman, Y. (1985). Kidwatching: Observing children in classrooms. In A. Jaggar & M.T. Smith-Burker (Eds.), *Observing the language learner* (pp. 9–18). Newark, NJ: International Reading Association.

Goodwin, C.D., & Nacht, M. (1988). *Abroad and beyond: Patterns in American overseas education.* New York: Cambridge University Press.

Larke, P. (1990). Cultural diversity awareness inventory: Assessing the sensitivity of pre-service teachers. *Action in Teacher Education, 12*(3), 23–30.

Larsen-Freeman, D., & Long, M.H. (1991). *An introduction to second language acquisition research.* New York: Longman.

Macian, J.L. (1986). An analysis of state adopted foreign language textbooks used in first- and third-year high school Spanish classes. *Foreign Language Annals, 19,* 103–118.

MacIntyre, P.D., & Gardner, R.C. (1991). Language anxiety: Its relation to other anxieties and to processing in native and second languages. *Language Learning, 41,* 513–34.

Met, M. (1989). Learning language through content: Learning content through language. In K.E. Müller (Ed.), *Languages in elementary schools* (pp. 43–64). New York: The American Forum, National Council on Foreign Languages and International Studies.

Met, M., & Galloway, V. (1992). Research in foreign language curriculum. In P.W. Jackson (Ed.), *Handbook of research on curriculum* (pp. 852–890). New York: Macmillan.

Müller, K.E. (1989). Policy and curricular implications of expanding language education in elementary schools. In K.E. Müller (Ed.), *Languages in elementary schools* (pp. 204–232). New York: The American Forum, National Council on Foreign Language and International Studies.

Nold, G. (1983). Grundzüge eines lernfordernden sprachverhaltens des lehrers im Fremdsprachenunterricht. In M. Heid (Ed.), *Literarische texte im kommunikativen Fremdsprachenunterricht.* München: Goethe Institut.

Pennycook, A. (1990). Critical pedagogy and second language education. *System, 18,* 303–314.

Petri, R. (1995). *Study abroad: Its impact on the intercultural perspective-taking ability.* Unpublished Master's thesis, University of Minnesota, Minneapolis.

Rhodes, N.C., & Snow, M.A. (1988). Foreign language in the elementary school: A comparison of achievement. In K.E. Müller (Ed.), *Children and languages: Research, practice, and rationale for the early grades* (pp. 204–232). New York: The American Forum, National Council on Foreign Language and International Studies.

Standards for foreign language learning: Preparing for the 21st Century. (1996). National Standards in Foreign Language Education Project. Yonkers, NY.

Valdes, J.M. (Ed.). (1986). *Culture bound: Bridging the cultural gap in language teaching.* New York: Cambridge University Press.

Van Lier, L. (1989). Reeling, writhing, drawling, stretching, and fainting in coils: Oral proficiency interviews as conversation. *TESOL Quarterly, 23,* 489–508.

Wesche, M., & Ready, D. (1985). Foreigner talk in the university classroom. In S.M. Gass & C.G. Madden (Eds.), *Input in second language acquisition* (pp. 89–114). New York: Newbury House.

CHAPTER 10

DEVELOPING INTERCULTURAL COMPETENCE IN THE LANGUAGE CLASSROOM

Janet M. Bennett, Milton J. Bennett, and Wendy Allen

As the oft-quoted saying goes, the person who learns language without learning culture risks becoming a fluent fool. And yet the pedagogy for infusing culture into the language curriculum remains elusive and we continue to debate the particulars of this complex learning and teaching task. This chapter is intended to make a contribution to this dialogue by suggesting a theoretical model for sequencing intercultural competence that parallels levels of language competence. The chapter is addressed to language teachers and others interested in how to place culture at the core of language teaching by systematically introducing intercultural competence into the classroom. Intercultural competence refers to the general ability to transcend ethnocentrism, appreciate other cultures, and generate appropriate behavior in one or more different cultures. While the focus in the chapter is on teaching intercultural competence in the language classroom, applications to other kinds of teaching and training can easily be derived from the material presented here.

Culture as the Core: Perspectives in Second Language Education, pages 237–270
Copyright © 2003 by Information Age Publishing
All rights of reproduction in any form reserved.

We, the authors, have thought a lot about you, the readers, and we have made the following assumptions:

- You believe that *culture* is inextricably linked to language.
- You are interested in how to think about *culture* in a way that helps you teach intercultural competence.
- You are committed to the idea that intercultural competence is as important as language competence in preparing students to live in the global village and multicultural societies.
- You are learner-centered in your classroom, placing emphasis on how students learn best rather than on just *covering the material*.

With these assumptions in mind, we have tried to address the following objectives in our discussion of this topic. We hope that this article will enable readers to:

- Place the discussion of intercultural competence into the professional context of language teaching.
- Recognize the distinction between *Big C* (objective culture) and *little c* (subjective culture) as these terms are used by language teachers and by interculturalists.
- Use the distinction of *culture specific* and *culture general* to see through the confusion of *what culture to teach* and to define *cultural intercultural competence*.
- Move with confidence toward teaching intercultural competence rather than exclusively focusing on any specific culture.
- Identify the stages of development that learners move through in their acquisition of intercultural competence, as described by the Developmental Model of Intercultural Sensitivity (DMIS) (M. Bennett, 1986, 1993).
- Recognize the developmental sequence of intercultural competence that parallels linguistic competence.
- Select intercultural learning activities appropriate to the readiness level of learners, both linguistically and culturally.
- Apply the learner-centered concept of *support and challenge* at each stage of the DMIS.

Our overall goal for this chapter, as it is for our work in general, is to contribute to preparing for life in a world that is profoundly different from that of our ancestors. Ours is now an interconnected world in which contact with those who are culturally different is inevitable. In this world, the skills that allow us to get along in our own cultures, while necessary, are now insufficient. Even the skill of a foreign language is, in itself, an insufficient guide for communicating with the wide range of cultural strangers who people our workplaces, our travels, and our daily social lives. We believe that educators have a particular responsibility to understand the new intercultural challenges facing us and to teach the new skills that are now demanded. We hope you share this goal.

INTRODUCTION: THE LANGUAGE TEACHING CONTEXT

The language teaching profession has, in the last decade, made significant progress in the teaching of language. The *ACTFL proficiency guidelines* (1986), research findings in the area of second language acquisition, and the call from both within and outside the profession for increased accountability have ushered in a new era in language teaching and learning. Language teachers at both secondary and post-secondary levels are putting the learner at the center of the classroom and there is a new focus on language *use*. Instructional sequences are being organized with a view to promoting learners' functional mastery rather than coverage of discrete-point grammar.

Of course, language-teaching professionals do not fully agree on the goals of teaching and learning language. But during the past decade the profession has engaged in intensive debate over major issues such as communicative competence vs. proficiency, the educated native speaker model, and the role of grammar. This debate has been positive for the profession as a whole as well as for individual practitioners. Language-teaching professionals have far more of a shared identity today than they did ten to fifteen years ago. While the solutions to the challenges that confront them are not all clear, there is substantial agreement as to what the key issues are. Increasingly, language teachers representing various levels of instruction— secondary teachers, coordinators of first- and second-year college/university programs, second language acquisition researchers, representatives from teacher education, and others—are coming together to look for solutions and to improve student learning.

The teaching and learning of culture have been affected by the debate and by changes in the teaching and learning of language. Indeed, various professional organizations (including the American Council on the Teaching of Foreign Languages, and the American Associations of Teachers of German, French, Spanish, and Portuguese) have sought to rethink the role of culture in the language classroom of today and tomorrow. Content-based instruction, especially at the post-secondary level, became one of the popular buzzwords of the 90s. The current dialogue about culture has begun to explore not only the definition of culture but also the role of culture in the language classroom and strategies for teaching it. The volume in which this piece appears represents an effort to bring to the attention of the profession at large the research and scholarly debate in the areas of culture and culture learning and thereby to expand the dialogue.

CULTURE AT THE CORE OF THE LANGUAGE CURRICULUM

In response to the question as to whether or not culture should be placed at the core of the language curriculum and of language instruction, many would respond with a rousing *no*. And there are a lot of reasons to support such a position. First, there is the language curriculum itself, which is already too full, especially in the light of available instructional time. Since there is not enough time to do justice to the language curriculum, is it reasonable to add another dimension to an already overloaded syllabus? Second, the teaching of culture poses numerous challenges to classroom teachers. For many, culture seems far more difficult to teach than language. As we will see, this may be due to confusing definitions of what *culture* (or what competencies) to teach. Often, teachers feel unprepared—even afraid—to teach either culture or intercultural competence. Since many teachers have never been taught intercultural competence, they have no model for teaching it themselves. Insofar as the goal is to teach a specific culture, teachers may have had little or no first-hand experience of the target language culture. Even if they have had experience in the culture, the culture keeps changing and they are continually faced with the challenge of keeping current. Cultural topics can also raise highly charged issues that may be difficult to deal within the classroom. Clearly, any successful effort to put culture at the core will have to include in-service training and faculty development opportunities for language teachers.

Even for the classroom teacher who can surmount the above hurdles, teaching culture still presents numerous challenges. Which kind of culture should be taught—civilization/history/fine arts? Contemporary culture/anthropology? Both? Neither? How should language teaching/learning and culture teaching/learning be integrated? Are there theoretical models or practical examples showing how to do this? While many instructional manuals deal with classroom exercises for teaching objective culture, there are very few instructional materials currently available that address subjective culture. This chapter is an effort to address these issues in a way that is both theoretically coherent and also practical for language teachers.

A final set of concerns relates to external pressures that affect the instructional decisions of classroom teachers. At the high school level, teachers may feel they have a responsibility to prepare their students to do well on Advanced Placement and other national exams. These exams are based on a *language and literature* model which views culture as largely irrelevant to the primary agenda of language study. Of course, examination is a two-way street; the examiners eventually accommodate to what is actually being taught.

For college and university language faculties, the external pressures are somewhat different. Traditionally, students learned another language in order to have access to the great works of literature written in that language. Some professors may be concerned that the recent shift to a communicative model (i.e., students learn another language in order to communicate with speakers of that language) has, to some extent, jeopardized the respectability of language study within the Academy. A move to place culture at the core of language teaching may be particularly threatening to these people, especially if the definition of *culture* is expanded beyond the *high culture* aspects of objective culture. The challenge in the academy will be to attain credibility for the underlying models of subjective-culture learning by showing their conceptual depth.

Notably, there are a growing number of other voices in the language-teaching profession calling for attention to an expanded treatment of culture. For instance, Claire Kramsch (1993) is eloquent in her call for attention to the personal issues that must be addressed as part of intercultural competence:

> The realization of difference, not only between oneself and others, but between one's personal and one's social self, indeed between different perceptions of oneself can be at once an elating and a deeply troubling experience. . . . In most foreign language classrooms, interculturality is not being taught as a systematic apprenticeship of difference nor is it generally integrated into a multicultural view of education. (pp. 234–235)

And in *The Cultural Component of Foreign-Language Learning*, produced in 1993 by the Cultural Commission of the American Association of Teachers of French, Wendy Allen and others make a substantial contribution to integrating culture and language. They define four stages of cultural competence and propose instructional objectives, topics, and methods appropriate to each stage.

The location of culture at the core of the curriculum grows naturally out of a series of developments that have occurred over the past ten to fifteen years, beginning with the recognition of a competency-based model for language learning first put forth in the *ACTFL proficiency guidelines* (1986). The competency-based model gradually expanded to integrate the concepts of content and language, creating an impetus for learning content through language and learning language through content and giving rise to content-based instruction, language for special purposes, and languages across the curriculum.

Finally, The National Standards in Foreign Language Education Project resulted in publication of *Standards for foreign language learning: Preparing for the 21st century* (1996). This volume defined the five C's (communication, cultures, connections, comparisons, and communities), making clear the central role of culture as content in the language curriculum. The introduction to the cultures standard states:

> American students need to develop an awareness of other people's world views, of their unique way of life, and of the patterns of behavior which order their world, as well as to learn about their contributions to the world at large and the solutions they offer to the common problems of humankind. Such awareness will help combat the ethnocentrism that often dominates the thinking of our young people. (p. 39)

Having established the saliency of *culture* effectively, *Standards* leaves some major questions unanswered:

- What is the definition of culture? The definition of culture adopted by *Standards*—the interplay among perspectives, practices, and products—is a significant advance over earlier definitions. But the definition still has the disadvantage of defining culture as something *out there*—a body of material to be explored and eventually mastered—as opposed to an interactive process between learners and cultural contexts. As well, it mixes elements of subjective culture (*perspectives*) and elements of objective culture (*products*) into a single definition, which further complicates the existing confusion between these two.
- How is culture learning implemented? While providing a sound conceptual overview of culture, the five standards are far less explicit when it comes to suggesting how to structure culture learning.
- How exactly can culture learning and language learning be integrated? This needs to be addressed on both the conceptual and practical levels.
- How do language teachers assess their success in implementing the integration of culture learning and language learning?

WHAT KIND OF CULTURE?

At the 1996 CARLA conference of interculturalists and language educators that gave rise to this volume, a telling exchange occurred on the second day of discussion. We had all agreed that culture was an important topic in the language teaching profession, when we suddenly realized that we all meant different things by the term *culture*! So, to avoid the same thing from happening in this chapter, we shall provide some short definitions. One of the advantages of CARLA's cross-disciplinary approach to language and culture is the opportunity to select or synthesize definitions from a larger arena.

The distinction between *Big C* and *little c* culture is used by both language teachers and interculturalists, although the two fields define these aspects of culture somewhat differently. In the *Standards for Foreign Language Learning* (1996) volume, Culture is defined as *formal* culture, including "the formal institutions (social, political, and economic), the great figures of history, and those products of literature, fine arts, and the sciences that were traditionally assigned to the category of elite culture" (p. 40). In contrast, culture is defined as "those aspects of daily living studied by the sociologist and the anthropologist: housing, clothing, food, tools, transportation, and all the patterns of behavior that members of the culture regard as necessary and appropriate" (p. 40). Lafayette (1997) uses more or less this distinction when he suggests goals for teaching culture in the foreign language classroom. Those that fit the *Big C* category include recognizing and explaining geographical monuments, historical events, major institutions (administrative, political, religious, educational, etc.), and major artistic monuments. The *little c* goals he suggests include recognizing and explaining everyday *active* cultural patterns such eating, shopping, greeting people, etc.; everyday *passive* patterns such as social stratification, marriage, work, etc.; and acting appropriately in common everyday situations.

Interculturalists such as Cushner and Brislin (1996) and Bennett (1998) are more likely to associate the *Big C* and *little c* distinction with *objective culture* and *subjective culture* respectively, in the manner of sociology (Berger & Luckmann, 1966) and psychology (Triandis, 1994). Objective culture not only refers to cultural creations—the institutions and artifacts that were defined above as formal culture, but it also includes institutionalized patterns of everyday behavior such as eating, shopping, artifacts, and clothing that were categorized by Lafayette as *little c* culture. As Cushner and Brislin (1996) suggest, "It is relatively easy to pick up, analyze and hypothesize about the uses and meanings of objective elements of culture." (p. 6).

For interculturalists, subjective *(little c)* culture refers the invisible, less tangible aspects of culture (Cushner & Brislin, 1996). It focuses on the world view maintained by members of a society. This world view is the set of distinctions and constructs that can variously be described as cultural values, beliefs, assumptions, or style. There is a significant overlap of this notion of subjective culture and the idea of *deep culture*, as described by Brooks (1997) based on his reading of Edward T. Hall's *The silent language* (1959). But in the continuing development of Hall's seminal work, interculturalists today typically define the elements of subjective culture as language use (the social contexting of language), nonverbal behavior (as it generates context for language, and as stand-alone signs), communication style (patterns of rhetoric or discourse), cognitive style (preferred forms of logic, information-gathering, etc.), and cultural values (assignment of goodness for certain ways of being, such as individualism or collectivism). It is the apprehension of this subjective culture—temporarily "looking at the world through different eyes"—that underlies the development of intercultural competence, as defined by interculturalists. As described in greater detail below, behavior that is adaptive to everyday culture is assumed by interculturalists to emerge from successfully making this shift in perspective.

WHAT KIND OF COMPETENCE?

For the purposes of this paper, intercultural competence refers to the ability to relate effectively and appropriately in a variety of cultural contexts. It requires culturally sensitive knowledge, a motivated mindset, and a skillset. The literature on intercultural communication competence focuses on the attributes and skills needed by the communicator. The competencies suggested for each stage of the curriculum design section of this paper were synthesized from a wide range of these publications on intercultural competence (Collier, 1989; Cui & Awa, 1992; Dinges, 1983; Dinges & Baldwin, 1996; Hammer, 1987, 1989; Kim, 1991; Lustig & Koester, 1996; Martin, 1989; Spitzberg, 1989; Wiseman & Koester, 1993) and organized into the appropriate developmental stages by the authors.

Another distinction about intercultural competence made by interculturalists that would be useful in the language-teaching context is that between *culture-specific* and *culture-general* approaches to effective interaction. Culture-specific approaches are similar in many respects to those stressed in ethnographic, or *emic*, approaches to culture learning in language classrooms (e.g., Jurasek, 1995). The goal of culture-specific approaches is to achieve competence in a target culture (C2); that is, to gain mastery of the world view and behavior specific to a particular culture. In this sense, specific-culture learning is a direct parallel to specific-language learning, where competence in L2 is the goal. Even the idea of competence is parallel between language learning and this kind of culture learning. In language learning, knowing grammar and vocabulary alone does not equal competence, and it is equally the case that knowing the objective aspects of C2 is insufficient for specific intercultural competence. The goal for competence in both L2 and C2 is to internalize the target sufficiently for appropriate behavior to be generated naturally.

Culture-general approaches to intercultural competence are not targeted on a particular culture. They are *etic* in the sense that they depend on *universal categories*, which in intercultural work are general distinctions about cultural difference that can be used to make cross-cultural comparisons. Culture-general approaches to intercultural competence focus on internalizing cognitive frameworks for cultural analysis, overcoming ethnocentrism, developing appreciation and respect for one's own culture and for cultural difference, understanding and acquiring skills in basic cultural adaptation processes, and dealing with the identity issues that attend to intercultural contact and mobility. The culture-general focus is consistent with several aspects of the discussion of culture learning in the language education literature. For instance, Kramsch (1993) calls for a focus on culture as context, where "Cultural awareness must then be viewed both as enabling language proficiency and as being the outcome of reflection on language proficiency" (p. 8). Crawford-Lange and Lange (1984) state that "To study culture as a body of facts is to study the characteristics of culture; to study culture as process is to study its essence" (p. 142). And several of the goals listed by Lafayette (1997) refer to this culture-general aspect. He suggests, for example, that learners should be able to "Value different peoples and societies; Evaluate validity of statements about culture; and Develop skills needed to locate and organize information about culture" (pp. 125–126).

It should be clear that developing intercultural competence is different from "teaching culture in the language classroom," as that subject has sometimes been treated in the language education literature. The goal of intercultural competence is not simply the knowledge of another culture, nor is it just the ability to behave appropriately in that culture. Developing intercultural competence demands a mix of culture-specific approaches that stress the apprehension of a particular subjective culture combined with culture-general approaches that address the larger issues of ethnocentrism, cultural self-awareness, and general adaptation strategies.

The mix of culture-specific and culture-general approaches is likely to be different in each language-learning situation. The level and sophistication of the learners is certainly a factor in how much the target language can be used to explain the complex frames of reference used in the culture-general approach. Also, the readiness of language teachers themselves to embark on this task is a factor. And, as noted in the introductory section, the demands of an educational system that stresses test achievement and *Big C* content may be an impediment to devoting the time necessary to develop skills beyond basic linguistic competence. That said, the task of developing intercultural competence is one that is natural to the language classroom and it is probably one of the most important contributions any of us can make to ensure a more peaceful and livable future. The rest of this chapter describes one way in which language educators can approach this task.

THE DEVELOPMENT MODEL
OF INTERCULTURAL SENSITIVITY

The Developmental Model of Intercultural Sensitivity (DMIS) (M. Bennett, 1986, 1993) describes stages that people move through in their acquisition of intercultural competence. The idea of *intercultural competence* in the DMIS is exactly as stated above—the ability to recognize oneself operating in cultural context, the identification and appreciation of cultural differences, and the development of general strategies for adapting to cultural difference. The model is thus *culture-general* in the sense that it describes how learners overcome ethnocentrism regarding their own culture and how they achieve sensitivity to other cultures in general. The model is *developmental* because it assumes that issues at each stage need to be resolved in some way before the learner can move on to deal with more complex issues at later stages. As a culture-general developmental model of intercultural competence, the DMIS offers a way for language teachers to (1) assess the *developmental readiness* of their students to pursue certain kinds of intercultural learning and (2) select and sequence learning activities that contribute to their students' development of general intercultural competence.

The purpose of the following sections is to demonstrate how this model can guide educational support and challenge for the language learner. First, the DMIS is summarized with reference to its theoretical and empirical support, including some discussion of how it fits theoretically into the language learning effort. Then, for each stage of the model, the developmental task and some stage-appropriate activities for supporting and challenging learners are explored. The goal is to provide language teachers with a practical and theoretically sound way to expand linguistic competence to include general intercultural competence.

Theoretical Background

The DMIS brings together two kinds of research. One is the systematic observation of actual behavior—how people act when they are faced with cultural difference. The second is the testing of a coherent theoretical explanation for that behavior. Based on testing, the theory is refined and becomes a better and better predictor of actual observed behavior.[1] The initial observations that led to formulating the model focused on students as they struggled with intercultural issues in workshops, language classrooms, and cultural exchange programs. Since then, these observations have been expanded to include business persons, social service and health care personnel, K–12 teachers, and college faculty, among others.

It appears that learners progress through six discernible stages that can be explained by principles of *constructivism*. Constructivist theory, an amalgam of cognitive psychology and post-positivist philosophy, holds that our experience of reality occurs largely through *constructs*, or complex categories, which together make up our *world view* (Watzlawick, 1984). In other words, our notions of reality are generated by the categories that we use to describe it, and those categories are the medium through which we experience events. As the constructivist psychologist George Kelly (1963) stated:

> A person can be a witness to a tremendous parade of episodes and yet, if he fails to keep making something out of them . . . , he gains little in the way of experience from having been around when they happened. It is not what happens around him that makes a man experienced; it is the successive construing and reconstruing of what happens, as it happens, that enriches the experience of his life. (p. 73)

This perspective is usually well known to linguists, since it is the basis of the so-called Sapir/Whorf Hypothesis (Whorf, 1956):

> The categories and types that we isolate from the world of phenomena we do not find here because they stare every observer in the face; on the contrary, the world is presented in a kaleidoscopic flux of impressions which has to be organized by our minds—and this means largely by the linguistic systems in our minds. (p. 213)

Although theorists continue to argue about the extent to which the Sapir/Whorf Hypothesis might be true, most language teachers and interculturalists know from their personal experience that the language one is speaking facilitates certain perceptions of the surrounding world and inhibits others (M. Bennett, 1998a).

Constructivism, then, provides an understanding of how people develop in their ability to construe, and thus to experience, cultural difference. The DMIS uses observed behavior (verbal statements) to indicate an underlying condition (world view state) that enables people to experience cultural difference in a certain way. The more sophisticated (complex) their world view constructions of cultural difference, the more interculturally sensitive and competent they become. Once a more sophisticated experience of cultural difference is achieved, that world view state is applied to any phenomenon that fits the category *culture*; in other words, the skills at each stage are generalizable to any kind of cultural difference. Further, it appears that the world view states are fairly stable; people maintain the same general orientation to cultural difference, no matter what the culture.

Overview of Stages

The Developmental Model of Intercultural Sensitivity is divided into two sets of stages, Ethnocentric and Ethnorelative (see Figure 10.1). In Ethnocentrism, people unconsciously experience their own cultures as central to reality. They therefore avoid the idea of cultural difference as an implicit or explicit threat to the reality of their own cultural experience. In Ethnorelativism, people consciously recognize that all behavior exists in cultural context, including their own. They recognize the restriction this places on their experience, and they therefore seek out cultural difference as a way of enriching their own experience of reality and as a means to understand others.

Denial. In the first stage of Ethnocentrism, Denial, people have not yet constructed the category of *cultural difference*. To them, the world is completely their current experience of it, and alternatives to that experience are literally unimaginable. People of other cultures, insofar as they are perceived at all, seem less human, lacking the *real* feelings and thoughts of one's own kind. Cultural strangers exist as simpler forms in the environment to be tolerated, exploited, or eliminated as necessary. This world view state is the default condition of normal socialization. People can stay in Denial their whole lives, as long as they don't have much contact with cultural difference. They can maintain this state by living in total *isolation* from people who are culturally different or, as is more common, by maintaining *separation* from difference through artificial means such as apartheid.

Diagnosing Denial. In most cases, the expression of Denial appears thoughtless, but benign, as in the statement "live and let live." Learners may appear extremely naïve and ask "stupid" questions, such as "do you live with wild animals (in Nairobi)?" The purpose of the question is not to denigrate urban Africans; it is simply uninformed. Students have difficulty differentiating cultures, leading them to lump all Asians, or all people of color, together. And learners at this stage are profoundly unaware of their own cultures. Any inquiry into how their cultural *lens* influences perception is likely to be met with bewilderment. Teachers are less likely to see the virulent form of Denial, which is the active dehumanization of others associated with genocide. Still, it may come up around certain political issues.

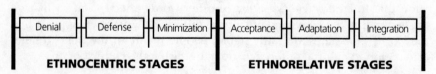

Figure 10.1.   The developmental model of intercultural sensitivity. *Source:* Bennett, M.J. (1993).

Defense.   In the second stage of Ethnocentrism, Defense, people have become more adept at perceiving cultural difference. Exposure to media images of other cultures, or the kind of casual contact that occurs in a multicultural classroom may set the stage for this level of experience. Other people still seem less real (i.e., less human) than one's own kind, but they now exist in perception as stereotypes and so must be dealt with. Because one's own culture is still experienced as the only true reality, the existence of the other cultures is threatening to that reality. To counter the threat, the world is organized into *us and them*, associated with the *denigration* of *them* and the *superiority* of *us*. Occasionally, people at this stage may go into *reversal*, wherein they exalt an adopted culture and denigrate their own primary socialization (*going native*, or *passing*). On the surface, this may appear to be more interculturally sensitive, but in terms of the dualistic perception characterizing this stage, it is an equivalent kind of Defense.

Diagnosing Defense.   Students in Defense tend to polarize any discussion of cultural difference. An attempt to contrast cultures in a non-evaluative way may be met with defensive statements, such as "so what do you have against America?" Jokes that denigrate other cultures and ethnic slurs are accepted as *normal*, and a lot of attention may be given to the relative intelligence or ability of different cultural groups. Reversal (in the United States) may accompany the discovery by someone that he or she is one one-thousandth Cherokee. Suddenly, he or she is *of the people*, as opposed to being one of those despicable Anglos. People of dominant co-cultures are likely to experience Defense as an attack on what they see as their *values—positions that others often see as *privileges*. People of non-dominant co-cultures may experience Defense as an opportunity to discover and solidify a separate cultural identity in contrast to the dominant group (Banks, 1998; Parham, 1989). In either case, learners will acknowledge and often attack the other group while continuing to avoid contact with it.

Minimization.   In the third and final stage of Ethnocentrism, Minimization, the threat of Defense has been resolved by assuming a basic similarity among all human beings. Either in terms of *physical universalism* (e.g., all humans have the same needs) or in terms of some principle of *transcendent universalism* (e.g., everyone is a child of God), the differences that were threatening in Defense are subsumed into already-existing, familiar categories. People in Minimization recognize cultural variation in institutions and customs (objective culture) and may be quite interested in those kinds of differences. However, they hold mightily to the idea that beneath these differences beats the heart of a person pretty much like them. Because they are still lacking cultural self-awareness, people in Minimization cannot see that their characterizations of similarity are usually based on their own culture.

Diagnosing Minimization. Learners in Minimization are *nice*. They make statements such as "we are all one under the sun," and they may be sincerely motivated to include culturally different others into their activities. However, they cannot fathom why people of other cultures might not *want* to engage in the proffered activities. This is the *melting pot* stage, where (in the United States) a lot of emphasis may be placed on *becoming American*. Older learners in this stage may argue for universal human rights or world capitalism, without reference to how such a position might be perceived by others as a form of cultural imperialism. People of dominant co-cultures may assume that all people have *equal opportunity*, failing to perceive that institutions fashioned in their own culture's image may offer them advantages while hindering the achievement of others who are culturally different.

Acceptance. In the first stage of Ethnorelativism, Acceptance, people have discovered their own cultural context, and therefore they can accept the existence of different cultural contexts. People at this stage can construct culture-general categories that allow them to generate a range of relevant cultural contrasts among many cultures. Thus, they are not necessarily experts in one or more specific cultures (although they might also be that); rather, they are adept at identifying how cultural differences in general operate in a wide range of human interactions. Acceptance does not mean agreement—some cultural difference may be judged negatively—but the judgment is not ethnocentric in the sense of withholding equal humanity. People at Acceptance first attain *respect for behavioral differences*, which involves only the more tangible aspects of subjective culture such as language use, nonverbal behavior, and communication style. *Respect for value differences* follows, wherein people experience their own values as but one *good way* of organizing the ethical dimension of reality. This is not the same as saying *anything goes*, the common allegation lodged by antagonists of cultural relativity. The focus is on recognition of the cultural context of behavior, not on the acceptance of all behavior as appropriate in all contexts.

Diagnosing Acceptance. Learners in Acceptance are able to see their own behavior in cultural context. Consequently, they tend to use self-referential statements such as "As a Japanese person, I am inclined to believe that...," or "This may be mainly a *guy thing*, but..." They are likely to be curious about cultural differences, seeking out information about the subjective cultural behavior and values of other groups and initiating contrasts with their own cultures. Many learners will be questioning the absolutism of certain values inculcated by early socialization. This may lead them to flirt with the *whatever* response to value questions, on their way to discovering that values can exist in cultural context and still command their commitment.

Adaptation.   In the second stage of Ethnorelativism, Adaptation, people are able to shift their cultural frames of reference; that is, they are able to look at the world *through different eyes* and intentionally change their behavior to communicate more effectively in another culture. This is a conscious act, necessitating an awareness of one's own culture and a set of contrasts to the target culture. Shifting cultural frames of reference can be thought of as intercultural *empathy*, which involves temporarily setting aside one's own world view assumptions and intentionally taking on a specific, different set of beliefs (M. Bennett, 1998b, p. 207). The result of employing empathy in an intercultural event is to generate *natural* behavior that is appropriate to the target culture. In other words, adaptive behavior emerges from successfully looking at the world from the other culture's perspective. *Pluralism* is an extension of empathy, referring to the routine shifts in frame of reference practiced by people who are *bicultural* or (in the case of several cultures) *multicultural.* But not all biculturalism is culturally sensitive. In the case of *accidental biculturalism*, people have simply received primary socialization into two cultures. Such people may be able to act appropriately in two different cultural contexts, but they cannot necessarily generalize that ability to a third culture.

Diagnosing Adaptation.   Learners in Adaptation are able to interpret and evaluate situations from more than one cultural perspective. They are likely to initiate statements such as, "I think a Japanese view of this situation would be...," or "Let's imagine how a Moslem might react to..." Learners at this stage are often those who seek out contact with cultural difference, and they are notable in their ability to change behavior in different cultural contexts. For example, a person's behavior may be more objective and detached from feelings in male or European American contexts, while the same person may be more *subjective* and attached to feelings in female or African American contexts. Learners also may act as *cultural liaisons* between two cultural groups that they know well. They are perceived as belonging to both groups, although there may be some people in each group who cannot accept the *disloyalty* of such dual membership.

Integration.   In the last stage of Ethnorelativism, Integration, people extend their ability to perceive events in cultural context to include their own definitions of identity. For these people, the process of shifting cultural perspective becomes a normal part of self, and so identity itself becomes a more fluid notion. One begins to see one's self as *moving around in cultures*, no longer completely at the center of any one or combination of cultures—a *cultural marginal.* This change in identity can be a profoundly alienating experience for people who have not been intentionally developing their intercultural sensitivity—*encapsulated marginality* (J. Bennett, 1993). But when this identity develops as an extension of Adaptation, it is more likely to become *constructive marginality.* Integration is not necessarily better than Adaptation in most situations demanding intercultural competence, but it is descriptive of a substantial number of non-dominant minority group members, long-term expatriates, *global nomads,* and other people who may see themselves as *citizens of the world.*

Diagnosing Integration. Learners in the encapsulated marginality form of Integration are likely to appear self-centered, alienated, and unsure of their values, while at the same time exhibiting a high degree of knowledge and competence regarding other cultures. The major difference between encapsulated marginality and normal alienation is the extent to which experiences in different cultures are involved. In constructive marginality, learners are characterized by their positive attitude toward intercultural activities of all kinds. They are more likely to be sophisticated in intercultural ethics, to be inclined toward deep cross-cultural interpretation, and to be skilled in intercultural mediation. Whether encapsulated or constructive, people at this stage of development are very complex in their constructions of cultural difference and in their definitions of self. The question "Who are you?" is likely to elicit a very long story, filled with examples of intercultural experience.

THE RELATIONSHIP OF THE DMIS
TO LANGUAGE LEARNING

The DMIS offers much that can be of benefit to language teachers because of its developmental nature and because of the applicability of its central principles to both culture learning and language learning. The model suggests that the essence of culture learning is not the acquisition of content or a body of knowledge, but rather the ability to shift cultural perspectives. As a result, the DMIS has the following advantages:

- The idea of cultural learning in the model is not the acquisition by the learner of discrete facts, but the development of an intercultural mind—a mindset capable of understanding from within and from without both one's own culture and other cultures. Thus defined, cultural learning resonates positively with communicative competence and proficiency-related theories of language learning.
- By taking a culture-general approach to intercultural competence, the model provides a way of teaching *culture* when it is not appropriate to teach any one particular culture. Even if a particular culture is clearly the target, the model suggests how to place culture-learning into a general framework that is more likely to provide learners with generalizable intercultural skills.

- The model posits that culture learning must begin with cultural self-awareness, a notion compatible with views regarding the interrelatedness of first-language and second-language learning. It is not until we study a second language that we come to know our native language.
- The model focuses on the importance of how one approaches cultural similarity and difference, and the centrality of cultural difference to the development of intercultural awareness. Tension between similarities and differences exists in the language learning domain as well; teachers must decide when it is appropriate to underscore similarities and when to focus instead on differences. The issue of timing is critical, and the model provides a guideline for presenting this material in a way that is intentionally developmental.

Although language proficiency is not a specific element of the DMIS, the model nevertheless supports the view of language learning as a communication endeavor and as a humanistic enterprise. As a communication endeavor, language competence is defined as the ability to use the language as an *insider*. The DMIS creates a parallel to language competence by defining cultural competence as the ability to interpret and behave within culture as an *insider*. As a humanistic enterprise, language learning creates an awareness and appreciation of language itself. The DMIS parallel is that intercultural sensitivity involves an awareness and appreciation of culture itself.

Having explored the conceptual foundation for sequencing culture into the language curriculum, we will now suggest stage-sensitive approaches to teaching culture. These methods have been selected not only for their appropriateness to developmental stages, but also for their fit with language proficiency levels.

CURRICULUM DESIGN

The Support and Challenge Framework

As we explore culture learning in the language classroom, Nevitt Sanford's (1966) framework for promoting development in our students provides a useful perspective. He suggests that the educational process involves a careful balance of support and challenge. As the students encounter and respond to the new knowledge and skills required in the learning process, they require a balance between the challenge represented by the new stimuli and the necessary support to take the risks and develop mastery. If the challenge is excessive, the learner will resist or engage in flight, psychologically or even physically. If the support is excessive, the learner stagnates, or sleeps blissfully through the course.

For the educator, it is possible to separate the challenge of the content of the material (grammar patterns in a foreign language, for instance) from the challenge of the process, the teaching methods used in the classroom. Each language teacher is familiar with the topics in the course that tax the students the most; each is familiar with those lessons that are sure winners, because the content is readily absorbed, or the subject is so intriguing. Depending on the learning styles, cognitive styles, and communication styles of the students we teach, we can also make a reasonable assessment of the methods they will find most challenging and those which are more comfortable (Jonassen & Grabowski, 1993). In general, learners find activities that are high risk, or high disclosure, more challenging. For instance, many adult learners find role-plays in front of a class quite challenging. Figure 10.2 represents a model for balancing content and process challenges for the learners (J. Bennett, 1993). What it suggests is that if we are presenting a topic that we know to be very demanding, we balance this out with a method that is user-friendly. In other words, we support the students with the process, while challenging them with the content. In contrast, if our topic is relatively boring, or routine, we can select extremely challenging methods for the lesson, balanc-

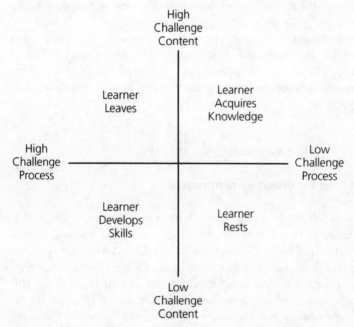

Figure 10.2.   Content and process: Balancing challenge. © Janet M. Bennett, 1993

ing a low-challenge topic with a high-challenge process. Students are quite comfortable with more demanding methods (such as simulations) if the topic is less threatening. By maintaining this balance, we support the learners to take risks and develop.

As intercultural educators, we can be reasonably sure that learners in ethnocentric stages will, in general, find the discussion of cultural differences quite challenging, perhaps even threatening to their world view. Culture becomes a less challenging topic as the learner moves into acceptance and beyond. Our methods can then become more complicated and we can involve the learners in higher risk activities, such as role-plays and simulations.

Development of Intercultural Sensitivity in the Language Classroom

How is the language teacher to determine the probable level of intercultural sensitivity at any given language level? Figure 10.3 illustrates the typical fit between language proficiency levels and developmental levels of intercultural sensitivity. The figure suggests that the DMIS model can

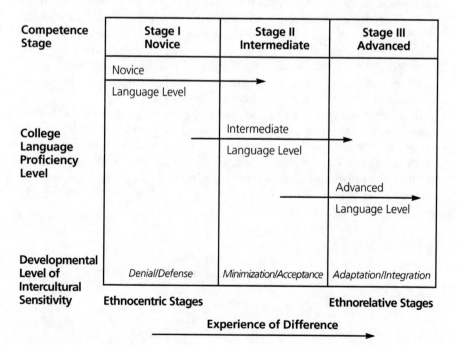

Competence Stage	Stage I Novice	Stage II Intermediate	Stage III Advanced
	Novice		
	Language Level		
College Language Proficiency Level		Intermediate	
		Language Level	
			Advanced
			Language Level
Developmental Level of Intercultural Sensitivity	*Denial/Defense*	*Minimization/Acceptance*	*Adaptation/Integration*
	Ethnocentric Stages		**Ethnorelative Stages**

Experience of Difference

Figure 10.3.   Development of Intercultural sensitivity[1] © 1998 Janet M. Bennett and Kazuko Ikeda.

readily be divided into three stages, by combining Denial and Defense into Stage I: Novice; Minimization and Acceptance into Stage II: Intermediate; and Adaptation and Integration into Stage III: Advanced. Novice language learners most frequently fall into Stage I, where their novice language skills match their intercultural development. While it is to be hoped that they might reach Minimization before they reach intermediate language skills, this is by no means assured. The language instructor at the intermediate level should therefore presume some residual issues from Defense, as the learners move more comfortably into Minimization and Acceptance. Finally, advanced language learners have most likely internalized cultural frame-of-reference shifting, resolved the remaining Acceptance questions, and moved into Adaptation. Only at the most advanced stages or in the most unusual circumstances (for instance, a whole class of learners studying their third or fourth language) would a language teacher expect a class to be in the Integration stage.

By assessing the learners' stages of both language and culture learning, the instructor can increase the level of cultural complexity in direct relationship to language proficiency. In keeping with this model, suggested activities for each stage have been selected based on the challenge of the cultural concepts explored as well as the linguistic demands of the method. This model of sequencing culture and language learning developmentally is for purposes of designing curriculum, not for individual diagnosis. In any given class, a teacher may have students at all levels of intercultural sensitivity. Nevertheless, any curriculum must focus on a probable pattern of development for students. In this case, our supposition is that culture can be integrated into the language curriculum by addressing levels of intercultural competence in tandem with language proficiency.

In the following discussion, we will apply this framework to the task of culture learning in the language classroom, suggesting for each stage of the model the developmental tasks the learners face, the existing level of challenge as it relates to culture learning, support and challenge patterns for the instructor, and stage-appropriate intercultural competencies. For each stage, appropriately sequenced culture learning activities will be suggested, as illustrated in Figure 10.4.

The following classroom activities have been selected as appropriate to develop intercultural competence for language learners at specific levels of intercultural sensitivity and language proficiency. (Citations for each item are in bibliography.)

STAGE I: NOVICE

Addresses Intercultural Sensitivity Levels: Denial and Defense

Appropriate for: Early and Late Novice Language Learners

- "Grocery Store Ethnography" by Randy Kluver in T.M. Singelis (1998) *(Denial)*
- "The Tag Game" by Norine Dresser, George O. Enell, and Kay Hardman from Simulation Training Systems (Gary Shirts) *(Denial)* (Available from Simulation Training Systems: 1-800-942-2900)
- "Aba-Zak" by Alvino Fantini (1997) *(Denial)*
- "Hollow Square: A Communication Experiment" in J.W. Pfeiffer and J.E. Jones *(Defense)*
- "One Way—Two Way Communication" in M.D. Pusch (1979) *(Defense)*
- "Building a Tower" in H. Fennes and K. Hapgood (1997) *(Defense)*

STAGE II: INTERMEDIATE

Addresses Intercultural Sensitivity Levels: Minimization and Acceptance

Appropriate for: Early and Late Intermediate (Second and Third Year) Language Learners

- "U.S. Proverbs and Core Values" by L. Robert Kohls in N. Seelye (Vol. I, 1996) *(Minimization)*
- "Personal Maps" and "Piece of Culture" in H. Fennes and K. Hapgood (1997) *(Minimization)*
- "Description, Interpretation, Evaluation" by Janet and Milton Bennett (available from The Intercultural Communication Institute) *(Minimization)*
- "Collage" and "Magazines" in J. O'Mara (1994) *(Minimization)*
- "The Cocktail Party: Exploring Nonverbal Communication" by Judy Blohm in A. Fantini (1997) *(Acceptance)*
- "Conversational Constraints as a Tool for Understanding Communication Styles" by Min-Sun Kim in T.M. Singelis (1998) *(Acceptance)*
- "The Culture Compass" by Paula Chu in N. Seelye (Vol. I, 1996) *(Acceptance)*

STAGE III: ADVANCED

Addresses Intercultural Sensitivity Levels: Adaptation and Integration

Appropriate for: Early and Late Advanced (Fourth Year) Language Learners

- "Case Study: Salman Rushdie and The Satanic Verses" by Janet M. Bennett in S.M. Fowler and M.G. Mumford (1995) *(Adaptation)*
- "Critical Incidents in an Intercultural Conflict Resolution Exercise" by Milton J. Bennett in S.M. Fowler and M.G. Mumford (1995) *(Adaptation)*
- "The Public and Private Self" by Janet and Milton Bennett (available from The Intercultural Communication Institute) *(Adaptation)*
- "Negotiating Across Cultural Boundaries" by Joseph C. Ady in T.M. Singelis (1998) *(Adaptation)*
- "Decoding Indirectness" in C. Storti and L. Bennhold-Samaan (1998) *(Adaptation)*
- "Beyond Ethnocentrism: Promoting Cross-Cultural Understanding with BaFá BaFá" by Gary Shirts and "BARNGA: A Game for All Seasons" by Barbara Steinwachs in S.M. Fowler and M.G. Mumford (1995) *(Adaptation)*

Figure 10.4.   Teaching culture in the language classroom.

Developing Intercultural Competence at the Denial Stage

Stage I: Early-Novice Language Learners

At this stage the learners typically find the subject of cultural difference quite challenging; having merely enrolled in a language class, they may see little reason to study the subjective cultural patterns of the target culture. They may be saying things like: "As long as we speak the same language, that's all that really matters" or "What I need to know is how to get around during my semester abroad." In the face of this denial, the instructors should emphasize methods of teaching culture that support the students and pursue the developmental task of teaching them to recognize the existence of cultural difference, and overcome initial anxieties about experiencing such differences.

It is not surprising that a vast amount of the material on teaching culture in the language classroom focuses on this stage, where lessons focus on *everyday culture* (Lafayette, 1997), and *big C* culture (Byram & Morgan, 1994, among others). Language teachers would probably not be far off in suspecting that most beginning students reside in the Denial stage. The content that is supportive to those anxious about cultural difference converges on what we have defined as objective culture—the sociopolitical and arts institutions of the target culture—as well as the functional culture of getting through a day. Lessons may celebrate heroes and holidays, or suggest *do's and taboos* for casual social interaction in the target language. These nonthreatening topics can easily be handled with pleasant, engaging classroom activities, such as culture fairs, shopping simulations, or various *show and tell* activities. Numerous resources exist to assist instructors in designing this curriculum.

While these approaches support the students, additional stimulation must be added to promote their development toward the next stage. Therefore, to challenge the learners, instructors need to introduce the concept of subjective culture, and selectively acquaint the students with values or communication behaviors that will not present an excessive challenge, but that may stimulate their curiosity. For instance, in teaching students about culture, the instructor can use creative but nonthreatening activities such as "The Grocery Store Ethnography" (Kluver, 1998). This glimpse into the potential complexity of cultural observation is designed to develop in the learners the initiative to explore other aspects of subjective culture that will increase their cultural competence.

Other classroom activities which require limited vocabulary and grammar proficiency include *Aba-Zak*, (Fantini, 1997, pp. 47–51), and *The Tag Game* (see Figure 4). These activities explore the topic of *difference* in a learner-friendly fashion, yet simulate developing greater sensitivity. Frequently, those of us who teach intercultural competence often aim too high for learners in denial. In fact, the stage-appropriate intercultural competencies are measured and limited; the learner should desire and be able to gather appropriate information about the target culture, to recognize cultural differences, and maintain an attitude of trust, friendliness, and cooperation during the exploration of difference. More complex outcomes should be reserved for students at later stages.

Developing Intercultural Competence at the Defense Stage

Stage I: Late-Novice Language Learners

Students who appear to be at the Defense stage often present the greatest obstruction to exploring cultural difference. Setting up various barriers to exploring other cultures, they may find other cultural patterns inferior, repulsive ("They eat WHAT?") or even immoral. Finding great security in the comforts of their own culture, any mention of cultural difference seems to challenge them excessively. Learners at Defense are sometimes labeled *resistant,* but in fact they may simply be fearful of needing to change, to take risks. Hence, the language instructor needs to emphasize maximum support for these individuals, as she moves them toward the developmental goal of discovering human commonalties.

Lesson plans therefore should avoid cultural contrasts and provide reassurance to the threatened student in Defense. For this stage, and this stage only, the focus of the message is on similarity, and how many things the students have in common with people of the target culture. Rather than correcting statements of pride in one's own culture, the instructor recognizes such comments as emblematic of the stage. The student in Defense can benefit from reframing an experience he has had (e.g., moving from high school to college) as a cultural transition, and assessing the skills he developed in this process that are relevant to culture learning (for instance, the ability to manage anxiety). Further support can be achieved by cooperative learning strategies in the classroom (Johnson, Johnson, & Smith, 1991; Kagan, 1994), where the goal is to provide the anxious student a safe peer group for taking risks later. Students at this stage perform best when they are involved in cooperative activities with students who are not in this same stage, who can model more sensitive behaviors and responses that will influence them to move ahead to the next stage. Methods that require little language and that focus on communication, such as "Hollow Square: A Communication Experiment," (Shedlin & Schmidt, 1974, pp. 32–40); "One Way—Two Way Communication," (Pusch, 1979, pp. 155–159); and "Building a Tower," (Fennes & Hapgood, 1997, pp. 264–266) comfortably address the learner's stage by building strategies for more effective interaction regardless of the cultures.

The challenge for this stage develops for the students as they examine similarities with those seemingly *weird* others. For the student of the Chinese language to discuss his commonalities with a native speaker from China presents an essential prerequisite step toward willingness to recognize and value differences. Once again, the teacher cannot be overly optimistic in designing unrealistic outcomes for the learners at this stage. Since the topic of cultural difference engenders a high degree of challenge, the emphasis can be placed more on personal characteristics. Thus, for students in Defense, the stage-appropriate competencies include the characteristics of anxiety management, tolerance, patience, and self-discipline.

Developing Intercultural Competence at the Minimization Stage

Stage II: Early-Intermediate Language Learners

Once students have determined that indeed, the people of the target culture are *just like them*, they have reached the stage of Minimization, in which they may be heard to say, "The key to getting along in any culture is to just be yourself!" Students who have become well versed in *Big C* culture may acknowledge that the art, music, and politics are different, "but deep down, we're really all the same." Having arrived at Stage II, the intermediate language learner may insist that honesty is a virtue the world over, so "just be direct and honest." There is sometimes a Disneyesque quality to this position—"It's a small world after all!" While this is an improvement over the Defense attitudes, it nevertheless represents an ethnocentric position. The basis for the assumed global commonalty is unquestioningly one's own culture! The goal of the language instructor is twofold at this stage. First, the learners must be consciously brought into awareness that they too possess a subjective culture. Then, acknowledging the shared humanity of the cultural other, they must learn to differentiate categories for cultural comparison between their own culture and the target culture. These categories can be explored through frameworks for identifying nonverbal patterns or communication styles. Mastering cultural self-awareness in terms of such frameworks is the prerequisite competency for moving into ethnorelativism.

At this stage, the language instructor faces less challenge in discussing cultural difference; blessed with only a moderate level of challenge about difference, it becomes appropriate to de-emphasize support somewhat. Supportive topics at this stage emerge from *safe* cultural differences, such as those noted above, and from having clear definitions of culture, race, ethnicity, stereotypes, and generalizations. For the language learner not sufficiently fluent in the target language, frameworks for these discussions may need to be in their own language, as homework readings. Certain cultural concepts may need to be discussed briefly in class in the first language.

Challenge for the minimizer materializes beyond the *safe* topics, when the lessons begin to explore perception, world view, and how world view emerges from a set of deep cultural values. Examination of their own culture calls into question the students' comfortable assumption of similarity and eventuates in the recognition that differences do exist. Perception exercises, style inventories, and value analysis (Kramsch, 1997) raise the students' awareness of their own cultures, which provides the necessary foundation for moving to Acceptance. Typical examples of cultural self-awareness methods include *Collage* and *Magazines* (O'Mara, 1994, pp. 83–85, 201–203); *U.S. Proverbs and Core Values* (Kohls, 1996, pp. 79–81), which can be readily adapted to any culture group; and *Personal Maps* (Fennes & Hapgood, 1997, pp. 175–176) and *Piece of Culture,* (Fennes & Hapgood, 1997, pp. 203–205), which are based in European culture, but also readily adapted. These exercises provide opportunities for examining their own culture using intermediate language skills. One of the more widely used perception exercises is the *Description, Interpretation, and Evaluation Exercise*, which was developed by Janet and Milton Bennett in 1979 (Bennett, Bennett, & Stillings), and is currently available on the Intercultural Communication Institute website (www.intercultural.org). This exercise forces the students to focus on what they see rather than their judgment about it, and to recognize the inevitability of conflicting meanings. The Minimization stage is often considered the first appropriate opportunity to use ethnorelative cultural informants from the target culture, since students' receptivity to other cultural perspectives is only now forming. Such guest speakers are best used in structured contact, such as role-plays, or facilitated discussion.

The expected intercultural competencies at this stage are quite a bit more demanding of cultural sensitivity. In addition to knowledge of one's own culture, the learners can be expected to have knowledge of cultural general frameworks, the ability to perceive others accurately, the ability to maintain a nonjudgmental interaction posture, as well as personal characteristics of open-mindedness and listening skills.

Developing Intercultural Competence at the Acceptance Stage

Stage II: Late-Intermediate Language Learners

After students have developed cultural self-awareness, they are prepared to undertake the more complicated cognitive tasks of the ethnorelative stages. Now they have developed sufficient awareness of their own world view to be able to recognize the equal complexity of other cultures. Instead of avoiding difference, they become difference seekers, and are given to making statements such as "How can I learn more about Mexican culture before my trip?" "When my French host family talks like that I'm really not sure what they mean but it will surely be interesting to try and figure this out!" "I know how the Taiwanese do this. Is it different in Hong Kong or Singapore?" The educator's developmental goal for these learners is to systematically increase the complexity of the categories they use for analyzing difference and to begin to develop their skills for frame-of-reference shifting. At this stage, learners find cultural difference an intriguing content element (nonthreatening), and therefore a rather low challenge. Thus, the instructor can increase the challenge of the methods, and ask the students to take more complex risks.

To support these students, the instructor selects topics which are now quite stimulating to them: complex value analysis, cultural comparison and contrast, cognitive, cultural, and communication styles interaction, etc. The challenge for the learners in this content area is frequently stated as a concern about cultural relativity as it relates to moral relativity: "if I 'accept' the Chinese culture, does this mean I think everything they do is right?" The delicate developmental task here is to assist the students in understanding another culture's behavior in the context of that culture, as a system which makes sense to the members of that culture regardless of how it might fit with their own values or morals.

The process challenge should employ structured experiential learning, including homestay opportunities, drop-offs (Batchelder, 1993, pp. 135–141), simulations, and exercises requiring intercultural empathy (Fowler & Mumford, 1995; Gochenour, 1993; Pusch, 1979; Seelye, 1996). For instance, for learners in the early stages of Acceptance, "The Cocktail Party: Exploring Nonverbal Communication" (Blohm, 1997, pp. 80–84) offers a quick exploration of cultural contrasts. While more demanding of linguistic competence, "Conversational Constraints as a Tool for Understanding Communication Styles" (Kim, 1998, pp. 101–109) and "The Culture Compass" (Chu, 1996, pp. 155–170) present complex examinations of values and communication styles.

The practice of delaying these experiential methods until the students are developmentally ready has only recently been widely recognized. Early intercultural training often began with a quick simulation or role-play, for which the students were not adequately prepared. Current pedagogical practice now supports a more measured approach, based on learner readiness. This sequencing content and method comes naturally to the language educator, who is familiar with detailed standards for measuring language competency.

In teaching to learners at the Acceptance stage, instructors can finally move toward the list of skills often suggested as prerequisites for intercultural effectiveness. The stage-appropriate competencies include cognitive flexibility, contextual analytic skills, tolerance of ambiguity, as well as culture-specific knowledge of the target culture, and culture-general frameworks for analysis.

Developing Intercultural Competence at the Adaptation Stage

Stage III: Early-Advanced Language Learners

After mastering the foundation competencies at Stage I and Stage II, the students are ready to engage in intercultural communication. This Stage III mastery requires them to shift perspectives, and actively use empathy skills. They can be heard commenting on the value of internalizing another world view: "The more I understand this culture, the better I get at the language." They might even be saying, "I'm beginning to feel like a member of this culture." While many language learners may stop short of internalizing a second culture, it is not unrealistic to expect them to function at an adaptation level during the course of mastering a language, usually at an advanced stage of language proficiency. Their cultural category system is now well developed and complex and they demonstrate a willingness to maintain flexible boundaries, allowing for the existence of other cultural constructs within their identity. (For example, "I'm enjoying learning to bargain in Spanish!" or "I'm now able to solve problems at work appropriately in Japanese.")

The developmental goal the instructor must address at this level is mastery of intercultural competence and skills at personal boundary formation. The students experience cultural differences as low challenge, and therefore the educator can emphasize nearly unlimited levels of challenge in both content and process. For the first time, activities can be less structured, and the students can learn more autonomously.

To support them, the curriculum can address such relevant issues as culture shock and adaptation, or such seldom-discussed matters as humor across cultures. The use of cultural informants in small groups or informal discussions can help to prepare the students to continue learning on their own. These *learning-to-learn* methods ground the students in necessary skills for ongoing culture learning after their years of formal study are complete. By practicing participant observation, intercultural interviewing, and various ethnographic techniques, they can acquire skills for continued development. For practice in frame-of-reference shifting and intercultural empathy, culture-specific case studies and critical incidents can provide

useful stimuli. A wide variety of exercises exist, including "Case Study: Salman Rushdie and *The Satanic Verses*" (J. Bennett, 1995, pp. 207–214); "Critical Incidents in an Intercultural Conflict Resolution Exercise" (M.
Bennett, 1995, pp. 147–156); "Negotiating Across Cultural Boundaries"
(Ady, 1998, pp. 111–120); and "Decoding Indirectness" (Storti & Bennhold-
Samaan, 1998, pp. 96–97). Simulations such as BARNGA and BaFa-BaFa
(as described by Steinwachs in Fowler & Mumford, 1995, pp. 101–108), provide the opportunity for skills practice and empathy.

To challenge the learners, content units on cultural identity development and intercultural sensitivity are addressed at this stage. The instructor
also faces the task of designing particularly sophisticated methods for challenging students at the adaptation stage. Often these students have experienced the typical methods, and are seeking deeper explorations of more
profound issues at higher levels of language proficiency. The use of autobiography, culture-specific fiction, and video can stimulate exploration of
identity issues of bicultural people.

For students in the Adaptation stage, the appropriate intercultural competencies include risk-taking skills, problem-solving skills, interaction management skills, social adaptability, and empathy.

Developing Intercultural Competence at the Integration Level

Stage III: Late-Advanced Language Learners

At the sixth stage of development, students are at least bicultural/bilin-
gual and familiar with discussing intercultural identity issues; this is neither
unusual nor particularly challenging for them. Frequently they feel supported by such explorations and gratified that they are not the only marginals in the world. They may say "I'm not a perfect Japanese, nor a perfect
American anymore, but I am me!" "I enjoy being a mediator between other
Americans and my Mexican hosts." "Problem-solving is a lot easier when
you have two frames of reference to bring to bear." When the learner has
reached this stage, the developmental goals relate to identity management
of what has been called the *multicultural self*, or the marginal identity (J.
Bennett, 1993). This fluid self, living at the margins (or edges) of at least
two cultures, presents challenges to the individual to maintain a personal
commitment to a set of values in the context of cultural relativism, and to
participate in a peer group that shares these commitments. All of this
avoids the sense of terminal uniqueness that often plagues marginals and,
instead, helps them to construct boundaries in their intercultural context.

For content support, the language instructor can explore models for
constructing a multicultural identity. While many existing models focus on

U.S. domestic identity development, there are several which lend themselves to international contexts as well (Banks, 1998; J. Bennett, 1993; M. Bennett, 1993). For supportive processes, the educator can involve these bicultural/bilingual marginals as resource persons in other language classes, preparing students for study abroad, facilitating small groups in the target language, etc. In addition, the marginal needs to be a member of a peer group of other multicultural people who understand the complex cultural issues of participating deeply in a number of cultures.

To stimulate further development, the instructor can present content challenges in the form of models of a multicultural self, or society; models of cultural mediation; or models of ethical development. These content elements can promote challenging processes, such as exploration of self-as-process, and patterns of ethical commitment.

Stage-appropriate intercultural competencies include a culturally appropriate sense of humor, the ability to create new cultural categories, and the skill to manage both role and identity flexibility.

CONCLUSION

It is our contention that by sequencing subjective culture topics in the language classroom, teachers can parallel the learners' development of intercultural competence with their language competence. Further, by recognizing the degree of challenge in the material at different developmental stages, instructors can balance appropriate methods within their curriculum. It is only through such theoretically grounded development and balance that culture can achieve its rightful place at the core of the language curriculum.

NOTE

1.   The process of observation and theory refinement is called grounded theory. In the case of the DMIS, initial observations were organized into theoretical world view states. These states were then tested by content analysis studies, which showed that statements made by respondents did indeed fall into particular stages of development. Experimental studies on the DMIS using content analysis showed that development through stages associated with a dependent variable such as an exchange program was observable in pre/post studies. Recently, Mitchell Hammer successfully replicated the content analysis studies with extremely high interrater reliability (Hammer, 1999). In the development of an instrument (the Intercultural Development Inventory, IDI) based on the Hammer study, factor analysis showed that statements about cultural difference *loaded* into categories according to DMIS theoretical prediction. Additionally, the pattern of correlation among

IDI scales indicates the world view states exist in a developmental sequence as posited by DMIS theory.

REFERENCES

Ady, J.C. (1998). Negotiating across cultural boundaries: Implications of individualism-collectivism and cases for application. In T.M. Singelis (Ed.), *Teaching about culture, ethnicity, & diversity* (pp. 111–120). Thousand Oaks, CA: Sage.

American Association of Teachers of French. (July, 1993). *The cultural component of foreign language learning: A common core defined at four levels of competence with pedagogical aids applied to the French-speaking world* (draft). San Diego, CA: San Diego University.

American Council on the Teaching of Foreign Languages. (1989). *ACTFL proficiency guidelines.* Yonkers, NY: Author.

Aarup Jensen, A., Lorentsen, A., & JÆger, K. (Eds.). (1995). *Intercultural competence: A new challenge for language teachers and trainers in Europe. The adult learner* (Vol. II). Language and Cultural Contact series. Aalborg, Denmark: Aalborg University Press.

Banks, J. (1998). *Multiethnic education: Theory and practice* (2nd ed.). Newton, MA: Allyn & Bacon.

Batchelder, D. (1993). The drop-off. In T. Gochenour (Ed.), *Beyond experience* (2nd ed., pp. 135–141). Yarmouth, ME: Intercultural Press.

Bennett, J.M. (1993). Cultural marginality: Identity issues in intercultural training. In R.M. Paige (Ed.), *Education for the intercultural experience* (2nd ed., pp. 109–135). Yarmouth, ME: Intercultural Press.

Bennett, J.M. (1995). Case study: Salman Rushdie and *The Satanic Verses.* In S.M. Fowler & M.G. Mumford (Eds.), *Intercultural sourcebook: Cross-cultural training methods* (Vol. 1, pp. 207–214). Yarmouth, ME: Intercultural Press.

Bennett, J.M., Bennett, M.J., & Stillings, K. (1979). *Intercultural communication workshop: Facilitators' guide* (revised ed.). Portland, OR: Portland State University.

Bennett, M.J. (1986) Towards ethnorelativism: A developmental model of intercultural sensitivity. In R.M. Paige (Ed.), *Cross-cultural orientation: New conceptualizations and applications.* New York: University Press of America.

Bennett, M.J. (1993). Towards ethnorelativism: A developmental model of intercultural sensitivity. In R.M. Paige (Ed.), *Education for the intercultural experience* (2nd ed., pp. 21–71). Yarmouth, ME: Intercultural Press.

Bennett, M.J. (1995). Critical incidents in an intercultural conflict-resolution exercise. In S.M. Fowler & M. G. Mumford (Eds.), *Intercultural sourcebook: Cross-cultural training methods* (Vol. 1, pp. 147–156). Yarmouth, ME: Intercultural Press.

Bennett, M.J. (1998a). Intercultural communication: A current perspective. In M.J. Bennett (Ed.), *Basic concepts of intercultural communication* (pp. 1–34). Yarmouth, ME: Intercultural Press.

Bennett, M.J. (1998b). Overcoming the golden rule: Sympathy and empathy. In M.J. Bennett (Ed.), *Basic concepts of intercultural communication* (pp. 191–214). Yarmouth, ME: Intercultural Press.

Berger, P.L., & Luckmann, T. (1966). *Social construction of reality: A treatise in the sociology of knowledge.* New York: Doubleday.

Blohm, J. (1997). The cocktail party: Exploring nonverbal communication. In A. Fantini (Ed.), *New ways in teaching culture* (pp. 80–84). New Ways in TESOL Series II: Innovative Classroom Techniques. Alexandria, VA: TESOL.

Brooks, N. (1997). Teaching culture in the foreign language classroom. In P.R. Heusinkveld (Ed.), *Pathways to culture: Readings on teaching culture in the foreign language class* (pp. 11–37). Yarmouth, ME: Intercultural Press.

Byram, M., & Morgan, C. (1994). *Teaching-and-learning language-and-culture.* Clevedon, Avon: Multilingual Matters.

Chu, P. (1996). The culture compass. In H.N. Seelye (Ed.), *Experiential activities for intercultural learning* (pp. 155–170). Yarmouth, ME: Intercultural Press.

Collier, M.J. (1989). Cultural and intercultural communication competence. *International Journal of Intercultural Relations, 13,* 287–302.

Cui, G., & Awa, N.E. (1992). Measuring intercultural effectiveness: An integrative approach. *International Journal of Intercultural Relations, 16,* 311–328.

Crawford-Lange, L.M., & Lange, D.L. (1984). Doing the unthinkable in the second-language classroom: A process for the integration of language and culture. In T.V. Higgs (Ed.), *Proficiency: The organizing principle* (pp. 139–177). The ACTFL Foreign Language Education Series. Lincolnwood, IL: National Textbook.

Cushner, K., & Brislin, R. (1996). *Intercultural interactions: A practical guide* (Vol. 9). Cross-cultural research and methodology series. Thousand Oaks, CA: Sage.

Damen, L. (1987). *Culture learning: The fifth dimension in the language classroom.* Reading, MA: Addison-Wesley.

Díaz-Rico, L.T., & Weed, K.Z. (1995). *The cross-cultural, language, and academic development handbook.* Boston: Allyn and Bacon.

Dinges, N.G. (1983). Intercultural competence. In D. Landis & R. Brislin (Eds.), *Issues in theory and design* (Vol. I., pp. 176–202). Handbook of intercultural training. New York: Pergamon.

Dinges, N.G., & Baldwin, K.D. (1996). Intercultural competence: A research perspective. In D. Landis & R. Bhagat (Eds.), *Handbook of intercultural training* (2nd ed., pp. 106–123). Thousand Oaks, CA: Sage.

Ellis, R. (1990). *Instructed second language acquisition: Learning in the classroom.* Colchester, VT: Blackwell.

Fantini, A.E. (Ed.). (1997). *New ways in teaching culture.* New Ways in TESOL Series II: Innovative Classroom Techniques. Alexandria, VA: TESOL.

Fantini, A.E. (1995). Introduction—Language, culture and world view: Exploring the nexus. *International Journal of Intercultural Relations, 19,* 143–153.

Fennes, H., & Hapgood, K. (1997). *Intercultural learning in the classroom.* London: Cassell.

Fowler, S.M., & Mumford, M.G. (Eds.). (1995). Intercultural sourcebook: Cross-cultural *training methods* (Vol. 1). Yarmouth, ME: Intercultural Press.

Fowler, S.M., & Mumford, M.G. (Eds.). (1999). *Intercultural sourcebook: Cross-cultural training methods* (Vol. 2). Yarmouth, ME: Intercultural Press.

Gochenour, T. (Ed.). (1993). *Beyond experience: The experiential approach to cross-cultural education* (2nd ed.). Yarmouth, ME: Intercultural Press.

Hall, E.T. (1959, 1981). *The silent language.* Garden City, NY: Anchor/Doubleday.

Hammer, M.R. (1987). Behavioral dimensions of intercultural effectiveness: A replication and extension. *International Journal of Intercultural Relations, 11*, 65–88.

Hammer, M.R. (1989). Intercultural communication competence. In M. K. Asante & W. B. Gudykunst (Eds.), *Handbook of international and intercultural communication* (pp. 247–260). Newbury Park, CA: Sage.

Hammer, M. R., (1999). The intercultural developmental inventory: A measure of intercultural sensitivity. In S.M. Fowler & M.G. Mumford, (Eds.). *Intercultural sourcebook: Cross-cultural training methods* (Vol. 2, pp. 61–79). Yarmouth, ME: Intercultural Press.

Hammerly, H. (1986). *Synthesis in language teaching: An introduction to linguistics* (Vol. 1). Blaine, WA: Second Language Publications.

Hammerly, H. (1985). *An integrated theory of language teaching and its practical consequences* (Vol. 2). Blaine, WA: Second Language Publications.

Huber, J., & Huber-Kriegler, M. (n.d.). *Language and culture education (LaCE): An attempt to combine language teaching, general communicative abilities and inter-/cultural learning.* Graz: Zentrum für Schulversuche und Schulentwicklung.

Johnson, D.W., Johnson, R.T., & Smith, K.A. (1991). *Active learning: Cooperation in the college classroom.* Edina, MN: Interaction Book Company.

Jonassen, D.H., & Grabowski, B.L. (1993). *Handbook of individual differences, learning, and instruction.* Hillsdale, NJ: Lawrence Erlbaum.

Jurasek, R. (1995). Using ethnography to bridge the gap between study abroad and the on-campus language and culture curriculum. In C.J. Kramsch (Ed.), *Redefining the boundaries of language study* (pp. 221–251). Boston: Heinle & Heinle.

Kagan, S. (1994). *Cooperative learning.* San Juan Capistrano, CA: Kagan Cooperative Learning.

Kelly, G.A. (1963). *A theory of personality: The psychology of personal constructs.* New York: Norton.

Kim, M. (1998). Conversational constraints as a tool for understanding communication styles. In T.M. Singelis (Ed.), *Teaching about culture, ethnicity, & diversity* (pp. 101–109). Thousand Oaks, CA: Sage.

Kim, Y.Y. (1991). Intercultural communication competence: A systems-theoretic view. In S. Ting-Toomey & F. Korzenny (Eds.), *Cross-cultural interpersonal communication* (pp. 259–275). Newbury Park, CA: Sage.

Kluver, R. (1998). Grocery store ethnography. In T.M. Singelis (Ed.), *Teaching about culture, ethnicity, & diversity* (pp. 23–28). Thousand Oaks, CA: Sage.

Kohls, L.R. (1996). U.S. proverbs and core values. In H.N. Seeyle (Ed.), *Experiential activities for intercultural learning* (pp. 79–81). Yarmouth, ME: Intercultural Press.

Kramsch, C.J. (1993). *Context and culture in language teaching.* Oxford: Oxford University Press.

Kramsch, C.J. (1997). Culture and constructs: Communicating attitudes and values in the foreign language classroom. In P.R. Heusinkveld (Ed.), *Pathways to culture: Readings on teaching culture in the foreign language class* (pp. 461–485). Yarmouth, ME: Intercultural Press.

Kramsch, C.J., & McConnell-Ginet, S. (Eds.). (1992). *Text and context: Cross-disciplinary perspectives on language study.* Lexington, MA: D.C. Heath.

Lafayette, R. (1997). Integrating the teaching of culture into the foreign language classroom. In P.R. Heusinkveld (Ed.), *Pathways to culture: Readings on teaching culture in the foreign language class* (pp. 119–148). Yarmouth, ME: Intercultural Press.

Lustig, M.W., & Koester, J. (1996). *Intercultural competence: Interpersonal communication across cultures* (2nd ed.). New York: HarperCollins.

Martin, J.N. (Ed.). (1989). Intercultural communication competence [Special issue]. *International Journal of Intercultural Relations, 13.*

McConeghy, P. (1990). The German program and international education. *Die Unterrichtspraxis/Teaching German, 23,* 5–13.

Meyer, M. (1991). Developing transcultural competence: Case studies of advanced foreign language learners. In D. Buttjes & M. Byram (Eds.), *Mediating languages and cultures: Towards an intercultural theory of foreign language education* (pp. 136–158). Clevedon, Avon: Multilingual Matters Ltd.

Müller, B.-D. (1995). An intercultural theory of teaching German as a foreign language. In A. Aarup Jensen, K. Jæger, & A. Lorentsen (Eds.), *Intercultural competence: A new challenge for language teachers and trainers in Europe. The adult learner* (Vol. II, pp. 59–76). Language and Cultural Contact series. Aalborg, Denmark: Aalborg University Press.

Müller, B.-D. (1995). Steps towards an intercultural methodology for teaching foreign languages. In L. Sercu (Ed.), *Intercultural competence: A new challenge for language teachers and trainers in Europe. The secondary school* (Vol. I, pp. 71–116). Language and Cultural Contact series. Aalborg, Denmark: Aalborg University Press.

O'Mara, J. (1994). *Diversity activities and training designs.* San Diego, CA: Pfeiffer.

Parham, T.A. (1989). Cycles of psychological nigrescence. *Counseling Psychologist, 17,* 187–226.

Padilla, A.M. (1980). *Acculturation: Theories, models and some new findings.* Boulder, CO: Westview.

Pavlovskaya, A. (Ed.). (1995). *Language, culture and communication.* Moscow: Moscow State University, Faculty of Foreign Languages, Centre of Cross-Cultural Studies.

Pusch, M.D. (Ed.) (1979). *Multicultural education: A cross-cultural training approach.* Yarmouth, ME: Intercultural Press.

Reid, J.M. (Ed.). (1995). *Learning styles in the ESL/EFL classroom.* Boston, MA: Heinle & Heinle.

Richards, J.C., & Lockhart, C. (1994). *Reflective teaching in second language classrooms.* New York: Cambridge University Press.

Robinson-Stuart, G., & Nocon, H. (1996). Second culture acquisition: Ethnography in the foreign language classroom. *The Modern Language Journal, 80,* 431–449.

Sanford, N. (1966). *Self and society.* New York: Atherton Press.

Seelye, H.N. (Ed.). (1996). *Experiential activities for intercultural learning Vol. 1.* Yarmouth, ME: Intercultural Press.

Shedlin, A., & Schmidt, W.H. (1974). Hollow squares: A communication experiment. In J.W. Pfeiffer & J.E. Jones (Eds.), *A handbook of structured experiences for human relations training* (Vol. II., Rev. ed., pp. 32–40). San Diego, CA: Pfeiffer.

Shumway, N. (1995). Searching for averroes: Reflections on why it is desirable and impossible to teach culture in foreign language courses. In C.J. Kramsch (Ed.), *Redefining the boundaries of language study* (pp. 251–260). Boston, MA: Heinle & Heinle.

Singelis, T.M. (Ed.). (1998). *Teaching about culture, ethnicity, and diversity: Exercises and planned activities.* Thousand Oaks, CA: Sage.

Singerman, A. (Ed.). (1996). *Acquiring competence: Four stages for students of French.* AATF National Commission on Cultural Competence. Lincolnwood, IL: National Textbook.

Spitzberg, B.H. (1989). Issues in the development of a theory of interpersonal competence in the intercultural context. *International Journal of Intercultural Relations, 13,* 241–268.

Standards for foreign language learning: Preparing for the 21st century. (1996). Yonkers, NY: National Standards in Foreign Language Education Project.

Steinwachs. B. (1995). BARNGA: A game for all seasons. In S.M. Fowler & M.G. Mumford (Ed.), *Intercultural sourcebook: Cross-cultural training methods* (pp. 101–108). Yarmouth, ME: Intercultural Press.

Storti, C., & Benhold-Samaan, L. (1998). *Culture matters: The Peace Corps cross-cultural workbook.* Washington, DC: Peace Corps.

Tedick, D.J., Walker, C.L., Lange, D.L., Paige, R.M., & Jorstad, H.L. (1993). Second language education in tomorrow's schools. In G. Guntermann (Ed.), *Developing language teachers for a changing world* (pp. 43–75). The ACTFL Foreign Language Education Series. Lincolnwood, IL: National Textbook.

Triandis, H.C. (1994). *Culture and social behavior.* New York: McGraw-Hill.

Valdes, J.M., (Ed.). (1986). *Culture bound: Bridging the cultural gap in language teaching.* New York: Cambridge University Press.

Watzlawick, P. (Ed.). (1984). *Invented reality: How do we know what we believe we know? (Contributions to constructivism).* New York: W. W. Norton.

Whorf, B. L. (1956). *Language, thought and reality: Selected writings of B. L. Whorf.* J.B. Carroll. (Ed.). New York: John Wiley.

Wiseman, R. L., & Koester, J. (Eds). (1993). *Intercultural communication competence: International and Intercultural Communication Annual, 17.* Newbury Park, CA: Sage.

Wolcott, H.F. (1982). The anthropology of learning. *Anthropology & Education Quarterly, 8,* 83–108.

CHAPTER 11

IMPLICATIONS OF THEORY AND RESEARCH FOR THE DEVELOPMENT OF PRINCIPLES FOR TEACHING AND LEARNING CULTURE IN SECOND LANGUAGE CLASSROOMS[1]

Dale L. Lange

We believe that moving toward a conceptualization of language and culture learning as promoting 'multicultural literacy' requires a fundamental shift in how language and culture are viewed, explored, utilized, and ultimately, integrated into the complex lives of learners. (Tedick & Walker, 1996, p. 215)

INTRODUCTION

Assertion: As a result of new National Standards for language and culture (Standards, 1996), culture in the second language curriculum can no

Culture as the Core: Perspectives in Second Language Education, pages 271–336
Copyright © 2003 by Information Age Publishing
All rights of reproduction in any form reserved.

longer receive superficial treatment. To support this assertion, we can say that for 30 years a more serious attention to culture has been called for by a variety of individuals (e.g., Brooks, 1968; Crawford-Lange & Lange, 1984; Lafayette, 1988; Nostrand, 1974; Seelye, 1972, 1976/1993). The new National Standards have taken up the challenge (Standards, 1996; Phillips, this volume). These Standards directly address culture learning in two goal areas: 2. *Culture (Gain Knowledge and Understanding of Another Culture) and 4. Comparisons (Gain Insight into the Nature of Language and Culture).* The three remaining goal areas are closely related to culture learning—*Communication (Communicate in Languages Other Than English), Connections (Connect with Other Disciplines and Acquire Information),* and *Communities (Participate in Multilingual Communities at Home and Around the World)*—and provide the mechanisms and context for culture learning. The National Standards have made explicit the assumption that culture is an essential core of language learning.

In such a context with an emphasis on culture, it is important to examine the implications of these new standards in second language programs for curriculum, instruction, and assessment with emphasis on culture. The outcome of this examination is the development of principles that speak to more appropriate assessment, the development of new curricula, and the broadening of instructional practice for students as they learn another culture in a language program. In order to complete this task, it is necessary to provide some context. By way of foundation, I first offer some basic assumptions about language and culture learning and introduce several theoretical frames of reference for understanding culture learning. These ideas are then applied to each of the three targeted areas: curriculum, assessment, and instruction. I conclude the article by presenting a set of seven principles for exemplary culture and language teaching.

BASIC ASSUMPTIONS

In order to provide a context for the development and presentation of principles for the teaching and learning of culture in second language classrooms, some basic assumptions must be presented. In each of these cases, I provide what I believe to be provocative and strong beliefs that, I hope, challenge some of our thinking as well as support what may be underlying suppositions in other chapters in this book. The assumptions are as follows:

1. If second language programs are going to flourish in the future, culture must be the core of assessment, curriculum, and instructional practices *with* language. This sentence means, and I say it directly,

that culture is the driving force in process and the content of language learning. A milder version of this assumption is that culture and language are equals in the pursuit of culture and language learning. This is not a new orientation, but it is one that is finally coming to the recognition that it deserves (see Crawford-Lange & Lange, 1984; Crawford & McLaren, 1998). Furthermore, it is supported by the importance given to culture in the new National Standards already discussed above.

2. If the appropriate vision can be developed among teachers, curriculum developers, researchers, and assessment specialists, second language programs have a unique opportunity to contribute to student development of intercultural sensitivity for both U.S. cultures and the culture of the language being studied (see discussions by Fantini, 1999; Tedick, Walker, Lange, Paige, & Jorstad, 1993). Such a vision could make second language education the core of the curriculum in P–12 schools, as well as the core of liberal arts preparation in undergraduate education and graduate education. We have literally not explored such a role for second language education in these contexts. Yet, the natural link to that role is accessible through the Standards.

3. If second language programs are going to flourish in the future, there must be a serious expansion in the understanding of how language acquisition is accomplished when language and culture have equal weight in the curriculum. Currently, linguists, applied linguists, and psycholinguists dominate the field. While their input to the field is clearly important, it is not sufficient because interdisciplinary, not single field, approaches to language and culture learning are required to move our understanding forward. Current work in intercultural communication (Bennett, M. 1993; Bennett et al., Section 2, this volume), cognitive psychology (Gardner, 1993a, b, 1995), and neuroscience (Sylwester, 1995) is a prerequisite to a fuller understanding of language and culture acquisition. These perspectives provide complementary and even somewhat new foci for language educators to think about as we contemplate the future of second language education.

4. As language programs include deeper aspects of culture, conceptual development of the language/culture programs will require significant work on the part of the field. Teachers, curriculum developers, materials publishers, teacher educators, and researchers will need to change the course of language programs. I make this statement because there is extremely little in the literature as far as actual research on specific aspects of assessment, curriculum, and instruc-

tion that is helpful in making viable a language/culture program, providing equal status between language and culture. An examination of the Paige, Jorstad, Siaya, Klein, and Colby chapter in section 2 of this volume very clearly demonstrates this fact.

THEORETICAL FRAMEWORKS FOR CULTURE LEARNING

The basic theoretical orientation of Section 2 of this volume is M. Bennett's (1993) model of intercultural development. While this chapter applies that framework to second language education, it also puts it into a broader context of general learning. The expectations for learning in the form of national standards, for example, inform learners of what is anticipated of them, as well as give guidance to teachers in arranging the curriculum, assessing student learning, and conducting instruction. The importance of this and other frameworks cannot be underestimated if we expect learners to reach high standards in culture learning. Lack of stated goals and outcomes, absence of curricular organization, deficient or nonexistent assessment tools, and unfocussed learning strategies are some of the major reasons why culture learning has not been successfully included in language instruction. In other words, the requirements of student learning, approaches to assessment, and use of learning strategies must connect with what students are learning (see Lange, 1999, pp. 63–70 for further discussion of this issue, including explicit analysis of the National Standards for culture).

In order to overcome these deficiencies, culture learning must be placed in a context where the appropriate planning can take place. Frameworks for learning can help that planning. There are two major frameworks that we will consider here: one for general educational development (Egan, 1979); the other for the development of intercultural sensitivity (M. Bennett, 1993; J. Bennett, 1993; Bennett et al., this volume). Other frameworks will be briefly considered as well.

Egan's (1979) theory of educational development and M. Bennett's (1993) developmental model of intercultural sensitivity are important because both are based upon the precepts of continuity, progression, and expansion of competence. These two frameworks are dynamic and interact with the maturational levels of learners. The frameworks also provide direction for teachers by helping them assess the students' developmental level and then structure the curriculum accordingly. The other conceptual frameworks that will be briefly reviewed in this chapter are those of Byram (1989), Byram and Morgan (1994), and Kramsch (1993).

Educational Development.   Since narrative is so important to language development and because narrative automatically includes culture as defined here, the work of Egan (1979) cannot be ignored. Theoretical underpinnings of the importance of narrative in human learning can also be found in Bruner (1990). Egan's four stages of development give meaning to expression in language through a link to educational growth that learners demonstrate at a particular stage. The framework provides the link between maturational level of the learner and the appropriate curriculum, the most suitable assessment, and the most applicable learning and teaching strategies. As a result, adaptation of curriculum, assessment, and instruction to student characteristics, needs, and interests can and should be anticipated. In this context, the primacy of the learner's development and

Mythic Approximate ages: 4/5 to 9/10 years	Mythic thinking provides absolute accounts of why things are as they are, and fixes the meaning of events to sacred models. Myth stories and children lack a sense of otherness, e.g. concepts of historical time, physical regularities, logical relationships, causality, and geographical space. Mythical thinking lacks a clear sense of the world as autonomous and objective. The child's world is full of meaning by those things the child knows best: love, hate, joy, fear, good, bad. Myth is articulated on binary oppositions such as big/little, love/hate, security/fear, etc.
Romantic Approximate ages: 8/9 to 14/15 years	The move from the mythic to the romantic state is noticed in the development of "otherness" and the development of historical time, geographical space, physical regularities, logical relationships, and causality which come from experience of the outside world. It is in this framework that children develop their sense of distinct identity.
Philosophic Approximate ages: 14/15 to 19/20 years	The move from the romantic to the philosophic stage strengthens the realization that all the important bits and pieces of experience and knowledge are interconnected parts of a general unit. The major defining characteristic then is the search for the truth about human psychology, for the laws of historical development, for the truth about how societies function—the general laws whereby the world works.
Ironic Approximate ages: 19/20 through adulthood	The transition from the philosophic to ironic stage is that students' appreciation of the general schemes cannot fully accommodate all the particulars and that no general scheme can adequately reflect the richness and complexity of reality. General schemes are seen as useful, but not true. There is reference and recognition of the "other" in this stage.

Figure 11.1. Egan's stages of educational development. *Source:* Taken from Egan (1979).

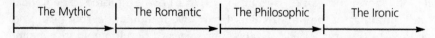

| The Mythic | The Romantic | The Philosophic | The Ironic |

Figure 11.2.   Egan's educational development model. *Source:* Based on Egan (1979).

the continuance of that development become crucial to the learning of language and culture. Moreover, culture learning is organized within a knowledge base rather than guided by guess or by individual teacher preference.

Egan's (1979) work has been applied previously to foreign language education. Byrnes (1990) uses Egan's developmental model as the basis for articulation in foreign languages and Pesola (1995) develops a model for the creation of curriculum in foreign languages in the elementary school using Egan's framework as a core element.

Intercultural Development.   While Egan provides us with an understanding of educational development, M. Bennett (1993) provides us with a conceptualization of the development of intercultural sensitivity. That development is outlined in a set of six stages that lead a person to evolve from an ethnocentric perspective to one that is ethnorelative. This framework is discussed in greater detail in Bennett et al. (Section 2, this volume). In this part, I briefly introduce each stage and then provide suggestions for stage appropriate instruction. The six stages of the model are classified under two rubrics: ethnocentric (denial, defense, and minimization) and ethnorelative (acceptance, adaptation, and integration).

Denial of difference is the inability of the individual to recognize cultural differences because the constructs to which the differences refer are not part of the individual's repertoire; thus, the differences are denied. "As long as we speak the same language, there's no problem." In this context, Bennett et al. suggest the importance of support, trust, friendliness, and cooperation in the classroom for learners as they begin to develop their ability to recognize difference, to gather appropriate cultural information, and to explore aspects of culturally different beliefs and behaviors. Some of the content includes objective, or formal, culture (art, music, literature, theater, dance), heroes, holidays, as well as selected beliefs and behaviors. Cultural contrasts are to be avoided here.

Defense against difference operates when the individual sees differences, but evaluates them negatively through overt stereotyping. "How stu-

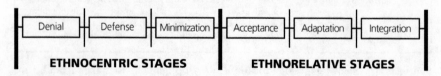

| Denial | Defense | Minimization | Acceptance | Adaptation | Integration |

ETHNOCENTRIC STAGES   **ETHNORELATIVE STAGES**

Figure 11.3.   The Bennett model. *Source:* Bennett, M.J. (1993).

pid to say 'grandmother' in that way? Our way is better!" The focus of instruction at this stage should be on helping learners develop attitudes of patience and tolerance. Difference is managed through attention to commonalities, as well as some existing distinctions within the in-group, in this case, within the class or even broader within one's own culture. Attention is given to the mediation of conflict and to team building through the promotion of cooperative activities that center on shared needs and goals between the in-group and the out-group. Some cultural contrasts may be useful.

In **Minimization of difference**, the individual sees superficial cultural differences, but wants to minimize those differences by suggesting that, "Deep down, we are all the same, no matter where we are from." The appropriate intercultural skills to be cultivated in this stage are listening, culture general knowledge, knowledge of one's own culture, ability to perceive others with accuracy, and the maintenance of a nonjudgmental posture. These skills are enhanced through contact with cultural informants, opportunities to seek out difference, emphasis on one's own cultural awareness, and expansion of curiosity from in-group to out-group. Excessive use of cultural contrasts should be avoided.

In **Acceptance**, the first ethnorelative stage, individuals appreciate cultural difference and acknowledge that other cultures provide alternative resolutions to human existence. "The more difference the better! More difference equals more creative ideas!" In this stage, individuals can understand cultural phenomena within context and elaborate on them. Moreover, learners refine categories of cultural contrast as they make cultural difference the focus of their learning. They handle issues of cultural relativity, distinguishing them from those of a moral or ethical relativity (Bennett et al., Section 2, this volume). The skills that learners work with at this stage, beyond culture specific knowledge, are knowledge of and sensitivity toward cultural context, respect for the values and beliefs of others, as well as tolerance of ambiguity.

In **Adaptation to difference**, individuals have the ability to see through the eyes of the *other*, and the communication skills necessary to communicate with the *other*. "The more I understand this culture, the better I get at the language." In the adaptation stage, the individual is learning how to take risks, solve problems, be flexible, adapt socially, and adjust to different communication patterns. The strategies to learn such behavior are the use of informants, case studies, and research strategies. Topics for consideration are humor, cultural deviance, and more sophisticated examples of difference.

In the final stage, **Integration of difference**, individuals find themselves in the process of creating an adaptable identity, not based on any one culture, which allows them to evaluate situations from multiple perspectives and communicate constructively with the *other*. "Whatever the situation, I can usually look at it from a variety of cultural points of view." This stage would probably be difficult to attain in the classroom. In this stage, the learner addresses the self as a process. "Am I able to interact culturally with others? Do I know how I will behave culturally? Can I act flexibly? Can I adapt to certain roles in a different culture, yet be true to my own cultural values?" The content through which this examination takes place is a framework of ethical and multicultural behavior as learners cross cultures.

One of the contributions of this model is that it points out the critical importance of the balance between challenge and support in engaging the student in the content and process of culture learning (Bennett et al., Section 2, this volume). Content is what is to be learned (cultural patterns such as friendship, respect, heroes, holidays, and the like). Process is what is done with content in the classroom (arousing curiosity, identifying skills to deal with difference, promoting cooperative activities, preparing learners to function autonomously using research strategies). A low-challenge process could be the memorization of facts and information to which the learner has easy access. A high-challenge process might be the use of research techniques when the learner is not clear on what research techniques are. On the other hand, low-challenge content is content that is already familiar, while high-challenge content is information that is largely unknown to the learner. The key to effective instruction is the adequate balance between supporting and challenging the learner. Thus, if both the process and the content are low-challenge, the learner, in the words of J. Bennett, "rests." Confronted with both high-challenge process and high-challenge content, the learner *leaves*, intimidated by the enormity of the task. It is the combination of high-challenge content and low-challenge process, or high-challenge process and low-challenge content that is conducive to the learner's developing skills and knowledge. For instance, using the evening news or the front page of a newspaper to demonstrate how over-generalizations come about might be a good way to approach a high-challenge topic of cultural stereotypes through a relatively low-challenge process (small group or large group discussion).

In summary, the value of the Bennett model for educators is in its explication of intercultural development; it helps teachers observe development taking place, plan for it, teach toward it, and evaluate learners within that developmental framework. Both the Egan and the Bennett developmental models help us better understand how we can include culture in the second language classroom. They provide us with decision-making capacity that is interactive with the needs of learners at various stages, thereby giving teachers, curriculum developers, and assessment specialists appropriate guidance.

Other Frameworks. Kramsch (1993) and Byram (1989,1994) provide us with two other major statements on the inclusion of culture in the foreign or second language classroom. In her approach to this important matter at the college/university level, Kramsch (1993) elaborates on the concept of critical dialog, i.e., the need for students to interact with language *and* the context(s) within which that language is found. Those broadly conceived contexts are the culture of text, including those of an oral and a written nature, the responses of other students to such text, the culture of the classroom itself, and the teacher-student-teacher relationship. In this dialectic, learning language is not aimed at the learning of listening, reading, speaking, and writing per se, but at the interrelationship of speakers and listeners, writers and readers, instructors, or any combination thereof with the object of the dialectic which is cultural context or *text*. In this way, Kramsch has integrated language and culture.

An important concept in this dialectic is that of subjectivity, in the form of inter-subjectivity, inter-textuality, and inter-culturality. The *inter-subjectivity* among speakers in the classroom, including teachers, brings an awareness of multiple voices, different experiences, and the diversity of race, gender, sexual orientation, and other sources of identity to the dialog. The result is the creation of multiple layers of meaning brought to the discussion.

Particularly in the teaching of literature, the voices of readers and the intended voice(s) of the text may not be the same. *Inter-textuality* allows the reader to interact with the author's intended text. When readers exchange meaning with the text, the dialog offers a variability of interpretations, perceptions, and experiences. As a result, the learner's world is opened to a variety of attitudes and values that make literature and culture inseparable (Kramsch, 1993, p. 175).

The concept of *inter-culturality* recognizes the subjectivity of both the home and other cultures. Individual experiences and perceptions can easily fracture the stereotypes that are created through the passing down of information. In this context, culture and language can be taught and learned through interpersonal processes, by an examination of difference, and via interdisciplinary examination of culture and language. The emphasis on the individual in the processing of literature, the connection of literature to the social sciences, and the examination of differences in language and culture are what Giroux (1992) calls 'border crossing.' It is a pedagogy which "points to the need for conditions that allow students to write, speak, and listen in a language in which meaning becomes multiaccentual and dispersed and resists permanent closure" (Giroux, 1992, p. 29). Traditional pedagogy recognizes the teacher as the master of the subject and the giver of knowledge. However, as we allow learners to focus on the perspectives, practices and products of others, the learners will have and will want to voice their own perspectives. In this regard, they will have crossed the border between given information and personal participation. Once that border has been crossed, it is the students who are recognized as the creators of their own learning.

The result is the opening of learning to difference, many voices, and a negotiation of meaning in the variety of texts and contexts wherein learning takes place. It is the essence of what might be called critical language pedagogy (Kramsch, 1993, pp. 244–47). In language programs, such border crossing makes language and culture inextricably intertwined. Moreover, it provides the basis for a personal understanding of culture that cannot be given through transmitted information (see Crawford & McLaren [Section 1, this volume] for further discussion of this issue).

Kramsch's orientation to the integration of language and culture in a way similar to that of Crawford-Lange and Lange (1984) in foreign languages and Wallerstein (1983) in ESL has so far failed to attract major attention of teachers. Teachers are generally unfamiliar or uncomfortable with these ideas originating from critical pedagogy and discourse analysis. Most teachers have not been prepared to teach in these learner-centered ways, nor are they prepared to help the learners negotiate meaning. Their focus has been on themselves. Teachers often feel that they must have full control of language/culture learning, give meaning to what is taught, and impart the required information to the learners. However, if culture learning is to be meaningful to the learner, then the focus must shift from the teacher to the learner. Here, the wise council of Freire and Faundez (1989) and Friere (1996) could be helpful to teachers. They recommend the creation of an atmosphere of exploration for learners in the classroom. The need for changes in teacher education to accommodate the learner's perspective have also been discussed by Lange (1990a), Tedick et al. (1993), and Tedick and Walker (1996).

Byram's framework (1989, 1994) is a result of an extensive consideration of the literature on language, culture, and their relationship to the social sciences. The main premise of Byram's argument is that language is both an object and a medium of study. In other words, the learning of language is a means to the "learning about the people and culture associated with it" (Byram, 1989, p. 51). In this regard, similar to Kramsch, Byram sees the interrelationship of language and culture as a natural one. Yet, his conceptualization of this interrelationship is somewhat different. Byram sees culture as actualized by the group and is not as concerned with individual perceptions or meaning. For him, culture is already marked through identities and boundaries. Moreover, he argues that the full integration of language and culture only comes in advanced classes with the examination (description, analysis) of literature. The integration of language and culture at the advanced level suggests that younger learners, because they can only express themselves in the foreign language in simple ways, will use the native language (for our purposes English) to describe and analyze culture, including C_1 as well as C_2. Gradually, they progress to the point where they can express cultural ideas in the foreign language.

Byram's framework is presented as a circle divided into four quarters, which contain the following elements: (1) *Language Learning*. The bottom left quarter of the circle represents language learning, a communicative, "skills" oriented foreign language focus; (2) *Language Awareness*. The top left quarter contains language awareness, a sociolinguistic, knowledge oriented, comparative focus, in the L_1; (3) *Cultural Awareness*. The top right quarter consists of cultural awareness, a knowledge-oriented comparative $[C_1-C_2]$ focus in the L_1 (see Triandis et al., 1972); and (4) *Cultural Experience*. The bottom right quarter of the circle embraces cultural experience (CE or a knowledge-oriented foreign culture focus in the FL).

This framework allows the use of the native language for comparative analysis of one's own and other cultural meanings. It combines the learning of a foreign language with the experiencing of foreign cultural phenomena in four recurring phases: (1) Communicative skills acquisition which is (2) enhanced through language awareness, an idea similar to that of Stern's (1982) linguistic syllabus; (3) The study of language is combined with the study of culture in an L_1 comparative mode in which the home and foreign cultures are described, analyzed, and compared; and, (4) the direct experience of some aspects of the C_2 is accomplished from the viewpoint and within the perspective of the foreign peer group in L_2. There is both a flow and a balance among the elements in this framework. The framework is intended to be fluid, not linear, as indicated by the arrows on the outside.

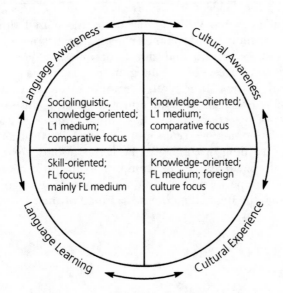

Figure 11.4.   Byram's language/culture model. *Source:* Taken from Byram (1989)

The importance of the Byram contribution is that it includes the *contrast of cultural knowledge* as an important content in the learning of both C_1 and C_2. Contrast serves as the basis for experiential work. Cultural experiences are incorporated into language and cultural learning *after* the contrast has been understood. These experiences could be through educational visits, home-stays, family trips, and the like. Yet, not all cultural experiences require living or traveling in or to the foreign culture. They can be achieved in a *section biculturelle* of a language course where content is taught through the foreign language.

Further elaboration of the framework can be found in Byram and Morgan (1994). The theory behind this framework includes the especially important issues of empathy, attitudes, and moral development as applied to the classroom. In this publication, the authors discuss the use of comparison as a method, explore the implications of comparison in teacher development, display nine case studies of cultural learning according to the principles of the model, and make recommendations for assessment. In this process, they provide a detailed understanding of the model.

Conclusion. The discussion in this section, while somewhat theoretical, provides the reader with frameworks that situate language/culture learning. Those settings include the educational development of a person from childhood through adult learning, the development of intercultural sensitivity, and two perspectives on the interrelationship of language and culture. For each of these frameworks, objections can be found. It can be argued that the Egan framework must be translated into a foreign language and that the concept of narrative is too unfamiliar as a basic teaching and learning strategy. A similar objection can be raised with the work of Bennett et al (Section 2, this volume) namely that it comes from the intercultural training literature and does not integrate language with it. Although Kramsch focuses on the integration of language and culture, her ideas may work at the college level, but not in elementary and secondary schools. Finally, Byram's ideas function well in the British context. The issue here is not objections, but rather the importance of frameworks in guiding the development of cultural competence of learners in culture and language learning programs. Without frameworks, there are no student expectations, no visible curriculum, and no instructional practices that guide student performance and direct related assessment. It is within this context that the Bennett model is examined further.

BENNETT FRAMEWORK:
QUESTIONS FOR LANGUAGE EDUCATORS

The major conceptual framework of Section 2 of this book is M. Bennett's (1993) developmental model of intercultural sensitivity, which is expanded into an analysis of culture as the core of a culture/language curriculum in the Bennett et al. chapter. This framework provides us with major propositions regarding the development of intercultural sensitivity and also the relationship of that developmental phenomenon with language learning. A number of questions arise related to the basic assumptions of this framework when culture and language are brought together. Those questions are as follows:

1. If individuals behave differently when visiting or living in another country because of their perception of events, can the examination of this behavior be integrated into second language curriculum, assessment, and instruction?

2. If the key to ethnorelativism is the process of deciphering or understanding difference, will the process of language and culture learning have to change significantly to make difference its core?

3. With ethical choices inherent in the development of intercultural sensitivity, will language educators accept the responsibility of providing ethical cultural choices within a curriculum that gives as much credibility to culture as to language?

4. What is the appropriate level of intercultural sensitivity of the educator? What does the answer to this question suggest for the development of language teachers? In total, what does the incorporation of the model into language and culture learning, teaching, and acquisition mean for the development of teachers?

These questions are difficult ones. Yet, I think that such questions should be in our minds as we continue to consider the potential of this framework for its viability for student learning in K–12 schools. They are not all answered here, but should scaffold our thinking.

THE BENNETT FRAMEWORK: ETHICAL CONSIDERATIONS

At this point, I would like to briefly mention a few basic ethical considerations, issues associated with the ways we affect the lives of our students when we begin to integrate culture and language learning. While these may only be tangentially addressed by Bennett et al., the implications of combining culture and language raise important ethical issues in my view.

Previously, I mentioned my concern that language learning is dominated by linguistic science and that we are therefore shortchanging students by focusing largely on verbal-linguistic and logical mathematical
orientations to language and culture learning. The works of Bennett
(1993) and Bennett et al. (Section 2, this volume) have raised in my mind
an additional set of ethical questions and concerns:

1. Are we really exhibiting ethical behavior when it comes to providing
   a fruitful learning environment by limiting learning to linear
   approaches to language and knowledge about culture? Should we
   not provide more balance to our assumptions about learning? (See
   Bloom, 1956; Krathwohl et al., 1964; and Appendix B.)

2. As educators, we send messages to students that language and culture learning are for everyone; yet, we limit the ways students learn,
   and in so doing, limit the number of students able to participate in
   our programs. I ask myself, if all students are capable of learning
   albeit in different ways, modes, and intelligences, have already
   learned a language, and have some understanding of their own culture, why do we continue to indicate that special talents are required
   to learn a second language and its culture? Isn't language/culture
   learning for everyone? In another example, the culture standards of
   the American Association of Teachers of French (Singerman, 1996;
   see Appendix A for a brief description of the AATF culture standards) on culture learning project a continuing elitism in relation to
   the cultures of the French language.

3. In becoming sensitive to another culture, a broad range of experience is necessary. Keys to culture certainly involve understanding
   through language, as well as understanding how language works.
   Yet, are these the only keys? If the acceptance of the framework provided by Bennett is something that we agree to, will we not be
   required to expand our basically verbal and scientific/analytical orientations to include activities that promote the development of
   intercultural sensitivity?

4. If language learning, intercultural development, and the integration
   of the two are the ultimate goals of language programs, then the purpose of language programs should exist beyond utilitarian intents
   such as an ability to function in business, industry, international
   commerce, government, and the military. If language learning and
    intercultural sensitivity are at the core, the real function of language
   programs is the understanding of and interaction with a wide range
   of human dimensions and their expression. Culture, like language,
   is not static; neither are our interactions with people. Language and
   intercultural sensitivity allow us to go beyond language structure,

use, and cultural facts alone; they permit us to know ourselves and to understand, accept, respect, and have empathy for the other. Thus, language and intercultural development bestow a responsibility on both the teacher and the learner for the relationship of the self to the other, which expands their awareness and insight into the language and culture worlds they inhabit. Such an ethical position puts language/culture programs directly in the middle of questions of diversity. It makes language/culture programs a natural contributor to the exploration, understanding, and interaction with the multiculturalism in this country and with the multiculturalism of the broader world.

5. With respect to culture, the separation of culture by Bennett et al. into objective and subjective forms (Big C and little c culture) highlights a problem in language/culture education: a greater value is placed on the C behaviors (objective culture) than on the c behaviors (subjective culture). Such assignment perpetuates the elitism, separatism, and defensive perspectives, which I believe, abound in language/culture programs, and which are found the AATF National Commission on Cultural Competence report (Singerman, 1996). The use of the terms *objective* and *subjective* culture, as suggested by the Bennetts and Allen, should turn us away from such elitism by in fact broadening our concept of culture.

6. Probably the most important ethical consideration is the treatment of the learner. We are seeing so much violence in our society that is transferred to schools. As educators, we owe respect to the learner and the learner owes respect to the teacher. To me, this mutuality suggests that teacher and student are learners together. In this instance of mutuality, teachers and students work together, but they are not equals (Shor & Freire, 1987). In this mutual learning context, both teacher and learner are responsible; the learner for discovering what needs to be learned, and the teacher for discovering how others learn as they discover what needs to be learned. Both learn, but differently. Both respect each other. Both learn from each other. This mutual respect is a requirement of both learners and teachers in a language/culture program.

7. Finally, I urge those of us in leadership positions in language learning and acquisition to honor a perspective on language as a means of cultural and personal expression that allows for a comprehension of the self and the other. Such a perspective greatly expands the opportunities for research and development on language/culture learning well beyond, but not excluding the linear, scientific tradition. It includes a more interpretive, respectful, and ethical orientation to the under-

standing of the many processes and complications in what it means to learn another language and to be sensitive to its culture(s).

Having explored the Bennett et al. framework and expanded the discussion to include ethical considerations, it is now appropriate to begin the discussion of *curriculum, assessment,* and *instruction* as they connect to the context of learning in general and to the learning of culture in the foreign language classroom. We will draw upon the new National Standards for Culture (*Standards*, 1996), the literature on culture learning in foreign language education (Paige et al., Section 2, this volume), Bennett et al. (Section 2, this volume), Sylwester (1995), and Gardner (1993a, b, 1995). A specific cultural example will be taken through the curriculum, assessment, and instruction processes to demonstrate how planning for culture learning can be accomplished within the theoretical context already discussed.

CURRICULUM

Curriculum is the organization of what is to be learned. There are several aspects to the language/culture curriculum that need our initial attention: orientations, content, process, and the integration of content and process with language, structure, standards, and design. In the design area, we begin the discussion of a specific example that will be carried on through the assessment and instruction sections.

Orientations.   Much of the foreign language literature on curriculum has been based on a technical orientation of curriculum, assessment, and instruction derived from the scientific nature of the area of study. Curricular organization has also been directed by the curriculum literature in English as a Second Language (ESL). In his description of the foreign language curriculum crisis, Lange (1990c) outlines four categories of curricular inquiry: the scientific-technical, the connective, the practical, and the critical or emancipatory.

The *scientific-technical curriculum* is a linear, objective, and scientific-technical approach to curriculum where the breakdown of elements to be learned is based on a scientific analysis of the field of study. For language, this scientific analysis comes through the science of linguistics. This analysis guides learning decisions from a broad mission statement to goals, objectives, specification of content and tasks, ordering of content and tasks, choice of learning materials, designation of instruction, and selection of assessments (Banathy & Lange, 1972 in foreign languages; Brown, 1995 in ESL).

The connection between a scientific-technical and a communicative approach to curriculum and program development is labeled *connective inquiry.* It allows for the development of language proficiency as a means of discovering and expressing the individual's personal meaning but within a scientific-technical framework (see Dubin & Olshtain, 1986; Johnson, 1982; Nunan, 1989; Yalden, 1987; all for ESL). As a result, the processes of scientific-technical curriculum are applied to the development of the ability to communicate personal meaning, i.e., discourse rules are the basis for competence in language use.

Practical curriculum inquiry does not refer to the practical, every day concerns for teaching language. Instead, it is "a quest for meaning and comprehension of the world as individuals strive to grasp an awareness of their own worth and identification" (Lange, 1990c, p. 91). This highly personal orientation to curriculum recognizes the individual's knowledge and experience as central to an understanding of oneself, the group, and society as a whole. Stevick (1976) is the best representative of this curriculum type.

Finally, *emancipatory inquiry* brings unity to reflection and action within a social, economic and political context. In this context and in this unity, individuals and groups reflect on their society and act on it to correct social inequities and to support fairness, justice, and emancipation for all persons regardless of race, creed, age, gender, sexual orientation, or social class. Friere (1996) is the best general example of this inquiry, while Crawford-Lange and Lange (1984) and Kramsch (1993) are foreign language examples and Wallerstein (1983) is one for ESL.

The importance of this discussion is that, although there are some distinctions in the different curricular orientations, these orientations overlap. If there is concentration on any one, single orientation, student abilities will be limited to that orientation. In the current learning climate, it is also clear that the most prevalent curriculum disposition is still the scientific-technical. In this climate, if students are limited to the scientific elements of language (phonology, morphology, syntax, and discourse rules) in the four language modalities, they will be able to function mainly with those elements. However, if the orientation is toward overlapping curricular directions (connective, practical, or emancipatory), then learners will be capable of communicating personal meanings, understanding their relationship to a broader culture, and expressing and acting upon the need to better the human condition. In addition, when culture is the focus and content of language learning, it is my firm belief that curriculum will be directed beyond the pure scientific-technical orientation. In other words, the organization of the curriculum that includes culture will automatically relate to connective, practical, and emancipatory curriculum perspectives.

Content. In the context of this chapter, culture is the content of language learning. It is not my particular purpose to argue for a particular cultural content, although there probably is a need for a mixture of both objective and subjective culture as defined by Bennett et al. Cultural themes which present specific cases of cultural behavior, information, and/or attitudes have been suggested by a number of individuals. Brooks (1968) discusses biological growth, personal refinement, literature and the fine arts, patterns for living, and the sum total of a way of life. Nostrand (1974) talks about the culture, the society and its institutions, conflicts, ecology, and the individual. I do not think there is any shortage of thematic material from which to choose.

Process.   This is the means by which learners interact and interpret cultural phenomena. One such process, suggested by Allen and Lange (1996; see Figure 5) has four elements: Observation, Exploration, Expansion, and Evaluation. It is applied to both C_1 and C_2, with analysis of the home culture coming before the second culture.

In the *Observation* phase of the process, cultural phenomena of both C_1 and C_2 are recognized as belonging to a theme that has been selected. These phenomena are then identified as to the contribution they make to the theme and described in detail. Reactions to the phenomena are also recorded. In the *Exploration* phase, the learner compares and contrasts the descriptions related to the phenomena for both C_1 and C_2, examining them in relation to original perceptions as well. As a result of this activity, the learner formulates a hypothesis as to why the phenomena in both cultures exist in the way they do. With this hypothesis and original perceptions in mind, the learner then gathers more information in order to confirm or reject the hypothesis. During *Expansion*, learners examine the data, describing what has been found. This description is then added to original observations. At this time, an initial analysis of the data allows the

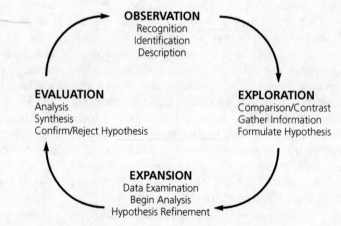

Figure 11.5.   Allen and Lange's process of culture learning.

learner to refine the original hypotheses for both C_1 and C_2 and again examine original perceptions. In the final stage, *Evaluation,* learners carefully analyze and synthesize information on the theme across both cultures and come to a confirmation or rejection of their original hypothesis. They also compare their confirmation or rejection with their original perceptions to determine whether those perceptions need to change.

Similar to the process of Allen and Lange (1996) is that of Crawford-Lange and Lange (1984) which has eight interactive steps or phases. Those eight phases are:

1. Identification of a cultural theme (employment, family, friends)

2. Presentation of cultural phenomena (Use of any presentational means)

3. Dialog (Dialog is used to help students locate and state perceptions on the theme.)

4. Language needs (What language is needed to pursue the theme?)

5. Language learning (Once needs identified, learning proceeds to language use.)

6. Verification of perceptions (Pursuance of original perceptions to see if they continue to work. Verification is pursued through any and all means of information available.)

7. Cultural awareness (Have the perceptions changed? Why? How?)

8. Evaluation of language and cultural proficiency. (What can students now do that they couldn't do before with language? What demonstration of cultural awareness is now possible?) (p. 147–154).

Integration of Content and Process with Language.   Language is the vehicle by which both the content and process of culture learning takes place. By the same token, the content and processes of culture learning are the vehicles by which language learning takes place. The process of culture learning is surrounded by the use of language and language is constantly used to express culture. Vocabulary is learned; communication strategies are discovered in talking with, interviewing people, and examining documents; the teacher prepares students to meet some of the language difficulties before they occur. Language is acquired for a purpose, namely the discovery of one's own and the other culture. This approach to language and culture learning is quite different from present thinking. In many ways, it is close to the concept of language learning across the curriculum in college/university programs (Krueger & Ryan, 1993). In this context, language learning has a purpose, the discovery and development of one's awareness of the other.

Structure.   If the curriculum is not linear or purely related to the scientific aspects of language, thereby including culture as defined by the National Standards, the structure of curriculum will not be linear either. In this context, I propose that curriculum be *recursive* and *thematic* (Lange, 1996). What does that mean? Simply stated, it means that culture learning will be organized around cultural themes and that these themes will reoccur throughout the curriculum. Once a theme has been introduced at the developmental level that is appropriate for learners (see Egan, 1979, or Figures 1 and 2 as an education developmental framework), it can be repeated at another developmental level with appropriate expansion of experience and necessary complexity of concept. Some general themes to consider are those that follow: family and relatives; relationships, such as friendships; transportation; education; manners; role of food preparation and consumption; work; play and recreation; the neighborhood; health; money. If, for example, the theme of family were chosen, it might be treated at the Egan *Mythic* level (see Figure 1) in the following manner: learners might listen to a story about a family of goats, traveling through the mountains to get the other side where there is food and water, where the mother and father protect 'kids' from the wolves who want to capture and eat the 'kids.' Learners might tell their own simple stories about a trip they have taken with their own families.

In the above example, the story deals with the theme of family and the subtheme of family as providing security and protection from the fear that children normally have of elements outside themselves, as well as a place of comfort and safety. Stories like this one and Red Riding Hood demonstrate the importance of family as a sacred model, where the focus of the listener is on self, where meaning is on things that the child knows such as love, fear, and security.

At the Egan *Romantic* Stage (see Figure 1), the story would certainly change significantly. Here, the story and activities could be set in the foreign culture and involve logical family relationships through the development of a family tree where the story involves some elements of the past and different geographical places, thus demonstrating how the family evolved. Such stories direct the learners to concerns outside of themselves, such as the family and its history. Learners could then develop their own family tree.

When the learners reaches the Egan *Philosophic* Stage (see Figure 1), their energy would be directed to a deeper level of comprehension. They would be involved in understanding the psychology of family through literatures that deal with family in a social sense. Here, they could read authentic materials on family in newspapers, magazines, and journals, as well as stories, poetry, and extracts from novels all demonstrating how families function. Family in one's own culture could be compared with that in the other cultures.

In the Egan *Ironic* Stage (see Figure 1), the learners would recognize the stories about family in the previous stages as contributing to their knowledge about family. However, at this stage, they would recognize that those stories were their own truths, realities, and perceptions. In this stage, learners are free to play with the mythic, romantic, and philosophic stages as a means of creating an imaginary story about family. Furthermore, such stories could certainly be extended to the creation of stories about families in other cultures. It is for the teacher to provide the necessary knowledge and information for the learner to include in this creation.

The several stages of the Bennett Model could also be given this same treatment. Using just one theme within this particular framework, namely that of "Friendship in X Culture," the following could exemplify recurrence by using the theme with differing activities which move the learner through the stages. An important caveat: *Students should be moved through the stages of ethnocentrism and ethnorelativism mindfully; teachers must recognize when students are ready to move on developmentally.*

Here is the example of the friendship theme in the different stages. In the ethnocentric *Denial of Difference* stage, learners could be asked to gather information and recognize differences in the manner in which friendships are established. In *Defense against Difference*, the theme of friendship could be directed toward how friendships are made in U.S. culture(s) and the pride one takes in friendships. In *Minimization of Difference*, friendship in both U.S. and in the X culture could be described with an emphasis on similarities and without any judgmental position taken. Moving to the ethnorelative stages, in *Acceptance of Difference* learners would be asked to contrast how friends are made in both U.S. culture and the X culture with the specific purpose of finding differences, analyzing those differences, and understanding that the concept of difference relates to issues of cultural relativity. The *Adaptation to Difference* stage in the curriculum would be devoted to an understanding of differences between the two cultures in establishing friendships through the examination of case studies of successful and unsuccessful instances of friendship creation. And, finally, in the *Integration of Difference* stage, the learner might have contact with those in the X culture with the purpose of working toward the establishment of a friendship. It is expected that learners could get into the adaptation stage, but would rarely get through the integration stage. Yet, the example serves the purpose of explication of how the Bennett framework could be used in a recursive curriculum.

There are other means by which a recursive curriculum in the foreign language classroom can be structured, as in the following examples:

- *By year.*   Here, similar thematic material would provide expansion of the learners' perceptions, knowledge, and understanding.
- *By semester.*   Similar themes could recur, which could expand on previously acquired knowledge and perceptions. Such a structure would be particularly useful in the modular, four-period school day that has become so popular in the United States in recent years.
- *By specific design.*   Curriculum or text materials could establish principles upon which themes would reappear and be expanded.
  Another variation: Several connected themes could be interwoven in text materials to expand on learners' perceptions and knowledge.

The most important aspect of these examples is to demonstrate that the recursive curriculum expands learners' knowledge and comprehension as they progress through their educational development. Few foreign language culture programs are organized in this manner. If we intend to take advantage of learner development, time availability, and learner curiosity about other cultures, the proposal for a recursive curriculum needs serious consideration.

A recursive thematic curriculum design has several aspects that are important to us in this discussion:

1. Such a design is developmental for both language and culture. As learners grasp aspects of language and culture on a particular theme, this language and those cultural aspects can be met in other contexts of the language/culture curriculum so that experience with them is broadened.

2. In relationship to the previous point, a recursive design allows both the processing of language and the development of cultural sensitivity to occur more or less naturally. We meet similar aspects of language and culture in different environments; such occurrences permit conceptualization and extrapolation from experience to result.

3. A recursive thematic curriculum allows for different aspects of a theme to be experienced at different times. The parceling out of the many complications of cultural development or language use to the several times that the same or similar theme is approached allows for review of earlier experienced learning and adds to what is already known.

4. A recursive thematic curriculum allows learners to enter learning at almost any time, thereby meeting some of the challenges of placing people in the exactly appropriate course; and, in addition, it meets some of the challenges of a transient school population.

Having argued in favor of a recursive curriculum, it is important to realize that it is easier to talk about than actually construct. A fully operative example of a recursive thematic curriculum is probably not available. It is an issue that needs to be seriously pursued to provide the most appropriate curriculum design for language/culture programs. In addition, a recursive thematic curriculum design allows this field to embark on an excursion into research and development which is supported by forms of curriculum inquiry not examined by any field to this point (Short, 1991). Those forms are, among others, ethnographic, narrative, aesthetic, phenomenological, hermeneutic, critical, integrative, and action oriented forms of inquiry.

It appears that the stages of the Bennett model fit into the concept of a recursive thematic curriculum particularly because the model is one that can accommodate *the dynamic learning* that is facilitated by a recursive thematic curriculum. In other words, the developmental nature of both language competence and cultural sensitivity fits a recursive thematic curriculum. The real issue, which will ultimately need to be treated in detail, is specifically how we bring these two aspects of a curriculum together. More specific thinking and actual development will be required so that such curricula are worked out, implemented, and evaluated.

Standards.   Within a recursive framework, standards for performance can characterize curriculum. As mentioned earlier, The National Standards (*Standards*, 1996) provide both overarching goal areas and specific standards for culture in both the *Culture* and *Comparisons* categories (see *Standards*, 1996, p. 9). The standards set both content and a general level of performance. In essence, students are to demonstrate an understanding of the *practices, products, and perspectives* of the culture being studied, as well as a demonstration of understanding of the *concept of culture* through comparisons of the culture studied and their own. Practices, products, and perspectives, and the concept of culture are the content. *Understand, demonstrate, compare* are the performances that are enunciated in the standards. These words can have more concrete meaning. For example, *understand* means to see, grasp, accept, digest, interpret, and learn. It is not a concept that lends itself to easy exemplification. But, it is a particular human trait and it represents both cognitive and affective learning. *Demonstrate* means to show, describe, explain, illustrate, make clear, and even teach. *Compare* means to liken, contrast, relate, match, equal, and associate among other meanings. These are the general achievements identified in the National Standards. Within the iterative, recursive curriculum structure, we need to see how they can be realized within the very general designated content.

Design.   For this discussion, I have drawn heavily on the presentation "Understanding By Design" (Wiggins & Kline, 1998). How do we design a curriculum that allows our students to meet the standards? The general principle is easily stated, but is not necessarily that easy to carry out. The principle has basically three parts: first, determine the *performance* (level of knowledge/skill) that all students have to demonstrate for each unit of learning; second, determine how that performance is to be assessed; and, third, determine what lessons or activities support the students in developing their performance knowledge and skills. Put another way, we can ask: What are the desired results for learning (standards or targeted achievements)? What evidence of results will be accepted (assessment)? What activities and experiences contribute to the desired evidence and results (instruction)? These three questions are the basis for what is conceptually labeled, "backward curriculum design" (Wiggins, 1998). This label is used to refer to a curriculum based on student performance rather than on predetermined content. A backward curriculum design poses some key questions that can assist teachers in designing their programs, courses, and lessons:

- Toward what standards and tasks does the content point, as a means to an end?
- Do the proposed final tasks require the key understandings, knowledge, and skills at the heart of the syllabus?
- Are there sufficient rehearsal and refinement opportunities built in?
- Are there lessons to provide enabling knowledge and skills?

A design that addresses these questions leads us away from the traditional approach to curriculum, where the text is accepted as the curriculum and the emphasis in instruction is on covering the material. Instead of focusing on student performance, teachers announce how many chapters of the book they are covering in a month, a semester, or a school year. In the context of covering the material, assessment is mostly a series of tests to determine if learners have learned it. However, in the backward design logic, the targeted performance and the assessment drive the curriculum. It is neither the content nor the instruction that determines what is learned; it is the learners' performance that is the key to instruction. The teacher is no longer a person who simply covers the material, but a coach who mentors learners toward the designated performance. Because the new role of coach may be difficult for some teachers to assume, continuing teacher development to focus on these aspects will be important as a vehicle for change.

As we think about this concept of curriculum design for culture, let me work through an example with you to demonstrate how such a design comes about. In this example, I am going to choose a key word from the above discussion of the National Standards for culture, namely *understanding*. I am going to link that word to the "demonstration of an understanding of practices." And, within the "demonstration of an understanding of practices," I am going to choose a more specific *practice* within which to create my example, namely *understanding friendships*. In this context, the example will be a general one and not tied to any particular culture.

The design tasks are three in number. The first is to determine the specific standards related to understanding the relationship between practices and perspectives, products and perspectives, and the concept of culture through comparisons between C_1 and C_2. The questions that need answering in order to design a curriculum and determine standards are the following:

- What practices in this culture should students learn?
- What perspectives will they have of these practices?
- Upon learning more about these practices, how will these perspectives change?
- What products should students learn about?
- What perspectives will students have of these products?
- Upon learning more about these products, how will these perspectives change?
- How are these practices, products, and perspectives related?

Answers to these questions give details to the local culture curriculum. Further decisions need to be made as to how the answers to the questions are distributed throughout the curriculum.

My second task is to specifically state the knowledge and skills that learners need in order to fulfill the performance requirement. The quality of how learners perform is another aspect that needs attention. Questions that need to be answered in this regard are the following:

- What knowledge and skills are important for learning the practices, products, and perspectives of another culture?
- What knowledge and skills will lead learners to give us authentic performances?
- To what tasks will we have learners respond?
- To what prompts will we have learners respond?
- What authentic performances will give us evidence that learners meet the standards?
- How will we document the quality of the performances to know that the standards have been met?

My third design task is that of arranging instruction so that learning tasks contribute to the desired performances. The basic purpose of instruction is to guide learner progress toward the desired performances through activities that will help reach the desired performance, to give feedback on learner progress, and to judge the learners' readiness to meet established standards. Answers to the following questions and those decided by the reader will inform instructional strategies:

- How do we guide learners toward determined performances?
- What learner strategies relate to the determined performances?
- Which of our multiple intelligences help expand learner functioning with any performance? (See Gardner, 1993a, b; Gahala & Lange, 1997.)
- By what processes do we give learners feedback on progress toward meeting the standards?
- What kinds of assessments contribute to giving learners feedback leading up to determined performances?

Let me provide an example with *Understanding Friendships*. This theme is different from the usual topics of food, music, and dance. It is also an abstract theme that requires more than surface knowledge. It combines both thought and feelings. In working through this example, I have found the topic difficult because I have had to create the example as it relates to curriculum, assessment and instruction. The flow of the example has been created to help the reader's understanding. Note that language is not dealt within these examples. The complexity of cultural issues is a sufficient challenge (see Crawford-Lange & Lange, 1984 on this matter). Note also that I have kept the example in the *home culture* to allow the example to be as comprehensible as possible. Yet, even with these caveats, it is my intent to push us beyond the usual topics. Without examples in new and different areas of culture, it is not possible to move away from the familiar and help learners grow as a result.

Example of Standard and Evidence. With this example, I have already determined that the theme of *friendship* fits into the National Standard 2.1 *understanding the practices and perspectives of the culture studied.* Similarly, I have determined the evidence that I would need to know to show how the theme could be assessed. The theme in the form of a classroom standard is stated below, along with the categories of evidence: knowledge, skills, attitudes, processes, and experience (see Pratt, 1994, pp. 65–101, particularly pp. 74–93).

Standard: In this case, the standard or what I expect learners to do may be stated as: *Explain your understanding of friendship in this culture.*

Evidence: Primary evidence will be student responses to prompts or academic tasks, activities, papers, simulations, and authentic tasks. The importance of the evidence as a contribution to the learner's developing competence with the standard (critical, important, or desirable) has also been indicated. Most of the following activities would be classified as prompts or academic activities.

Knowledge

- Obtain basic information on friendship in your own culture (Critical)
- Obtain basic information on friendship in the other culture (Critical)
- Outline and sort information for both cultures (Important)

Skills

- Define friendship in *your* culture (Critical)
- Define friendship in the other culture (Critical)
- Explain how kids in *your* culture make friends (Critical)
- Explain how kids in the other culture make friends (Critical)
- Dramatize friendship in *your* culture (Desirable)
- Dramatize friendship in the other culture (Desirable)

Attitudes

- Recognize differences in friendship patterns (Critical)
- Help others understand differences in friendship (Critical)
- Plan to respect differences in friendship (Critical)
- Seek further information on friendship voluntarily (Important)

Process

- Distinguish friendship in the other culture from *your own* (Critical)
- Compare/contrast being friends in the other culture with *your own* (Critical)

Experience

- Create/imagine/develop a situation between you and a person in the other culture in which you would become friends. (Critical— Here is the authentic task one that simulates real life.)

Knowledge, Skills, and Activities.   In the *backward* design of curriculum and instruction for performance assessment, Wiggins and Kline (1998) show how the designation of standards leads to assessment evidence. Yet, a couple of more detailed steps in this design for instruction/assessment are also necessary such as determining the enabling knowledge and skills necessary for basic understanding of any concept and enabling and engaging activities to help the student meet the standard.

In our example of friendship, the enabling knowledge and skills would be associated with activities regarding some very basic questions that individual learners would answer for themselves (Who is a friend to you? How do you know a friend? When is a friend a friend? When is a friend not a friend?). In this instance, knowledge and skills are stated in response to the questions and other activities. The first activity could be an outline of the knowledge obtained from answering the questions. From the outline, each student creates a definition of friendship. From the definition, learners explain, according to their experience, how friendships are made. That explanation can be actualized in a dramatic presentation of how friendships are made. Here are the *knowledge and skills* needed for this example:

- What is friendship to me?
- What questions did we answer about "friendship?"
- What words did you use? What words did you need to learn?
- How did you define "friend?"
- Explain what a friend is?
- With a partner, show us what a friend is!

Responses to the first three activities could be assessed through observation of the group. A list of responses, words used, and words needed to learn could be established. The needed words could be then pursued in further learning and the used words could be reentered later. The responses could be directed toward the creation of the definition of a friend.

Some process skills are also appropriate to the learning about friendship, such as indicated in the following questions:

- What is the structure of a concept like friendship? Is there only one?
- What tool(s) can we use to explain friendship?
- How do we know when we have explained a concept like friendship?

The activities connected with these questions are the basis upon which definitions, explanations, and dramatic performances could be improved. Moreover, these more cognitive and strategic activities also provide a basis upon which performances can be strengthened. Evidence can be associated with these activities as well in evaluating the improvement of the definitions, explanations, and dramatizations of friendship in the other culture.

Enabling and engaging activities consist of both *prompts* and *authentic tasks* which draw upon basic knowledge and skills to challenge learners to perform in more sophisticated ways which allow them to demonstrate their competence in relationship to the standard. Although *prompts* are more associated with academic problems, they are intended to prepare learners for authentic tasks. Prompts tell the learners what is required and what they are supposed to do. Examples of prompts would be the following for our friendship example: Prepare an oral presentation that describes the differences/similarities between friendship in a nation or community with that of X culture. For this presentation, gather information on teen-age friendships in X culture, summarize and evaluate that information, and present your summary and evaluation to the group in your class that is working on friendship among adults.

Authentic tasks provide a challenge to the learner that is based in real life. It may be in a real or simulated context. What would be an authentic task for our culture example? Take the example, "Create/imagine/develop a situation between you and a person in the other culture in which you would become friends." I would argue that this represents the experience category in the outline of evidence for meeting the standard, *Explain your understanding of friendship in this culture,* because it meets the requirement of a simulation of a real life situation.

ASSESSMENT

If we look into the mirror to examine the current state of culture learning in our classrooms, we find a lack of standards; we find assessment that is meager. What assessment there is of culture learning may be focused on facts and information which are *tested* by objective means. However, the National Standards Project clearly outlines what is to be learned and brings language and culture into a natural alliance. With sample progress indicators, the project also provides us with directions for the assessment of culture/language learning. As a result of setting standards for culture learning, we are obliged to map out our intentions, indicate what students are to learn and perform, and indicate how we will assess them. For the learning of culture, this is an enormous step forward. Since the onus is now on learners and their performance, we will need to think beyond the narrow focus of tests. That is our next step. Let me provide some background.

Background.   In the history of testing and assessment until recently, much of the work has been associated only with testing. In particular, language testing has emphasized the creation of objective, standardized forms of tests to mainly isolate language *skills*. Lado (1961) was the first person to seriously pay attention to the testing of language. Although his work was focused mainly on English as a Second Language, he did use examples in other languages. His main orientation was the testing of listening, reading, writing, and speaking. Lado also focused on the qualities of tests such as reliability and validity, as well as on issues related to the construction and analysis of items, since most of the tests tended to be of a standardized nature. The testing of culture was mentioned, but received limited attention.

In the decades that have followed, major publications on language testing have generally continued this orientation. A sampling of those publications suggests three basic categories of work on testing with some attention to assessment: (1) major focus on the qualities of tests; (2) major focus on the evaluation of language and language skills; and (3) major orientation to proficiency that mixes testing and assessment. In the first category, the literature concerns itself mainly with testing and its various features, including item creation, item analysis, item discrimination, reliability, validity, use of machines with testing, and research on testing (Bachman, 1990; Henning, 1987; Oller & Perkins, 1978, 1980; Spolsky, 1978, 1979). In this category, culture as defined by the National Standards Project is not included, although the sociolinguistic context is mentioned in several references. While the sociolinguistic context is important for communication as defined by the National Standards Project, it does not provide the content of culture perspectives, products, and practices.

The second category, evaluation of language and language skills, is represented by Valette (1977). In this work, the concentration is on *classroom tests*: types of tests; how to prepare them; and, how to analyze results. However, the emphasis here is on tests for the four language modalities of listening, reading, writing, speaking, and for literature. A very short chapter on culture defines culture largely as information, and shows some interrelationship between language and its social uses. The item types represented are largely objective in nature.

In the third category, there is a mixture of testing and assessment. This mixture results from a carry-over of the strong tradition of testing characteristics of American educational culture. It happens because of a relatively new direction in language teaching, namely teaching for language proficiency or communicative competence. This trend resulted in the translation of the Foreign Service Oral Proficiency Interview for the academic world through a project of the Educational Testing Service and the American Council on the Teaching of Foreign Languages (Byrnes & Canale, 1987). This same project led to the development of proficiency guidelines in listening, reading, speaking, and writing (Byrnes, et al., 1987). While originally there were guidelines for culture in the ACTFL Provisional Proficiency Guidelines, those guidelines were subsequently eliminated because they were unwieldy. The literature represented in this category (Jones & Spolsky, 1975; Lowe & Stansfield, 1988; Omaggio, 1983) examines some of the technical issues of the oral proficiency interview, explores the translation of the oral interview as a model for classroom testing for other modalities, and relates some of the problems and research issues which need addressing in order to make this new direction a viable one. Again, in this literature, culture is referred to in the *sociolinguistic* sense, but not as a content. Beyond this literature, there are three references in foreign languages that are particularly oriented toward assessment (Cohen, 1994; Genesee & Upshur, 1996; Shohami & Walton, 1992).

What is Assessment? In his introduction to *Approaches to Language Testing*, Spolsky (1978) argues that language testing finds itself in a post-positivistic, post-scientific state that concentrates on the creative aspects of language and that is directed toward the individual's understanding of varieties of language and their use in a variety of contexts. To me this argument suggests that the concept of testing has to be broadened beyond a narrow, scientific orientation to assessment and has to include culture. Even though some 20 years have passed since Spolsky's statement, the narrow focus of testing still persists and culture is hardly included. In my own reaction to testing priorities at the 1990 ACTFL Priorities Conference (Lange, 1990b), I argued for the use of assessment in language learning. I suggested that assessment includes the following:

> observation of production (taped and written samples) which are reviewed holistically; triangulated examination of responses to oral, written, and cultural texts; connected use of more than one modality to receive and express meaning of events, people, institutions, and relationships which concern the individual; collaborative use of language in situations where the second culture (C2) context is made problematic (in some dissonance with that of the native culture C1), and reacted to by more than one person ... outcomes associated with personal understanding and expression. (Lange, 1990b, p. 404)

It is in the work of Wiggins (1993), who is not a foreign language specialist, but whose thinking and work in assessment must be considered, that the concept of assessment is fully elaborated. But what do we mean when we talk about assessment?

According to Richards, Platt, and Weber (1985), assessment is "the measurement of the ability of a person ... For example, assessment of the comprehension of an immigrant child may be necessary to discover if the child is able to follow a course of study in a school" (p. 18). In general terms, this definition points to what the student is actually capable of doing with the process of comprehension. Madaus and Kelleghan (1992) confirm this definition when they state that assessment "may be defined as an activity designed to show what a person knows or can do. Thus, it is concerned with the appraisal of individuals. As we shall see, assessment in the classroom is based largely on a teacher's observations of students as they go about their normal learning activities" (p. 120). Madaus and Kelleghan discuss the range of assessments that can occur from oral examinations, the use of the essay exam, to multiple-choice questions used particularly in standardized exams (pp. 124–25). In foreign languages, the American Council on the Teaching of Foreign Languages Oral Interview is an example of an assessment of oral competence that is judged against a set of guidelines (Met & Galloway, 1992). Concomitant guidelines for listening, reading, and writing have been developed for the purpose of assessing those modalities in similar ways in the ACTFL Proficiency Guidelines (Brynes et al., 1987). The University of Minnesota has developed profi-

ciency assessments in speaking, reading, and writing from the oral interview procedure and the guidelines for speaking, reading, and writing
(CARLA, 1997). These are examples of assessment in foreign languages
which point specifically to "what the learner can do." Yet, we must remember that there is still a healthy discussion and some confusion between testing and assessment. In this chapter, we are concentrating mainly on
performance assessment, which is defined, as "our ability to perform [cre-
atively] with knowledge" (Wiggins 1993, pp. 209 ff.).

Wiggins (1993) provides deep background to the concept of assessment.
In his discussion of assessment, Wiggins is not friendly to the kind of standardized testing that occurs on a one time basis to determine one's capabilities such as IQ tests, or the National Assessment of Education Progress
(NAEP) or even classroom tests. Wiggins is concerned about lack of feedback on such tests, the use of standardized procedures in examining competence, and issues of reliability and validity of the measures. Throughout
the following discussion, keep in mind that the concept of assessment has
its own problems of validity and reliability. Liskin-Gasparro (1996) reviews
some of the issues in her article on the assessment of standards.

For what reasons and how do we give tests? According to Wiggins
(1993), we give them (1) for information; (2) for transmission of knowledge only; (3) to examine a standardized knowledge; (4) with distrust of
students in mind; (5) for objective knowledge when knowledge is never
neutral; (6) for student control over knowledge first before creative use;
(7) for largely utilitarian knowledge; and (8) without incentives to reach
expectations (pp. 38–46). Such reasons and manners concentrate on a less
thoughtful *education,* or on learning that is mainly information focused. A
more thoughtful assessment system provides resolution to the tensions created
with the current system of testing.

Assessment Postulates.   A more thoughtful assessment system assumes
that:

1. Learners are asked to justify their understanding of their learning
   and skill. Assessments should provide the opportunity for the asses-
   sor, through questions, probes, and cues, to understand what learners' abilities are and how the learners are misleading themselves. In
   this context, learners are rewarded for self-corrections.

2. Because students are novice learners, they are given access to models
   of how the subject of study functions and opportunity to work with
   real problems in the subject area. There is no secret how assessment
   works since learners are given sample tests or assessments in advance
   of any assessment event. Students know how and why they are being
   assessed. In this context, Wiggins (1993) says, "All assessment should
   be thought of as 'formative'" (p. 51).

3. Learners know that the assessment system is based on "known, clear, public, non-arbitrary standards and criteria" (Wiggins, 1993, p. 51). There is nothing mysterious about the assessment system. And, it is also not used as a reward or punishment system.

4. Self-assessment is key to an *authentic* education. Learners apply the "known, clear, public, non-arbitrary standards and criteria" to their own performances. Such opportunity allows learners to be their own best critics and prepares them for self-judgments that will have to be made in adult life.

5. Learners are engaged in the field in which they perform; they are not bystanders.

6. Learners develop confidence and the ability to express themselves as they read, understand, function with, and resolve authentic problems in a particular field. Confidence in learning does not arrive overnight, nor does ability to express oneself in the language of a field. Working with authentic problems of a field, expressing perceptions, and receiving probing feedback generates sophisticated learning.

7. Learners understand that their comprehension of the field is best assessed when their answers are probed. A field is not understood through one question, but through extensive series of questions. Probing questions begin at the commencement of learning in any new field and continue to be formed as part of the learning process, hence, the importance of the recursive curriculum concept.

8. Learners learn that ideas, theories, and systems are not fixed. They can and should be challenged. A critical aspect of all human endeavors (practices, products, perceptions, ideas, theories, and systems) is to engage them in a dialog with potential action to resolve inconsistencies, generate new perspectives, and create new knowledge.

9. Through the assessment of others, as well as self-assessment, learners' intellectual honesty, personal character, and attitudes toward knowledge and learning distinguish what they know and what they don't know.

Extensive discussion of these postulates is available in Wiggins (1993, pp. 46–69). They are the key issues that form the major discussion in the book. Here, they provide a context in which we can question our own assessment practices.

Implications for Culture Learners and Cultural Assessment. These postulates have the following implications for *understanding* and also apply specifically to the National Culture Standards (see Wiggins & Klein, 1998) and the Bennett framework as well:

- Understanding means the student can apply, predict, adapt, demonstrate, avoid misconceptions, verify, defend, critique, make qualified and precise judgments, and make connections with other ideas and facts. These expectations go well beyond information and establish important expectations for understanding, one of the major arguments for culture learning.
- The learner can answer key questions: What? Why? How? Whose? Which? When? Where? What if? So what? These questions reveal the core of cultural understanding. *What* is only the first question. While the accuracy of knowledge per se is important, assessment focuses more on the ability of the learner to verify and critique information and ideas. Process is crucial in the development of understanding another culture. Facts and information are only one basis for such understanding.
- Interaction of teacher and learner in assessment provides evidence of progress to both and furnishes the teacher with the opportunity to detect important learning errors. Ongoing teacher-learner interaction in processing cultural knowledge and understanding shows how process is being applied and where misconceptions may arise.
- Assessment is anchored in authentic and contextualized problems as opposed to highly focused tests of information. In order for learners to have deep cultural understanding, culture is presented in the form of authentic problems that have several resolutions. The example of "organization of adolescent sports programs in the French culture" in Crawford-Lange and Lange (1984) and the many examples in Wallerstein (1983) indicate that problems in a process context yield sophisticated cultural understanding whereas information out of context in the traditional tests does not.
- The use of rubrics and recurring tasks across time gives learners an understanding of the sophistication of their learning. In developing cultural understanding, the importance of growth of that understanding cannot be underestimated. Use of a recursive curriculum, authentic performances within that curriculum, and assessment strategies (similar rubrics) demonstrate growth in the learner's cultural understanding.

These are some of the implications from the discussion on assessment that give us pause to think not only about assessment, but also curriculum, and instruction related to cultural understanding.

Rubrics.   While the postulates and their implications give us a broad context within which to work, they are only guidelines to carry out assessment. They establish a more ethical attitude toward students, an attitude that allows students to understand what is to be learned as well as how well it is to be learned in an atmosphere that honors student learning. In this context, assessment actually occurs using the student performance as evidence to be judged against a *Standard*. That judgment comes through the application of a rubric to the performance. What is a rubric? A rubric is "a guideline for scoring that consists of descriptors of each level of performance on a scale. The scale is applied to elements of the performance that have been determined in advance [as contributing significantly to the performance and thereby to meeting the standard]" (Gahala & Lange, 1996). Consequently, to create rubrics in the context of assessment that are intended to give feedback to the student, several principles apply:

- Use numerical and/or descriptive categories;
- 4–3–2–1–0 or Very Good to Excellent, Good, Acceptable, Weak, Unacceptable;
- or a three-point scale (3–2–1–0 for no response—Excellent, Acceptable, or Weak) or on a continuum of Naïve-Sophisticated or Novice-Expert.
- Scales larger than 5 levels become difficult to define; three levels with a no response or 0 category may be more manageable.
- Define categories to reflect learning that is deep, insightful, and that recognizes differences among learners.
- Determine descriptors after the task has been determined but *before* it has been performed.
- Involve learners in the development of the categories within the rubric so that they understand fully how they are being assessed.
- Provide opportunity for outsiders to view and critique assessments to make sure they are authentic.

I am using the assessment postulates, their implications for culture learning, and the principles for the development of rubrics in my example of assessment of the standard, *Explain your understanding of friendship in this culture.*

Assessment Example. Among many ways, one way of assessing this standard is to allow ongoing, formative assessment through a number of activities. However, for demonstration purposes, I would like to take a specific example of one form of evidence already mentioned above for this example. Here is what an assessment might look like.

You will remember our example had several categories leading to the fulfillment of this standard: knowledge, skills, attitudes, processes, and experience(s). For the assessment example, as well as for instruction, I have chosen to focus on: "Explain how kids in your culture make friends."

Since the class will be divided into groups, the first assessment task to be developed jointly with students is the assessment of group functioning, something they do regularly with us. The assessment and the rubric look something like the one following.

Class _____	Date ___/___/___				

Group Members: _____

Task _____

In our group:	Strongly Disagree				Strongly Agree
• Everyone was on task	1	2	3	4	5
• Every one helped complete the task	1	2	3	4	5
• We helped each other	1	2	3	4	5
• We are proud of the product we created	1	2	3	4	5

What we did best was _____

What we could have done better is _____

We needed help and still need help on _____

Next time we should _____

Student Signatures:

_____

_____

Teacher Comments

Teacher Signature

Student Reactions:

_____

Figure 11.6.   Cooperative group task assessment.

The second assessment (see instruction example in F below) is that for the creation of a definition. The task is an individual task that involves reflection, discovery, and feelings that learners record in their journals, feeling diaries, and/or personal histories. In this class, we have used similar criteria for assessment as with other tasks of this kind that have been negotiated with learners. The assessment of the definition has been added to the usual assessment form.

The third assessment (see instruction example in F below) is for a group presentation to "explain what a friend is in your culture." This task involves the development of a group product as well as verbal explanation of that product.

Criteria for Journaling

	Strongly Disagree				Strongly Agree
I expressed my feelings completely	1	2	3	4	5
I gave appropriate examples to reflect my feelings	1	2	3	4	5
My feelings represent my behavior	1	2	3	4	5
I learned new things about myself	1	2	3	4	5

Summarize here what you have learned about yourself in reflecting about friendship.
Important Points:
1.
2., etc.

On another sheet of paper, use that summary to answer the question, *What is a friend?*

Criteria for Assessing the Definition of a Friend

3. Exceptional

The definition is based on reflections, discoveries, and feelings from a journal, a feeling diary, and/or a personal history with several elaborated indicating a fully-developed and perceptive understanding of what you define as a friend. The writing of the definition is carefully constructed to reflect your experience and your meaning.

2. Acceptable

The definition is based on reflections, discoveries, and feelings from a journal, a feeling diary, and/or a personal history. The definition is written with minimal examples to express your personal meaning of friendship and it shows only an adequate reflection of your understanding of what you define as a friend. The writing of the definition is sufficient in reflecting your experience and your meaning.

1. Poor

While the definition is based on a journal, a feeling diary, and/or a personal history, the examples mentioned have not been developed in the definition to show an understanding of what you define as a friend. The writing lacks clarity and reflects misunderstanding of your experience and its relationship to your meaning.

Figure 11.7.   Assessment of journaling and definition of a friend.

As you will see in the section on instruction, the same items that have been developed for assessment are also the subject of instruction. The purpose is to show consistency between standard, assessment, and instruction.

5.5 Exceptional

The group presents a fully developed definition of friendship, indicating how the knowledge and examples of individual group member definitions of friendship are represented in the group's one clearly articulated definition. The representation of the group product (mime and dance, collage, story) demonstrates a high degree of clarity between the product and the definition, thereby representing a mature and confident understanding of friendship in our culture.

4. Accomplished

The group presents a carefully developed definition of friendship, indicating some of the knowledge and examples from group member definitions that are articulated with care. The representation of the group product (mime and dance, collage, story) demonstrates careful attention to the relationship of product and definition, thereby representing a very useful understanding of friendship in our culture.

3. Adequate

The group presents a somewhat developed definition of friendship. The illustration of knowledge and examples of group member definitions, though relatively few, show that the group considered their importance in the definition. Although the relationship of the product to the definition is visible in the presentation of the group product (mime and dance, collage, story), the presentation lacks clarity.

2. Limited

The group presents a definition of friendship. The examples and knowledge from individual group members are limited. While the explanation of friendship is given by the group (mime and dance, collage, story), it is not clear how the knowledge and examples of the definition are related to it.

1. Inferior

The group presents a definition of friendship. There is little or no cohesion to the definition although knowledge and examples of individual group members is presented. The explanation of friendship (mime and dance, collage, story) is so limited that its message is hardly understood and has little or no relationship to the definition presented.

Figure 11.8.   Group presentation: Explain what a friend is.

INSTRUCTION

In working with the concept of assessment being the engine for curriculum development and instruction, I have had my own struggles with this concept. In some of my own work (Banathy & Lange, 1972), I have seen curriculum as that engine; and, assessment has always been a derivative of curriculum. Yet, I also know the importance of efficiency and effectiveness, and how the reduction of knowledge serves those purposes (see Giroux, 1988; Lange, 1990c). For example, if the goal is to learn the dates of the major holidays in the French culture, which is what the students will learn. What will be left out is any understanding of what the holidays are about, why they are important, how they came to be, the value they have within French culture, or how they relate to holidays in the U.S. culture. And, certainly the scientific-technical-rational curriculum does not ask the question, "To what end is this learning important?" It only asks, "What can you reproduce?"

The role of instruction in a fully rationalized curriculum is to present the learner with the knowledge that is to be reproduced in steps that are manageable. The learning tasks required within the breakdown of this knowledge tend to be predictive of the learning outcome and prescriptive of the learning process. As a result in language teaching, we have seen a variety of *rational methods* that have proven restrictive of student learning. It is important to at least name a few here that fall into the category of rational-scientific-technical: Direct Method (Coleman, 1929), Audio-lingual (Lado, 1964), Individualized Instruction (Strasheim, 1972), and Total Physical Response (Asher, 1977).

Other language teaching methods like Communicative Language Teaching (Richards & Rodgers, 1986) and Proficiency Oriented Language Learning (Omaggio Hadley, 1993) fall into a bridge category between the rational-scientific-technical and more humanistic approaches to language instruction, the practical and the emancipatory (Lange, 1990c). They can be characterized in a set of contrasts between communicative and rational-scientific-technical instructional principles (Finochiaro & Brumfit, 1983). I am providing only a few important contrasts:

Communicative	Rational-Scientific-Technical
1. Meaning is paramount	1. Attends to structure and form
2. The ability to use the linguistic system effectively and appropriately.	2. Linguistic competence is the desired goal.
3. Drilling may occur, but peripherally.	3. Drilling is a central tecechnique.
4. Students are expected to interact with other people, either in the flesh, through pair and group work, or in their writings	4. Students are expected to interact with the language system, embodied in machines or controlled materials.

In communicative language teaching culture becomes more visible (Omaggio Hadley, 1993), but it still remains an after thought with few real designated outcomes. However, culture plays a larger role in practical learning. It is here that learner choice becomes more important (see Stevick, 1980, for a discussion of Counseling Learning, The Silent Way, and Suggestopedia). In Emancipatory learning (Crawford-Lange & Lange, 1984), culture is the content. Here, the purpose for language study is highly individual and learner choice is optimal. It is also where the learner asks the question: "Why is this culture important; and, how can I use language to act upon cultural knowledge?"

The Role of Instruction.   In any approach to the development of communicative ability, the focus must be on the individual learner's need to become a competent user of the language because each arrives at the process of language and culture learning with a unique background and set of experiences. As a result, instruction is an adaptation to individual learners to meet mutually agreed upon outcomes. The attention to the learner is not just for the learning of language. It applies to the learning of culture through language just as well. Here, in the context of National Cultural Standards, the practices and products of another culture are given meaning through language, and, perceptions are created and communicated through language. For the learner, the expectation is to perceive and communicate meaning and understanding of the products, perspectives, and practices of others. For the teacher, the expectation is to guide learners toward that goal and to assess their competence. While the goal for each is the same, the role is different. While the role of both is an active one, the teacher is no longer *saddled* with the need to produce the outcome when the attention is on student performance. That is the learner's role.

It is the teacher's responsibility to guide the learner through the needed performances with the prompts and tasks that reflect the standard. Here is where instructional guidance and assessment come together where knowledge is connected to receive, respond, value, organize, and characterize (see Appendix B); where learning requires application, analysis, synthesis, and evaluation *in addition to* knowledge and comprehension (see Appendix B); and, where assessment in the learning framework provides honest feedback and authenticity of task to bring learners to a fuller understanding of the culture about which they are learning.

The *backward design* of Wiggins (1998) that I have used as a major frame in this article is especially important because of its emphasis on learner performance rather than teacher behavior. In this way, curriculum, assessment, and instruction are aligned on learner performance in a different kind program articulation: curriculum = assessment = instruction. This internal articulation avoids isolated and self-contained cultural instructional strategies that have been part of culture teaching: culture capsules (Miller & Bishop, 1979; Miller, Drayton, & Lyon 1979; Miller & Loiseau, 1974), culture clusters (Meade & Morain 1973), and cultural incidents and assimilators (Fiedler, Mitchell, & Triandis, 1971). These instructional strategies emphasize information and facts about another culture with little stress on understanding. Facts and information are simply not enough. Certainly such instructional tools could be useful IF they are used in connection with more sophisticated performances *other than* reporting information, such as gathering more information and applying critical operations to that information through analysis, synthesis, and evaluation.

Instruction, like curriculum, is in certain ways related to the comprehensive theoretical principles of learning like those of Egan (1979) or M.J. Bennett's (1993) and J.M. Bennett's (1993) theory of culture learning. I believe very strongly that theory is related to practice and practice generates theory. Under the umbrella of curriculum = assessment = instruction, we must be constantly aware of how these three are related so that student performances linked to cultural understanding reach expected standards. There are two relatively new books on the teaching of culture that include a variety of activities for culture learning (Fantini, 1997; Seelye, 1996). While both of these publications are very useful in generating ideas, it is still important that any teacher integrate the actual or derived ideas into the curriculum = assessment = instruction framework for understanding culture, which includes not only presentation of information, but the more critical operations as indicated above. We must not recreate the past focus on information and random activity, when the future holds so much promise through the new National Standards as well as through the Bennett framework.

An **Ethic of Instruction**.   Primary to any learning in the approach that Wiggins (1993, 1998) has outlined is the learner. In instruction/assessment, the ethic related to this instructional philosophy is summarized in the following statements:

- Learners are honored for their knowledge, their processes, and their mistakes.
- Learners know and practice with the knowledge and skills that they use in the learning activities and also the assessments within which they are assessed.
- Learners are involved in the development of activities and choice of learning strategies as a result of learner differences (Breen, 1987).
- Learners are given honest, immediate, and appropriate feedback in both learning and assessment conditions.
- Learners know the means of assessment and the rubrics applied to them in advance of both instruction and assessment.
- Learners individually apply both the means of assessment and appropriate rubrics to their own learning.

These statements outline the basic relationship between learner and teacher. They suggest an environment where the learner is respected, honored, and treated as a valuable human being, as is the teacher. This environment empowers the interaction of language with culture and culture with language in an atmosphere where quality teaching and quality learning can occur.

Instruction as Guidance. In our quest for the one magic solution to teaching foreign languages, the "Holy Grail" as Higgs (1984) called it, a variety of options have been explored. In this chapter and elsewhere (Lange 1990c), I have mentioned some of them. None of those options hit the mark. As a result, we have turned to an eclectic approach to instruction, applying what we think is appropriate mostly from either logic or experience. To some degree, the research on learning strategies in foreign language learning and acquisition has received important attention and inclusion in our eclecticism (Oxford, 1990).

With the development of National Standards for foreign languages, including culture, an eclectic, somewhat haphazard global approach to instruction is inappropriate. If the curriculum is planned around standards and performance evidence presented by learners, then instruction is no longer targeted completely to the whole group, but much more related to the needs and talents of individual learners. Here, more individual interaction with learners is required to process the knowledge and skills that contribute to performances. As a result, the situation calls for an important shift in instruction from major focus on the large group controlled by the teacher to extensive teacher involvement with individual learning controlled by learners.

This approach raises an important question, "If instruction isn't telling, giving, or drilling cultural information, then what is it?" Clearly, the new direction in culture learning is on learner performance with products, practices, and perspectives. We've already established that fact. The new direction places teachers in a role of guiding learning. That direction strongly places learning within the abilities, attitudes, and capacities of learners themselves.

There is corroboration of this aspect of guidance in instruction from the research on how the brain functions in learning (see Figure 9). Sylwester (1995) has summarized for educators the research on "how the brain learns," showing how learning takes place from sensory input to problem solving or from input to output. Input comes through the several senses (sight, hearing, touch, smell, taste), including movement. The brain's own biological processes bring the characteristics of redundancy, connections, flexibility, and efficiency to any learning task. Let us not forget one of the basic elements of learning, the emotions, is the continuum between flight (survival) and the ability to focus (attention) that prompts learning to take

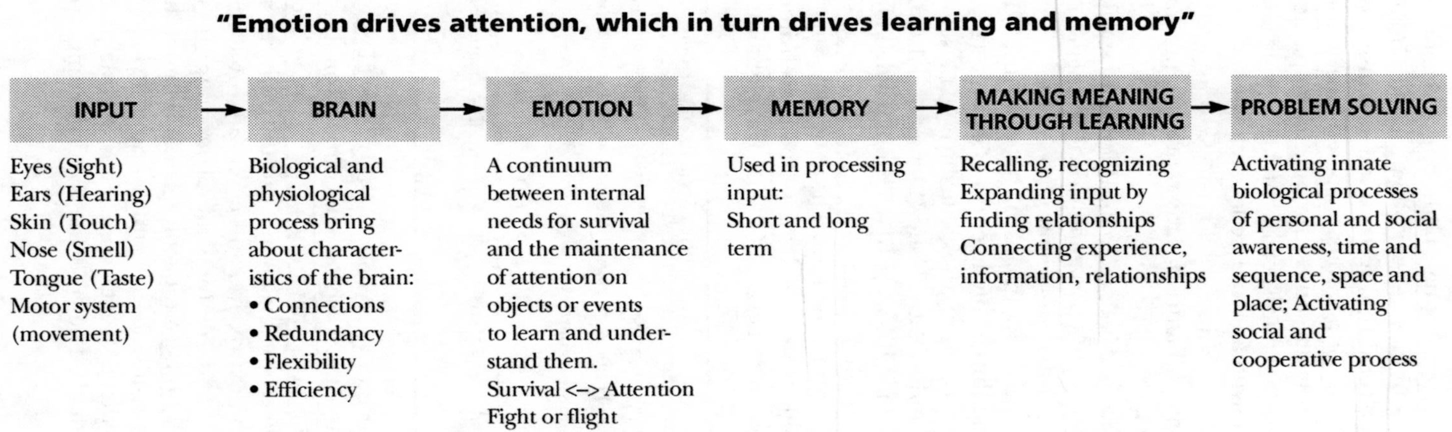

"Emotion drives attention, which in turn drives learning and memory"

INPUT	BRAIN	EMOTION	MEMORY	MAKING MEANING THROUGH LEARNING	PROBLEM SOLVING
Eyes (Sight) Ears (Hearing) Skin (Touch) Nose (Smell) Tongue (Taste) Motor system (movement)	Biological and physiological process bring about character-istics of the brain: • Connections • Redundancy • Flexibility • Efficiency	A continuum between internal needs for survival and the maintenance of attention on objects or events to learn and under-stand them. Survival <–> Attention Fight or flight	Used in processing input: Short and long term	Recalling, recognizing Expanding input by finding relationships Connecting experience, information, relationships	Activating innate biological processes of personal and social awareness, time and sequence, space and place; Activating social and cooperative process

Figure 11.9.   Model of learning from research on how the brain functions in learning.

313

place. Input is processed through both long and short-term memory. The characteristics of the brain's biology allow the individual to make meaning out of input through recall and recognition, expansion of input in locating relationships, and the connections of experience, information, and relationships. Problem solving comes through the application of meaning in order to act on personal and social contexts of time and sequence, space and place, both individually and collectively. In such contexts, the brain uses its capacities, its multiple intelligences, to approach and resolve the problems it encounters. Figure 9 is my representation of Sylwester's analysis of how learning takes place here.

Sylwester (1995) and Wiggins (1993, 1998) both speak specifically about the role of the teacher in *guiding* individual learners to perform. Howard Gardner (1993a, b, 1995) contributes to our understanding of what it means to guide learning by means of his discourses on multiple intelligences. What are multiple intelligences? Gardner (1993a) mentions two very important dimensions of an intelligence: (1) a set of skills to "resolve genuine problems or difficulties"; and (2) a set of skills for "finding or creating problems" (Gardner 1993a, p. 61). Through a delimiting process, Gardner arrives at multiple intelligences as a set of core processes or abilities that can be observed as brain functions. These unique functions can be developed and expanded. He originally described seven intelligences (1993a) and has since argued for an eighth (1995). The eight intelligences are:

Personal Intelligences	*Expressive Intelligences*
• Intrapersonal/Introspective—Self Smart	• Bodily/Kinesthetic—Body Smart
• Interpersonal/Social—People Smart	• Visual/Spatial—Picture Smart
• Musical/Rhythmic—Music Smart	
Academic Intelligences	*Emerging Intelligence*
• Logical/Mathematical—Logic Smart	• Naturalist—Nature Smart
• Verbal/Linguistic—Word Smart	

According to Gardner, everybody has this array of intelligences. Because schooling and language learning concentrate on the academic intelligences, they are the ones that most people assume accompany learning. However, if we reflect on the matter carefully, we recognize that we can involve the personal, expressive, and emerging intelligences as we involve learners with new standards for cultural learning. In some way, culture learning involves all of these capacities. Yet, it is important to comprehend that the multiple intelligences are not learning styles. They are capacities that are expanded through active use. They provide pathways for learning for different individuals. They provide understanding of complex individuals with whom we teachers can work better. Yet, they are not a label and should not be used to categorize individuals. Multiple intelligences interact with each other in interesting ways. Not all are used with any one learning task; but they can be intermingled. Most importantly, they allow us to guide students to take responsibility for their own learning.

Example of Instructional Guidance with Multiple Intelligences. As we help learners work through the matter of *friendship,* in our example of the standard, **Explain your understanding of friendship in this culture**, multiple intelligences can help us guide learners as they process the tasks. In the *Knowledge and Skill* Activities in the section on Curriculum, several activities were oriented toward answering the questions, "How do you define a friend?" and "Explain what a friend is in your culture?" In getting to this point, learners have had to draw on their own *intrapersonal/introspective intelligence* to reflect on, to discover, and to feel what a friend is. We have guided them to express such reflection, discovery, and emotions through activities such as autobiographical journals, feeling diaries, and personal history on which we have given them feedback.

Then, in cooperative groups, where they have used their *interpersonal/interactive intelligence,* we have asked students to share their reflections, self-discoveries, and feelings about friends. Moreover, through their email communication, they have gotten a wider range of information from learners in other schools. As a result, they have begun to consolidate the information they have pursued individually. We have asked the learners to form different groups where they will use different talents to arrive at a definition of friendship. Once that definition has been finished, we will ask them to explain their definition in a group presentation to the entire class.

Two groups have chosen to represent their understanding of friendship through a combination of mime and dance using their *bodily/kinesthetic intelligence.* In this process, they will use their *verbal/linguistic intelligence* to describe how the mime and dance express the knowledge they have shared and how they define friendship. Their explanation of friendship will come through both body moment and verbal expression.

Two other groups are expressing their knowledge through two separate collages, electing to use their *visual/spatial intelligence* to indicate how they would define friendship. They, too, will be using their *verbal/linguistic intelligence* to explain how the making of the collage represents their collective knowledge and their definition. These groups will use a collage and a verbal explanation of their collage to explain their understanding of friendship.

Finally, two groups are using their *verbal/linguistic intelligence* and their *logical/mathematical intelligence* to read stories of friendship, look up friendship in dictionaries and encyclopedias, interview others, and to write in their journals, feeling diaries, and personal histories. From this activity, they will write a story about friendship and present it to the class as a written document, representing their view of friendship. They will also give their own definition of friendship.

While the groups are doing their work, it is obviously our responsibility to provide them with the needed materials and equipment, such as computers, and make sure everything is working. It is also our obligation to attend to the needs of individuals as they work through the problems by answering questions, giving feedback to assumptions, asking questions, and serving as a sounding board. We are providing the kind of atmosphere where learners to work with each other, albeit in different ways according to their talents, and to resolve problems.

When each group finishes its explanation of friendship, we will open each group's presentation to probing questions from other groups and from the teacher(s). The kinds of questions that might be asked are the following:

- Why did you choose to represent your explanation in this way?
- What role did the personal reflection of individual learners play in the development of the explanation?
- What did you learn from your presentation?
- What do you still need to know?
- How will you pursue what you still need to know?

Assessment will be accomplished with the rubric developed previously. Before we use this rubric, we will give learners input and make necessary changes from that input. Once the rubric has been applied, we will give the groups feedback on what has been done well and what needs improvement. The opportunity to redo any aspect of the definition or presentation will also be allowed.

This example is brief and partial, but it demonstrates the use of multiple intelligences in instruction where teachers guide learners to use their talents in completing a classroom task to develop a definition and to explain it. It also shows the close relationship of classroom tasks and their assessment. This relationship allows constant feedback to learners on their progress. In their workshops on the use of multiple intelligences in both language and culture learning, Gahala and Lange (1996) have developed some materials that show how activities to promote learning with the multiple intelligences generally relate to assessments with those same intelligences. That relationship is summarized for each intelligence in Appendix C.

Obviously, the next step in reaching the Standard, **Explain your understanding of friendship in this culture**, could be a similar process whereby learners develop a definition of friendship in the culture that they are studying. Here, they would be more limited and be required to use much more of the language they are learning as well. Learners would go to teen magazines to read articles on friendship. Or they could conduct interviews in class with native speakers focusing on "What is a friend?" They could email their pen pals and ask questions about what it means to be a friend in the other culture. Beyond the development and explanation of a definition of friendship in the other culture, a further step would be the comparison of definitions, leading ultimately to the development of situations where learners would imagine how friends are made in the other culture, the authentic performance.

Understanding Friendships has taken us through an entire example of how curriculum relates to assessment and instruction (curriculum = assessment = instruction). This theme contributes significantly to an understanding of how more complex aspects of culture can be dealt within the classroom. The example shows us how planning for culture learning using classroom standards links curriculum, assessment, and instruction directly to student performance. In this regard, the ultimate outcome of such planning should be an increased awareness of *the other* and progress toward the development of intercultural sensitivity.

PRINCIPLES FOR TEACHING AND LEARNING

The final result of this discussion is a determination of its meaning for the teaching and learning of culture in the second language classroom. From my point of view, that meaning is best established through the development of a set of principles that apply to culture teaching and learning. In devising this set of principles, I have chosen to state them broadly, not linking them to any particular theoretical perspective, as a means to stimulate thought and discussion. However, the several previous pages certainly provide a backdrop for the meaning of these principles.

Seven Principles

1. The National Standards for culture provide a much more complete picture of the content of culture learning, as well as some indicators of what should be accomplished at grades 4, 8, and 12. The testing of cultural competence is suggested as well. Almost every state has a set of standards, including those for culture. Locally, the *standards should be used as the vision of what a program of language and culture learning may ultimately become at different grade levels in language learning,* but they are not a curriculum. Further, it is important that the National Standards for culture, and all of the National Language Standards for that matter, reflect a quality that can truly improve the learning

of language and culture (see Lange, 1999, and Ohanian, 1999 for further discussion of this issue.)

2. The most important principle is *the utilization of a framework* for the conceptualization of what is to be learned, how that learning is to be evaluated, and how learning is to be guided. Several frameworks were presented in this chapter, but those with emphasis on the learner's development were highly stressed. The National Standards have already been mentioned in this regard. For general educational development, Egan's framework provides a representation of learning from early childhood to mature adult through a set of stages. For the development of intercultural sensitivity, the Bennett (1993) framework offers a vision of the culture learner's growth from Denial of Difference to an Integration of Difference. Other frameworks were also discussed. Such frameworks overcome the haphazard directions that curriculum, assessment, and instruction (learning) have demonstrated to the present.

3. With the use of both standards and frameworks, *the ethical questions of who, what, when, where, how, and why we learn culture in a second language classroom must be addressed.* Is language and culture learning for all or only the few? Do we direct language and culture acquisition beyond the utilitarian intents that we currently espouse IF the goals include the development of cultural sensitivity? Can we move away from narrow views of culture in the contrast of C/c and move toward the broader terminology of objective and subjective culture? If we respect learners, as well as their learning and their responsibilities, can we also respect our knowledge about learners and our responsibilities to them? Are we capable of envisioning the development of language use and cultural sensitivity as a means for personal and cultural expression that allows for the comprehension of the self and of the other?

4. *The curriculum, more broadly conceived, contains the dimensions of orientations, content, process, integration of content and process with language, structure, use of standards and frameworks, and design.* If we move beyond a scientific/technical orientation toward the curriculum and think of the development of intercultural sensitivity, then learners' cultural content will include more abstract concepts, relationships, and understandings that they can process within a language framework. A recursive structure will also give learners a depth of understanding beyond superficial, surface features of culture. Standards, as well as other frameworks, provide the vision for the very practical work of designing a curriculum that includes the relationship of curriculum = assessment = instruction—what is to be learned at what

level, how learning is to be assessed, and how instruction guides learners to reach the desired learning.

5. Within the design of content for culture learning, *learners need to know what knowledge, skills, attitudes, processes or activities, and what experiences will be required of them as they learn about another culture.* The intent of this principle is to bring the learner closer to real life encounters with culture so that learners' understanding of *the other* can be stretched and deepened. The example of Understanding Friendships was my attempt to show how a deeper understanding of friendship can be accomplished. The knowledge, skills, attitudes, processes, and experiences for this purpose were carefully outlined as an example.

6. While including testing, *assessment is the appraisal of what a person knows or can do in relationship to a set of standards.* The ACTFL Oral Interview is one such example. In a carefully developed assessment system, learners move beyond basic knowledge to critiquing, forming judgements, and making connections with other ideas and facts. They answer what, why, how, whose, which, when, where, what if, and so what questions which go beyond simplistic, objective tests. They are accurate in their responses, but they also verify and critique information and ideas; they constantly interact with the teacher in processing their understandings of their own and another culture. Learners' assessments are based on authentic problems that can have several resolutions. The recurrence of similar tasks over time with more sophisticate rubrics assesses greater depth of understanding. This view of assessment is one that gives learners the opportunity to demonstrate how they can apply learning to the real world.

7. *Instruction is the guidance of learners toward desired performances, while engaging their abilities, attitudes, and capacities.* It is not the telling, giving, or drilling of cultural information. Instead, Each learner is different because of different genes, capacities to use background, experience, and abilities, as well as attitudes toward language and culture learning. The guidance of learners to use their several abilities or multiple intelligences opens learning input to wider connections with other knowledge and experiences. The categories of personal (Intrapersonal/Introspective and Interpersonal/Social), expressive (Bodily/Kinesthetic, Visual/Spatial, and Musical/Rhythmic), and emerging intelligence (Emerging) enhance and expand the processes of learning beyond the usually called-upon academic intelligences (Logical/Mathematical and Verbal/Linguistic) upon which language teachers rely so heavily. It is in guiding the use of

these several abilities that teachers assist students in their achievement of more quality outcomes.

CONCLUSION

This chapter provides an extension to the discussion of the application of the Bennett framework for the development of intercultural sensitivity in the second language classroom. While there may not be a complete explication of how this framework is carried out in the second language classroom, its existence gives guidance to the example of *Understanding Friendships*. Framed by the notion of curriculum = assessment = instruction, this example moves our thinking beyond the status quo of superficial cultural stereotypes. The importance of National Standards, the necessity of frameworks to give guidance to learning, the resolution of ethical questions around who learns (language and) culture, as well as the development of curriculum, the application of assessments to determine how well learning and the curriculum function, and the role of guidance in instruction form seven principles to guide the future of culture learning in the second language classroom. If these principles are applied to the learning and teaching of language and culture in the future, it will be to the ultimate benefit of our students.

NOTE

1.   Some parts of this chapter were originally published in Lange, D.L. (1999). Planning for and using the new national culture standards. In J.K. Phillips & R.M. Terry (Eds.), *Foreign language standards: Linking research, theories and practices* (pp. 57–133). The ACTFL Foreign Language Education Series. Lincolnwood, IL: National Textbook. Permission to reprint was granted from NTC/Contemporary Publishing Group, Inc.

REFERENCES

Allen, W.W., & Lange, D.L. (1996). *Integrating culture and learning: Theory and practice.* Unpublished manuscript.

Asher, J.J. (1982). *Learning another language through actions: The complete teacher's guide book* (2nd ed.). Los Gatos, CA: Sky Oaks Productions. Nd.

Bachman, L.F. (1990). *Fundamental considerations in language testing.* Oxford: Oxford University Press.

Banathy, B., & Lange, D.L. (1972). *A design for foreign language curriculum.* Lexington, MA: D. C. Heath.

Bennett, J.M. (1993). Cultural marginality: Identity issues in intercultural training. In R.M. Paige (Ed.), *Education for the intercultural experience* (pp. 109–135). Yarmouth, ME: Intercultural Press.

Bennett, M.J. (1993). Towards ethnorelativism: A developmental model of intercultural sensitivity. In R.M. Paige (Ed.), *Education for intercultural experience* (2nd ed., pp. 21–72). Yarmouth, ME: Intercultural Press.

Bloom, B.S. (Ed.). (1956) *Taxonomy of educational objectives: The classification of educational goals, handbook I: The cognitive domain.* New York: David McKay.

Breen, M. (1987). Learner contributions to task design. In C.N. Candlin & D. Murphy (Eds.), *Language learning tasks* (Vol. 7, pp. 23–46). Lancaster Papers in English Language Education. Englewood Cliffs, NJ: Prentice-Hall.

Brooks, N. (1968). Teaching culture in the foreign language classroom. *Foreign Language Annals, 1,* 204–217.

Brown, J.D. (1995). *The elements of language curriculum: A systematic approach to program development.* Boston: Heinle & Heinle.

Bruner, J. (1990). *Acts of meaning.* Cambridge, MA: Harvard University Press.

Byram, M. (1989). *Cultural studies in foreign language education.* Philadelphia: Multilingual Matters.

Byram, M., & Morgan, C. (1994). *Teaching and learning language and culture.* Philadelphia: Multilingual Matters.

Byrnes, H. (1990). Priority: Addressing curriculum articulation in the nineties. A proposal. *Foreign Language Annals, 23,* 281–92.

Byrnes, H., & Canale, M. (Eds.). (1987). *Defining and developing proficiency: Guidelines, implementations, and concepts.* The ACTFL Foreign Language Education Series. Lincolnwood, IL: National Textbook.

Byrnes, H., Child, J., Levinson, N., Lowe, P. Jr., Makino, Seichi, Thompson, I., & Walton, R. (1987). ACTFL proficiency guidelines. In H. Byrnes & M. Canale (Eds.), *Defining and developing proficiency: Guidelines, implementation, and concepts* (pp. 15–24). The ACTFL Foreign Language Education Series. Lincolnwood, IL: National Textbook.

Center for Advanced Research in Language Acquisition. (1997). *MLPA: The Minnesota Language Proficiency Assessments.* Minneapolis, MN: University of Minnesota, The Center for Advanced Research on Language Acquisition. (Email: MLPA@tc.umn.edu).

Coleman, A. (1929). *The teaching of modern languages in the United States.* New York: Macmillan.

Cohen, A. D. (1994). *Assessing language ability in the classroom* (2nd ed.). Boston: Heinle & Heinle.

Crawford-Lange, L. M., & Lange, D. L. (1984). Doing the unthinkable in the second-language classroom: A process for the integration of language and culture. In T. V. Higgs (Ed.), *Teaching for Proficiency, the Organizing Principle* (pp. 139–177). The ACTFL Foreign Language Education Series. Lincolnwood, IL: National Textbook.

Dubin, F., & Olshtain, E. (1986). *Course design: Developing programs and materials for language learning.* Cambridge: Cambridge University Press.

Egan, K. (1979). *Educational development.* New York: Oxford University Press.

Fantini, A. E. (1997). *New way in teaching culture.* Alexandria, VA: TESOL.

Fantini, A. E. (1999). Comparisons: Towards the development of intercultural competence. In J. K. Phillips & R. M. Terry (Eds.), *Foreign Language Standards: Linking Research, Theories, and Practice* (pp. 165–218). The ACTFL Foreign Language Education Series. Lincolnwood, IL: National Textbook.

Fiedler, F. E., Mitchell, T., & Triandis, H. C. (1971). The culture assimilator: An approach to cross-cultural training. *Journal of Applied Psychology, 55*, 95–102.

Finocchiaro, M., & Brumfit, C. (1983). The functional-notional approach: From theory to practice. New York: Oxford University Press.

Freire, P. (1996). *Pedagogy of hope.* New York: Continuum.

Freire, P., & Faundez, A. (1989). *Learning to question.* New York: Continuum.

Gahala, E. M., & Lange, D. L. (1996, April). *Toward classroom assessment of oral performance for new foreign language standards.* Paper presented at the Southwest Conference on Language Teaching, Albuquerque, NM.

Gahala, E. M., & Lange, D. L. (1997). Multiple intelligences: Multiple ways to help students learn foreign languages. *Northeast Conference on the Teaching of Foreign Language Newsletter, 41*, 29–34.

Gardner, H. (1993a). *Frames of mind: The theory of multiple intelligences* (2nd ed.). New York: Basic Books.

Gardner, H. (1993b). *Multiple intelligences: The theory in practice* (2nd ed.). New York: Basic Books.

Gardner, H. (1995). Reflections on multiple intelligences: Myths and messages. *Phi Delta Kappan, 77*, 200–209.

Genesee, F., & Upshur, J.A. (1996). *Classroom-based evaluation in second language education.* Cambridge: Cambridge University Press.

Giroux, H.A. (1992). *Border crossings: Cultural workers and the politics of education.* London: Routledge, Chapman, and Hall.

Henning, G. (1987). *A guide to language testing: Development, evaluation, research.* Cambridge, MA: Newbury House.

Higgs, T.V. (1984). Introduction: Language teaching and the quest for the Holy Grail. In T. V. Higgs (Ed.), *Teaching for proficiency, the organizing principle* (pp. 1–9). The ACTFL Foreign Language Education Series. Lincolnwood, IL: National Textbook.

Johnson, K. (1982). *Communicative syllabus design and methodology.* Oxford: Oxford University Press.

Jones, R.L., & Spolsky, B. (1975). *Testing language proficiency.* Washington, DC: Center for Applied Linguistics.

Kramsch. C. (1993). *Context and culture in language teaching.* Oxford: Oxford University Press.

Krathwohl, D.R., Bloom, B.S., & Masia, B.B. (1964). *Taxonomy of educational objectives, the classification of educational goals, Handbook II: Affective domain.* New York: David McKay.

Krueger, M., & Ryan, F. (Eds.). (1993). *Language and content: Discipline and content-based approaches to language study.* Lexington, MA: D.C. Heath.

Lado, R. (1961). *Language testing: The construction and use of foreign language tests.* London: Longman.

Lado, R. (1964). *Language teaching: A scientific approach.* New York: McGraw-Hill.

Lafayette, R. (1988). Integrating the teaching of culture into the foreign language classroom. In A.J. Singerman (Ed.), *Toward a new integration of language and culture* (pp. 47–62). Northeast Conference Reports. Middlebury, VT: The Northeast Conference.

Lange, D.L. (1990a). A blueprint for a teacher development program. In J.C. Richards & D. Nunan (Eds.), *Second language teacher education* (pp. 245–268). Cambridge: Cambridge University Press.

Lange, D.L. (1990b). Priority issues in the assessment of communicative language abilities. *Foreign Language Annals, 23,* 403–407.

Lange, D.L. (1990c). Sketching the crisis and exploring different perspectives in foreign language curriculum. In D.W. Birckbichler (Ed.), *New perspectives and new directions in foreign language education* (pp. 77–109). The ACTFL Foreign Language Education Series. Lincolnwood, IL: National Textbook.

Lange, D.L. (1996, May). *Principles for the application of a conceptual framework for the teaching and learning of culture.* Paper presented at the conference of the Intercultural Studies Project, The Center for Advanced Research on Language Acquisition, Minneapolis, Minnesota.

Lange, D.L. (1999). Planning for and using the new national culture standards. In J.K. Phillips & R.M. Terry (Eds.), *Foreign language standards: Linking research, theories, and practices* (pp. 57–135). The ACTFL Foreign Language Education Series. Lincolnwood, IL: National Textbook.

Liskin-Gasparro, J. (1996). Assessment: From content standards to student performance. In R.C. Lafayette (Ed.), *National standards: A catalyst for reform* (pp. 169–196). The ACTFL Foreign Language Education Series. Lincolnwood, IL: National Textbook.

Lowe, P., Jr., & Stansfield, C.W. (Eds.). (1988). *Second language proficiency assessment: Current issues.* Englewood Cliffs, NJ: Prentice Hall.

Madaus, G.F., & Kellaghan, T. (1992). Curriculum evaluation and assessment. In P.W. Jackson (Ed.), *Handbook of research on curriculum* (pp. 119–154). New York: Macmillan.

Meade, B., & Morain. G. (1973). The culture cluster. *Foreign Language Annals, 6,* 331–338.

Met, M., & Galloway, V. (1992). Research in foreign language curriculum. In P.W. Jackson (Ed.), *Handbook of research on curriculum* (pp. 852–890). New York: Macmillan.

Miller, J.D., & Bishop R.H. (1979). *USA-Mexico culture capsules.* Rowley, MA: Newbury House.

Miller, J.D., Drayton, J., & Lyon, T. (1979). *USA-Hispanic South American culture capsules.* Rowley, MA: Newbury House.

Miller, J.D., & Loiseau, M. (1974). *USA-France culture capsules.* Rowley, MA: Newbury House.

Nostrand, H.L. (1967). *Background data for the teaching of French: Part A. La culture et la société française au Xx^e siècle.* Seattle: University of Washington.

Nostrand, H.L. (1974). Empathy for a second culture: Motivations and techniques. In G.A. Jarvis (Ed.), *Responding to new realities* (pp. 263–327). The ACTFL Foreign Language Education Series. Lincolnwood, IL: National Textbook.

Nunan, D. (1989). *Designing tasks for the communicative classroom.* Cambridge: Cambridge University Press.

Ochsner, R. (1979). A poetics of second-language acquisition. *Language Learning, 29,* 53–81.

Ohanian, S. (1999). *One size fits few: The follow of educational standards.* Portsmouth, NH: Heinemann.

Oller, J.W., Jr., & Perkins, K. (1978). *Language in education: Testing the tests.* Rowley, MA: Newbury House.

Oller, J.W., Jr., & Perkins, K. (Eds.). (1980). *Research in language testing.* Rowley, MA: Newbury House.

Omaggio, A.C. (1983). *Proficiency-oriented classroom testing.* Washington, DC: Center for Applied Linguistics.

Omaggio Hadley, A.C. (1993). *Teaching language in context* (2nd ed.). Boston: Heinle & Heinle.

Oxford, R.L. (1990). *Language learning strategies: What every teacher should know.* New York: Newbury House [Boston: Heinle & Heinle].

Paige, R.M. (Ed.). (1993). *Education for the intercultural experience* (2nd ed.). Yarmouth, ME: Intercultural Press.

Pesola, C.A. (1995). *Background, design and evaluation of a conceptual framework for FLES (Foreign Languages in the Elementary School) curriculum.* Unpublished doctoral dissertation, University of Minnesota, Minneapolis.

Pratt, D. (1994). *Curriculum planning: A handbook for professionals.* Fort Worth: Harcourt Brace College Publishers.

Richards, J.C., Platt, J., & Weber, H. (1985). *Longman dictionary of applied linguistics.* London: Longman.

Richards, J.C., & Rodgers, T.S. (1986). *Approaches and method in language teaching: A description and analysis.* Cambridge: Cambridge University Press.

Seelye, H.N. (1972). Analysis and teaching of the cross-cultural context. In E.M. Birkmaier (Ed.), *Foreign language education: An overview* (pp. 37–81). ACTFL Foreign Language Education Series. Lincolnwood, IL: National Textbook.

Seelye, H.N. (1976/1993). *Teaching culture: Strategies for intercultural communication.* Lincolnwood, IL: National Textbook.

Seelye, H.N. (1996). *Experiential activities for intercultural learning* (Vol. 1). Yarmouth, ME: Intercultural Press.

Shohamy, E., & Walton, R. (Eds.). (1992). *Language assessment for feedback: Testing and other strategies.* Dubuque, IA: Kendall/Hunt.

Shor, I., & Freire, P. (1987). *Pedagogy for liberation: Dialogues for transforming education.* South Hadley, MA: Bergin & Garvey.

Short, E. C. (Ed.). (1991). *Forms of curriculum inquiry.* Albany: State University of New York Press.

Singerman, A.J. (Ed.). (1996). *Acquiring cross-cultural competence: Four stages for students of French.* American Association of Teachers of French National Commission on Cultural Competence. Lincolnwood, IL: National Textbook.

Spolsky, B. (Ed.). (1978). *Some major tests* (Vol. 1). Advances in Language Testing Series. Washington, DC: Center for Applied Linguistics.

Spolsky, B. (Ed.). (1979). *Approaches to language testing* (Vol. 2). Advances in Language Testing Series. Washington, DC: Center for Applied Linguistics.

Standards for foreign language learning: Preparing for the 21st century. (1996). Yonkers, NY: National Standards in Foreign Language Education Project.

Stern, H.H. (1982). Toward a multidimensional foreign language curriculum. In R.G. Mead, Jr. (Ed.), *Foreign languages: Key links in the chain of learning* (pp. 120–46). Northeast Conference Reports. Middlebury, VT: The Northeast Conference.

Stevick, E.W. (1976). *Memory, meaning, and method: Some psychological perspectives on language learning.* Rowley, MA: Newbury House [Boston: Heinle & Heinle].

Stevick, E.W. (1980). *Teaching languages: A way and ways.* Rowley, MA: Newbury House [Boston: Heinle & Heinle].

Strasheim, L.A. (1972). A rationale for the individualization and personalization of foreign language instruction. In D.L. Lange (Ed.), *Individualization of instruction* (pp. 15–34). ACTFL Foreign Language Education Series. Lincolnwood, IL: National Textbook.

Sylwester, R. (1995). *A celebration of neurons: An educator's guide to the human brain.* Alexandria, VA: Association for Supervision and Curriculum Development.

Tedick, D.J., Walker, C.L., Lange, D.L., Paige, R.M., & Jorstad, H.L. (1993). Second language education in tomorrow's schools. In G. Guntermann (Ed.), *Developing language teachers for a changing world* (pp. 42–75). The ACTFL Foreign Language Education Series. Lincolnwood, IL: National Textbook.

Tedick, D.J., & Walker, C.L. (1996). Teaching all students: Necessary changes in teacher education. In B.H. Wing (Ed.), *Foreign languages for all: Challenges and choices* (pp. 187–220). Northeast Conference Reports. Lincolnwood, IL: National Textbook.

Triandis, H.C., Vassiliou, V.G., Tanaka, Y., & Shanmugam, A.V. (1972). *The analysis of subjective culture.* New York: Wiley.

Valette, R.M. (1977). *Modern language testing.* New York: Harcourt Brace Jovanovich.

Wallerstein, N. (1983). *Language and culture in conflict: Problem-posing in the ESL classroom.* Reading, MA: Addison-Wesley.

Wiggins, G.P. (1993). *Assessing student performance: Exploring the purpose and limits of testing.* San Francisco: Jossey-Bass.

Wiggins, G.P. (1998). *Educative assessment: Designing assessments to inform and improve student performance.* San Francisco: Jossey-Bass.

Wiggins, G.P., & Kline, E. (1998, January). *Understanding by design.* Paper presented at the Collaborative Seminar, Headquarters of the American Council on the Teaching of Foreign Languages, Yonkers, NY.

Yalden, J. (1987). *Principles of course design for language teaching.* Cambridge, MA: Cambridge University Press.

APPENDIX A: AATF CULTURE STANDARDS

UNDERSTANDING CULTURE

A. EMPATHY TOWARD OTHER CULTURES

Indicators of Competence

Upon completing Stage 1, the learner:
- Is curious about similarities and differences between the home and the target culture.
- Shows willingness to understand the differences encountered.

Upon completing Stage 2, the learner:
- Is tolerant of differences between the home and target culture.
- Is open and accepting of different peoples.
- Recognizes the depth and complexity of cultural differences.
- Shows an active interest in the search for understanding of the target culture.

Upon completing Stage 3, the learner:
- Is aware of the problem of accepting the norms of another culture while maintaining one's own values and identity.
- Shows fair-mindedness and tolerance in trying to solve an embarrassing situation or a cross-cultural conflict.
- Can adjust behavior and conversation according to the situational context and to the expectations of participants.

Upon completing Stage 4, the learner:
- Recognizes the importance of understanding manifestations of the target culture in terms of its own context.
- Is aware of his/her own cultural perspective and of how this perspective influences one's perception of phenomena.
- Can act and react in a culturally appropriate way while being aware of his/her "otherness."

B. ABILITY TO OBSERVE AND ANALYZE A CULTURE

Indicators of Competence

Upon completing Stage 1, the learner:
- Can give examples of the relationship between language and culture (e.g. different forms of oral address, depending on social relations and situation).
- Can identify a few characteristics of the target culture as cultural patterns (e.g., businesses and government offices in France may close for as long as two hours at lunch time).
- Can identify a few common cultural differences between home and target cultures (e.g., the presentation of American and French meals).
- Can identify some commonly-held images of the target culture as stereotypes (e.g., "the French drink wine with their meals").

Upon completing Stage 2, the learner:
- Can demonstrate understanding that cultural values, patterns, and institutions cannot be used to predict the behavior of all individuals (e.g., not all French people avoid creating relations with their neighbors to preserve their privacy).
- Can give examples of an observer's own cultural biases interfering with understanding of the target culture (e.g., being embarrassed by kissing on the cheek between female friends in France).
- Can give an example of how cultures change over time (e.g., in some workplaces in France, the noon mealtime has been shortened considerably).
- Can discuss ways in which cultural norms and values are transmitted (e.g., the role of parents as models and teachers of values).
- Can give examples of one culture influencing another (e.g., the popularity of American-style fast-food restaurants in France).

Upon completing Stage 3, the learner:
- Can give examples of social behaviors that express the target culture's underlying value system (e.g., the reluctance of French people to invite casual acquaintances into their homes is an expression of their concept of friendship, their value of privacy, and their general distrust of outsiders).
- Can describe and explain important elements of major institutions in the target culture (e.g., can describe the baccalaureate exam and its importance in the French educational system).

- Can interpret social phenomena within the context of the target culture (e.g., understands how the frequent recourse to public demonstrations in France is related to administrative centralization).
- Can describe several instances of major change within the target culture (e.g., fewer and fewer French people attend religious services regularly).
- Can describe some major forces that influence culture and cultural change (e.g., the role of technology: the Minitel, television, etc.).
- Recognizes that a culture is not uniform and can identify the principal subcultures of the target culture (e.g., the increasing importance of Moslem culture in France).

Upon completing Stage 4, the learner:
- Can critique phenomena of the target culture with a minimum of bias (e.g., can discuss the various political parties in France objectively, whether on the *left* or on the *right*).
- Can interpret social phenomena at several levels of generalization (e.g., can discuss the development of the role of women in the world, in France in general, and in a given French social class).
- Can describe the multi-faceted character of sociocultural phenomena (e.g., the historical, social, religious, economic, and political dimensions of the growing North African population in France).

KNOWLEDGE OF FRENCH-SPEAKING SOCIETIES

- France
- North America
- Sub-Saharan Africa
- The Caribbean
- North Africa

Within each of these areas, culture is broken into seven categories of cultural knowledge:

- Communication in Cultural Context
- The Value System
- Social Patterns and Conventions
- Social Institutions
- Geography and the Environment
- History
- Literature and the Arts

Each of the areas of competence is locked into 4 levels as indicated in *Understanding Culture*. They apply to the *Knowledge of French-Speaking Countries* as well. Those four levels are:

- Stage 1: Elementary
- Stage 2: Basic Intercultural Skills
- Stage 3: Social Competence
- Stage 4: Socioprofessional Capability

The AATF Culture Standards are available from National Textbook, 4255 West Touhy Avenue, Lincolnwood, IL 60646–1975. The full citation is as follows:

Singerman, A.J. (Ed.). (1996). *Acquiring cross-cultural competence: Four stages for students of French.* American Association of Teachers of French National Commission on Cultural Competence. Lincolnwood, IL: National Textbook.

APPENDIX B: COGNITIVE LEARNING, AFFECTIVE LEARNING, AND THE RELATIONSHIP OF COGNITIVE AND AFFECTIVE LEARNING

COGNITIVE LEARNING

Cognitive Learning is... The learner...

1. Knowledge

Terminology; Facts—Acquires cultural meaning of words; Recalls important cultural facts.

Conventions; Trends and Sequences; Categories; Criteria; and, Methodology—Knows culture's rules for general behavior; Knows forces which shape cultural behavior; Knows categories of cultural behavior; Knows criteria for the evaluation of cultural behavior; Knows methods for the study of cultural behavior.

Principles and Generalizations; and, Theories and Structures—Knows important principles of cultural difference; Recalls major theories of cultural difference.

2. Comprehension

Translation; Interpretation; and, Extrapolation—Comprehends cultural behavior in context; States its potential meaning to others; Indicates its future consequences.

3. Application (Problem Solving)

Employs principles of cultural behavior from own culture to understand a new one.

4. Analysis (Breakdown into Constituent Parts)

Elements; Relationships; and, Principles—Distinguishes facts of cultural behavior from generalized statements about cultural behavior; Checks consistency of hypotheses about cultural behavior with information; Recognizes the bias of "the other" in a description of cultural behavior.

5. Synthesis (Putting elements together to form a new whole)

Create a Unique Communication; Develop a plan; Derive abstract relations—Writes a definitive description of cultural behavior for "x" culture; Proposes ways of researching cultural behavior; Formulates a theory about learning cultural behavior.

6. Evaluation (Making Judgments about the value of ideas, works, solutions, methods, materials, etc.)

Judgments on Internal Evidence; and, Judgments on External Evidence—Indicates fallacies in arguments in publications about cultural behavior; Compares major theories about cultural behavior.

AFFECTIVE LEARNING

In..., the individual develops...—or s/he ...

1. Receiving

Awareness—Recognizes cultural differences
Willingness to Receive—Tolerates differences
Selected Attention—Becomes sensitive to differences

2. Responding

Compliance—Forces self to see difference
Willingness—Seeks information voluntarily
Enjoys Response—Finds pleasure in information

3. Valuing

Acceptance—Increases recognition of difference
Preference—Helps others understand difference
Commitment—Accepts difference as part of life

4. Organization

Conceptualization of a Value—Identifies the characteristics of difference.
Organization of a Value System—Plans to respect difference in dealing
with other cultures.

5. Characterization by a Value or Value Complex

Predisposition to Act—Willingness to revise attitudes on difference with
new evidence.
Acting on a Value System—Develops consistent behavior related to cultural difference.

THE RELATIONSHIP BETWEEN
COGNITIVE AND AFFECTIVE LEARNING

Cognitive	*Affective*
1. Recalls and recognizes *knowledge*	1. *Receives* knowledge and attends to it.
2. *Comprehends* knowledge	2. *Responds* on request; Takes satisfaction in responding
3. *Applies* comprehended knowledge	3. *Values* activity; Responds voluntarily
4. *Analyzes* knowledge; and	4. *Conceptualizes* values responded to
5. *Synthesizes* it in new ways	5. *Organizes* values into systems and a single system which
6. *Evaluates* knowledge to judge value	6. *Characterizes* an individual

APPENDIX C

MULTIPLE INTELLIGENCES: ACTIVITIES AND ASSESSMENTS

Personal Intelligences

Intrapersonal Intelligence: Understanding Oneself
"Self Smart"

Activities to Promote Learning:

reflection	goal setting	visualization
metacognition	self-discovery imagery	autobiography
surveys	problem solving	independent tasks
journals	open-ended	independent learning times
relaxation	expression	family heritage
personal graphics		
"me" collage or		
T-shirt, mood cube,		
cultural heritage		
poster, etc.)		

Environment:

time to think/give and get positive feedback
gallery of student work/identification of one's strengths

Assessments (Psychological-Based Instruments):

Personal application scenarios, autobiographical reporting, metacognitive surveys and questionnaires, higher-order questions and answers, feeling diaries and logs, personal projection, personal history, personal priorities and goals.

Interpersonal Intelligence: Individuals in Social Groups
"People Smart"

Activities to Promote Learning:

cooperative tasks	creative group tasks
(think-pair-share,	(mobiles, collages, songs, poems,
round robin, jigsaw, etc.)	comic strips, story books, etc.)
technology: e-mail, CD-ROM,	
Internet rating scales	

Environment:

instructional variety / learning centers
cooperative guidelines / social skills instruction
collaborative problem solving
management tactics for cooperative groups
debriefing / learning that is fun

Assessments (Relational-Based Assessments):

Group jigsaws, think-pair-share, explaining to or teaching another, giving and receiving feedback, interviews, people searches, questionnaires, empathetic processing, random group quizzes, assess your teammates.

Expressive Intelligences

Bodily/Kinesthetic Intelligence: Skillful Control of Bodily Motions
"Body Smart"

Activities to Promote Learning:

active learning   projects   interviews
  (mime, TPR,   simulations   role playing
  manipulatives,   field trips   creative movement
  games, sports,   whole-body learning
  creating things)

Environment:

creating dramatics ("pretend", "what if...")
hands-on environment (not worksheets and lectures)
whole-body movements in exercise or stretch breaks
learning that is fun

Assessments (Performance-Based Instruments):

Charades, mimes, TPR, dramatizations, dance, impersonations, human tableaux, invention projects, physical routines and games, demonstrations, illustrations using body language and gestures.

Visual/Spatial Intelligence: Accurate Comprehension of the Visual World
"Picture Smart"

Activities to Promote Learning:

visuals	graphic organizers	
(photos,	(outlines, charts, matrices, grids, webs,	
paintings,	clusters, timelines, sequence charts, maps,	
drawings,	Venn diagrams, etc.)	
illustrations)	video	
props	demonstrations	imagery
manipulatives	role play	sketches
overhead	chalkboard	color-coding systems
sculpting	constructing	active imagination

Environment:

classroom walls that stimulate by color, design, and pattern, but not a bombardment of the senses
verbal instructions that appeal to vision ("See, Visualize, Imagine, Picture this...")
...and learning that is fun

Assessments (Image-Based Instruments):

Video recording, photography, flowcharts, graphs, murals, montages, collages, graphic representations, mind maps, manipulative demonstrations, visual illustration

Musical/Rhythmic Intelligence: Musical Abilities
"Music Smart"

Activities to Promote Learning:

songs	dances	mnemonics
raps	cheers	poems
song, movement, or		
dance to illustrate		
ideas or concepts		

Environment:

sound tapes to prepare the mind for learning, reviewing, imaging, creating, relaxing, energizing, awareness, etc.
choral readings (poems, stories, popular songs)
theme music
learning that is fun

Assessment (Auditory-Based Assessments):

Creating concept songs and raps, illustrating with sound, linking music and rhythm with concepts, discerning rhythmic patterns

Academic Intelligences

Logical/Mathematical Intelligence: Scientific and Reasoning Ability, Mathematical Ability
"Logic Smart"

Activities to Promote Learning:

graphic organizers (see list under Visual / Spatial)
cognitive organizers (lists, summaries, outlines, comparisons, contrasts, metaphors, analogies, paradigms, categories, patterns, relationships)
problem solving   experiments   challenge tasks
research projects   manipulatives
                         (puzzles, board games, etc.)

Environment:

well-ordered and sequenced lesson design
clear lesson objectives and connections among parts of lesson
instruction that demonstrates, models, provides guided practice, checks understanding and evaluates
authentic applications
...and learning that is fun

Assessments (Cognitive Pattern-Based Assessments):

Higher order reasoning, logic and rationality exercises, mental menus and formulas, deductive reasoning, inductive reasoning, logical analysis and critique, cognitive and graphic organizers

Verbal/Linguistic Intelligence: Uses of Language
"Word Smart"

Activities to Promote Learning:

personal expression (opinions, reactions, experiences)
speakers   interviews   peer teaching
field trips   debate   discussion
role play   dramatization   simulation

reading (outcome prediction, dramatic reading, seek and
   organize information, etc.)
writing (logs, journals, student-made books, webs or clusters to
   brainstorm ideas, etc.)

Assessments (Language-Based Instruments):

Vocabulary quizzes, written essays, recall of verbal information, audio
recordings, poetry writing, linguistic humor, formal speech, cognitive
debates, listening and reporting, learning logs and journals

Emerging Intelligence

Naturalist Intelligence: See Deeply into the Nature of Living Things
"Nature Smart"

Activities to Promote Learning:

data collection	data analysis	logs
demonstration	awareness projects	video
research projects	reports	charts
identification of flora and fauna		

Environment:

outdoors	horticultural gardens	zoos
farms	parks	forests
wildlife preserves	ecological models	

Assessments (Nature-Based Assessments):

Observation of phenomena, recognition of events and conditions, identification of elements, classification of materials and events, problem solving,
demonstration of findings.

   Environmental/ecological issues are a rich context for multi-disciplin-
ary studies that utilize all the intelligence.

CHAPTER 12

FUTURE DIRECTIONS FOR CULTURE TEACHING AND LEARNING

The Implications of the New Culture Standards and Theoretical Frameworks for Curriculum, Assessment, Instruction, and Research

Dale L. Lange

INTRODUCTION

In the four chapters of this section, important ideas and concepts have been presented about the teaching and learning of culture in the second language classroom. Phillips explains the importance of new National Standards (1996, 1999) and the dominant role of culture in both the content and process of language learning. As a consequence, the direction given by standards toward what students *should know and be able to do* leads

Culture as the Core: Perspectives in Second Language Education, pages 337–354
Copyright © 2003 by Information Age Publishing
All rights of reproduction in any form reserved.

us to a future beyond a mechanistic view of both language and culture. In the Bennett, Bennett, and Allen chapter, a theory for the development of intercultural sensitivity provides a context for the outcomes of culture learning. This framework allows us to understand how intercultural development progresses across stages. By showing how language and intercultural sensitivity relate to each other, the authors suggest ways in which these two elements may fit together in the curriculum for the future development of both language and culture learning. Lange's contribution takes culture learning one step further by showing how several conceptual frameworks, including that of Bennett (1993) and Bennett et al. can be used to plan a culture curriculum, create meaningful assessment tools for culture learning, and guide students in learning how to understand another culture. This addition brings the potential for the integration of language and culture learning even closer. The Paige, Jorstad, Siaya, Klein, and Colby chapter presents a discussion, based on a review of the research literature, of many of the important variables in culture learning that need attention if we are going to fulfill the long term goals of the National Standards for language and culture learning. The purpose of this final chapter is to distill salient issues that will make a significant impact on the future of culture teaching and learning in the second language classroom. Questions relating to future directions will be pulled from each of the four core chapters. A final section will bring all of these questions together in one place.

NATIONAL STANDARDS

The national standards (National Standards, 1996, 1999) particularly those focusing specifically on culture, direct culture learning and teaching beyond its current marginalized existence as a fifth skill (where it is often viewed as a trivialized conglomeration of names, places, and things). Culture is actually the core of language learning for both process and content. The two goal areas related to culture (Culture and Comparisons) and two of the other goal areas (Connections and Communities) give us a sense of direction regarding content, while the Communication goal area helps us envision the process. As articulated by Phillips and the National Standards Project (1996, 1999), such a vision is extremely forward-looking. It is not a vision that is being carried out by the profession at this point, but it is truly one of the future (Lange & Wieczorek, 1997, p. 270) for K–12 and possibly post-secondary levels of learning. Yet, in this very visionary context, we must constantly and carefully review both national and state standards to ascertain their quality (see the discussion in Lange, 1999, pp. 63–70), assure their implementation, and encourage the appropriate articulation of programs. In particular, post-secondary education will need to incorporate the standards, or at least articulate programs with them.

Phillips provides important assertions about the importance of the standards as a guide to the teaching and learning of culture:

- Culture is a driving force within the standards because it interacts with all goal areas.
- The standards within the culture goal areas (Culture and Comparisons) spell out the development of "understanding of meanings, attitudes, values, and ideas" through interaction with practices, products, and perspectives of the cultures studied. As demonstrated in the progress indicators and learning scenarios, the potential for in-depth study and demonstration of the acquired understandings will lead learners to see the complexity of culture, suspend judgment, and seek broader explanations for cultural phenomena.
- Within the language learning context, culture learning is achieved by both *knowing* and *doing* through an interweaving of cultural content with the *interpersonal, interpretive,* and *presentational* modes of communication, as defined in the Standards document. In turn, the modes of communication also interact with the language system, critical thinking strategies, learning strategies, and technology. Although the *weave* is complex, it does represent the elements considered in the creation of a language/culture curriculum.
- As a result of such characteristics and linkages, culture learning is so "[infused] in a standards-driven curriculum . . . that it can never again be treated as an aside."[1]
- Phillip's one caveat to a culture-driven curriculum is the lack of knowledge and experience teachers may feel they have with the other culture. Yet, she firmly believes that learners who are given opportunities to observe, analyze, suspend judgment, and confirm hypotheses can overcome the tendency to sustain stereotypes.

The significance of Phillip's assertions suggests that the standards provide a broad system within which culture learning can take place in language learning programs. The standards provide visionary direction through goal statements, progress indicators in grades 4, 8, and 12, and learning scenarios at the same grade levels. As a general plan, these goals, indicators, and scenarios are indicative of what teachers may teach and learners may learn. Yet, the standards are not complete because they have not been localized and thus present only an indication of the processes, content, and possible outcomes that could result (see Wiggins, 1993, pp. 282–285; 1998). Moreover, they do raise questions for our consideration, particularly in the light of the Bennetts and Allen framework:

- How do the standards relate to the objective and subjective meanings of culture presented by Bennett et al.? (See learning scenarios for a variety of languages in National Standards Project, 1996, 1999.)
- How can we know that the interpersonal, interpretive, and presentational modes of communication are interacting sufficiently with the Bennett (1993) framework to develop intercultural competence?

THE DEVELOPMENT OF INTERCULTURAL COMPETENCE: RELATIONSHIP TO LANGUAGE LEARNING

Working from Bennett's (1993) developmental model of intercultural sensitivity (DMIS), Bennett et al. show us how intercultural development relates to general levels of language competence (see ACTFL Guidelines, Byrnes et al., 1987). They provide selected intercultural learning activities that match linguistic and cultural readiness. In addition, they introduce us to the terms *culture specific* and *culture general* and avoid over utilizing the Big C and little c culture distinction so often used in language learning discussions.

While pointing out a gradual acceptance of culture as the core of language learning by the profession, Bennett et al. essentially concur with Phillips that the national standards enhanced that stance. But they have important questions, generated by the standards, questions which, when answered, give us a definition of culture and cultural competence, a framework for developing cultural competence, and suggested classroom activities for such development as related to language learning.

1. What is the definition of culture?

Perceiving potential confusion in the definition of culture, in the words of the standards *perspectives*, *practices*, and *products*, Bennett et al. define culture in terms *objective culture* and *subjective culture*. These terms orient learners to an interactive process in culture learning between the objective and subjective, thereby avoiding the exploration and mastery of only the bits and pieces of culture. In this context, objective culture is defined as: "cultural creations including institutions (administrative, political, religious, literary, educational, etc.) and artifacts of formal culture (eating, shopping, artifacts, clothing, marriage, work, behavior, etc.)." Subjective culture is defined as: "language use, nonverbal behavior, communication style, cognitive style, and cultural values." Such a perspective avoids the conflicts and separations that arise with the *C* and *c* distinctions.

2. How is culture learning implemented?

The answer to this question lies in the development of intercultural competence. Such competence evolves through a mix of culture-specific and culture-general approaches. Similar to an ethnographic view of culture in language classrooms and to language learning itself, the culture-specific approach wants learners to gain mastery of the world view and behavior of a particular culture. The culture-general approach is more universal and process oriented; it focuses on "overcoming ethnocentrism, developing appreciation for one's own culture and for cultural difference, understanding and acquiring skills in cultural adaptation, dealing with identity in intercultural contact and mobility." The combination of these approaches results in a *not-as-usual* approach to teaching culture in the language classroom, one that is more process than concrete fact oriented. This orientation, in itself, raises a set of important questions:

- Will the profession accept the Bennett et al. definition of culture as a combination of objective and subjective culture?
- By what means can we know that the definitions of objective and subjective culture are being accepted in language and culture instruction in schools? In colleges and universities?
- By what means can we be assured that language teachers will shift their perspective of culture from *parts and pieces* to be mastered to a process of developing intercultural competence?
- How does the development of intercultural competence and language learning interact in the use of target language in the classroom?
- Are teachers prepared to embark on the development of competence in both language and culture as viewed by Bennett et al.? (See the section on the Relationship of the DMIS to Language Learning.)

3. How can culture and language learning be integrated?

In the Bennett et al. chapter, there is a two-part answer to this third question. A first answer to this question comes through the development of intercultural sensitivity, a culture-general framework Bennett (1993) refers to as the developmental model of intercultural sensitivity (DMIS). This carefully outlined framework suggests that people proceed in their development of intercultural sensitivity through two basic states, *ethnocentrism* (denial, defense, minimization) and *ethnorelativism* (acceptance, adaptation, integration).

A second answer to the question comes in the relationship Bennett et al. posit between the levels (or stages) of intercultural development and the levels of language competency in the ACTFL Proficiency Guidelines (Byrnes et al., 1987). This association is further clarified by suggestions for the kinds of classroom activities that would be linked to the different levels: Novice-Denial, Intermediate-Minimization/Acceptance, and Advanced-Adaptation/Integration stages.

As the profession attempts to integrate language and culture, a number of issues will need to be addressed:

- If intercultural competence is developmental, does the DMIS truly represent that development? Are its stages accurate? Are they reliable and valid?
- How do we know that the activities for the development of intercultural competence in the classroom are appropriate by level and by category?
- How do we know that the competence in various stages of language competence per the ACTFL Guidelines is commensurate with the stages of intercultural competence in the manner hypothesized by Bennett et al.?
- Are the examples of progress indicators in the Standards (1996, 1999) at grades 4, 8, and 12 commensurate with the definition of culture, which combines objective and subjective dimensions, presented by Bennett et al.?
- If one accepts Bennett's (1993) framework for the development of intercultural competence, what kind of modifications of the Standards will have to be made in the future?

PRINCIPLES FOR TEACHING AND LEARNING CULTURE IN SECOND LANGUAGE CLASSROOMS

The core message of Lange's chapter is the necessity of having a plan for culture learning and teaching. That message is reflected in the concept of the linkage of curriculum = assessment = instruction and is exemplified in the seven principles that are derived from the discussion. These three elements are so closely related that they require almost simultaneous attention when planning for classroom instruction. But, most important, the three elements are in opposition to conventional practice in the language classroom, namely the lack of planning for culture learning outcomes. They are fully represented in the seven principles. The seven principles also raise issues for further consideration:

1. The national standards provide a "vision of what a program of language and culture learning may ultimately become at different grade levels in culture learning."

- How do we know that the national standards represent outcomes for culture learning that depict the expected quality?
- As a vision of culture learning, does the definition of culture in the culture standards relate well to that of Bennett et al.?

- How do we know that the framework for the development of inter-cultural competence functions well with the culture standards?
- How well do the culture standards fit with the frameworks discussed in this volume such as the one regarding general learning (Egan, 1979) or those related specifically to culture (Byram, 1989; Crawford-Lange & Lange, 1984; Kramsch, 1993)?

These same questions could be asked of the American Association of Teachers of French guidelines for the learning of culture (Singerman, 1996).

2. The most important principle is "the utilization of a framework." Without a learning and/or a cultural framework, there is no clear understanding of what is to be learned, how that learning is to be evaluated, and how learning is to be guided.

- What is the effect of any framework—general educational, culture specific, or intercultural development—on the curriculum = assessment = instruction relationship when preparing a curriculum for learning language and culture?

3. There are still many questions of ethical nature on the learning of language and culture, which require resolution. Those questions are:

- Who learns language and culture? Why?
- Which culture is to be learned? When? Why?
- How are language and culture to be learned? Where? How?

These questions continue to be asked because of the elitist attitudes that remain prevalent in schools and colleges, which prevent learners from having an opportunity to learn other languages and cultures. In the current and future world context, both language and culture are needed to understand *the other,* both within and outside the framework of national borders.

4. Much of language and culture learning is based on the scientific-technical approach to language and culture, or the observable parts and pieces (facts, information, analyses—objective truth). As we begin to use the culture standards, develop culture learning around frameworks, and make use of a recursive curriculum structure, it will become evident that all of culture learning cannot rest on the traditional vision of what language and culture consist. In that light, the following questions come to mind:

- What can practical and emancipatory inquiry provide for the learning of culture in addition to that of the scientific-technical approach?
- What is the contribution of a recursive, thematic curriculum to the learning of culture?

Because principles 5, 6, and 7 deal with the relationship of content (knowledge, skills, attitudes, processes, and experiences), assessment, and instruction (curriculum = assessment = instruction) they will be dealt with together. In Lange's article, these three concepts were unified through an example of how to develop the concept of *friendship* both in the learners' culture as well as in that of *the other*. These three principles together generate the following questions:

- Within any recurring cultural theme, what are the knowledge, skills, attitudes, processes, and experiences that learners need to encounter? Are the knowledge, skills, attitudes, processes, and experiences generalizable beyond a specific theme?
- What are the ways in which assessment can evaluate the learner's accomplishments? What are the "what, why, how, whose, which, when, where, what if, and so what" questions that go beyond simple objective measures to assess learner knowledge, skills, attitudes, processes, and experiences in intercultural encounters?
- How do teachers guide individual learners toward desired performances in the development of intercultural competence?

CULTURE LEARNING IN LANGUAGE EDUCATION: A REVIEW OF THE LITERATURE

In their impressive review of the literature on culture learning in language education, Paige et al. have brought us up-to-date on the theoretical and research literature on the teaching/learning of culture. While the review is extensive, it has to rely on inference from a more general literature to make statements about the teaching/learning of culture. This is not a criticism of the review, but rather of those of us who are researching and writing on this subject. The writing about the subject is more extensive than the actual research and may be reflective of the tendency to place culture in a very secondary role in the language classroom.

This review, along with the Bennett et al. and Lange chapters, was commissioned by the Intercultural Studies Project (one of the projects associated with the Center for Advanced Research on Language Acquisition and the National Language Resource Center at the University of Minnesota) for its 1996 conference, *Culture at the Core*. It is used in this chapter to summarize the needs of culture teaching and learning in the future. The areas reviewed in the Paige et al. article also serve as the framework for the summary of questions in this chapter that need to be addressed through research, curricular development, instructional practice, the advancement of assessments, and theoretical writing. They include: Context, Setting,

Teacher Variables, Learner Variables, Curricular Materials and Instructional Methods, and Assessment.

Context

It appears that context has been defined in the literature as containing an extremely broad set of variables. Second, context seems to also emphasize the impact of immersion "in the host culture versus classroom instruction," which can and does take place in study abroad programs, and in limited ways, in elementary classrooms and language across the curriculum courses. Third, the most studied variables of context seem to be the teacher and learner variables. However, the many variables of context, such as setting, teachers, learners, curricular materials, instructional methods, and assessments make it extremely difficult to develop a quantitative research response without hundreds of subjects. Perhaps, in terms of context, we might focus instead on the following questions:

- Have we effectively articulated the language and culture relationship so that both can be learned in the language classroom?
- As we contemplate the broad context of language learning in schools, colleges, and universities, how do we know we have carefully established the need for culture in the language classroom for the general public, parents, teachers, and learners?

Setting

The most important emphasis in the literature on context seems to be study abroad programs in naturalistic settings, while immersion programs have been stressed in the classroom. And, the *normal* classroom is an important third setting. In all three settings (external contexts), learners interact with culture. Yet, there is very little understanding of how learners can encounter the other in more than just superficial ways (internal contexts) in any of the three settings. Motivation and attitudes may play an important role in each of these settings, but the setting by itself does not "guarantee increases in either language or culture beyond what can be provided by the classroom." Often, what is learned is largely facts and information about the target culture, indicating that any deep understanding of the other may be limited at best. The questions that require attention under this heading are the following:

- How can we replicate natural elements of a culture under study in the classroom and in immersion programs?

- What is the balance between external and internal cultural contexts for this purpose?
- What is the impact of the normal classroom and immersion on the development of cultural competence?
- How do we determine if the impact is similar to learning culture in natural settings, such as in study abroad programs?

Teacher Variables

The literature reviewed clearly demonstrates the importance of the role of the teacher in what learners accomplish in the language classroom. Yet, the literature is somewhat contradictory. Many teachers believe that language study is more than just the language, including understanding the other; and, their knowledge, attitudes, and beliefs impact their pedagogical practice. Yet, because a large number of teachers feel insufficiently prepared to teach "the whole of the culture," they focus largely on linguistic objectives, believing that culture learning will be a byproduct of such instruction. Such is the case in spite of the fact that teachers seem to feel that "their field [is] composed of a well-defined body of knowledge on which they can agree." It is difficult to make sense out of such contradictions, but they do exist in the complicated world of pedagogical practice. The contradictions raise the following questions about teacher variables, which can probably apply to natural, immersion, or normal classroom settings:

- How and when do teachers use stated objectives for culture learning?
- How do teachers translate their objectives for culture learning into practice?
- How do teachers' knowledge, attitudes, motivation, and beliefs about culture inform their practice?
- What is the nature of the relationship between the teaching of culture and the development of intercultural competence? Does this relationship vary according to the setting?
- How do teachers use the students' individual, multiple abilities and talents in developing intercultural competence?
- What is the role of the teacher preparation programs in helping teachers reach culture-learning goals with their students? [One might think of both national standards and state standards for culture in regard to their translation to the local level.]

Learner Variables

This area of consideration has been dominated largely by the research on motivation and attitudes, i.e., characteristics that can affect the "manner and depth of [learners'] attention while they study [another language; here I would also add learning another culture]." Even though much stress has been placed on the importance of attitudes and motivation in the contact with the other, there are important questions about the cause and effect relationship between these variables, success in language learning, and the development of intercultural competence. Studies with these variables contain significant problems related to "definition, measurement, and interpretation of findings," particularly in learning another culture. Further, other learner variables such as contact with people from the target culture, the intelligence(s) discussed by Gardner (1993, 1995), previous language learning background, language aptitude, and strategy use have hardly been examined. The lack of attention to such variables and the stress on attitudes and motivation lead us to the following questions:

- What is the role of personal contact with persons from other cultures in the learner's development of intercultural competence?
- What role do attitudes and motivation have in the development of the learner's intercultural competence?
- How do attitudes and motivation combine with other learner variables such as the several intelligences, previous culture learning, amount of personal contact, and the use of general learning strategies in the development of the learner's intercultural competence?
- What role does each of these categories of learner variables play in developing intercultural competence?

Curricular Materials and Instructional Methods

There is no doubt in anyone's mind that the textbook is the curriculum for the language and culture classroom. The literature review has established that in the classroom setting culture learning is largely assumed to be the accumulation of facts (food, dress, holidays, etc.) about a specific culture. In other words, there is little in the curriculum that moves learners toward the development of intercultural competence. While the review indicates that alternative materials are used, they are considered "time-consuming, less efficient, and more difficult to use." Methods of instruction are hardly addressed in the review, except for the use of the computer to assist with simulations. These results lead us to the following questions:

- How can the profession work more closely with textbook publishers to ensure that students are more engaged in the development of intercultural competence than in learning the facts of a particular culture?
- How can authentic materials be more integrated into the curriculum of the language program to support the development of intercultural competence?
- What is the role of computer software and of computer-assisted learning in the development of intercultural competence beyond visualization of the context and immediate feedback? What other technologies can assist in the development of intercultural competence?
- What are the particular pedagogical methods that are effective in the development of intercultural competence?
- Since publishers include a variety of media with text materials today, how can we work with publishers to determine the role of the technology in the development of intercultural competence?
- How do authentic materials fit into a package of pre-published materials?

Assessment

The assessment of culture is largely associated with the concept of objective testing, according to the review. This means of assessment is congruent with the perspective of culture as factual knowledge. Therefore, assessment is focused on geography, food, and festivals, to cite a few examples. Some newer developments in assessment focus on a deeper cultural knowledge and different aspects of culture learning, yet they use some of the same techniques. Even though assessment is now being defined in broader terms (e.g., portfolios, self-reports of progress, journaling of culture learning, simulations, experiential techniques such as role plays, critical incidents, case studies, and culture immersions), the literature indicates only scant use of such tools. The importance of the connection of assessment with the curriculum and instruction as indicated by Wiggins (1993, 1998) leads to the following questions:

- What is the role of traditional assessments (multiple choice tests, true-false tests, etc.) in the development of intercultural competence?
- What is the contribution of alternative means of assessment (portfolios, self-reports of progress, journaling of culture learning, simulations, experiential techniques such as role plays, critical incidents, case studies, and culture immersions) in the development of intercultural competence?

- What is the effect of alternative means of assessment on student motivation to develop intercultural competence?
- What is the relationship of the system of curriculum = assessment = instruction to the development of intercultural competence?

SUMMARY OF QUESTIONS NEEDING TO BE ADDRESSED

The final section of this chapter restates and reformulates the questions that have been raised above, organized according to the framework used by Paige et al. in their chapter. The purpose is to bring all of the questions together as a means of focusing our attention as a profession on the future of culture in the language classroom. It should be noted that the Bennett et al. perspective on intercultural competence heavily influences the questions. It is my conviction that this concept will significantly change how the profession addresses culture in the future.

Context

- Who learns language and culture? Why?
- What is to be learned? When?
- How are language and culture to be learned? Where?
- Have we effectively articulated the culture and language relationship so that both can be learned in the language classroom?
- As a vision of culture learning, is the definition of culture in the culture standards congruent with Bennett's (1993) model of intercultural development?
- Will the profession accept the Bennett et al. definition of culture as a combination of objective and subjective culture?
- How well do the culture standards fit with the frameworks discussed in this volume such as the one regarding general learning (Egan, 1979) or those related specifically to culture (Byram, 1989; Crawford-Lange & Lange, 1984; Kramsch, 1993)?
- How can we know that the interpersonal, interpretive, and presentational modes of communication are interacting sufficiently with the Bennett (1993) framework to develop intercultural competence?
- By what means can we know that the definitions of objective and subjective culture are acceptable in language and culture learning in schools? In colleges and universities?
- By what means can we be assured that language teachers will shift their perspective of culture from *parts and pieces* to be mastered to a process of developing intercultural competence?

- Are teachers prepared to embark on the development of competence in both language and culture as viewed by Bennett et al.? (See the section Relationship of the DMIS to Language Learning.)
- If cultural competence is developmental, does the DMIS truly represent that development? Are its stages accurate? Are they reliable and valid?
- How do we know that the competence in various stages of language development per the ACTFL Guidelines is commensurate with the stages of intercultural competence in the manner hypothesized by Bennett et al.?
- If one accepts the Bennett (1993) framework for the development of intercultural competence, what kind of modifications of the standards will have to be made in the future?
- As we contemplate the broad context of language learning in schools, college, and universities, how do we know we have carefully established the need for culture in the language classroom for the general public, parents, teachers, and learners?

Setting

- How can we replicate natural elements of a culture under study in the classroom and in immersion programs?
- What is the balance between external and internal cultural contexts for this purpose?
- What is the impact of the classroom and immersion on the development of intercultural competence?
- How does the impact of the classroom and immersion programs compare to culture learning in natural settings, such as in study abroad programs?

Teacher Variables

- How do teachers guide individual learners toward desired performances in the development of intercultural competence?
- How and when do teachers use stated objectives for culture learning?
- How do teachers translate their objectives for culture learning into practice?
- How do teachers' knowledge, attitudes, motivation, and beliefs about culture inform their practice?

- What is the nature of the relationship between the teaching of culture and the development of intercultural competence? Does this relationship vary according to the setting?
- What is the role of the teacher preparation programs in helping teachers reach culture learning goals with their students? [One might think of both national standards and state standards for culture in regard to their translation to the local level.]

Learner Variables

- What is the role of personal contact with people from other cultures in the learner's development of intercultural competence?
- What role do attitudes and motivation have in the development of the learner's intercultural competence?
- How do attitudes and motivation combine with other learner variables such as the several intelligences, previous culture learning, amount of personal contact with another culture, and the use of general learning strategies in the development of the learner's intercultural competence?
- What role does each of these categories of learner variables play in developing intercultural competence?

Curriculum Materials and Instructional Methods

- How do we know that the national standards represent outcomes for culture learning that depict the expected quality?
- How do the development of intercultural competence and language learning interact in the use of the target language in the classroom?
- How do we know that the activities for the development of intercultural competence in the classroom are appropriate by level and by category?
- Are the examples of sample progress indicators of the Standards (1996, 1999) in grades 4, 8, and 12 commensurate with the definition of a combination of objective and subjective culture as represented by Bennett et al.?
- What is the effect of any framework—general educational, culture specific, or intercultural development in nature—on the curriculum = assessment = instruction relationship when preparing a curriculum for learning language and culture?
- What can practical and emancipatory inquiry provide for the learning of culture in addition to that of the scientific-technical?

- What is the contribution of a recursive, thematic curriculum to the learning of culture?
- Within any recurring cultural theme, what are the knowledge, skills, attitudes, processes, and experiences that learners need to encounter? Are they generalizable beyond a specific theme?
- How can the profession work more closely with textbook publishers to ensure that students are more engaged in the development of cultural competence than in learning the facts about a particular culture?
- How can authentic materials be more integrated into the curriculum of the language program to support the development of intercultural competence?
- What is the role of computer software and of computer-assisted learning in the development of intercultural competence beyond visualization of the context and immediate feedback? What other technologies can assist in the development of intercultural competence?
- What are the particular pedagogical methods that are effective in the development of intercultural competence?
- Since publishers include a variety of media with text materials today, how can we work with publishers to determine the role of technology in the development of intercultural competence?

Assessment

- What are the ways in which assessment can evaluate the learner's accomplishments? What are the "what, why, how, whose, which, when, where, what if, and so what" questions that go beyond simple objective measures to assess learner knowledge, skills, attitudes, processes, and experiences in cultural encounters?
- What is the role of traditional assessments (multiple choice tests, true-false tests, etc.) in the development of intercultural competence?
- What is the contribution of alternative means of assessment (portfolios, self-reports of progress, journaling of culture learning, simulations, experiential techniques such as role plays, critical incidents, case studies, and culture immersions) in the development of intercultural competence?
- What is the effect of alternative means of assessment on student motivation to develop intercultural competence?
- What is the relationship of the system of curriculum = assessment = instruction to the development of intercultural competence?

The outcome of this summary suggests an enormous amount of work that needs to be done in order for the development of intercultural competence to become an integral part of the language classroom. These questions provide a map of the issues to be addressed. With these questions, we have a better sense of what needs significant attention in the development of intercultural competence.

NOTE

1. It should be assumed that all quotations in this chapter come from the chapters discussed namely those of Phillips, the Bennetts and Allen, Paige, Jorstad, Siaya, Klein, and Colby, and Lange. This assumption avoids heavy use of citations that take up unnecessary space.

REFERENCES

Byram, M. (1989). *Cultural studies in foreign language education.* Philadelphia: Multilingual Matters.

Byrnes, H, Child, J., Levinson, N., Lowe, P., Jr., Makino, S, Thomson, I., & Walton, R. (1987). ACTFL proficiency guidelines. In H. Byrnes & M. Canale (Eds.), *Defining and developing proficiency: Guidelines, implementation, and concepts* (pp. 14–24). The ACTFL Foreign Language Education Series. Lincolnwood, IL: National Textbook.

Crawford-Lange, L.M., & Lange, D.L. (1984). Doing the unthinkable in the second-language classroom: A process for the integration of language and culture. In T. V. Higgs (Ed.), *Teaching for proficiency, the organizing principle* (pp. 139–177). The ACTFL Foreign Language Education Series. Lincolnwood, IL: National Textbook.

Egan, K. (1979). *Educational development.* New York: Oxford University Press.

Gardner, H. (1993). *Multiple intelligences: The theory in practice.* New York: Basic Books.

Gardner, H. (1995). Reflections on multiple intelligences: Myths and messages. *Phi Delta Kappan, 77,* 200–202, 206–209.

Kramsch. C. (1993). *Context and culture in language teaching.* Oxford: Oxford University Press.

Lange, D.L. (1999). Planning for and using the new national culture standards. In J.K. Phillips & R.M. Terry (Eds.), *Foreign language standards: Linking research, theories, and practices* (pp. 57–135). ACTFL Foreign Language Education Series. Lincolnwood, IL: National Textbook.

Lange, D.L., & Wieszorek, J. (1997). Reflections on collaborative projects: Two perspectives, two professionals. In J.K. Phillips (Ed.), *Meeting new goals, new realities* (pp. 243–272). Northeast Conference Reports. Lincolnwood, IL: National Textbook.

National Standards in Foreign Language Education Project. (1966). *Standards for foreign language learning: Preparing for the 21st century.* Yonkers, NY: The National Standards Education Project.

National Standards in Foreign Language Education Project. (1999). *Standards for foreign language learning in the 21st century: Including Chinese, Classical Languages, French, German, Italian, Japanese, Portuguese, Russian, and Spanish.* Yonkers, NY: The National Standards Project.

Singerman, A.J. (1996). *Acquiring cross-cultural competence: Four stages for students of French.* Lincolnwood, IL: National Textbook.

Wiggins, G.P. (1993). *Assessing student performance: Exploring the purpose and limits of testing.* San Francisco: Jossey-Bass.

Wiggins, G.P. (1998). *Educative assessment: Designing assessments to inform and improve student performance.* San Francisco: Jossey-Bass.

INDEX

A

Acculturation, 6
Agency, 143–144
American Association of Teachers of
    French
    culture standards/ability to observe
        and analyze, 327–328
    culture standards/empathy, 326
    culture standards/knowledge of
        French-speaking societies,
        328–329
    Proficiency Guidelines, 19–20, 239,
        241
        cultural competence categories,
        19–20, 58
American Council on the Teaching of
    Foreign Languages, 239
    guidelines, 19
Anthropological perspectives on cul-
    ture, xiii, 12, 39–40, 49, 59–61
    classroom implications, xiii–xiv, 38
    cultural meaning of metaphors, 43
    and linguistic anthropology, 42
    and second language education,
        37–38, 55–56, 61, 74
        awareness, 61–62
        comparison, 62–63

other dependent learning,
    63–64
Apology, study of in cross-cultural prag-
    matics, 22–23
Assessment issues in culture learning,
    212, 214–216, 225–226, 299,
    348–349
    assessment models, 216–218,
        300–302
    assessment postulates, 302–303
    challenges
        academic insularity, 220
        content and criteria, 218
        intercultural competence and
            the teacher, 220
        misinterpretations, 218–219
        positivistic tradition, 219–220
    example, 305–308
    historical overview, 212–214,
        299–300
    in National Culture Standards and
        Bennett framework, 303–304
    nature of assessment, 214
    open questions, 352–353
    rubrics, 304–305
Audio-lingual movement, 54
Autonomous linguistics, 3
    linguistic competence, 4
Auxiliary language, 6, 14

Culture as the Core: Perspectives in Second Language Education, pages 355–362
Copyright © 2003 by Information Age Publishing
All rights of reproduction in any form reserved.

CPSIA information can be obtained at www.ICGtesting.com
Printed in the USA
LVOW05s1150221113

362401LV00002B/363/A